HINDU ENCOUNTER WITH MODERNITY

R

Hindu Encounter with Modernity

Kedarnath Datta Bhaktivinoda

Vaiṣṇava Theologian

SHUKAVAK N. DASA

श्री
SRI
Los Angeles

SRI
<www.sanskrit.org>

This edition is a major revision of
The Life and Thought of Kedarnath Dutta Bhaktivinode:
A Hindu Encounter with Modernity

Library of Congress Cataloging-in-Publication Data

Dasa, Shukavak N.
Hindu encounter with modernity: Kedarnath Datta Bhaktivinoda, Vaiṣṇava theologian / Shukavak N. Dasa.
p. cm.
Includes bibliographical references and index.
ISBN 1-889756-30-X (hardcover)
1. Thākkura, Bhaktibinoda.
2. Chaitnya (Sect)–Doctrines.
3. Hinduism–India–Bengal.
4. Bengal (India)–Religion–19th century.
I. Title.
BL1175.T47D37 1999
294.5'512'092
[B]–DC21 97-2565
CIP

5 4 3 2 1
Printed in the United States of America on acid-free paper.

To Joseph T. O'Connell

Acknowledgements

A special thanks to those who helped publish this volume

Milan and Tara Chakrabarty
Alok Sindher
Naina Sindher
Akhil A. Sheth
Pankaj and Suman Agarwal
Kavita and Kapil Mishra
Hiren and Nomita Mukherjee
Neelesh and Annika Karody
Roshan and Kulwant Khandpur
Gopal and Archana Chaturvedi
Shwetha, Shilpa, and Shanta Hareesh
Arriane Devi Kalra
Vijay and Bharti Mathur
Vijay and Meenu Kumar
Rajgopal and Jai Shri Krishnan
Sai and Priya Upadhyayula
Vikram and Sheila Chandrashekar
Suresh and Veena Jhawar
Mahesh and Usha Gupta
Rohit and Nishey Wanchoo
Shambhu and Meera Rai
Harish and Meenu Chauhan
Darsh and Ranju Aggarwal
Aditya and Sushma Agarwal
Kulin and Vibha Dalal
Sudeep, Charu and Virat Mathur
Sreesha and Champa Rao
Quentin E. Monnin
Meghna and Nishli Panjabi
Lata Saxena and family
Anand Lingayat
Dristadyumna Dasa
Shibu, Sabrina & Preeanka Mazumder
Taradas and Bharati Bandyopadhyay
Kali and Sunanda Chaudhuri
Rita Mediratta
Kathleen and Douglas Marvin
Surender and Indira Vuthoori
Shilpa and Ravi Vuthoori
Asha and Badri Narayan Nath
Sharath and Uday Reddy
Shachi Hamendra Rana
Kul and Swaren Bhushan
Laxman and Devi Panjwani
Katie and Jenifer Marvin
H. K. and Shantha Mariyappa
Shobhan and Swati Sengupta
Tarsem and Kiran Singhal
Jugal and Sangeeta Ralli
Harish and Neera Dang
Robert and Rosy Dang
Vrindavana Dasa
Jerri Herring

In memory of:
Suresh Ghiya
Om and Shanti Dixit
Rama Shanker and Usha Dubey
Sundernan M. Vakil
Taraben S. Vakil
Kalpesh Vardhan
Smt. Priyambada Rajpoot
Shivender and Sumitra Sahgal
Sridhar and Suneeta Rao
Chandra and Sri Krishna Agarwal
Kaushalaya Dhingra
Vishwanath More
Smt. Pushpaben V. Sodha

Foreword

I have read Shukavak's work with great interest and enjoyment. I find it to be an excellent work of scholarship: carefully researched, convincingly argued, and very well written. This book is an important scholarly contribution to our knowledge of modern India and of the Hindu tradition in the modern world.

I admit to a personal self-interest in this judgment, because I have been for many years a great admirer of the role of Kedarnath Datta (Bhaktivinoda Ṭhākura) in the renaissance of Caitanya Vaiṣṇavism during the nineteenth and twentieth centuries. Some dozen years ago, I tried to assess that role in an article on "The Social and Religious Background for the Transmission of Gauḍīya Vaiṣṇavism to the West," using all of the material I could find on the life and work of Bhaktivinoda Ṭhākura and the cultural setting of his career. Material on the latter was not hard to come by for my purposes, but I could find surprisingly little on Bhaktivinoda himself—and much of that was from suspect sources that often had the quality more of hagiography than of factual biography.

Thanks to Shukavak, most of what I wanted to know at that time has now been made accessible. There is of course much more to learn about Bhaktivinoda, as about any great person, but the basic facts about his life have now been carefully winnowed out from the husks of hagiography and the sources for further study have been tracked down. I have nothing but admiration for the persistence with which this has been done, since the search for evidence has led Shukavak not only to archives in India and England but to Bengal villages and individual homes to locate essential pieces of the puzzle and make them available for future scholars and devotees.

Beyond this reconstruction of Bhaktivinoda's personal life history, Shukavak has laid out in clear fashion the cultural context of his life in terms of the social, political and intellectual changes taking place in Bengal in the nineteenth century. This part of the book is less original than the biographical research, but it is very ably done and is creatively integrated with the biography to identify the problems that Bhaktivinoda was struggling to overcome in the course of his career. Moreover, we now know many of the cast of characters who intersected with Bhaktivinoda at various stages in his development, many of them well-known in more familiar histories of the Bengal Renaissance. One would like to know more about the roles played in Bhaktivinoda's development by such figures as Iswar Chandra Vidyasagar, Keshab Chandra Sen, the Tagores, Alexander Duff, Charles Dall, and Bankim Chandra Chatterjee, to mention only a few of the more famous, but we at least have now a better idea of where to pursue this question. It is evident from Shukavak's account that Bhaktivinoda was in contact with many of the key figures who carried the Renaissance forward from the early Brahmo Samaj movement to the social reform and nationalist movements of the late nineteenth century, and that his personal world included not only Bengali traditionalists and modernizing intellectuals but Christian missionaries as well. The larger history is not new, but Bhaktivinoda's place in it is much more clearly defined.

To this more general history, Shukavak adds two important new sets of data: a careful record of Bhaktivinoda's publications year by year, and evidence of his relations with a range of religious communities and teachers outside both Calcutta *bhadraloka* circles and the Gauḍīya mainstream. The record of publications has never before to my knowledge been authenticated in such detail, and the latter evidence has hitherto either been overlooked or suppressed by the orthodox Gauḍīya hagiographers who have until now largely controlled the story of Bhaktivinoda's religious life. Shukavak demonstrates both excellent research skills and scholarly integrity in bringing to light a much more complete—and much more compelling—account of Bhaktivinoda's religious development that recognizes the influences of his Śākta family background, Christian teachings, the Kartābhajās and Jāti-Vaiṣṇavas, and the Bāghnāpāḍā Vaiṣṇavas whose leader Bipin Bihari Goswami initiated him and later gave him the title of "Bhaktivinoda" by which he was known from 1880 onward. It is clear from what Shukavak has provided that Bhaktivinoda's religious journey was more complex than hagiographies have told us, and that he had perhaps the broadest-ranging religious experience of anyone in his generation—certainly more wide ranging and varied than any known member of the English–educated *bhadraloka*, because so much of his life was lived away from Calcutta in the more traditional regions of Bengal and Orissa.

Variety of experience, of course, does not in itself produce great religious thought; it must be synthesized in the mind of a spiritual genius. Shukavak leaves little doubt that Bhaktivinoda was such a genius, a devotee whose vision transcended his culture and his time. Raised in a traditional Śākta household in village India, exposed in Calcutta to Western rationalism and Christian devotion, charged by his profession as a magistrate to adjudicate British law, and gradually drawn to and then converted to Caitanya Vaiṣṇavism, Bhaktivinoda had the range of life experience from which a creative synthesis could emerge. The question is how Bhaktivinoda could evolve the synthesis he did when his contemporaries failed to do so, most of them clutching at one end of the traditionalist–modernist spectrum or finding themselves adrift in the middle. And how could he create a synthesis that not only accommodated both traditional Vaiṣṇava devotion and modern rationalism but transcended them both in a vision of universal salvation deeply rooted in Caitanya's devotional principles but open to the whole world?

Shukavak's assessment of these issues and his analysis of Bhaktivinoda's solutions is quite simply the best I have seen. He knows Bhaktivinoda's works thoroughly, and he knows the works of his contemporaries such as Bankim Chandra Chatterjee. He knows, moreover, the works of modern Christian theologians and historians of religion who have struggled with the problems of tradition and modernity. With these various perspectives, he is able to identify the inner logic of Bhaktivinoda's approach as it points backward to Caitanya and the gosvāmīs and forward to the challenges of rationalism and universalism while remaining rooted in Bhaktivinoda's own religious experience. The result is a clarification of Bhaktivinoda's own thought from a scholarly perspective without in the least infringing on his integrity as a devotee. Both scholars and devotees should equally appreciate the product of Shukavak's efforts.

Thomas J. Hopkins
Professor of Religious Studies (Emeritus)
Franklin & Marshall College,
Lancaster, Pennsylvania

Prologue

This study of Kedarnath Datta Bhaktivinoda is the result of my personal involvement with Krishna Consciousness over the last thirty years. As I grew up in Toronto during the late 1960s, I became influenced by the social currents of those times. I began to experiment with new ideas and religious sentiments, particularly from cultures more exotic than my own. Somehow I became touched by the sweet chanting of Hare Kṛṣṇa, which eventually matured into a long and deep involvement with Krishna Consciousness or, as it is more properly known, the Caitanya Vaiṣṇava movement. These last thirty years have been a time of great discovery and personal development, but they have not been easy years. What began as a simple process of Kṛṣṇa worship led to an intense interaction with medieval Hindu culture. My involvement with Krishna Consciousness was not simply a religious conversion, but something much more dramatic, a cultural conversion that involved the transformation of my entire personality.

As I gradually moved into the world of the Caitanya Vaiṣṇavas, I faced a Herculean task—the need to assimilate a new world-view. Of course, in those days I was propelled by a youthful zeal and the social currents of the 1960s and 1970s, so I did not perceive my passage from West to East in such dramatic terms. It was a great adventure, but, nonetheless, I now perceive the inherent difficulties in making that transition. I moved from my cultural and intellectual homeland in the modern world to the traditional world of the Caitanya Vaiṣṇavas, and in so doing I challenged some of my most fundamental beliefs and conceptions.

From the outset I was confronted with the problem of applying my acquired Vaiṣṇava outlook within a modern context. Could I play a meaningful role in modern society and at the same time maintain integrity as a Vaiṣṇava? It appeared that I was confronted with two great worlds. One was the modern and secular world that I had grown up in, which demanded rational thought and conformity to standards that seemed godless and uncompromising. The other was a traditional world of Vaiṣṇava faith and piety, which seemingly allowed little room for critical thought. The two worlds appeared mutually exclusive and I soon discovered that I had two conflicting identities, the modern rational thinker and the old-world Vaiṣṇava.

My first attempt to resolve this conflict was to deny my indigenous culture altogether. I tried to become a Vaiṣṇava of 500 years ago, but I soon learned that there was no escaping the modern world. I lived in Toronto, Canada, not Vrindavan, India. Even more importantly, after spending time in India, I discovered that within my deepest core I was a product of the modern world and to deny this was to be dishonest. On the other hand I felt that Vaiṣṇava faith, with its ancient traditions, did indeed have something important to offer, something which I dearly wanted. But before I could have it, I needed to reconcile these two opposing views.

My need to integrate tradition and modernity eventually led to my study of Kedarnath Datta Bhaktivinoda (1838–1914), who during his own lifetime faced a similar predicament. Born near Calcutta during the Bengal Renaissance, when English influence was at its height in India, Bhaktivinoda was British–educated and largely European in his outlook. In his mid-twenties he became attracted by Caitanya Vaiṣṇavism and eventually immersed himself in that culture. Gradually he became an important nineteenth-century Vaiṣṇava leader in Bengal. For most of his life he lived as a Vaiṣṇava and yet continued his contacts with the British, working as a deputy magistrate in the Provincial Civil Service. Bhaktivinoda achieved a workable balance between tradition and modernity. Instead of relinquishing modernity, he utilized it in his writings; instead of rejecting Vaiṣṇava tradition, he strengthened it in the presence of rational thought.

This study will help the present followers of Caitanya Vaiṣṇavism in the West deal with the problems of cultural implantation and adaptation, and enable others to understand more realistically what processes are at work in such a phenomenon. For individuals who have become members or sympathizers of Caitanya's movement, the life of Kedarnath Datta Bhaktivinoda serves as a great inspiration and guiding light. That Bhaktivinoda was a great Vaiṣṇava and simultaneously a respected magistrate of the British Indian Government, a philosopher and family man, provides the movement with a much needed role model. Vaiṣṇavas throughout the world can take inspiration and guidance from Bhaktivinoda. I hope that an exposition of his life and thought will facilitate the process of cultural conversion and broaden the movement's intellectual and social range.

SvDasa
May 1998

Cover design and book layout: Sukulina Devi Narayan Das

Pictures of Kedarnath Datta Bhaktivinoda on pages 60, 84, 117, 118 and 250 published courtesy of the Bhaktivedanta Archives.

Picture of Theodore Parker (*circa* 1850) published courtesy of the Theodore Parker Unitarian Church, West Roxbury, Massachusetts.

Map of India 1836, C. Colin Davies, *An Historical Atlas of the Indian Peninsula* (New Delhi: Oxford University Press, 1959). Reprinted by permission of Oxford University Press, New Delhi.

Table of Contents

Abbreviations

Publication data are included in the Bibliography.

ST – *Sajjana-toṣaṇī*

KS – *Kṛṣṇa-saṁhitā*

Jīvanī – *Svalikhita-jīvanī*

CS – *Caitanya-śikṣāmṛta,* Bengali edition

CS Eng – *Caitanya-śikṣāmṛta,* English edition

JD – *Jaiva-dharma,* Bengali edition

JD Eng – *Jaiva-dharma,* English edition

TS – *Tattva-sūtra,* Bengali edition

TS Eng – *Tattva-sūtra,* English edition

CC – *Caitanya-caritāmṛta*

Bhāg – *Bhāgavata-purāṇa*

BRS – *Bhakti-rasāmṛta-sindhu*

HC – *Hari-nāma-cintāmaṇi*

TV – *Tattva-viveka*

DK – *Datta-kaustubha*

BG – *Bhagavad-gītā*

Transliteration and Translation Notes

In rendering Sanskrit and Bengali into English I have used the commonly accepted system of transliteration that employs diacritic notation for Sanskrit. This rule applies for both Sanskrit and Bengali transliteration. See the transliteration tables in the appendices that describe this system. However, there are two notable exceptions.

In the case of geographic and modern personal or institutional names I have employed the commonly accepted form rather than the diacritic form. For example, "Śrī Rāmapura" is written as "Serampore." Similarly "Dvārakanātha" is anglicized as "Dwarkanath," and "Gauḍīya Maṭha" is written as "Gaudiya Math."

While transliterating the future tense of the Bengali verb I employ "b" instead of "v." For example, the literal transliteration, *karivena,* is transliterated as *karibena.* I have done this to account for the special characteristics of the Bengali language. Otherwise, the numerous Bengali passages are transliterated according to the same system of transliteration as Sanskrit.

As far as possible I have omitted the honorific titles, *Śrī, Śrīmad,* and *Śrī Śrī* that are commonly used at the beginning of Sanskrit and Bengali titles in both the text and bibliography. Finally, all Sanskrit and Bengali translations are my own unless otherwise stated.

শ্রীকেদারনাথ ভক্তিবিনোদ

Kedarnath Datta Bhaktivinoda (1838–1914)

Introduction

Perspective

Much has been written about the life of Kedarnath Datta Bhaktivinoda, but most of it is hagiographic. This is not surprising. The life of Bhaktivinoda is primarily a devoted religious life, around which a significant body of followers has arisen. These followers have tended to take an idealized approach to Bhaktivinoda's life. The emergence of hagiography is, of course, natural; its purpose is to nurture piety. At the same time, the existence of hagiography has created an important need within the Vaiṣṇava academic community for critical biographies.

One of the key issues in this study is the need to find a balance between critical scholarship and religious faith. Wilfred Cantwell Smith has pointed out that one of the objections most often directed to any scholarship undertaken by the religious insider is that the work is inherently unscholarly because it lacks necessary detachment and critical analysis. On the other hand, the religious adherent often says that any scholarship performed by the outsider lacks an understanding of the essence of religious faith and therefore cannot adequately comprehend a religious matter. On these grounds one could easily conclude that any scholarly study of religion is inherently inadequate, or that any study of religion is inherently unscholarly.

There are, no doubt, elements of truth in both arguments. The purpose of hagiography is to kindle faith, and to achieve this end there may be an emphasis on those facts and interpretations that nurture faith, and a tendency to disregard the data that do not. The hagiography is an appeal to the heart, whereas the critical biography is an appeal to the mind. While both have their respective places, it is important to distinguish between the two.

The present study is not hagiographic. Instead it is an attempt by a Vaiṣṇava adherent to write a critical biography and exegesis of Bhaktivinoda's thought. When I began this research I had two specific concerns. Was it possible for the religious insider to study his own tradition in a critical way and still maintain religious faith in the tradition? And if so, what was the precise nature of the critical approach that would permit such a study?

I eventually found the solution to my predicament in the writings of Bhaktivinoda. I chanced to find a copy of Bhaktivinoda's first major work, the *Kṛṣṇa-saṁhitā* (1879). As I gradually translated the document I was amazed to learn that Bhaktivinoda was attempting to analyze Indian history and show the development of Vaiṣṇavism according to what he called the *ādhunika-vāda,* or the modern approach. Here was Bhaktivinoda taking a keen and discriminating look at Indian history and Vaiṣṇava religious traditions according to the techniques of modern (nineteenth century) critical scholarship. He offered a plausible date for the *Bhāgavata* according to internal and extra-textual evidence; he pointed out corruptions in the text, and he brought attention to the human weaknesses of its author—all things that the religious insider seemingly should not do. At the same time, I saw a personality who obviously maintained firm faith in the Vaiṣṇava tradition. In his *Kṛṣṇa-saṁhitā* Bhaktivinoda was showing that it was indeed possible to take a critical look at one's own tradition, and at the same time maintain a deep and abiding faith within that tradition.

I was impressed, and I wondered how it was possible. I had never seen a practicing Vaiṣṇava assume such a bold position as critical historian. I sensed that some of Bhaktivinoda's basic theological assumptions must be essentially different from my own or from what I had experienced as a Caitanya Vaiṣṇava. Perhaps the tradition-modernity issues that confronted Bengal's elite during the nineteenth century had something to do with Bhaktivinoda's seemingly radical approach. On this basis I felt that I had found the necessary license with which to proceed. Not only could I draw on Bhaktivinoda for support, but now I was especially interested to discover the basic theological perspective that allowed him to write his *Kṛṣṇa-saṁhitā*.

Situation and Significance

Born of a wealthy *kāyastha* family near Calcutta in 1838, Kedarnath Datta Bhaktivinoda grew up in a traditional Śākta household of rural Bengal. In his youth he moved to Calcutta where he was English-educated. Eventually he took a position in government service as a district sub-magistrate for the British administration. In his late twenties he discovered his "Eastern Savior," Caitanya Mahāprabhu (1486–1533), and eventually became a theologian and leader within the Caitanya Vaiṣṇava movement[1] in Bengal. He made a lifelong study of Vaiṣṇava philosophy, theology, and literature; and he wrote or edited almost a hundred books in Bengali, Sanskrit, and English. He was an associate of such noteworthy men as Kashiprasad Ghosh, his maternal uncle; Ishwar Chandra Vidyasagar, his college teacher and lifelong friend; Keshub Chandra Sen, a classmate; Michael Madhusudan Datta, a literary associate; Bankim Chandra Chatterjee, a civil service colleague and eminent novelist; and Sisir Kumar Ghosh, a prominent newspaper publisher in Bengal. Kedarnath Datta Bhaktivinoda was also a great family man and the father of fourteen children. In 1908 he adopted the lifestyle of a Vaiṣṇava recluse. He passed away in his Calcutta home at age 76 on June 23, 1914.

Although this work primarily describes the life and thought of Bhaktivinoda—through his writings, theology, religious practices —it also addresses the influences of modernity and how they affected Bhaktivinoda's life. From his reactions to these influences we learn about his conception of religious faith and his theological per-

1. The Caitanya Vaiṣṇava Movement is also known as the Gauḍīya Vaiṣṇava Movement. I have elected to use the term Caitanya instead of Gauḍīya in order to avoid the geographic reference that is implied by the term Gauḍīya.

spective in a modern world. In addition, we learn about religious adaptation and how a spiritual tradition can evolve in the light of intense intellectual and cultural change.

The Bengal Renaissance was a time of radical change and rapid growth for most areas of Bengali society. Urban culture and mass media had become distinct features, and as industrial, commercial and economic life expanded so did social and cultural life. During those times Hindu religious life, and Vaiṣṇavism in particular, became vibrant and underwent great change. Ramakanta Chakrabarty points out, "There is no evidence of languor, neglect or depression of Hinduism at any time during the nineteenth century. The impressive durability of Hinduism as a religion and a way of life remained unquestionable. . . . But the educated Bengali elite felt the need of modernizing Hinduism. They wanted to clip off the superfluities and the superstitions for their own benefit."[2] Therefore, this is an ideal time to study the religious life of Bengal as it adapted to the changes of modernity.

Usually when we recall the religious personalities of that period, the names of Rammohun Roy, Debendranath Tagore, Bankim Chandra Chatterjee, Sisir Kumar Ghosh, Keshub Chandra Sen, and Protap Mazumdar come to mind. These were the "superstars" of the Bengal Renaissance. Less frequently do we hear the names of Bijoy Krishna Goswami, Bhudev Mukhopadhyay, or Kedarnath Datta Bhaktivinoda. But these "second echelon" personalities were no less important than their more famous counterparts. In fact, they are perhaps more representative of how the *bhadraloka* in general reacted to the pressures of modernization. There were more of them and they generally held closer to tradition than did the "superstars." Therefore, the study of this second echelon of Bengal's elite and their reactions to the strains of modernization may actually tell us more of what the intelligentsia in general did, and still do, under the pressures of modernization. In the case of Bhaktivinoda, we

2. Ramakanta Chakrabarty, *Vaiṣṇavism in Bengal* (Calcutta: Sanskrit Pustak Bhandar, 1985), 402.

have a personality who was as fully articulate in English, Sanskrit, Persian and Bengali as the "superstars", but who, unlike most of them, was willing to nurture and reveal his personal spirituality and his identification with traditional Hindu culture and religious life.

There are two features of Bhaktivinoda's religious trajectory that make the study of his life particularly rewarding. First, he left an autobiography that outlines the course of his religious transformation. In other words, he left an effective "road map" of his religious development. Second, he was not born into a family of Vaiṣṇavas. Instead, he came to Vaiṣṇavism after a gradual and thoughtful study of the tradition at a time when Hindu and Western traditions were converging. The life of Kedarnath Datta Bhaktivinoda, therefore, presents a unique opportunity to study the religious development of a prominent member of Bengal's cultural elite through his own eyes at a critical moment of cultural confrontation.

That Bhaktivinoda was generally loath to involve himself in secular affairs beyond his strictly professional duties is perhaps the main reason why his influence has been largely overlooked. He was, however, no less a creative personality than his more famous colleagues. Compared to Bankim Chandra Chatterjee and Sisir Kumar Ghosh, who certainly considered themselves followers of Kṛṣṇa, Bhaktivinoda's practice of Caitanya's teachings was far more spiritual and less socially and politically activist. Bhaktivinoda and Sisir Kumar jointly edited a Vaiṣṇava periodical entitled *Viṣṇu-priyā-patrikā,* until Bhaktivinoda withdrew on the grounds that his esteemed friend was mixing too many secular and topical issues into the journal. Bhaktivinoda refused to attend a drama on the life of Caitanya, even at the request of its well known playwright, Girish Chandra Ghosh, on the grounds that the drama mixed contemporary social and political concerns with what should be a strictly spiritual subject. Bhaktivinoda was a purist, which tended to separate him from the less deeply religious mainstream of elite society.

At the same time, Bhaktivinoda's influence was still a force to be reckoned with. Bankim Chandra acknowledged his influence as a

Vaiṣṇava leader in the introduction to his *Gītā* translation.[3] Bhaktivinoda was able to rally the influence of Sisir Kumar Ghosh and the *Amṛta Bazaar Patrikā,* one of Calcutta's most important newspapers, in support of his plans to construct a large temple of Viṣṇupriyā-Caitanya in Mayapur.[4] Bhaktivinoda's popular *nāma-haṭṭa* preaching program often included the names of prominent Bengalis and Europeans, and for this reason it was instrumental in shaping the public's attitude towards Caitanya Vaiṣṇavism. The conservative and purist influence of Bhaktivinoda should not be underestimated. Personalities like Bhaktivinoda became the spiritual conscience and, in effect, the new priests for Bengal's elite.[5] Consequently, he had a major influence in shaping public opinion on many important issues of cultural and religious significance.

Current Scholarship

The Bengal Renaissance was a period of intense literary output. The British demonstrated a passion for documentation in their administrative zeal. Missionaries recorded their thoughts and accomplishments for their patrons back home. Bengal's intellectual elite, likewise, were a prolific literary group. The literature of the time is replete with newspapers, journals, and autobiographies – all filled with commentary. There is, therefore, a wealth of written material emanating from this period of British-Bengali interaction.

---

3. *Baṅkima Racanāvalī,* edited by Yogesh Chandra Bagal (Calcutta: Sahitya Samsad, n.d.), 680.
4. The Viṣṇupriyā-Caitanya Mandir is the temple that Bhaktivinoda helped to construct over the birth site of Caitanya in Mayapur.
5. M. N. Srinivas, in his *Social Change in Modern India,* rightly notes that modernization often led to the gradual erosion of the authority of the traditional *brāhmaṇa* Hindu priests. They were, in effect, left behind by modernity. They failed to learn English and consequently lost their relevance and ability to understand the intellectual and spiritual needs of the Westernized Hindu elite. Speaking of the traditional priesthood, Srinivas writes: "They did not have the intellectual equipment or the social position to undertake a reinterpretation of Hinduism that would suit modern circumstances. Since the beginning of the nineteenth century, such rein-

On the religious front Narendra Sinha records that there were over ninety Vaiṣṇava journals and related organizations in Bengal between 1870 and 1900. Similarly, Ramakanta Chakrabarty records that Bhaktivinoda was at the very center of this Vaiṣṇava revival: "Vaiṣṇava journalism as well as Gauḍīya Vaiṣṇava organization in Bengal really became meaningful under the guidance of a dynamic Vaiṣṇava Deputy Magistrate named Kedarnath Datta Bhaktivinoda."[6] In the West, Thomas Hopkins recognizes Bhaktivinoda for playing a fundamental role leading to the appearance of ISKCON in the modern world.[7]

Within the Gaudiya Math and ISKCON[8] much information about Bhaktivinoda is available, although these sources are largely hagiographic. From the Gaudiya Math the most prolific and scholarly works were presented by Sundarananda Vidyavinoda between 1936 and 1938. His works include the *Gīti-sahitye Śrī-bhaktivinoda, Chātradera Śrī-bhaktivinoda, Bhaktivinoda-prasaṅga, Ṭhākura Bhaktivinoda* and *Bhaktivinoda-vāṇi-vaibhava.* All of these works are in Bengali. More than anyone else, Sundarananda has been responsible for shaping the image of Bhaktivinoda within the Gaudiya Math and ISKCON. In addition, the Gaudiya Math has produced many short biographical essays in English. However, most of these publications contain information extracted from Sundarananda's works.

From ISKCON and similar organizations, one monograph has

---

terpretation has come from the Westernized Hindu elite." Individuals like Kedarnath Datta and Bijoy Krishna Goswami, therefore, assumed *de facto* such priestly roles.

6. Chakrabarty, *Vaiṣṇavism in Bengal,* 394.

7. Thomas J. Hopkins, "The Social and Religious Background for the Transmission of Gauḍīya Vaiṣṇavism to the West". A paper presented in New Vrindavan (1985) and published in: David G. Bromley and Larry D. Shinn, eds., *Krishna Consciousness in the West* (Lewisburg: Bucknell University Press, 1989), 35-54.

8. The Gaudiya Math is a Vaiṣṇava organization established in India by Bhaktivinoda's son, Bhaktisiddhanta Sarasvati (Bimal Prasad Datta). ISKCON is an acronym for the International Society for Krishna Consciousness established in 1966 by A.C. Bhaktivedanta Swami, a disciple of Bhaktisiddhanta Sarasvati.

recently appeared by Rupavilas Das entitled *The Seventh Gosvami.* This work is a biographic study of the life of Bhaktivinoda and like the publications of the Gaudiya Math it is written as a hagiography. There is also an assortment of song books and other short biographical sketches that have been self-published in recent years by numerous Western followers of Bhaktivinoda.

During his lifetime Bhaktivinoda wrote, translated or edited over a hundred works.[9] In preparing this study I have used the following works: *The Bhagavat, Its Philosophy, Ethics and Theology* (1869), *Datta-kaustubha* (1873), *Kṛṣṇa-saṁhitā* (1879), *Sajjana-toṣaṇī* (volumes 1–22), *Caitanya-śikṣāmṛta* (1886), *Āmnāya-sūtra* (1890), *Tattva-viveka* (1893), *Jaiva-dharma* (1893), *Tattva-sūtra* (1893), *Gītā-mālā* (1893), *Svalikhita-jīvanī* (1896), *Sri Chaitanya Mahaprabhu, His Life and Precepts* (1896) and *Harināma-cintāmaṇi (1900)*. Together these works span the entire length of Bhaktivinoda's writing career from the late 1860s to the early twentieth century and represent his progressive theological development.

The Bhagavat, Its Philosophy, Ethics and Theology is one of the few pieces of English writing from the pen of Bhaktivinoda. Since so much of Bhaktivinoda has to be presented in translation, I have added *The Bhagavat, Its Philosophy, Ethics and Theology* as a supplement to give the reader a direct appreciation of Bhaktivinoda's early thought through his own words.

The Gaudiya Math has been instrumental in keeping Bhaktivinoda's writings available since the late 1930s. Some of his major works were translated into English during the 1960s. Periodically I have consulted these publications.

In preparing this study I have especially relied upon Bhaktivinoda's *Kṛṣṇa-saṁhitā,* his autobiography *Svalikhita-jīvanī,* and his journal *Sajjana-toṣaṇī* for the following reasons.

9. Many of these works are small collections of verses with commentary. Others are songs, and others are works by old authors that have been edited and published by Bhaktivinoda. Depending on what is considered a major work, I suggest that about twenty of these publications can be considered major works that Bhaktivinoda penned himself. Appendix I lists all of his known publications.

The *Kṛṣṇa-saṁhitā*[10] is one of Bhaktivinoda's earliest historical and theological works (the other one being the *Datta-kaustubha*). The *Kṛṣṇa-saṁhitā* was written while Bhaktivinoda lived in Puri, which was a formative phase of his life. The *Kṛṣṇa-saṁhitā* is fundamental to the study of Bhaktivinoda's theological development because it represents, more than any other work, the foundations of his reconciliation of tradition and modernity. I have made my translation from two sources: the serialized edition published in Bhaktivinoda's *Sajjana-toṣaṇī* during 1903 and the third edition of the Gaudiya Math's 1946 Bengali publication.

Bhaktivinoda's autobiography, *Svalikhita-jīvanī,* is a warm and human narration portraying the life of a great spiritual seeker in a unique and turbulent time of Bengal's history. Much of the biographic information is new and provides a fresh basis for interpreting Bhaktivinoda's life. The *Svalikhita-jīvanī* allows an excellent opportunity to step beyond the hagiographic perspective and see Kedarnath Datta Bhaktivinoda in human terms.

The *Svalikhita-jīvanī* was written in the form of a letter to Bhaktivinoda's son, Lalita Prasad Datta, who later published the work in 1916 for close friends and followers.[11] The story is a compelling account of Bhaktivinoda's life from his birth in 1838 to his retirement at age 56 in 1894. It was never republished and conse-

10. The *Kṛṣṇa-saṁhitā* is found in the following volumes of ST: vol. 14, 1903, numbers 10, 11, and 12 (Jan., Feb., Mar.); vol. 15, 1903 numbers 1, 2, and 3, (Apr., May, June).

11. I originally received a copy of *Svalikhita-jīvanī* through a friend, Mr. Abhiram Dasa, and subsequently found a published edition in the London India Office Library. Since the *Svalikhita-jīvanī* would have a critical bearing on how Bhaktivinoda's developing life was interpreted, I traveled to West Bengal to authenticate the text. To my delight I found the original handwritten manuscript in the possession of one elderly lady, Bhakta Ma. She allowed me to photograph the handwritten text. To determine authenticity, I compared its handwriting with handwriting from other manuscripts by Bhaktivinoda. I also compared the printed edition with the original handwritten manuscript. I am convinced that the printed edition is a true rendering of the original text and has not been altered or corrupted by the editor, Lalita Prasad Datta.

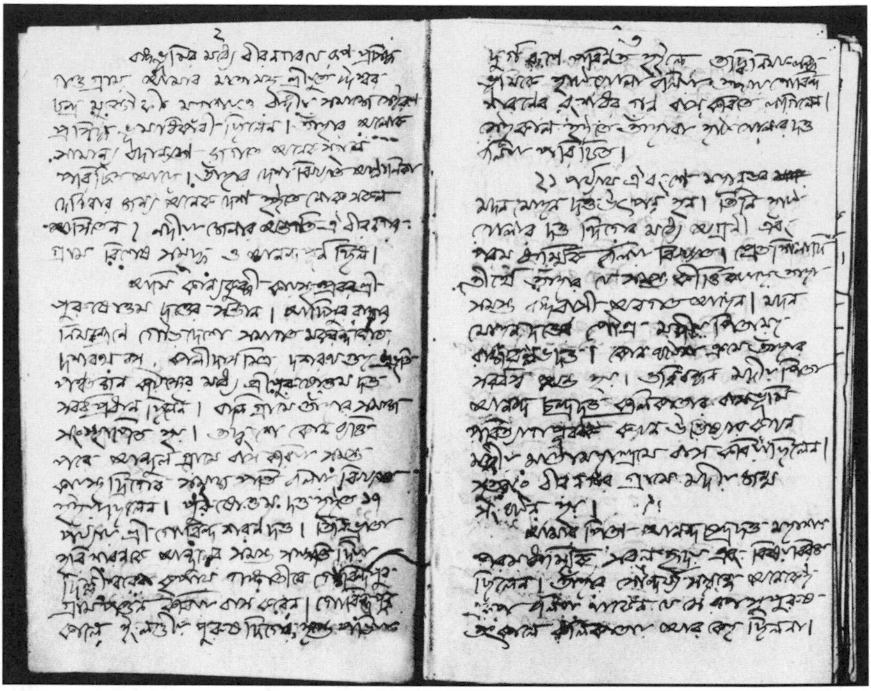

A handwritten page of Kedarnath Datta's autobiography, *Svalikhita-jīvanī.*

quently, the work is largely unknown.[12]

The other important source of information about Bhaktivinoda and his times is his journal, *Sajjana-toṣaṇī,* published between 1882 and 1904. The journal is especially valuable because it contains a wealth of information about Vaiṣṇavism in the nineteenth century as seen through the eyes of Bhaktivinoda. The early volumes, issues one through nine (1882-1891), are particularly topical because they provide information on the events of Caitanya Vaiṣṇavism during that time period. They record Bhaktivinoda's commentary on the state of Vaiṣṇava society and *varṇāśrama-dharma,* announcements of new journals, published books, and upcoming events within the

12. Sundarananda Vidyavinoda refers to the work in an oblique manner citing Bhaktivinoda's "*ātmā-carita.*"

Vaiṣṇava community. They also contain the summaries of various fund-raising and *nāma-haṭṭa* programs. After 1891 the journal begins to dedicate more and more pages to serializing Bhaktivinoda's published writings. After the turn of the century the journal becomes exclusively a presentation of his writings. Unfortunately, this makes the journal increasingly less interesting in terms of topical Vaiṣṇavite news, but it does allow us to see how Bhaktivinoda originally published his own works.[13] Apart from the *Sajjana-toṣaṇī,* the only other access to Bhaktivinoda's writings is through the published editions of his works by the Gaudiya Math.

Another valuable source of information on Bhaktivinoda's life is his service records with the Government of Bengal found at the National Library in Calcutta. With these records I was able to trace his working career and compare these records with the information provided in his autobiography. These government records provide further witness as to the accuracy of Bhaktivinoda's autobiography.[14]

In addition to these sources there are many smaller publications that have been helpful. One is a Bengali work entitled *Bhaktivinoda-carita*[15] by Krishna Dasa, who is purported to have been a close servant of Bhaktivinoda. Another useful source is Pundit Satkari Chattopadhyay's *A Glimpse into the Life of Thakur Bhakti-vinode* written in English in 1916.[16] Finally, from the Shauri Prapanna Ashram near Khargpur in Southern Bengal, a work entitled *Śrila Bhaktitīrtha*

---

13. The *Sajjana-toṣaṇī* was originally edited by Bhaktivinoda's son, Radhika Prasad Datta, until 1904. This is the year of the last extant edition of the journal. Later, after Bhaktivinoda's passing away in 1914, the journal was published by the Gaudiya Math and edited by Bhaktisiddhanta Sarasvati. I obtained complete photocopies of the *Sajjana-toṣaṇī* from the Bangiya Sahitya Parishad in Calcutta in 1987.

14. Kedarnath Datta's service records were found in two sources: History of Services of Gazetted Officers Employed under The Government of Bengal (corrected up to 1st July 1888), 114; and History of Services of Officers Holding Gazetted Appointments Under the Government of Bengal (corrected to 1st July 1894), chapter 9, Sub-Executive Officers, 604-5. See Appendices.

15. I found the *Bhaktivinoda-carita* at Kedarnath's maternal family's home in Birnagar. It was given to me by Bhakta Ma.

16. Pundit Satkari Chattopadhyay was a friend of Bhaktivinoda. His short sketch

Ṭhākurera Saṅkṣipta Jīvanī has been published, containing valuable information on Bhaktivinoda's life. This work is a biography, as its title suggests, of Bhaktitirtha Thakur, a disciple of Bhaktivinoda. The Shauri Prapanna group is a line of spiritual descendants from Bhaktivinoda that is important in tracing the *guru-paramparā* and *sādhana* practices of Bhaktivinoda.

There are many aspects of Bhaktivinoda's life that could have been examined, but were not. These include Bhaktivinoda's career as a magistrate working with the British Indian government. Bhaktivinoda had a long career in public service, and in the course of his work he had to hear many difficult and important cases that involved Hindu-Muslim relations, political terrorism, and sedition within Bengal, Bihar, and Orissa. The proceedings of these trials are available in the West Bengal Government Archives and I am certain that Bhaktivinoda's role as a magistrate and a supporter of British rule would make a fascinating study.

Bhaktivinoda was also a literary man. He experimented with various literary forms, including blank verse and the novel. During the nineteenth century many new forms of literary presentation, including the novel, were borrowed from European literature. Many Bengalis, including Michael Madhusudan Datta, Kashiprasad Ghosh, and Bankim Chandra Chatterjee, experimented with these new forms. Bhaktivinoda himself was no less a literary writer than his more famous colleagues. His *Jaiva-dharma* is a prime example of his use of the didactic novel in Bengali literature. Recently, Banarasinath Bharadwaj has drawn attention to the literary side of Bhaktivinoda in his work entitled, *Kedāranātha Datta.*[17]

In London I came across five other writings by an unknown person named Kedarnath Datta. Four of these may be found at the

---

was published in English in 1916 by the Bhaktivinoda Memorial Committee. It includes an introduction by Sarada Charan Mitra, an ex-judge of the Bengal High court and junior contemporary of Bhaktivinoda.

17. Banarasinath Bharadvaj, *Kedāranātha Datta* (Calcutta: Śrī Caitanya Research Institute, 1989).

India Office Library and one at the School of Oriental and African Studies Library. None of these writings are listed in any of the Gaudiya Math lists of works by Bhaktivinoda. These writings are semi-secular. Two of them are novels, which shows their author experimenting with the novel as a literary form. Further research is needed to determine the authorship of these works.[18]

During the nineteenth century, Vaiṣṇava arts, including music, dance, and song experienced a renaissance. Bhaktivinoda played an important role in this development. Included within his works are some major collections of Bengali devotional songs. These include the *Kalyāṇa-kalpa-taru* (1881), *Śaraṇāgati* (1893), and *Gītāvalī* (1893). Except for a few references to his devotional practice, I do not mention his role as a songwriter or musician.

Finally, Bhaktivinoda was a great family man. He had fourteen children. However, I have not attempted to follow their lives except where they have a bearing on his devotional life.

18.The names and description of these works are as follows: *Deva-dāsa* (1909, pp. 152) is described as the story of a religious life; *British Māhātmya Kāvya* (1903, pp. 66) is described as the glorification of British rule in India; *Priyamvadā* (1857, pp. 211) is described as a love story; and *Bañcaka-carita* (1863, pp. 52) is the story of a swindler. In the School of Oriental and African Studies Library I found a work entitled *Bhārata-varṣera Itihāsa*, described as a history of India in Bengali. This work was published in 1859 and includes an introduction by the Reverend J. Long. In preparing this volume I have not utilized any of these texts because none relate directly to Vaiṣṇavism, nor have they been authenticated as actual works of Bhaktivinoda.

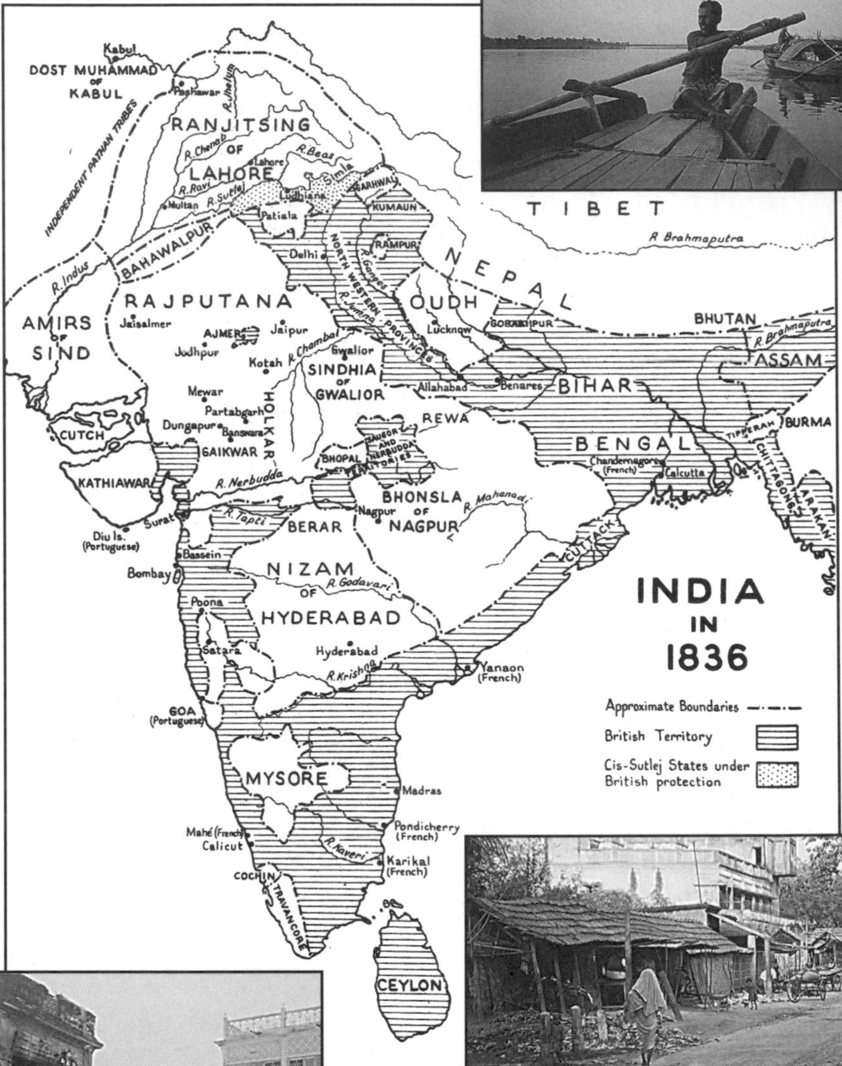
INDIA
IN
1836
Approximate Boundaries
British Territory
Cis-Sutlej States under British protection
Kabul
DOST MUHAMMAD OF KABUL
Pashawar
INDEPENDENT PATHAN TRIBES
RANJITSING OF LAHORE
R. Jhelum
R. Chenab
R. Beas
Lahore
R. Ravi
R. Sutlej
Multan
Simla
Ludhiana
Patiala
GARHWAL
KUMAUN
TIBET
R. Brahmaputra
BAHAWALPUR
R. Indus
Delhi
RAMPUR
NORTH WESTERN PROVINCES
R. Ganges
R. Jumna
NEPAL
RAJPUTANA
Jaisalmer
AJMER
Jaipur
AMIRS OF SIND
Jodhpur
Kotah
R. Chambal
Gwalior
SINDHIA OF GWALIOR
OUDH
Lucknow
GORAKHPUR
BHUTAN
ASSAM
Allahabad
Benares
BIHAR
Mewar
Partabgarh
HOLKAR
Dungapur
Banswara
CUTCH
GAIKWAR
REWA
SAUGOR AND NERBUDDA TERRITORIES
BHOPAL
BENGAL
Chandernagore (French)
Calcutta
TIPPERAH
BURMA
CHITTAGONG
ARAKAN
KATHIAWAR
R. Nerbudda
BHONSLA OF NAGPUR
Nagpur
R. Mahanadi
Surat
R. Tapti
BERAR
Diu Is. (Portuguese)
CUTTACK
Bassein
Bombay
NIZAM OF HYDERABAD
R. Godavari
Poona
Satara
Hyderabad
R. Krishna
Yanaon (French)
GOA (Portuguese)
MYSORE
Madras
Pondicherry (French)
Mahé (French)
Calicut
R. Kaveri
Karikal (French)
COCHIN
TRAVANCORE
CEYLON

Chapter One

Nineteenth Century Bengal

> You must yourself knock at the door of the inexhaustible store of truth from which the former ages drew their wealth. Go, go up to the Fountain-head of truth where no pilgrim meets with disappointment of any kind. Vyasa did it and obtained what he wanted. We have been advised to do so. Liberty then is the principle, which we must consider as the most valuable gift of God. We must not allow ourselves to be led by those who lived and thought before us. We must think for ourselves and try to get further truths which are still undiscovered. In the *Bhagavat*[1] we have been advised to take the spirit of the shastras and not the words. The *Bhagavat* is, therefore, a religion of liberty, unmixed truth, and absolute love.[2]

These words, found at the beginning of "*The Bhagavat, Its Philosophy, Ethics and Theology*," were originally spoken by Bhaktivinoda before an audience of Bengali intellectuals at Dinajpur in 1869. They are words of hope, and they reflect an attitude of religious freedom and reform that was characteristic of the Bengali elite during the nineteenth century. These words provide insight into an age of formative development in Bengal's modern heritage. In essence they reflect the attitude of eighteenth century universalism, rationalism, and cosmopolitanism that deeply affected

---

1. *phala-śrutir iyaṁ nṝṇāṁ na śreyo rocanaṁ param/*
śreyo-vivakṣayā proktaṁ yathā bhaiṣajya-rocanam// Bhāg. 11/21/23.
2. Kedarnath Datta, *The Bhagavat, Its Philosophy, Ethics and Theology*, ed. Bhaktivilas Tirtha, 2d ed., (Madras: Madras Gaudiya Math, 1959), 39.

the lives of Bengal's intellectual elite. The attitudes that are reflected in these words became the tools by which the Bengali intellectual approached the challenges of the nineteenth century.

The Rise of the *Bhadraloka*

In August 1765, eight years after the Battle of Plassey, Shah Alam, the Mughal Emperor, conveyed the regions of Bengal, Bihar and parts of Orissa to the East India Company. This granted the East India Company the right to collect taxes and rule these regions. The consequences of this transfer of power were substantial. The advent of British power greatly accelerated many of the economic and political changes that were already occurring throughout Northern India. Consequently, Bengal and its surrounding lands became the first regions in India to experience the direct impact of British rule and the beginnings of modernization.

For the remainder of the eighteenth century and throughout the early decades of the nineteenth century, the East India Company laid the foundations for civil administration. The British established communications, transportation systems, a modern bureaucracy, an army and police; furthermore, they instituted law courts, and opened schools and colleges. The nineteenth century became the high point of British-Indian interaction, particularly within Bengal. Historians refer to this era as the Bengal Renaissance —a period of intense cultural and technological advancement as well as a time of great social and political change.

The basis of the Bengal Renaissance was East-West contact. With the spread of European imperial influence around the world through the agency of the East India Company and similar organizations, many regions in the East, including India, experienced comparable interactions of culture and pressures to change. Bengal was the first region in Asia to have its culture radically transformed through this interaction with the West. As Tapan Raychaudhuri points out, "The nineteenth century Bengali experience is thus a part of a global phenomenon. Chronologically it is perhaps the earliest manifestation of the revolution in the mental world of Asia's elite groups."[3]

In particular, Calcutta was the focus of this cultural transformation. It became the center of British administration, trade, and commerce. In the process a class of Bengali elite developed that could interact with the ruling British. This was the *bhadraloka,* a socially privileged and consciously superior group, economically dependent upon landed rents and professional and clerical employment.[4]

Here we want to identify the most important factors that affected the life and thought of Bhaktivinoda as he faced the challenges of cultural change and modernization during the Bengal Renaissance. Some of these factors include the influence of Rammohun Roy and Henry Vivian Derozio, the establishment of Hindu College and English education, the rise and decline of British Orientalism, and the introduction of Christian and Utilitarian thought into Bengal.

Rammohun Roy and Modern Education

Perhaps the most prominent member of the early *bhadraloka,* at least on the intellectual front, was Rammohun Roy (1772–1833). Rammohun Roy is often credited with being one of the initiators of the Bengal Renaissance and the father of modern India. While this may not be entirely accurate, it is a fact that his personality and

3. Tapan Raychaudhuri, *Europe Reconsidered: Perceptions of the West in Nineteenth Century Bengal* (Delhi: Oxford University Press, 1988), ix.

4. The term *bhadraloka* is commonly used in Bengali literature to refer to any educated and respectable gentleman mainly of the three Bengali upper castes *(brāhmaṇas, kāyasthas* and *vaidyas*). In a more technical sense the word refers to the *abhijāta bhadraloka* and the *gṛhastha bhadraloka.* The *abhijāta bhadraloka* became permanent residents of Calcutta in the second half of the eighteenth century. Some rapidly acquired fortunes by working as junior partners with the British. The *gṛhastha bhadraloka* were the next layer of middle-income Bengalis that included small landholders, government employees, members of the professions, teachers, and journalists. Kedarnath and most of his colleagues were members of this latter class. For more information see Meredith Borthwick, *The Changing Role of Women in Bengal 1849-1905* (Princeton: Princeton University Press, 1984).

intellect were among the primary factors that influenced the direction of Bengali thinking during the early nineteenth century.

Rammohun Roy was important for many reasons, not the least of which was his insistence that the young elite of Bengal receive a modern education and that Sanskrit and Persian should *not* be the languages of instruction for the growing numbers of *bhadraloka*.

It is often thought that the British first introduced English education in order to create a new class of Bengalis who could fill the lower echelons of the new civil administration and thus help in their ruling of India. While it is true that English education was a key ingredient that led to the rise of the *bhadraloka* and set the wheels of modernization in motion, it is not true that it came about through British design alone. The desire to facilitate business and cultural contacts with the British prompted members of the *bhadraloka* to learn English on their own. The importance of English education increased with the establishment of British rule, but not until 1835 did the British make any formal commitments to teach English on a wide scale. English instruction was introduced by the *bhadraloka* themselves, first for economic reasons, and then for intellectual and cultural reasons. R. C. Majumdar points out, "Until 1835 the English Government was more enthusiastic about imparting education through oriental languages, i.e. Sanskrit, Arabic, and Persian in preference to English. On the other hand, many among the prominent Bengalee Hindus were in favor of the teaching of English."[5]

In 1817, Dwarkanath Tagore, Prasanna Kumar Tagore and others at their own initiative and expense took a major step along the path of modernization by establishing the first institution of Western education in Asia, Hindu College, using English as the medium of instruction.[6] The teaching of Western sciences, philosophy, English literature and grammar, and other Western subjects was the hallmark of Hindu College. There was no other institution

5. R.C. Majumdar, *History of Modern Bengal* (Calcutta: G. Bharadwaj & Co, 1978), 114.
6. Hindu College taught many vernacular languages in addition to English.

that even came close to the influence that Hindu College exerted in bringing about the awakening of Bengal to Western thought in the early nineteenth century. Through the efforts of Hindu College more than a thousand young men received education in English before the Government officially introduced its own program of English education in 1835.

When the government proposed to establish a Sanskrit College with the object of imparting higher education in the different branches of Sanskrit literature, Rammohun Roy vigorously protested. He wrote a letter to Lord Amherst, then governor of Bengal (1823–1828), in which he stated: "This seminary can only be expected to fill the minds of the youth with grammatical niceties and metaphysical distinctions of little or no practical use to the possessors or to society. . . . The Sanskrit system of education would best be calculated to keep the country in darkness . . . but as the improvement of the native population is the object of the Government, it will consequently promote a more liberal and enlightened system of instruction, embracing Mathematics, Natural Philosophy, Chemistry, Anatomy with other useful sciences."[7] Rammohun Roy was well aware that the key to the future lay in a modern education; consequently, he was one of the first to prefer modern subjects over the teaching of Sanskrit and Persian. And a modern education primarily meant an English education. In this way the stage was set for the introduction of European ideas to the *bhadraloka* through the medium of English. Thus, Rammohun Roy and the others acted collectively as an important bridge, transferring eighteenth century European ideals to the *bhadraloka.* The influence of these early members of the *bhadraloka* is, indeed, behind most of the great changes in religious, literary, political, and intellectual life in Bengal during the early nineteenth century.

Accompanying the establishment of Hindu College and English instruction was the powerful influence of Henry Louis Vivian

7. Majumdar, *History of Modern Bengal,* 115.

Derozio (1808–1831), a young professor at Hindu College. Born in 1808 of Portuguese–Indian descent, Derozio grew up in Calcutta. He was educated in the school of Mr. Drummond in the Dharmatala area of Calcutta. Drummond, Scottish by birth, was a dedicated rationalist. Inspired by Drummond's teachings, Derozio accepted an appointment to teach at Hindu College in May of 1826. Even though Derozio taught for only five years, his influence on the students of Hindu College was unprecedented.

At Derozio's request, Hindu College sponsored many seminars and journals to encourage the discussion of progressive views and ideas. One important entity was the Academic Association (1828). Through this forum Derozio expressed his views on civil administration, social reform, predestination, individual freedoms, the existence of God, idolatry, the priesthood, female education, and so on. Under Derozio's guidance the liberal writers of England and America—Francis Bacon, David Hume, and Thomas Paine—were introduced to the students of Hindu College, the more radical of whom became known as Young Bengal. Derozio encouraged his students to judge the customs, practices, and the rules of Hindu society according to the dictates of logic and reason alone. As a result, many members of Young Bengal began to condemn Hindu dietary laws, the authority of gurus and priests, caste divisions, women's status, image worship, and other traditional Hindu practices.[8] Above everything, Derozio encouraged his students to think for themselves. "To live and die for the truth" was the motto of Young Bengal.

As one might expect, many parents soon objected to Derozio's

8. The journals and newspapers of the day are filled with the comments of horrified parents who watched as their sons rebelled against Hindu tradition by the consumption of meat and alcohol, and a general disregard for all things sacred. Typically, one anguished father writes, "I am a poor man; my son used to look after household affairs and to come to me whenever I called him and answer all questions. But since his admission in the Hindu College, the picture has totally changed. He has given up the usual social and religious customs, behaviors and dress, and started keeping his hair uncut and putting on shoes; he has discarded his string of beads round the neck, goes without baths, eats whenever and whatever

influence on their sons and they refused to send their children to the school. The officials of Hindu College eventually pressured Derozio to resign from the College. He died of cholera a few months later (26 December 1831) at the young age of twenty-three. R. C. Majumdar points out that Derozio will forever be remembered as one of the pioneers in the annals of English education and Western thought in Bengal.

Although Derozio's influence on the young members of the *bhadraloka* was relatively short, the effects were powerful and long lasting. Many members of Young Bengal ultimately grew to have a major influence on Bengali society. As they matured they became the leaders of society and so the rationalism and independent thinking that they had imbibed from their English education and days at Hindu College gradually affected the norm. As the number of English language institutions grew, so did the number of English-educated *bhadraloka*. Gradually they became a strong and distinct class within Bengali society.

One such member of Young Bengal was Kashiprasad Ghosh (1809–1873). Kashiprasad was a poet and a vocal patriot. As early as 1828, the young Kashiprasad, a student of Derozio at Hindu College, lashed out in an essay at James Mill's *History of British India.* In a manner similar to that of the famed Orientalist H. H. Wilson,[9] Kashiprasad defended the Hindu past against Mill's criticism that the Hindus were a "rude and credulous people."[10] Describing Kashiprasad's defense of Hindu ideals, David Kopf writes: "He was the first known Bengali intellectual to defend a secular concept of a golden age among the Hindus. His arguments use evidence clearly derived from the work of the Calcutta Orientalists."[11] Later

---

he pleases, treats equally the pure and the impure, has lost national dignity and treats all advice as nonsense." Quoted in Majumdar, *History of Modern Bengal,* 142.

9. See: "The Wonder that was Orientalism: In Defense of H.H. Wilson's Defense of Hinduism". *Bengal Vaiṣṇavism, Orientalism, Society and the Arts,* ed. J. T. O'Connell. East Lansing: Asian Studies Center, Michigan State University, 1985, 75-90.

10. Quoted from David Kopf, *British Orientalism and the Bengal Renaissance* (Calcutta: Firma K. L. Mukhopadhyay, 1969), 264.

11. Ibid.

Kashiprasad became the editor of an outspoken English language newspaper, the *Hindu Intelligencer* (1846), that promoted Hindu nationalism and often attacked British rule in India.

Although the secular and free spirited thinking of Derozio and the members of Young Bengal including Kashiprasad Ghosh may seem worlds apart from the religious focus of Bhaktivinoda, there is in fact a direct link. Kashiprasad Ghosh was Bhaktivinoda's maternal uncle and it was at the home of Kashiprasad that Bhaktivinoda lived for six years while he himself was a student at Hindu College in the 1850s. At the home of Kashiprasad the young Bhaktivinoda helped his uncle edit and write articles for the *Hindu Intelligencer.* Through Kashiprasad, Bhaktivinoda was in contact with some of the greatest newspaper men of the time, including Kristo Das Pal, the editor of the *Hindu Patriot,* and Shambhu Chunder Mukhopadhyay, the founder of two English language papers, the *Reis* and the *Rayyet.* At Hindu College, the spirit of libertarian thinking that Derozio and Young Bengal had indelibly woven into the fabric of that institution was still present when Bhaktivinoda studied there. Bhaktivinoda's statement from his Dinajpur speech quoted at the beginning of this chapter clearly expresses the tone and ideals of Young Bengal—free thinking, liberty, and truth. These ideas would have a tremendous impact upon the future religious thinking of Bhaktivinoda.

British Orientalism and the College of Fort William

As much as English language education and Hindu College brought the ideas of the West to India, so did the era of Orientalism facilitate the transmission of new cultural attitudes to the *bhadraloka.* British Orientalism was a unique phenomenon in British Indian history that was inspired by the needs of the East India Company to train a class of British administrators in the languages and culture of India. In 1800 Governor General Wellesley established the College of Fort William as a training center in Calcutta for company-servants. In the words of Warren Hastings the idea behind the college was, "to rule effectively, one must love India; to love India, one must communicate with her people; to communicate with her people, one must acquire her languages."[12] This was the start of a short but remarkable era in Indian history characterized by what is known as British Orientalism.[13] In essence, the idea that traditional oriental learning could be combined with the rationalism of the West was the inspiration of British Orientalism. Intellectually it was one of the most powerful ideas of nineteenth century India.

Under the auspices of the College of Fort William, an elaborate and expensive program of literary patronage and research was undertaken. Faculty were trained, language instruction was initiated, an extensive library was established, and books were published in Bengali, Marathi, Urdu, Hindi, Persian, and Sanskrit. Over a hundred Sanskrit texts alone were translated and published by the college. Indeed, the effects of British Orientalism on Bengal were revolutionary. The College of Fort William was the first institution of its kind in India to employ the tools of modern comparative philology, textual criticism and historical analysis on a vast scale in conjunction with traditional learning. The college hired numerous Persian, Sanskrit and European scholars. The methods adopted by the Orientalists heralded a new approach to Indic studies that influenced Bengali intellectuals and men of learning well into the twentieth century.

For the most part, the British Orientalists were a unique group who reflected the eighteenth century notions of rationalism, classicism, and cosmopolitanism. Unlike many later British officers serving in India, the Orientalists were appreciative of the ancient religious and cultural traditions of classical India. Consequently, they made significant contributions to the fields of Indian philology, archeology, and history. In fact, the influence of British

---

12. Ibid., 95.

13. David Kopf points out that one of the distinct features of British Orientalism was that the Orientalists did not remove themselves from the people they ruled. Instead they formed long term relationships with members of the *bhadraloka* to whom they served as sources for knowledge of the West and with whom they worked to promote social and cultural change in Calcutta.

Orientalism was the reason why the British were initially inclined to promote Sanskrit and Persian studies in Bengal over modern English education.

Although the *bhadraloka* rejected the idea of Sanskrit and Persian education, they ultimately embraced the ideals of Orientalism more than the British. For the first time the *bhadraloka* gained a systematic overview of Sanskritic Hindu culture, making the *bhadraloka* keenly aware of the accomplishments of their cultural past. The results were impressive. David Kopf highlights some of the successes:

> Texts, heroes, and institutions were no longer relegated to the oblivion of sacred timelessness, but were endowed with existence in the annals of recorded civilization. That the Vedas were the scriptures of the Aryans, and that the Upanishads preceded the *Vedānta*, were the inventions of the Orientalists. The fact that Buddha was once a human being as well as Śaṅkara, that the Mauryas ruled a vast empire, and that classical civilization reached its peak under the Guptas, were also significant accomplishments of Oriental scholarship.[14]

However, by the 1820s the forces of racism and cultural imperialism within the ranks of the British administration began to overpower the ideals of Orientalism and this unique period in British Indian history began to wane. By the late 1830s Orientalism as official policy was all but gone from British India.[15] David Kopf notes:

> Cosmopolitanism, classicism, and rationalism were distin-

14. David Kopf, "Hermeneutics versus History," *Journal of Asian Studies*, 31 (May 1980), 31.

15. The success of British Orientalism was also the source of its downfall. Christian missionaries and other colonial interests soon began to wonder in whose favor Orientalism was tending, that of the rulers or the ruled. A struggle ensued that eventually saw the College of Fort William effectively shut down by William Bentinck in 1831 when he dissolved the College Council and began to disperse the library. The college was officially closed by Governor-General Dalhousie in 1853.

> guishing features of the enlightened eighteenth-century mind, but it was the idea of tolerance that proved crucial to British Orientalists seeking to transcend alienation from another culture. The high intellectual regard for non-European peoples and cultures (even primitive ones) was presumably as prevalent in the 1700s as it was to become rare in the 1800s.[16]

Here we are not concerned with what Orientalism accomplished in terms of British attitudes toward India, but with the philosophy behind Orientalism and how it achieved its remarkable successes in the minds of Bengali intellectuals. British Orientalism was based on two main principles, namely the acceptance of traditional learning and the use of rational and critical methods of scholarship. British Orientalism combined an attitude of globalism along with the acceptance of traditional values and knowledge. To use the words of David Kopf, Orientalism was based on the belief that modernization could be achieved by pouring the new wine of modern functions into the old bottles of Indian culture. In this way the attitudes of Orientalism promoted cultural equality and accommodation between British and Indian culture.

The idea that the rational techniques of modern scholarship could be combined with traditional learning was powerful, and it is clear that many prominent members of the *bhadraloka*, including Bhaktivinoda and Bankim Chandra, employed the techniques of British Orientalism in their search for Hindu religious and cultural identity. Both Bhaktivinoda's *Kṛṣṇa-saṁhitā* and Bankim Chandra's *Kṛṣṇa-caritra* are built on the principles of British Orientalism, although, as we shall see, they use them in very different ways.

Christianity and Utilitarianism in Bengal

Paralleling the attitudes of British Orientalism, the activities of the late eighteenth century and early nineteenth century missionaries went on just beyond the reach of British

16. Kopf, *British Orientalism*, 24-25.

administration. Prior to 1813 the British East India Company policy prevented Christian missions from being established in British held territory. As a result, the Danish enclave at Serampore, north of Calcutta, became the seat of early nineteenth century "Christian Orientalism." Famed missionaries William Carey, Joshua Marshman and William Ward formed the nucleus of an evangelical base that followed the practices undertaken by the College of Fort William. These missionaries eagerly learned Sanskrit, Bengali, and Urdu, pioneered the development of vernacular printing, and established a library of Hindu and Muslim manuscripts. The collection of Hindu texts, in particular, helped to promote the rethinking of Hindu religious and cultural traditions by both European and Indian scholars. In 1801 the College of Fort William even offered Carey a position to teach Bengali and Urdu.

However, the tone of the Christian missions changed considerably after 1813. The Charter Act of that year opened the door to a new breed of Christian evangelicals who quickly established themselves throughout Bengal. These "post–Orientalist" missionaries[17] were the very antithesis of British Orientalism. They viewed Hindu culture as backward and profane. To them the strength of European culture was its Christian foundations. Their goal was to obliterate as much of Hindu religion as possible and to replace it with as much of Christian values, English education, and Western ideas as they could. The following remarks by Reverend Alexander Duff (1806–1878) reflect the attitude of many of the missionaries towards Hinduism during this time:

> Of all the systems of false religion ever fabricated by the perverse ingenuity of fallen man, Hinduism is surely the most stupendous. Of all the systems of false religion it is that which seems to embody the largest amount and variety of semblances and counterfeits of divinely revealed facts and doctrines.[18]

17. Two notable exceptions were Reverends Charles Dall and James Long.
18. Reverend Alexander Duff, *India and Indian Missions,* Vol. X (Quoted in the *History and Culture of the Indian People,* 1822).

With such a demeanor, it is a wonder that Alexander Duff and men like him did as well as they did. Yet Duff was instrumental in making some of the most prominent Christian conversions. Krishna Banerjee and Michael Madhusudan Datta are the best examples. In general, however, the missionaries had only limited success in converting the *bhadraloka*. Nonetheless, they did play an important role in social change within *bhadraloka* society. They challenged the foundations of Hindu culture and thereby became one of the major forces that influenced it. The *bhadraloka* were compelled to answer their criticisms.

From the secular side another factor that worked to shape the character of *bhadraloka* society was the role of the British Utilitarians who promoted strong rationalist and democratic views. Individuals like James Mill and later his son, John Stuart Mill, expressed views that were similar in many respects to the later Christians who openly promoted the superiority of European culture. The views of the Utilitarians were often drawn upon for the support of social reform which included the teaching of English and Christianity over the teaching of Hindu religion, Sanskrit, and the other classical languages of India. In this respect the Utilitarians were also in contrast to British Orientalism.

In 1828 Lord Bentinck came to India as Governor-General; he was a sympathizer of Jeremy Bentham and James Mill. In 1829 Bentham wrote to Bentinck encouraging his progressive views on Western education and approving of his policy for English education. In February of 1835 Macaulay submitted his "Minute on Education" that criticized the old system of education that was founded on the principles of Orientalism and encouraged the teaching of English and vernacular languages. Until the time of Macaulay few government officials had publicly supported the spread of English education as a policy of Government in such strong terms. With the support of Macaulay, Bentinck issued the Government Resolution in 1835, which accepted the teaching of European arts and sciences through the medium of English. Consequently, English, as an instrument meant to strip away the classical foundations of Indian culture and society, found its way into the fabric of *bhadraloka* society. And although the rational and secular ideas of the British Utilitarians were opposed by the Christian evangelicals, the missionaries and Utilitarians jointly condemned Indian religion and culture.

British Orientalism and the establishment of Hindu College lit the fires of Hindu pride, while the attacks of the missionaries and Utilitarians created a powerful impetus to reformulate and understand past Hindu religious traditions in the light of modernity. As a result, many of the *bhadraloka* including Bhaktivinoda and Bankim Chandra attempted to redefine and defend Hindu culture. Both wrote in a way that was patterned after the ideals of British Orientalism.

The most obvious outcome of the intermixture of these forces of change was the emergence of the anglicized *bhadraloka* itself. Their British education had stripped them of their Indian identities, preventing them from being wholly Indian, and yet their racial origins disallowed them from being European or British. During the nineteenth century, family breakdown, alcoholism, and divorce were common amongst the *bhadraloka*.[19] The disturbed and shattered life of Michael Madhusudan Datta is a prime example. But this clash between cultures also produced tremendous cultural and social creativity. It is with this creative aspect of modernization that I am most concerned.

The relationships between tradition, modernity, and modernization are complex. One of the simplest ways to understand tradition and modernity is to view them as opposites. In between is an indeterminate area that must be crossed. Modernization is the process of transition from one side to the other during which the structures of traditional society are transformed or replaced by the structures of modern society. Modern society is characterized as industrial, urban, literate, and politically participatory. In contrast, tradi-

19. See Borthwick, *Role of Women*, for specific details concerning the domestic life of the *bhadraloka*.

tional society is characterized as agrarian, rural, illiterate, and politically non-participatory—the very opposite of modern society. Implicit in this understanding is the idea that a traditional society is culturally subordinate and at a lower stage of cultural and social evolution than a modern society. During the modernization process a traditional society is impacted by the dominant force of a more evolved society. Modernization is, therefore, synonymous with progress. It is a step forward in the evolution of human culture.[20]

In some ways the British–Bengali situation seems to fit this basic model. By the nineteenth century British society was predominantly urban and industrial, and it was well on the way to becoming literate and politically participatory. Bengali society, on the other hand, was pre-modern or traditional. The Bengali economy was largely rural and agrarian; literacy and political participation were restricted to the privileged minorities, and the vast majority of Bengalis received no formal education beyond the village level, nor had they any involvement in the political processes of their society. The years of British–Bengali contact saw virtually every aspect of traditional Bengali society gradually affected by the structures of modern society as the British surveyed the land, instituted a new system of law, established transportation, education, and administrative systems, and so on. By the end of the nineteenth century Bengal had been radically transformed; traditional society, it might be argued, had all but given way to modernity.

While many aspects of this model do indeed correspond to the

20. I am referring to the classical model of modernity developed in the 1950s and 1960s by David Lerner based on his study of Western interaction with the Middle East. Lerner argues that from medieval times Western man has been confronted with a series of influences which have resulted in catastrophic social, intellectual and economic changes in Western culture. History regards these changes as marking the Age of Exploration, the Renaissance, the Reformation, and the Industrial Revolution. These periods affected the peoples in all Western countries regardless of their political rulers. The overall effect of these changes has resulted in what we call Western Society. Lerner also points out that modernization often assumes various parochial forms, so named after the particular agent or model of modernization. Consequently we can talk about Westernization, Europeanization, Americanization, and so on.

British–Bengali situation, others do not and it would be a mistake to ignore them. One of the greatest problems with this approach is that it presents modernization as an external process in which one distinct culture impacts on another. This, however, is only one aspect of the process. The other aspect comes from within the depths of the affected culture itself. Modernization is also a process that occurs internally within the collective consciousness of the modernizing society. What created modernity within Bengal was not simply British economic and political culture impacting on Bengali society, but more crucially the interiorization of the processes of modernization by the *bhadraloka* themselves. Modcrnity in Bengal was not so much what happened to the *bhadraloka* as it was what they did with the factors of change that were affecting them. What occurred in Bengal during the Bengal Renaissance conforms well to Wilfred Cantwell Smith's observations concerning the internal effects of modernization. Smith writes: "The process of modernization is that process by which a country becomes conscious of itself and of its processes, and of the kind of country that it is possible for it to become, and by which it finds or constructs the technical means for executing such choices as it consciously or unconsciously makes."[21]

It is therefore incomplete to regard the tradition–modernity issue simply as modernity impacting traditional culture, as something new and separate transforming something old and remote. It is better to view tradition and modernity as mutually complementary phenomena in which tradition and modernity are continuous rather than separate. Tradition and modernity are not dichotomous; they are complementary. Accordingly, tradition can assume a much higher status in relation to modernity than we find in the dichotomous model. It also means that those sectors of traditional society that contain or express potentialities for change become critical for understanding the nature and processes of moderniza-

21. Wilfred Cantwell Smith, *Religious Diversity*, ed. Willard G. Oxtoby (New York: Harper and Row, 1976), 95.

tion.[22] The modernization process may be likened to the confluence of two rivers converging rather than the impact of a river rushing upon a rock, to use Wilfred Cantwell Smith's metaphor.

With both these approaches in mind, I am primarily looking at how the *bhadraloka* themselves responded to the transformations that were occurring within their own society. They were keen enough to perceive the need for change and, in fact, welcomed it. However, they wanted to change not as passive recipients of outside interventions—but in an inherently Bengali way. From the very beginning the *bhadraloka* were conscious of the changes that were occurring within their society and they wanted as far as possible to direct those changes. The early establishment of Hindu College by Bengal's elite is a prime example of this. Similarly, Bhaktivinoda's interpretation of Vaiṣṇava theology was not an attempt to model Vaiṣṇava theology according to Christian ideals, but it was an indigenous response to the intellectual changes that were occurring within Bengali culture. Bengal's elite had no desire to model their society as a mere imitation of British or European culture. Instead they wanted to build a distinctively Bengali society in step with the prevailing trends of modernity.

---

22. Here I am referring to the work of Lloyd and Susanne Rudolf and their "continuum model" of modernity. See *The Modernity of Tradition: Political Development in India,* Lloyd I. Rudolf and Susanne Hoeber Rudolf. (Chicago: Chicago University Press, 1967).

The entrance to Kedarnath Datta's maternal home
in Birnagar (Ula), West Bengal.

Chapter Two

The Early Years

1838 – 1858

Ula 1838

On Sunday, 2 September 1838, in the ancient village of Ula, Kedarnath Datta was born the third son of Ananda Chandra Datta and Jagat Mohini Mitra. Describing his birth, Kedarnath writes, "Mother told me that three days before my birth she suffered severe labor pains and that during my birth an astrologer recorded the time with both an hour glass and an English clock. Of all my brothers I was a little ugly, and so my mother prayed, 'Okay, let this boy be the servant of the rest, but just let him live.'"[1]

Kedarnath had two older brothers: Abhaykali, who had died years earlier while the family was in Calcutta, and Kaliprasanna, who was living when Kedar was born. Subsequently, there was a younger sister, Hemlata, and two younger brothers, Haridas and Gauridas.

The early days that Kedarnath spent in Ula were pleasant. He played in the paddy fields around his home and swam and fished in the ponds and streams.

In those days the village of Ula was situated on the bank of the river Bhagirathi, the most western mouth of the Ganges, about 100 kilometers upstream from Calcutta. Today, the river has shifted a few miles to the west and no longer passes through the village.

The origins of Ula are obscure, but the Reverend James Long, a well-known missionary and senior contemporary of Kedarnath,

---

1. Kedarnath Datta Bhaktivinoda, *Svalikhita-jīvanī.*, ed. Lalita Prasad Datta, deposited in the Indian Office Library Feb. 13, 1918 in Vern Tracts, Bengali biography 3584 (Calcutta: 1916), 6. The work is hereafter referred to as *Jīvanī.*

records a short description of Ula in his essay, "The Banks of the Bhagirathi." He informs us that the village received its name from the goddess Ulia, also known as Ula Caṇḍī, whose festival was held there annually. During the celebration many thousands of people would come to Ula and leave presents for the goddess. Kedarnath tells us that there were nearly 1400 *brāhmaṇa* families and many more *kāyasthas* and *vaidyas* living in Ula during his time. Reverend James Long records one peculiar detail about the village: "As Guptapara (the village across the river from Ula) is noted for its monkeys, Halishar for its drunkards, so is Ula for fools, as one man is said to become a fool every year at the *melā* (festival)."[2] Kedarnath affirms, "Everyone was expert at buffoonery. Many people received a reputation for being crazy. There was Isha *pāgala*, Ganga *pāgala*, Pesha *pāgala*, and Shambu *pāgala*.[3] Many respectable people had these names and would go to local and distant places to collect money by sly and crafty means for the public *pūjās*."[4]

Unfortunately, the happy village of Ula was devastated by cholera in 1857. Whole families were lost in a matter of days. Today the village is known as Birnagar and is located three rail stops south of Krishnanagar on the Sealdah rail line to Calcutta. When I visited the village in 1987 I was told that Ula remained vacant for almost forty years after the epidemic. What remained of Ula's residents after 1857 did not return until the turn of the century, when the town was renamed Birnagar.

In 1876 Kedarnath produced a Sanskrit work entitled *Datta-vaṁśa-mālā*.[5] There he gives a genealogical description of the Datta family and claims to be the twenty-fifth descendant from Puruṣottama Datta, who came to Bengal in the twelfth century at the request of King Ādiśura. According to Kedar the Dattas are *kāyastha*

2. Reverend James Long, *The Banks of the Bhagirathi*, ed. by Sankar Sen Gupta (Calcutta: Indian Publications, 1974), 22-23.

3. The Bengali word *pāgala* means crazy or fool. Here it is used in an affectionate sense.

4. *Jīvanī*, 36.

5. *The Datta-vaṁśa-mālā* (1876) is a collection of Sanskrit verses giving a genealogical description of the Datta family.

descendants of the original families who immigrated to Bengal. Today the *kāyasthas* have about 100 surnames among which Datta, De, Das, and Mitra are prominent.

Much less is known about the origins of Kedarnath's maternal family, the Mitras, except that his maternal grandfather, Ishwar Chandra Mustauphi, was a descendant of the noble Rameshwar Mitra from Mustauphi. Rameshwar Mitra was a prominent zamindar in the eighteenth century. The Mitras, like the Dattas, are also supposed to be *kāyastha* descendants of the original five families who immigrated to Bengal.[6]

From the time of Caitanya (1486-1533) the Dattas were mainly Vaiṣṇava. The fifteenth descendant from Puruṣottama Datta was Rāja Kṛṣṇānanda, the father of Narottama Dāsa Ṭhākura and an associate of Nityānanda Prabhu.[7]

The particular branch of Dattas to which Kedarnath belonged was known as the Hathkhola Dattas. They descended from Rāja Kṛṣṇānanda's grandson, Govindasharan Datta, who received a plot of land from the Sultan of Delhi on the banks of the Ganges in West Bengal. On this land Govindasharan established the town of Govindapur, named after himself. When the British wanted to construct a base at Govindapur, Govindasharan and his family moved to Hathkhola in the north. From that time onward the family became known as the Dattas of Hathkhola. Govindapur eventually became Fort William, which later combined with the neighboring villages of Kalighat and Sutanuti to form the site of the present-day city of Calcutta.[8]

Govindasharan's grandson was Ram Chandra Datta, the nineteenth in line from Puruṣottama Datta. Ram Chandra's son was

---

6. In Bengal the surname Mitra is also common among the *vaidya* caste. During the nineteenth century it was not uncommon for *kāyasthas* and *vaidyas* to intermarry, but in the case of Kedarnath's family, the Mitras were *kāyasthas* and not *vaidyas*. Later on, many of Kedar's children married *kāyastha* Mitras.

7. According to Dinesh Candra Sen, Caitanya's associate, Nityānanda Prabhu, used to visit the home of Rāja Kṛṣṇānanda.

8. The name "Calcutta" is thought to be an anglicization of the Bengali village of Kalighat.

Krishna Chandra whose son was the famous Madan Mohan Datta,[9] a contemporary of Lord Clive. Madan Mohan was a wealthy Vaiṣṇava merchant, ship-owner and zamindar in Calcutta. Madan Mohan Datta's son was Ramtanu Datta whose son was Rajballabh Datta, a well known Śākta living in Calcutta.[10] Rajballabh's son was Anand Chandra, the father of Kedarnath Datta Bhaktivinoda.

A few years before Kedarnath was born, his paternal grandfather, Rajballabh Datta, ran into financial problems in Calcutta and so moved to the village of Chutimangal near Cuttack in Orissa. At that time Kedarnath's father, Anand Chandra, moved from Rajballabh's home in Calcutta to the estate of his father-in-law, Ishwar Chandra Mustauphi, in Ula. For this reason Kedarnath grew up in the home of his maternal family, the Mitras, instead of his paternal family, the Dattas.

The Mitra family was one of the wealthiest in Ula. Kedarnath describes his maternal grandfather:

> As Birnagar was famous within Bengal as a wealthy village, so my maternal grandfather, Shri Ishwar Chandra Mustauphi was famous as a prosperous landowner. His wealth and liberal disposition were known throughout the region and people used to come from all over the countryside to see his famous palace. If anybody was in need they could go to the home of Mustauphi Mahashay and get whatever they needed without any difficulty.[11]

Kedar describes his father, Anand Chandra, as a straightforward, clean, religious man who people said was the most handsome man in Calcutta. Similarly, his mother, Srimati Jagat Mohini, was the

9. Madan Mohan built the famous 395 steps up the Pretshila Hill at Gaya for a cost of hundreds of thousands of rupees in 1774. He also traded regularly with American merchants in and around Boston.

10. Śāktas are followers of Śakti, the goddess Durgā. In Bengal the most popular form of Durgā is Kālī. During the eighteenth century there was an upsurge of Śāktism when many prominent zamindars adopted this faith. This accounts for the change from Vaiṣṇavism to Śāktism in Kedar's paternal line.

11. *Jīvanī*, 2.

daughter of a very rich man and "a sober woman possessed of many unique qualities." The role that Anand Chandra played in Kedarnath's life was more the result of his absence than presence. As soon as the family arrived in Ula, Anand Chandra left for Orissa while Kedarnath's mother was pregnant with him. Anand Chandra was away for almost two years after Kedar's birth. Kedar writes:

> When I was almost two years old my father returned from Orissa. My nurse said that a few days before my father's return I saw a crow flying and recited this nursery rhyme, "O crow! Kah! Kah! If my father is coming, show a sign. Move aside on your perch." As I spoke, the crow moved on his perch. Some people nearby saw this and said, "O Kedar! Your father must certainly be coming soon." It so happened that in a few days my father arrived in Ula.[12]

Throughout his autobiography Kedarnath recalls his early childhood in glowing terms. In the evenings he listened to the servants and guards reciting stories of tigers and ghosts and romance. Remembering the family festivals in the home of Ishwar Chandra, he fondly recalls:

> In my grandfather's home all kinds of festive occasions were celebrated. Jagaddhātrī *pūjā* was celebrated with much fanfare. I remember it well. During the night hundreds of chandeliers hung in rows by the lot outside the *pūjā* building. The door guards dressed themselves in Sepoy uniforms. From Ranaghat and Shantipur great crowds of stout men adorned in golden clothes would come. They were accompanied by bodyguards and soldiers. It was like a forest of people and with all the lights it looked like Kurukṣetra. The festival was celebrated with fireworks and rowdy pomp. The guests would become so overwhelmed with the fun that they would lose all sight of the religious occasion. Late at night *kavi-gāna* (song tournaments) would begin and last until dawn. I used to stay

12. Ibid., 7.

> up and listen and laugh at the fun. The gods and goddesses were all dressed in their finest splendor and the meal arrangements were the best. On this occasion many goats and buffalo were sacrificed and eaten. In those days the ladies would worship the goddess Durgā carrying pots of incense on their heads. Everybody used to enjoy this occasion except, of course, the goats and buffalo.[13]

Another popular festival was the *dola-yātra* or spring festival. Again Kedarnath reminisces:

> On *dola-yātra* there would be singing and all kinds of fun. Red dye was thrown everywhere. At this time even the guards took part in the festival. They would enter the temple courtyard singing and throwing dye. With all this commotion I would hide and watch from a distance. During the festival I especially enjoyed watching the bonfires.[14]

These tender years in Ula laid the foundations for Kedar's adult life. They were predictable and happy times and they provided a backdrop of faith and promise for his eventual acceptance of Vaiṣṇava traditions. Later on, when he was thrust into the urban world of the *bhadraloka* in Calcutta, he would find stability in the memories of these years.

But not all of his early life in Ula was happy and peaceful. After age five there were increasing difficulties and uncertainties. In 1843 at the age of five Kedarnath started school. The village schools in Ula, like most village schools at the time, were rough places for a young boy. William Adam, a Baptist missionary, describes the typical village school in a report on rural education in Bengal prepared in 1835. He writes:

> These schools were housed in shabby straw-built structures or held in open air under shady trees, and run by

13. Ibid., 8.
14. Ibid., 10.

> teachers who were little respected and poorly rewarded. Discipline was enforced in these institutions in a rough and ready manner by the lusty exercise of the cane as well as numerous forms of sadistic infliction.[15]

In Kedarnath's own school the teacher would use the older students to inflict terror on the younger ones. In one incident the teacher forced his students to steal various things from their parents' homes. Haridas, Kedar's younger brother, became so incensed by this constant harassment that he finally plotted to kill his teacher with a machete! Luckily, Kedarnath caught wind of the plot and managed to confiscate the knife, but the incident created such an uproar that the teacher apparently fled from Ula the same day.

Later an English school opened and during lunch Kedarnath would attend the classes. The headmaster was a Frenchman named Dijor Barrette. Kedarnath's interest in learning English endeared him to Monsieur Barrette, who requested his father to allow Kedar to attend the English school. Amongst the *kāyasthas*, attendance at an English school was a social asset, so his father readily agreed. This was Kedarnath's first European contact.

At age seven Kedarnath and his brothers moved to Krishnanagar for further education. The local *rāja* had opened an English school under the auspices of Captain D. L. Richardson, and he invited Ishwar Chandra to send his grandsons. Krishnanagar was about twenty-five kilometers northeast of Ula. As there were no trains in those days, the boys had to stay in Krishnanagar for the week and return home by palanquin on the weekends. During the first term, Kedarnath did well, so much so that he became the pride of his family and the talk of the town. He even received an official award from the king of Krishnanagar. However, such fame proved to be his undoing. He laments:

> Hearing all this praise simply inflated my pride to such an extent that soon all my reading and writing simply

---

15. *Report on the State of Education in Bengal*, cited in *The History of Bengal (1757-1950)*, ed. N. K. Sinha, (Calcutta: University of Calcutta, 1967), 273 & 480-1.

> amounted to nothing. I could no longer perform well in class, so the teacher gave me trouble. Using this as an excuse, the other students who were envious gave me nothing but trouble. I could no longer do my lessons; torment came from all sides. I would leave for school on the palanquin, but I would not go to class. Instead I would hide out in the woods until after school and then return home on the palanquin.[16]

Kedarnath's troubles at Krishnanagar however, were soon interrupted by a much greater calamity—cholera. One evening a friend came to their residence and cooked a meal. That night the boys became violently ill. The doctor said that Kaliprasanna's condition was dangerous and he should be rushed back to Ula. Within an hour of their return, Kaliprasanna died. Kedarnath somehow survived this bout with cholera. Not surprisingly this incident ended his education in Krishnanagar. His mother was so overwhelmed with grief that she refused to send any more of her children away for schooling. For the rest of Kedarnath's childhood he remained in Ula, where he received a mixture of Bengali and English education at the local village schools. During this time he also received training in astrology and tantra from a local ashram of *sādhus*.

In the mid 1840s increasing debt became a grave threat to the Mustauphi family. They retained extensive land holdings in the Murshidabad district north of Calcutta, but since the Permanent Settlement many of their properties had been lost in government auctions. The Permanent Settlement Act of 1793 was passed during the time of Lord Cornwallis (1786–1793) as a measure to stabilize land revenues and improve the condition of the land.[17] The settlement recognized the zamindars as the proprietors of the land so

16. *Jīvanī,* 28.

17. Prior to Permanent Settlement, land was leased for five years to the zamindar paying the highest price. This policy made the zamindar a temporary landholder under pressure to draw as much money as possible from the tenants during his short tenure. Recognizing the poor consequences of this policy, Lord Cornwallis decided to make a permanent settlement of the lands with the zamindars.

long as they paid the government an annual fee. Unfortunately, the fee was so exorbitantly high that many zamindars were hard pressed to pay the lease. On their default the zamindars' land was auctioned. This resulted in the total ruination of many landowners in Bengal, including the Mustauphi family.

To make matters worse, Kedar's two remaining brothers succumbed to cholera, leaving only Kedarnath and his sister, Hemlata, alive. Ishwar Chandra had to borrow heavily to maintain his social status in the village, especially during *pūjā* season. He even considered remarriage as a means to improve his situation. Kedarnath's father, Anand Chandra, was naturally concerned about the future of his family now that the financial situation of the maternal side was weakening. He considered moving back to Calcutta to find work, but dismissed the idea due to the high cost of living there. Finally, Anand Chandra made arrangements to move to Firashdanga,[18] a French colony in Bengal, where he had found work managing an estate. As fate would have it, however, Anand Chandra was also stricken with cholera and abruptly passed away.

In 1849, the eleven-year-old Kedarnath found himself plunged into confusion and depression. The death of his father marked the end of an important era in his life. Whatever trouble there had been in the Mustauphi family prior to this time had not affected him directly, but now the harsh realities of life weighed heavily on his shoulders. His future was uncertain. To make matters worse, he failed to receive some property north of Calcutta which might have come to him through an inheritance. Due to a dispute over the ownership it did not pass to him. Deprived of both his father and his inheritance, Kedarnath describes his plight:

> I was eleven years old when my father passed away, and I was forced to become independent. I constantly worried, "What would become of me?" I saw only darkness. There were no blood relatives to look after me. I was helpless and gradually sinking lower. At school I became listless. I

18. Firashdanga is present day Chandernagore.

> would even take caster oil in order to avoid attendance. Repeatedly my old fever returned.[19] The only redeeming feature of this period was that I avoided bad company. I thought many things over and tried to put my thoughts into poetry. At this time I wrote the *Ulacaṇḍī Māhātmya,* which is now unfortunately lost.[20]

Typical for a boy of this age, Kedarnath questioned the meaning of life, but in the wake of his father's death and the family's financial upheaval, his youthful questioning took on a tone of urgency. He asks, "What is this world? Who are we? Why must there be so much suffering?" He listened to the talk of the villagers about the creation of the world and concluded that they knew nothing of value. He heard the recitations of the *Mahābhārata, Rāmāyaṇa, Kālī-purāṇa,* and other *śāstras,* but it all seemed futile. With a tone of cynicism he questioned the reality of the temple gods and goddesses:

> I even went so far as to watch the image makers and the priests who installed the idols to see when they came alive. Sometimes I would enter a Śiva temple alone and call out to the idol, but there would only be an echo. I thought that perhaps Śiva was teasing me, so I would touch Him and run away. I thought that if Śiva was real then he would grab me, give me some pain or trouble, but he did nothing, so I concluded that the idol was useless.[21]

An old sculptor expressed his opinion to the young Kedar that the *brāhmaṇa* priests and idol makers were cheaters. The sculptor told him that the gods and goddesses were only imagination and that he should just worship *parameśvara* (God). At the same time another member of the Mustauphi family, an uncle named Akhil, reinforced the old sculptor's view. Akhil advised Kedar to have no faith in clay idols, and he especially warned him to beware of the

19. Throughout his life Bhaktivinoda was beset with recurrent bouts of malaria.
20. *Jīvanī,* 48-49.
21. Ibid., 43.

Brahmo Samaj, whose philosophy he considered nothing less than atheism. Daily Akhil would read *Vedānta*, recite the Muslim Kalama and finally kneel and pray as a Christian. He told Kedar that the God of the Veda was the same God of the Qur'an and the Bible. Later on an old Muslim guard and friend told him that Rahim and Rāma where the same. The guard also told him that ghosts were the sons of Satan who lived in fear of the name of Rahim (God).

At the same time Kedar met with many contrary views. Akhil's own son, Parashuram, was an avowed atheist who tried to convince Kedar that nature alone was the source of creation and that God was just another name for nature. On other occasions Kedarnath experienced "*advaitic* fantasies." He imagined that he himself was God, and that his sufferings were the result of his forgetfulness of his own divine nature. He thought that if he could just awaken from his slumber he would find that he himself was God. He even considered whether his sufferings were God's own pastimes (*līlā*)! On other occasions he questioned the *brāhmaṇas* and pundits, who gave him other answers that seemed just as incomprehensible. Bombarded with these opinions, Kedarnath found himself philosophically confused and frustrated.

During this period he describes a simple boyish event that served to calm his confused suffering. There was a tasty fruit grown in a nearby orchard. Unfortunately he was afraid to enter the orchard because it was thought to be haunted by ghosts. The stories that he had heard in his younger days had given him a fear of spirits. In order to allay these fears he went to an old family pundit. The old man confirmed his fears and strongly suggested that he stay away from the orchard altogether. Alarmed, but determined, he questioned an old exorcist, who assured him that if he recited the name of Rāma no spirits would ever disturb him. Somehow, Kedarnath took this old woman's advice and was able to get into the orchard and enjoy the fruit. Kedarnath comments that this old woman's advice about the name of Rāma more than anything else, gave him hope. "Since all the other conclusions were uncertain," he writes, "I never gave up the name of Rāma, which warded off the fear of ghosts."[22]

Although eating the fruit in the orchard was nothing more than a childhood adventure, in his turbulent state of mind, the incident assumed a greater significance. At a time when little else made sense, reciting the name of Rāma was advice that was tangible and effective, both practically and emotionally. It provided him with a sense of security. The advice of the old sculptor and the guard reinforced his confidence and provided an emotional basis for religious faith. Thus the seeds of faith, Vaiṣṇava faith, were planted in the heart of the young Kedarnath.

While Kedarnath wrestled with philosophy, his mother tried to help him, but without her husband's support, there was little she could offer her son. She reasoned that the family was suffering due to her own ill karma, so perhaps the children could be spared from suffering if they no longer belonged to her. She arranged to "sell" Kedarnath and Hemlata to a friend for nine rupees and five rupees respectively. In another attempt to secure a better future for her son, she arranged for him to marry Shaymani Mitra, the five year-old daughter of Madhusudan Mitra of Ranaghat. As before, his mother reasoned that she could improve Kedar's fortune by canceling the effects of her own karma with the good karma of a new family. Unfortunately, his mother had to borrow heavily to finance the marriage, which only made matters worse. Kedarnath describes:

> Acquiring gold from Mother, Nanda Kumar began to make various ornaments. He made enough to cover the whole body. Dashu Mama[23] gave the approval for everything. The expenses were enormous. There was a pleasure boat, a wedding palanquin, decorations, lights and even English music. The marriage was between a twelve-year-old boy and a five-year-old girl and it was exactly like a child's doll marriage, yet so much expense was incurred. On the day of the wedding I drank Ganges water and milk and arrived at the house of my father-in-law to face a huge

22. Ibid., 48.
23. Bhaktivinoda's maternal uncle.

> pompous crowd. The reception was grand. Many gentlemen of the *teli* (oil) caste dressed in bright and varied clothes and wearing *jari* outfits came to the reception. . . . Two speakers read out the family histories. My mother's portion of the cost of the wedding was more than Rs. 2,000, an incredible sum in those days.[24]

Unfortunately, the good luck that Kedarnath's mother worked so diligently for did not appear. Soon after the wedding Ishwar Chandra Mustauphi died, leaving the full weight of household responsibility on the shoulders of the twelve-year-old Kedarnath. He describes his predicament:

> I was living in Ula trying to study, but I could not. I worried too much. Everybody thought that my mother had a lot of money and jewelry, so no one would help. All her wealth was lost except for a few properties. There was so much debt and I was full of anxiety. I was unqualified to look after the affairs of the estate. My grandfather's house was huge. The guards were few and I was afraid of thieves at night so I had to give the guards bamboo sticks to carry.[25]

Shortly after the death of Ishwar Chandra, Kedarnath made his first trip to Calcutta to settle the estate. Calcutta was a strange and fearful place to the young Kedar. He had never seen so many kinds of people. He describes his trip: "By boat we came to Calcutta. Upon arriving my nose was struck by the foul smell of the place. This smell took away my appetite. We stayed in Bhavanipur[26] for a few days and from there we went to many places in Calcutta. We saw Kalighat, but I was so disgusted that I could not appreciate anything. When it was time to leave I was the first to get out."[27] Even though this was a short and unpleasant trip, Calcutta had an effect on the young Kedar. "After that time," he wrote, "I would put on white man's

---

24. *Jīvanī,* 52.
25. Ibid., 54.
26. Then a suburb of Calcutta, now a south central portion of the metropolis.
27. *Jīvanī,* 53.

pants and go and talk with the Europeans. I was very curious to see the finely dressed English ladies. When the missionaries came to town I would go and see them."[28] The youthful Kedar was gaining a taste for European life.

After this trip he spent the next two years in Ula struggling to maintain what was left of Ishwar Chandra's estate. He could not attend school regularly and his education suffered. Finally, in 1852, as he was just turning fourteen, a change for the better took place. His maternal uncle, Kashiprasad Ghosh, a well known poet and newspaper editor, paid a visit to Ula. When Kashi's wife met the young Kedar she immediately recognized the boy's potential and arranged for her husband to meet him. Kashi tested Kedar and concluded that he should come to Calcutta to further his studies. Kashi's wife spoke to Kedarnath's mother requesting that she send her son. At first his mother was hesitant, remembering her previous experience of sending children away to school, but finally she consented, recognizing the limitations of a life in Ula. After the *pūjā* season in the month of November 1852, Kedarnath left his mother and sister at Ula and went to live at the home of Kashiprasad Ghosh on Bidan Street in the heart of Calcutta.

Calcutta 1852

In those days Calcutta was an international hub and the most important city in the British Empire outside of London. It was populated by visitors from almost every part of the world: Chinese, French, Persians, Germans, Arabs, Spaniards, Jews, and Dutch. William Carey, an English missionary, describes Calcutta as:

> the most motley picture that can be imagined. On the streets can be seen at once Europeans in elegant carriages drawn by fine horses, children in carriages drawn by bullocks, and natives in old tattered coaches or indescribable carts, made with bamboo, covered with red curtains, and drawn by horses which can scarcely stand upright. On foot

28. Ibid., 55.

> are people of different nations with their respective national dresses, and all speaking the languages of their own countries.[29]

It was here that Kashiprasad Ghosh had his residence. The Ghosh family, like the Dattas and the Mitras, had moved to Calcutta in the eighteenth century to work with the British. In Calcutta they could enjoy their new wealth and power free from the restraints of Hindu orthodoxy. Kashiprasad, who was the greatest luminary of the Ghosh family, stood at the vanguard of Westernization. As a student attending Hindu College Kashi had become a member of Derozio's Young Bengal. He was now the editor of the *Hindu Intelligencer*, an English language journal that voiced the opinions of the *bhadraloka.*

In spite of its reputation for inducing radical social behavior, Hindu College produced some of the finest literary minds of the day, including Kashiprasad Ghosh. It was at Hindu College that Kashiprasad first began to write in English.[30] His patriotic poems are the first signs of nationalism in Bengal. Even in England he received good reviews. The British journal, *Fraser's Magazine*, referred to Kashiprasad in the following words:

> We may particularly notice the picture of that amazingly clever lad, Kashiprasad Ghosh, the Hindoo poet, whose poem in honor of the Gold River (Ganges) appears not only in *Fisher's Scrap Book,* but in Tom Roscoe's *Oriental Annual.* Kashiprasad ought therefore to feel much honoured. We are told he is a very excellent and worthy young fellow, who drinks brandy pawnee as orthodoxly as if he

---

29. William Carey's letter to his sister, dated 2 December, 1802. Found in *Memoir of William of Carey* (London: 1836), 460.

30. About 1830 Kashiprasad Ghosh contributed to the *Bengal Annual*, the *Literary Gazette* and the *Calcutta Magazine*, both in verse and prose. Many of his writings may be taken as the first patriotic cries roused in Bengal by the introduction of Western culture. There is little doubt that Kashiprasad and many of his contemporaries dreamt of independence.

were a Christian.[31]

It was in this environment that Kedarnath found himself when he came to live in Calcutta. Describing his residence in Calcutta Kedarnath writes:

> I stayed in the home of Kashiprasad Babu. This time I enjoyed Calcutta. The neighborhood, Simla, was beautiful and reminded me of my home village. The house of Kashiprasad was on the north side of the Heduya pond. The house had thick pillars and arches. On the banks of the pond were several missionaries' homes, the church of Krishna Mohan Bannerjee, Queen's College, and Bethune School. The house we stayed in was enjoyable and through the efforts of my aunt and uncle I did well.[32]

The six years (1852-1858) that Kedarnath lived with Kashiprasad had a major impact on his life. In sharp contrast to the rustic world of village Bengal, Calcutta was cosmopolitan. Calcutta was an international city pulsing with the industry of the West. It was a time of global awakening and secularization. Calcutta was London's intellectual colony and the abundance of English literature published in Calcutta led to an intense intellectual atmosphere rivaling any European capital. At the home of Kashiprasad, Kedarnath became deeply involved in the lives of the *bhadraloka*, and under his uncle's guidance he became a full member of the group.

He enrolled at the Hindu Charitable Institution where except for a few trips to Ula he remained until 1856. The Hindu Charitable Institution was one of a number of schools started by the *bhadraloka* to counteract attempts by the missionaries, notably Alexander Duff, to Christianize higher education in Calcutta. There Kedarnath began his life-long acquaintance with the famous Ishwar Chandra Vidyasagar. He writes:

31. *Fraser's Magazine*, November, 1834, 68.
32. *Jīvanī*, 57.

> What can I say? I had limitless faith in Ishwar Babu. He was truthful, sense-controlled, religious, knowledgeable in all the *śāstras* and well-spoken. Through his guidance I prospered well. At the annual examinations I received first prize and obtained a medal. Under his direction I studied English and read many books.[33]

Quickly Kedarnath began to interact in the literary world of Kashiprasad. He would read aloud to his uncle many of the articles that had been presented for publication in his newspaper. Within a short time his command of English improved and he could study most of the works in Kashiprasad's library. He freely availed himself of the Calcutta public library. Eventually Kedarnath began to write poetry in English.

After some time his health deteriorated because of the city's poor drinking water. His doctor advised him to return to Ula for a rest. At first he resisted, but after a particularly bad spell of dysentery he relented and boarded a boat back to Ula. In those days there was no rail service, so the 100 kilometer trip to Ula was a three-day ordeal. During his return the Ganges became rough and dangerous, but eventually he arrived safely in Ula. He comments, "I could not express my happiness when I arrived in Ula. I now understood the meaning of the expression: 'One's mother and mother-land are sweeter than heaven.'[34] I fell at the feet of my mother and cried."[35]

Seeing the frail condition of her son, Kedar's mother became alarmed. She immediately arranged for him to see a local doctor, a *fakir* from the leather worker's caste. He turned out to be a member of the Kartābhajā, a subsect of Vaiṣṇavas.[36]

Not far from Ula, at Ghoshpara, the Kartābhajā had their main center. They were especially reputed as doctors in rural Bengal, so

---

33. Ibid., 58.
34. "*janani-janma-bhumiś ca svargād api garīyasī*"
35. *Jīvanī*, 59.
36. For a study of the Kartābhajā see: Sumanta Banerjee, "From Aulchand to Satima: The Institutionalization of the Syncretist 'Kartā-bhajā' Sect in 19th Century Bengal," paper read at Indian Institute of Advanced Study, Shimla 1994.

it was not surprising that Kedarnath's mother sent her son to a local member of this group for medical treatment. The *fakir* put the boy on a strict regimen of herbal medicine, exorcism and mantras, and in due course, Kedar was cured. During the ordeal he was introduced to the *fakir's* guru at Gauntagram, where he learned the history and philosophy of the sect.

The eighteenth and nineteenth centuries saw a tremendous proliferation of religious sects throughout Bengal. In 1886, Akshay Kumar Datta compiled a list of over fifty heterodox sects that claimed links to Vaiṣṇavism. The Kartābhajā was one of the most powerful. They were even invited to send a representative to the Parliament of Religions in Chicago in 1893.[37]

Aulchand (c. 1686–1779) was the founder of the sect and it was his grand disciple Dulachand (1775–1833) who developed the sect's theology and made the Kartābhajā a powerful movement in Bengal. Dulachand himself was regarded as the incarnation of both Kṛṣṇa and Caitanya. In 1811 the Baptist missionary William Ward recorded that Dulachand had over 400,000 followers spread throughout Bengal. The Kartābhajā believe that they have a genuine link with Vaiṣṇavism and the Caitanya movement.

Interestingly, Kedarnath was soon initiated and given a Kṛṣṇa mantra from the *fakir's* guru, who advised him to avoid meat and the worship of gods other than Kṛṣṇa. Kedarnath responded by stating, "I had faith in the mantra and doctrine, and even though Gurudeva was a *muci* (from a low caste) I had strong faith in him as a guru."[38] Later on Gurudeva predicted that the village of Ula would soon be destroyed by disease.

Bhaktivinoda's relationship to the Kartābhajā has to be clearly understood. Towards the end of the nineteenth century, orthodox Gauḍīya Vaiṣṇavas mounted a massive assault on the Kartābhajā and

37. The Chicago Parliament of Religions was the famous conference attended by Swami Vivekananda, Protap Mazoomdar and others.
38. *Jīvanī,* 64.

other subsects. In the twentieth century the Gaudiya Math, founded by Bhaktivinoda's son, Bhaktisiddhanta Sarasvati, was one of the strongest opponents of the Kartābhajā. Consequently, most of Bhaktivinoda's biographers either totally deny or underplay Kedar's relationship with the Kartābhajā during these teenage years. However, his involvement with the Kartābhajā cannot be overlooked. The ghost in the orchard and his cure by the Kartābhajā are two incidents which contributed to his acceptance of Caitanya Vaiṣṇavism. Twelve years later, when Kedarnath seriously studied the life of Caitanya, he recalled the Kartābhajā as a group of rural men who represented the power of Vaiṣṇava dharma and who helped him to find faith in bhakti (devotion). Of course, Kedar's involvement with the Kartābhajā was at a time when he was young and impressionable. In more theological writings Kedar clearly points out the heterodox nature of the sect. His *Sajjana-toṣaṇī* has harsh criticism of the Kartābhajā. In his autobiography, however, he positively acknowledges the benefit they offered bringing him closer to the Caitanya movement.

After his contact with the Kartābhajā, Kedarnath returned to Calcutta with renewed health. Unfortunately the social influences of the day were just too much, and he could not keep many of the rules that his Kartābhajā guru had suggested. Again he became ill. Only this time, he did not have the heart to return to the Kartābhajā. He frankly admits eating meat which his guru had adamantly forbidden. Instead, with the help of Ishwar Chandra he found an Ayurvedic doctor to cure him.

By his third year in Calcutta Kedarnath was making good literary progress. He regularly wrote for the *Hindu Intelligencer* and with Kashiprasad's help his writing improved. During these days he was immersed in the ideas of the West. He attended many learned meetings and engaged in active social and philosophic debate. Benoy Ghose, in his collection of Indian periodicals from the nineteenth century, includes one of Kedar's speeches before a meeting of the Hogulkuria Debating Club on January 19, 1857. This speech, entitled "What Should be the True Aim of Education," is the earliest known sample of Kedarnath's thought. Interestingly, it is an attack on Young Bengal:

> Let us solve the question—why is Young Bengal all discussion and no action? Is it owing to a defective system of education or no regular education at all? They are learning everything and nothing. They talk morning and evening, noon and night, in the language of Shakespeare and Milton, Byron and Pope. In short, they look upon themselves as perfectly Europeanized and enlightened by English Literature. I admit that they have a good deal of intelligence, but what can that intelligence do while they learn from school to talk nonsense and humbug—to get many things by heart and understand little. What more do we expect from these ill-trained youths?[39]

I wonder whether this speech had the approval of Kashiprasad, who himself had been a notorious member of Young Bengal?

There is just one other sample of Kedarnath's writings that has survived from this period. It is a tract entitled, "The Marriage Systems of Bengal." The work is an historical description of marriage in Bengal that concludes with an attack on the *kulīna brāhmaṇas* and their system of marriage. At this time, Ishwar Chandra Vidyasagar was hotly contesting the issues of widow remarriage and polygamy. Perhaps echoing the views of his teacher, Kedarnath writes:

> Polygamy is the bane of native society—a curse that enslaves many of the softer sex. The Kulina Brahmins are inseparable companions of polygamy. In their society it is as firmly advocated as is American slavery in the Southern States. The Kulina women are no better off than the African blacks. But an African black has many advocates around: he has a voice in the "Anti-Slavery League" whilst a Kulina Brahmini has no zealous friend to tell of her sorrows and

39. Benoy Ghose, *Selections From English Periodicals,* vol. IV (Calcutta: Papyrus 1978), 258.

> relieve them. The legislature ought to hear the cries of the people as far as their interest is concerned. Reform in everything is sought for and as the first movement we desire the removal of polygamy by an enactment.[40]

The home of Kashiprasad was the center of activity for many important *bhadraloka,* including Kristo Das Pal, Shambu Mukhopadhyay, Baneshwar Vidyalankar, and many others who attended the meetings there. Kedarnath came to know these important men, and so formed his intellectual and moral opinions about many issues of the day.

At age eighteen, four years after coming to Calcutta, Kedarnath enrolled in Hindu School, Calcutta's best school. He remained there for the next two years until 1858. This time Ishwar Chandra taught him history. At the Hindu School Kedar found himself amidst an impressive group of classmates: Keshub Chandra Sen, Navagopal Mitra, Satyendranath Tagore and Gajendranath Tagore. Describing Keshub Chandra, Kedar writes:

> At that time Keshub Chandra Sen was a Hindu boy. He studied in the class above me and, like me, he was not good in math. He had no chance of passing that class, but he was very good in literature and established a *sabhā* called the British India Society.[41] Many English professors used to come to that *sabhā* and Keshub requested that I also become a member because I had some taste for literature.[42]

Immersed in the intellectual life of Calcutta, Kedar did well in this school. George Thompson, a well known British parliamentarian, gave public speaking lessons to Kedarnath, Keshub Chandra Sen, and Navagopal Mitra. Thompson told the boys how he prac-

---

40. Babu Kedarnath Datta, *The Marriage System of Bengal.* We have some photocopied pages of this speech, but the source is obscure. I would guess that this piece dates around 1857. He left Calcutta in 1858.

41. This is an obscure statement because the actual British India Society was started by Dwarkanath Tagore and George Thompson.

42. *Jīvanī,* 68.

ticed speech-making by speaking to the trees while on his way to parliament. Both Kedarnath and Keshub Chandra followed his example by gathering young children for an audience and making speeches to them. Kedarnath read everything on philosophy that he could find. He was helped in literature by his teacher and now senior friend, Ishwar Chandra Vidyasagar. Unfortunately, in this atmosphere he also acquired a hard rhetorical attitude. He writes, "We would wander about and go to the different societies like the Free Debating Club. On the strength of my learning I did not think that anyone else had any learning."[43]

Kedarnath soon published the first volume of his English poem *The Poriade,* which he presented to Alexander Duff, a prominent missionary of the day. *The Poriade* was Kedar's first serious piece of writing. It was a work written in English verse describing the wanderings of Porus (King Puru), who fought Alexander the Great and checked his advance into India. Kedarnath intended to complete

43. Ibid., 66.

Ishwar Chandra Vidyasagar
(1820 - 1891)

Keshub Chandra Sen
(1838 - 1884)

the poem in twelve volumes, but subsequently published only one other volume. The second volume was published in 1858. Duff said that he liked the poem, but suggested that he write something about the cruelty of the zamindars next time. Kedarnath was proud of his work and sold copies of it. This provided him with some extra income. With the help of Duff, Kedarnath read Milton, Macaulay, Hazlit, Carlyle, and Edison. He published regularly in the *Library Gazette* of Hindu College and soon acquired the name Mr. ABC.

The relative calm of Kedarnath's life in Calcutta ended abruptly during the fall of 1857 when he made a trip home to Ula.[44] After the second day of traveling he received news of the raging cholera epidemic in his home town. The prediction of his Kartābhajā guru had proved to be true. When he arrived he found that his sister had died along with most of the other members of his family. His mother was still alive, but gravely ill. He describes the pitiful scene:

> Traveling from Calcutta, I heard from one man that an epidemic had killed many people in the village. People from my own home had died. When I heard this I was shocked and I intensified my travel home. For protection I took a man who was skilled in stick fighting and on the way many people described the horrible state of the village. Reaching our home, I saw the main door open. I called out many times until someone answered, "Babu, come inside." By then I could barely stand up. Running towards the *pūjā* room I called out again and my aunt came and brought me to my room. She was hysterical. She told me that Hemlata had died and that my mother was very sick. I entered my mother's room and found that she had been delirious with fever for a week. Mother began to cry. I said that we must leave Ula at once. During the night I could not eat or drink and I slept only a little. Rising in the morning I heard that all the servants had died. On the day before we set out, I went to many places in Ula.

44. The year 1857 is, of course, most famous for the Sepoy Mutiny. Bhaktivinoda hardly mentions the mutiny, presumably because he is preoccupied with the destruction of Ula and other calamities in his own life.

> Everywhere the houses were empty. At some homes bodies were lying all around. At other homes there were the cries of pain from those who were dying. Others were making preparations to leave. It was the time of the Durgā *pūjā*, but there was no happiness. The fever was terrible and whoever got it could die within a few hours.[45]

After a few days Kedarnath, his mother and grandmother left Ula and reached Calcutta. There he sank into depression. He recalls his plight: "I was seventeen years old and I had to face terrible hardships. There was no money. I could hardly speak to anyone. Everyone thought that my mother had a lakh[46] of rupees; no one believed that we were poor. I saw no hope. My mind became apathetic, the house was empty, and I had no strength. My heart was dying of pain."[47]

Feeling helpless and devastated by the destruction of Ula and the loss of his family, Kedarnath could no longer maintain his previous haughty outlook. His life lay in shambles. He sought shelter at Jorasanko, the home of the Tagores. There he had two friends, Dvijendranath and Satyendranath Tagore. It was with Dvijendranath that Kedarnath found solace. He writes, "If ever among men there was a close friend, he was that friend. He was charitable, of good character, loving, and honest. My heart was uplifted being near him and all my troubles would go away. He was without attachment for worldly things and when I was with him I became happy and gave up my thoughts of material things."[48]

With the help of his friend, Kedarnath gradually overcame this crisis, but the destruction of Ula was the final step severing him from his childhood roots. Now he was alone in Calcutta with his mother and grandmother. He no longer had one foot planted in rural Bengal. The arrogant attitude that he had acquired under Kashiprasad had been crushed. He began to have religious feelings,

45. *Jīvanī,* 73-74.
46. 100,000 rupees
47. *Jīvanī,* 77.
48. Ibid., 78.

and together he and Dvijendranath studied Sanskrit and religion. They studied Kant, Goethe, Hegel, Swedenborg, Hume, Voltaire, and Schopenhauer and discussed various theological problems. Dvijendranath was impressed by his younger friend's discriminating abilities, and under his guidance Kedar often addressed the British Indian Society and other learned gatherings. Now he spoke on religious questions instead of political and social issues as he had done under Kashiprasad's tutelage.

At the home of the Tagores, Kedarnath intensely studied the books of the Brahmo Samaj, and for a time his faith in Brahmo philosophy grew. With great interest he studied with many Brahmo missionaries, but after some time he began to lose interest in their philosophy. He writes, "I studied the books and lectures of the Brahmo Samaj. Their belief in one God was good and for a while I accepted their philosophy, but in the end the theology and the worship of the Brahmos had no appeal for me."[49] During this time Kedarnath met an American Unitarian missionary, the Reverend Charles H. Dall, who had just arrived in Calcutta. Dall was to have a profound influence on Kedar's life.

On 18 June 1855, Reverend Charles Dall began his thirty-one year ministry in Calcutta representing American Unitarian interests in India. Prior to this, the Brahmo Samaj had made an impact in America by creating interest within the growing Unitarian movement in Boston. The American Unitarian Association of Boston sent Dall to India to investigate the Brahmo Samaj and find out how it might aid Unitarian concerns. Dall was requested to teach, sell, and give away books about the Unitarians to the educated Bengalis of Calcutta. Just a few weeks after his arrival in Calcutta, Dall wrote to his mission in America that he had an active congregation of fifty natives. He reports, "Some Hindoos of education, and a few of the Society of Rammohun Roy attend and also meet me during the week for conversation. Of these native gentlemen, some contribute towards our expenses, many purchase our Unitarian books, and a

49. Ibid., 80.

few look earnestly towards Christianity."[50] Kedarnath Datta was a member of Reverend Dall's congregation.

Kedarnath met daily with Reverend Dall, who personally directed his readings. Under Dall's guidance he studied the Bible and the Unitarian writings of Channing, Emerson, Parker, and Newman.[51] He soon developed strong sympathies toward Christianity. At the same time he read Sale's Qur'an. Kedar writes, "I discussed theology with Padre Dall and on his advice I read the Bible and various Christian books. Previously I read all books on philosophy, but now I preferred to read books on religion. I developed a deep faith in Jesus Christ. Whatever I read I discussed with Dvijendranath."[52]

Dall's brand of Unitarianism fascinated the young *bhadraloka.* The Unitarians admitted that God's truth had come to mankind at other times and places than in ancient Palestine. The era in India when the Vedas and Upanishads were revealed was one instance of God at work; however, darkness had fallen on India in recent centuries until at last Christ's truth had come. Compared with Alexander Duff and the other missionaries, Dall's theology was liberal and the writings of Channing and Parker appealed to both Kedarnath and Dvijendranath. The influence of Theodore Parker and Ralph Waldo Emerson are especially prominent throughout the writings of Kedar. But no matter how appealing, Dall's views were still Christian, and to Dvijendranath his efforts to convert Hindus into Unitarians were unacceptable.

There is little doubt that Dall's attempt to convert Kedarnath was blunted by Dvijendranath, who kept a tight watch on his vulnerable friend at this time. Apart from the influence of Unitarian

---

50. Spencer Lavan, *Unitarians and India: A Study in Encounter and Response* (Chicago: Exploration Press, 1991), 84.

51. William Ellery Channing (1780–1842) was one of the most eloquent preachers and prominent spokesman for American Unitarianism in the early 19th century. Ralph Waldo Emerson (1803–1882) was ordained as a Unitarian minister in 1829, but resigned his pulpit in 1832. Theodore Parker (1810–1860) attended the Harvard Divinity School and in 1837 became a Unitarian. Francis W. Newman (1805–1897) was the younger brother of the more famous John Henry Newman (1801–1890). Francis W. Newman was a Unitarian.

52. *Jīvanī,* 80.

ideas that became a part of Kedar's thought, Dall's efforts had one other important and lasting effect on the young Kedarnath. It stirred within him the sentiments of devotion, and although such feelings had been thwarted by Dvijendranath because of the negative Christian context, Kedar's sentiments of devotion had been kindled and left waiting for the appropriate moment to be set ablaze.

Late in 1857 Kedarnath tried to find work and rent a house in Calcutta. His young wife, who was still living with her family, had asked if she could come to live with him. Now that he had both his mother and wife to support he decided to set up his first household. He was nineteen. His wife was twelve. Jobs were hard to find in Calcutta, but eventually he found work as a private tutor for twelve rupees per month. He rented a house in the liquor dealers' (Shunri) district along with a servant and maid for eight rupees per month! Later that year he found a better job as a teacher at the Hindu Charitable Institution, his old school, making fifteen rupees per month. Unfortunately this was not enough income, and within a few months he accumulated a debt of over sixty rupees. In the end his mother had to sell a gold necklace to pay the debt. Kedarnath and his family moved back to a relative's house. Eventually he lost his teaching job. After that he found a job buying and selling sugar in the markets of Calcutta, but this work was so riddled with cheating that he soon quit. In the end he writes, "I was going around Calcutta trying to get a job, but it was impossible; there were so few jobs compared to the number of people needing them. I did not have a permanent residence in Calcutta and I simply could not live without money."[53]

Soon a message arrived from Rajballabh, Kedarnath's paternal grandfather in Orissa, requesting that he come at once. His grandfather stated that he would not live much longer and desired to see Kedar as soon as possible. Kedarnath consulted with his mother and decided there was nothing to gain by remaining in Calcutta. In the spring of 1858, with his mother and young wife, he set out for the village of Chutimangal in Orissa.

---

53. Ibid., 88.

An assembly of court magistrates *circa* 1890.
Kedarnath Datta Bhaktivinoda is seated in the middle.

Chapter Three

The Working Years

1858 – 1874

Orissa 1858

From the day Kedarnath left Calcutta in 1858 till he began his career in government service in 1866, he lived apart from the ferment of Calcutta and the overwhelming seduction of the modern world. It was a period of transition, a time to digest his college years spent with Kashiprasad and the Tagores. It was a time to reestablish and consolidate his traditional roots. Without this opportunity to rediscover and reflect on his past in the light of his Western education, he might have remained enmeshed in the onslaughts of modernity, alienated from his traditional roots. The move away from Calcutta allowed him time to synthesize his traditional roots and the modern world. During this period Kedar's views on the Brahmo Samaj, Positivism, Śāktism, Christianity and, of course, Vaiṣṇavism began to mature. By the time he re-emerged he was ready to face the modern world with a new sense of stability and direction. No longer would he simply react to its overwhelming influences as he had done in his teenage years.

Kedarnath came to the home of his paternal grandfather, Rajballabh Datta, at Chutimangal, fifty kilometers east of Cuttack in central Orissa. Life in the home of Rajballabh was the very antithesis of life with Kashiprasad and the Tagores. Rajballabh himself was a Śākta, a worshipper of the goddess Kālī. During the eighteenth century, Śākta and Tantric influences had attracted many Bengali zamindars away from Vaiṣṇavism, and although Rajballabh's grandfather, Madan Mohan Datta was a well known Vaiṣṇava, Rajballabh's father had introduced Śāktism into the family at that time. Kedarnath describes his grandfather as a *kālī-siddha* dressed in crimson cloth like a *sannyāsī,* reciting the names of *devī* during the day and smoking tobacco and *gāñjā* from a large hookah with friends in the evening. His reputation for pulling live cobras from their holes and killing them on his hard wooden shoes best illustrates Rajballabh's eccentric nature.

Kedarnath lived with his grandfather for six months until he obtained a job as an English teacher. At that time he moved to the nearby town of Kendra. The local superintendent of schools, Doctor Roer, was so impressed by Kedarnath that he encouraged him to take the teacher's certification exam in Puri. In the meantime Kedar taught school in Kendra during the week, returning to Chutimangal only on the weekends.

Soon Rajballabh asked Kedar to remain in Chutimangal because his death was fast approaching. Kedar describes Rajballabh's passing:

> Even though my grandfather said that he would die in a few days, I did not see any signs of illness. After three days he asked me to come to his bed. He had a small fever and was sitting up chanting and smoking tobacco from his hookah. He was surrounded by a dozen friends, who were chatting with him. Calling me to his side he spoke, "After I am gone, do not remain in Orissa. Whatever job that you get by age twenty-seven will be your main life's work. You are destined to become a famous Vaiṣṇava. You have my blessings." With that he passed away, releasing his vital breath through the top of his head (*brahma-randhram*). Such an amazing death is rarely seen![1]

After the passing of Rajballabh, Kedar moved to nearby Cuttack to work as a sixth grade English teacher. His salary was a mere twenty rupees per month, but he enjoyed living in Cuttack. He writes, "In Cuttack the eating was good. The price of ghee (clarified butter)

1. *Jīvanī,* 93.

was cheap. I was able to eat the best rice in the morning and all the *luci* one could desire in the afternoon."[2] In Cuttack he would regularly go to the library and read books on philosophy and religion.

In March of 1860, at age twenty-two, Kedar left Cuttack to become a school principal at Bhadrak in northern Orissa. This time his monthly salary was forty-five rupees. He stayed in Bhadrak for less than a year and during that time he wrote his first prose work, *The Maths of Orissa,* describing many of the monasteries that he had seen throughout Orissa. A few years later William Hunter utilized Kedar's book in his own work entitled, *History of Orissa* (1866).[3] In Bhadrak, Kedarnath's first son, Annada Prasad, was born.

Preferring to live in Bengal, Kedar soon gave up his position as principal and moved to Midnapore in southern Bengal to become a fifth grade English teacher. He was twenty-three years old. In Midnapore he stayed with Raj Narayan Basu, a well known Brahmo Samaj leader who later became the grandfather of Shri Aurobindo. Kedar describes the Bengali community in Midnapore as turbulent due to the constant struggle between the Hindus and the Brahmos. Although Raj Narayan was the headmaster of the school in Midnapore where Kedarnath worked, Kedarnath's sympathy lay with the Hindus. While living in Calcutta, he had made up his mind about the Brahmo Samaj and at this time he firmly sided with the Hindus. He recalls:

> In those days I was with the Hindus. I had decided that the philosophy of the Brahmos was incomplete. I also thought that the brotherly philosophy taught by Jesus Christ was best. I felt that the real taste of worship was devotion and unfortunately the Brahmos lacked this taste. All the time I read books by Theodore Parker and other Unitarians, which I obtained from Calcutta. From my childhood I had developed faith in devotion. In particular I was attracted by the devotion of Jesus.[4]

---

2. Ibid., 97.
3. N. K. Saha, *A History of Orissa by W. W. Hunter* (Calcutta: Susil Gupta, 1956).
4. *Jīvanī,* 101.

Even in later years Kedarnath often equates the devotion of Christianity with the bhakti of the Vaiṣṇavas. In his *Kṛṣṇa-saṁhitā* he describes Christianity as a *vaiṣṇava* type religion because of its theistic perspective and emphasis on devotion to God. For Bhaktivinoda the foundation of all religious life is *bhakti-rasa.*

Here he compares Śāktism, Vaiṣṇavism and Brahmo philosophy:

> The Śāktas would perform a sacrifice and kill animals and eat the meat, but the Vaiṣṇavas would not kill. I remember a Vaiṣṇava named Jaga, who used to come to our home dancing and singing and doing *nāma-kīrtana* with eyes crying like torrents of rain. All these incidents created great faith. When I was sick the Kartābhajā cured me and I realized the strength of the Vaiṣṇava dharma. There was substance in the Vaiṣṇava dharma, and it was the bhakti that gave me faith. I saw only low activities in Śākta dharma, and as far as I could see, the Brahmos were without dharma or *rasa* of any kind. Gradually I came to these conclusions.[5]

While visiting Calcutta, Kedar again read the *Tattva Bodhini,* the journal of the Brahmo Samaj, and talked with his old friends Dvijendranath and Satyendranath Tagore. This time he was not interested in Brahmo philosophy. He even preferred to visit with Reverend Charles Dall and the other missionaries than with the Brahmos. He frankly admits that his heart was captivated by the devotion of Jesus more than anything else. Surprisingly Kedar never fully embraced Christianity. It was a constant frustration to Dall and the other missionaries that in spite of all their efforts relatively few *bhadraloka* ever became Christians.

In Midnapore Kedarnath met a *jāti* Vaiṣṇava[6] who gave him some books on Vaiṣṇavism and told him about Caitanya. This was

5. *Jīvanī,* 101–102.

6. The *jāti* Vaiṣṇavas are followers of Caitanya originally taken from the lower classes of Bengali society. See: Joseph T. O' Connell, "Jāti-Vaiṣṇavas of Bengal: 'Subcaste' *(Jāti)* without 'Caste' (*Varṇa*)," *Journal of Asian and African Studies* XVII, 3-4, 1982.

his first substantial contact with Caitanya. He tried to find a copy of *Caitanya-caritāmṛta* and the *Bhāgavata*, but was unable. It would take another eight years before Kedar could secure a copy of these works. He concedes that during these days he developed a strong yearning for bhakti, but still he did not follow any Vaiṣṇava practices. There is a good possibility that had Kedarnath not eventually reposed his feelings of devotion in Caitanya he might well have embraced the love of Jesus and become a Christian. It was the nectar of devotion that he yearned for.

In Midnapore another calamity struck. Kedar's childhood wife passed away, leaving him in shock. He laments: "When my wife was sick all my friends helped me. I endured this grief like the warrior in Longfellow's *Psalm of Life*. In silence, I prayed telling God all my problems, but I could not understand how God was a person. Simultaneously I believed that God was formless and with form, but I could not reconcile the two views."[7]

There is a long standing debate concerning the nature of the Absolute within Hinduism. Vaiṣṇavas assert that ultimately God has form and is a person. The contrary view supposes that God is ultimately formless and impersonal. In his grief-stricken condition, Kedarnath wrestled with this problem. He admits that intellectually the formlessness of God was more agreeable, but emotionally, in his times of need, the idea of God in personal form was more appealing. He was unable to find solace in a God that was formless and impersonal. In these times of trouble it is clear that he was gradually being drawn towards the theistic conclusions of the Vaiṣṇavas.

Alone and with a ten-month-old child, Kedarnath could not remain single for long. Within a couple of months he arranged to marry the daughter of Gangamoy Roy from Jakpore. Her name was Bhagavati Devi. His plans to re-marry raised some eyebrows in Midnapore and Calcutta. His English friends and some of the *bhadraloka*, like his uncle Kashiprasad disapproved, suggesting that it was too soon.

Regardless of the objections, the marriage went ahead with just

7. *Jīvanī*, 104.

a simple ceremony. Soon he ended his short career as a teacher and moved to Burdwan, taking a job as a translator with the Land Revenue Service. Quickly he was repulsed by the ruthless practices of tax collection and within a short time he quit and took a clerical position for a mere thirty rupees per month. Somehow he survived in Burdwan acting as a clerk and a money agent, but the need for money and a steady job remained a constant problem.

In spite of his financial difficulties, his literary life carried on. He published two Bengali poems, one about the destruction of Ula called "*Vijanagrāma,*" and the other about a religious life entitled "*Sannyāsī.*" The style of these poems was excellent and they were appreciated by many literary men including Michael Madhusudan Datta, Nabin Sen, Hemachandra Bandyopadhyay and Bankim Chandra. *Vijanagrāma,* in particular, was noted for its literary merit. It was the first use of Bengali blank verse (*amitrākṣara-chanda*), incorporating the style of Milton and Byron. *Vijanagrāma* influenced Michael Madhusudan, who later perfected the style in his *Tilottamā-sambhava* and *Meghanāda-vadha. The Calcutta Review* published a critique of both of Kedarnath's poems.

> We have glanced at this little volume of Bengali verse, which we have no hesitation in recommending as suitable especially for Hindu women. We hope the author will continue to give his countrymen the benefit of his elegant and unassuming pen, which is quite free from those objectionable licenses of thought and expression which abound in many dramas recently published. The want of the day is the creation of a literature for Hindu ladies and we trust that many more educated natives will have the good sense to devote their time and abilities to the attainment of this most desirable end.[8]

Unfortunately, Kedarnath Datta has not been adequately appreciated as a writer of Bengali literature. Perhaps this is due to his exclusive Vaiṣṇava orientation. Kedarnath was a writer in his own

8. *Calcutta Review,* vol. 39 (1863), 452.

right and as good as any of his better known colleagues.

In Burdwan, Kedarnath often met with Lal Bihari De and Keshub Chandra Sen, old friends from his college days in Calcutta. Keshub Chandra Sen had become an impressive Brahmo leader and Lal Bihari an important Christian missionary. Like Midnapore, Burdwan was also in social turmoil, only this time the controversy was between Brahmos and Christians. Being friends of both, Kedar found himself caught in the middle. Sometimes he was asked to mediate, but this usually ended with his receiving the rage of both.

He made an attempt to compromise by starting his own group, the Bhratri Samaj (The Brotherly Society). Unfortunately this only made matters worse when many Brahmos and Christians left their respective groups to join him. The Bhratri Samaj met regularly in the Burdwan public library. One of Kedar's speeches entitled "Soul" attracted a lot of attention even in Calcutta and was published in the journal *Public Engagement.*

In those days lack of money was still one of Kedarnath's greatest problems. His wife was pregnant and he was without a decent job. In 1864 his second child, Saudamani, was born in Jakpur. Then an employment opportunity arose. A friend in the Registrar's office was planning a leave of absence and needed a replacement. The monthly pay was 140 rupees, and he would have to give half of the earnings to his friend, but it was better than his present salary. It also meant a possibility of future government service. Kedar gladly accepted the position.

Government Service 1866 – 1894

"In bad times," Kedar writes, "there is nothing but trouble; in good times the whole world is your friend. On 9 February 1866 I received three separate letters of employment for government service and the whole world became my friend."[9] At last it seemed that Rajballabh's prediction of a permanent career was coming true. The position Kedar finally accepted was Special Deputy Registrar of Assurances with Powers of a Deputy Magistrate and Deputy

9. *Jīvanī,* 116.

Collector of the 6th-grade of the Sub-executive service. Even though the position was in Bihar, it was a permanent job, and it meant the end of Kedar's financial problems.[10]

During the nineteenth century government service was the ambition of the *bhadraloka.* Michael Madhusudan was head clerk and interpreter to the police magistrate in Calcutta. Raj Narayan Basu was headmaster of a government school in Midnapore. Ishwar Chandra Vidyasagar was the principal of Sanskrit College. Bankim Chandra became a Deputy Magistrate, and above all, Ramesh Chandra Datta (1848–1909) belonged to the "heaven born" Indian Civil Service (I. C. S.).

The lot of those who secured government service was enviable compared with those who did not. Parents regarded their lives a failure if their sons did not receive government posts. Many resorted to bribing. The very association with government was a privilege; a government toll-keeper, receiving a meager salary of three rupees, was socially superior to a shopkeeper whose earnings were many times higher. Besides social status, government positions carried other attractions: a few weeks paid leave, free service of domestic workers, and a pension.

To run the affairs of India the British created an elaborate administrative system. On top were the covenanted civilians known as the Indian Civil Service. This group of only 900 men was almost totally British, and they controlled all the key positions from governor down to district officer. For many decades no Indians were admitted to any positions of government authority, but with an act passed at the urging of Dwarkanath Tagore in 1843,[11] the British

10. See Appendices for a summary of Bhaktivinoda's government work history.

11. The British had divided Bengal into a number of administrative districts. In charge of each region was a District Judge, Collector and Magistrate—all members of the Executive Service. Immediately below them was the Sub-executive Service, which was similarly headed by a Deputy Collector and Deputy Magistrate, etc. The positions of Deputy Magistrate and Deputy Collector were originally suggested by Dwarkanath Tagore, who urged that "they should be taken from the respectable class of people and should be stationed in the interior, and their powers in criminal cases should correspond with those of Moonsiffs."

created a second tier of bureaucratic service comprising educated Indians—the *bhadraloka*. This group of non-commissioned civilians, known as the Sub-executive Service, shadowed the Executive Service. Compared with salaries paid in the Executive Service, salaries paid in the Sub-executive Service were low, but by Indian standards, they were more than adequate. It was this unprecedented bureaucratic organization, with its relatively high wages, that allowed the British to control the affairs of India.

Kedarnath spent his career in the Sub-executive Service. During the next twenty-eight years he was employed in various districts of Bihar, Orissa, and Bengal. He does not mention his starting salary, but a fair estimate would be two hundred rupees per month. His English colleagues in the Executive Service made at least fifteen times this salary. By retirement in 1894 he had risen from sixth grade to second grade with a salary of four hundred rupees per month, a high and respected position by Indian standards. He retired with a pension of almost four thousand rupees per annum.

Like Kedar's early days in Calcutta, these working years were a time when he was in full contact with the British and the pressures of modernization. Only now there was a difference. As a youth he was vulnerable and easily swayed by the forces of modernization. His exposure to British education upset his confidence in his Bengali ancestory, making it impossible to accept the traditions of his forefathers. His family's declining fortune made him weak and insecure. Cholera dealt the final blow when it destroyed his ancestral home. In the end he was pulled away from the tormented world of the *bhadraloka* in Calcutta and given shelter under the ancestral traditions of his grandfather in Orrisa.

Kedar's years in government service reveal a different personality. Employed in the Sub-executive Service, he had social status. He was a proficient and loyal servant of the British Raj,[12] a man in step

12. Bhaktivinoda is renowned for his staunch support of the British. In his *Sajjanatoṣaṇī* he writes: *āmādera varttamāna adhīśvarī śrīmatī mahārāṇī bhikoriyā svacchanda śarīre o nirud-vighna antaḥkaraṇe eī bhārate rājya karite thākuna/* (ST vol. 4 p. 1) "May our present empress Victoria continue to rule over this India in a healthy body and tranquil spirit."

with his times. His demeanor was strong and commanding. These working years begin with Kedarnath standing firm, free of the deficiencies and confusion of his past student days.

Kedar's employment in government service was not the only reason for his change in demeanor. Deep within, a transformation was taking place. There was an emerging devotional personality. His days in Calcutta had forced him to grapple with Western philosophy, modern rationalism, and various Bengali polemics. He had even been pushed to the threshold of Christianity, where he had learned the importance of devotion. Now he began to search for devotional traditions within his own culture. During these working years he would come to accept bhakti as the heart of his religious life. For Kedarnath, bhakti would provide the key to his synthesis of modernity and tradition. These years in government service show Kedar reposing his devotional sentiments in Caitanya Vaiṣṇavism instead of Christianity and other ideas from the west.

On receiving his appointment, Kedar assembled his wife and family, including their family dog Tiger[13] and headed for Sharan in Bihar. There he rented a second–story apartment near the court house. The British practice of sending government officials to remote areas led to the custom of wives traveling with their husbands. Ordinarily the wives and children of Indian officers would remain in the joint–family home in Calcutta or the ancestral village, but with the changing times the adoption of English standards of family life became a common practice among the *bhadraloka.* So in 1867 Kedar's third child, Kadambani, was born in Bihar.

Kedarnath's position on the circuit court afforded him the opportunity to see the countryside and study local history. He was fond of learning regional matters. When he lived in Cuttack he wrote about the *maṭhas* of Orissa. The Sharan area of Bihar was the home of *nyāya,* Gautama's system of logic. When Kedar learned of this, he spoke on the topic and urged the establishment of a school

13. To consider dogs as family members was an unheard of practice by normal Indian standards. That Kedar kept Tiger as a family pet indicates the extent of his adoption of British domestic practices.

dedicated to preserving the traditions of *nyāya* in Bihar. Years later, the cornerstone for just such a school was laid by Sir Rivers Thompson, the Lieutenant Governor of Bengal. Kedar also prepared an Urdu translation of a manual for the Registration Department called the *Bāḷid-i-Registry*, which was soon circulated throughout the provinces of Agra and Oudh.

Much of Kedar's time in Sharan was spent embroiled in trouble with some local Europeans. When he arrived he found himself in a raging dispute with the indigo planters. Before he had come to Sharan the local European magistrate, whom he had replaced, along with the chief of police and an English doctor, had been regularly accepting payments from the indigo planters for preferential treatment. Kedar refused to go along with such a scheme. This put him at odds with the two remaining Europeans. He eventually navigated the mess with the help of his superior officer, Halliday Sahib. In the end he gained a reputation for honesty and firmness.

In his autobiography Kedar makes a number of frank statements about his diet in Bihar. Evidently the Sharan region was famous for a particular kind of hot pickle that he liked to eat with fish and goat meat. He comments, "At that time I ate fish and meat, but I knew that killing animals was not good. I persisted simply because I enjoyed the food. I would have liked to have eaten fish, but its quality was so poor that I ate more goat instead."[14] It was not until 1880, at the time of his Vaiṣṇava initiation, that Kedarnath finally gave up meat eating. Amongst Caitanya's followers meat eating is strictly shunned, so we must appreciate Kedarnath's candor in freely admitting this practice.

During the nineteenth century, beef eating and alcohol consumption caused great controversy among many *bhadraloka* families. In Hindu society beef eating and drinking had never been an accepted practice, but with the advent of the Europeans these practices became more common. Many students of Hindu College, as we have noted, experimented with alcohol and beef as a sign of their liberality. This understandably caused anguish to many parents.

---

14. *Jīvanī,* 120.

Amongst the Bengalis some degree of meat consumption was prevalent. This included most of the *kāyasthas* and the *vaidyas* unless a family was strictly Vaiṣṇava. It is not unusual to find Kedar's family eating goats and water buffalo during the Durgā *pūjā*. In Kedar's case, meat eating was the result of his *kāyastha* background and not his defiance of Hindu orthodoxy. There is no evidence that he ever ate beef or drank alcohol like his maternal uncle Kashiprasad Ghosh, and most of his associates.

One requirement of the Sub-executive Service was an annual law examination. In fact, career advancement depended on the successful outcome of these examinations. In preparation for the examination, Kedar studied English law, but when he took the exam he failed. These annual examinations were to become a constant headache for Kedarnath. Eventually, with the help of his supervisory officer, Beverley Sahib, his attempt in Patna was a success. The date was 5 June 1867. Kedar was twenty-nine years old.

Rail service had recently come to many parts of India, so Kedarnath and a few friends took an excursion to Vrindavan, 1500 kilometers to the west of Bengal. This was Kedar's first trip to Vrindavan. He writes, "In those days my faith in Hindu dharma was not so strong and whatever bhakti I had was mixed with *jñāna*. While in Vrindavan I could not appreciate the taste of devotion. I simply became sick from drinking Yamuna water."[15]

When Kedar returned from this trip he faced another set of law examinations and failed. Fortunately, the British soon reorganized the Sub-executive Service and he was allowed to transfer from the Sub-collectorate branch to the Sub-judicial branch where he did not have to face as many examinations. After a short stay at Purneah he became Deputy Magistrate in Dinajpur in northern Bengal. The date was 17 March 1868.

In Dinajpur the Vaiṣṇava community was large and dynamic, which offered many spiritual opportunities. In this environment his devotional sentiments sprang to life. Not since his teaching days in

15. *Jīvanī*, 228. The Yamuna river flows past Vrindavan and pilgrims eagerly drink her waters for blessings and purification.

Midnapore, seven years before, had he met so many followers of Caitanya. With the help of Pratap Chandra Roy, a local merchant, he finally obtained a copy of the *Caitanya-caritāmṛta* and the *Bhāgavata-purāṇa.* The life of Śrī Caitanya proved to be the turning point for Kedarnath. He comments:

> My first reading of *Caitanya-caritāmṛta* created some faith in Caitanya. On the second reading I understood that Caitanya was unequaled, but I doubted how such a good scholar with so high a level of *prema* could recommend the worship of Kṛṣṇa, who had such a questionable character. I was amazed, and I thought about this in detail. Afterwards, I humbly prayed to God, "O Lord, please give me the understanding to know the secret of this matter." The mercy of God is without limit and so I soon understood. From then on I believed that Caitanya was God. I often spoke with many *vairāgīs* to understand Vaiṣṇava dharma. From childhood the seeds of faith for Vaiṣṇava dharma had been planted within my heart and now they had sprouted. I experienced *anurāga* (spiritual yearning) and day and night I read and thought about Kṛṣṇa.[16]

Kedar's concern about the character of Kṛṣṇa has to be understood in the context of nineteenth century Bengal. It was a commonly held view that the character of Kṛṣṇa was flawed due to Kṛṣṇa's apparent moral lapses. From various texts like the *Mahābhārata* and *Bhāgavata-purāṇa* Kṛṣṇa is known to have lied, to have married numerous wives, and to have spent time alone with others' wives. Many *bhadraloka* felt that Kṛṣṇa's character was morally questionable. These concerns primarily arose from Christian and Utilitarian influences and were later discussed extensively by both Bhaktivinoda and Bankim Chandra in their respective writings.

In Dinajpur Kedar found his "Eastern Savior," Śrī Caitanya, and whatever philosophical and spiritual restlessness remained was

16. Ibid., 130.

finally put to rest. As Caitanya's life changed after his visit to Gaya, so Kedar's life changed with his reading of the *Caitanya-caritāmṛta*. Soon he began to write and speak on Vaiṣṇava topics. The oratory training he had received from George Thompson in Calcutta's debating clubs made him an eloquent speaker. At the request of some local Vaiṣṇavas he delivered his famous speech, *The Bhagavat: Its Philosophy, Ethics and Theology*, at a meeting in the home of a friend. Many *bhadraloka* were present and the speech was well received. In this speech we find the seeds of Kedar's synthesis of modern thought and Vaiṣṇava orthodoxy. He discusses the place of the *Bhāgavata* in Hindu philosophy and explains why the *Bhāgavata* had been misunderstood and rejected by such great thinkers as Rammohun Roy.

As usual there was a lot of competition between the Hindus and Brahmo Samaj in Dinajpur. The Brahmos tried to enlist Kedar. Only this time he sent them a letter stating that he was now a follower of Caitanya Mahāprabhu. From then on they left him alone.

In 1868 his wife gave birth to a son, who died within a few days. Kedar writes, "My wife was very sad and at the same time her father also died. I tried to keep the news of her father's death a secret for a few days, but I could not. Two calamities together make a very sad time. It was a difficult period for us."[17] A few days later he also failed another departmental law examination.

On 25 October 1869 Kedar was transferred to nearby Champaran, where another son, Radhika Prasad, was born. Again he attempted the law examination, but still he could not pass. His failure to pass these examinations eventually led to his transfer from Bengal, the main sphere of British activity, to Orissa. On 14 April 1870 Kedarnath was transferred to Puri in the Orissan district of Cuttack.[18] For Kedar his transfer from Bengal to Puri was no loss.

---

17. Ibid., 132.

18. Even as early as 1827 the British had adopted the practice of keeping only their best men in Calcutta. David Kopf reports in his research from the Proceedings of the College of Fort William, (National Archives, New Delhi) vol. DLIX (nd.) 630, that the College Council expelled thirteen students for "idleness" and sent them to remote stations in East Bengal and Orissa.

Puri was the earthly home of Jagannātha, one of the most important pilgrimage sites in all of India. It was also the spiritual home of Caitanya Mahāprabhu. His transfer to Puri was indeed a great blessing. There he would have access to the famous Jagannātha temple and the shelter of his beloved Caitanya. In the mood of a pilgrim Kedar writes, "At that time Radhika was a baby and so I decided to go ahead alone; taking one *Bhāgavata* and *Caitanya-caritāmṛta* I proceeded to Calcutta on my way to Puri."[19]

Puri 1870

On 8 August 1803 the British took possession of Orissa and the famous Puri Jagannātha Temple. Spelling out British policy towards the temple, Marquis Wellesley, the commander of British field forces, wrote to his commanding field officer:

> On your arrival at Jaggarnaut, you will employ every possible precaution to preserve the respect of the pagoda due to the religious prejudices of the brahmins and pilgrims. You will furnish the brahmins with such guards and shall offer perfect security to their persons, rites and ceremonies and to the sanctity of the religious edifices, and you will strictly enjoin those under your command to observe your order on this important subject with the utmost degree of accuracy and vigilance.[20]

Throughout British reign in India, Wellesely's policy was taken with the utmost seriousness. Later, Thomas Munro expressed the feelings behind such a policy, "In every country, but especially in this, where the rulers are so few and of a different race from the people, it is the most dangerous of all things to tamper with religious feelings."[21] The primary interest of the British was

19. *Jīvanī,* 134.

20. India, Governor-General, *Intercepted correspondence from India: containing Despatches from Marquis Wellesley During his Administration in India* (London: P Hand, 1805), 269–270.

21. Nancy Gardner Cassels, *Religion and Pilgrim Tax under the Company Raj,* South

commerce and so the East India Company took great care not to interfere with matters of religion. The company wanted daily life to continue as usual without any interference that might unsettle the population. Wellesley's directive was fashioned with this in mind.

Just how such a policy was to be enacted soon became a matter of great controversy between British authorities in India and their counterparts in Britain. Initially, Wellesley's policy was interpreted to allow the various religious shrines to function normally. It soon became apparent that this obligated the British to assist in the maintenance of temples and other religious institutions throughout India. As a result the British revived the former Maratha policy of maintaining these institutions through the collection of a pilgrim tax. The British never directly managed any religious institutions, instead they used local Indian authorities to manage these affairs. In the case of the Puri temple, the British allocated a liberal portion of the pilgrim tax to the local *rāja* for the upkeep of the temple.

Throughout the first half of the nineteenth century such a direct interpretation of Wellesley's policy forced the British to become involved in India's religious affairs. The British eventually aided in the construction of a "Jagannath Road" to help pilgrims reach Puri. Company troops often escorted religious processions, fired salutes on ceremonial occasions, and even printed the titles of Hindu gods at the head of official documents.

Such a policy enraged the British clergy both in India and at home. The collection of the pilgrim tax was dubbed the "wages of idolatry" and the Jagannātha Temple was castigated as the "seat of the Empire of Moloch." The missionaries charged that the British Government had no business acting as "wet nurse to Vishnu"[22] and the participation of British troops in religious events was viewed as a disgrace. Under this pressure, which peaked in the 1840s, the British gradually changed their interpretation of Wellesely's policy and withdrew entirely from religious affairs. The Pilgrim Tax was

Asian Studies No. xvii (Delhi: South Asian Institute, New Delhi Branch, Heidelberg University Monohar: 1988), 123.

22. J. W. Kaye, *Christianity in India: An Historical Narration* (London: Smith Elder, 1859), 381.

gradually cut and less money was given for temple maintenance, leaving the *rāja* in Puri to find his own funds. By the time the British withdrew all support for the temple in 1863, the affairs of the temple were in a mess. The matter was made even worse by the famine of 1866, which devastated the region, creating tremendous social and economic hardship. Kedarnath arrived in Puri in 1870, just when the problem had reached its peak.

The District Commissioner for Orissa, Mr. T. E. Ravenshaw, was pleased when Kedarnath arrived. Kedar's reputation for honesty had reached the ears of Mr. Ravenshaw and so he was delighted to receive his young magistrate. In Puri Kedar worked in two capacities, as Deputy Collector and Deputy Magistrate. He soon received a promotion to the fifth grade of service with a monthly salary of 300 rupees. His official duties were to represent the British Government and to oversee law and order in the district. As Puri was a large pilgrimage center, receiving thousands of visitors each month, the city occupied a major part of his time. During the numerous festivals it was his responsibility to arrange for the lodging, food, and medical services for the pilgrims.

Some biographers describe how Kedar assumed charge of the temple administration and corrected many of its internal problems. This is impossible. In his autobiography, Kedar does not mention any involvement with the internal affairs of the temple other than his official duties. As a representative of the British government he would not have been allowed any connection with the administration of the temple. By the 1870's, British policy towards the temple had been firmly established by the demands of the missionaries. Further, the history of the Jagannātha Temple from 1870 shows continued internal trouble, and so whatever changes Kedar was supposed to have made could not have been effective. What his autobiography does mention are certain conflicts that arose between himself and the local *rāja* and some of his ministers. But this was only in Kedar's official capacity, managing affairs outside of the temple as they pertained to the maintenance of law and order and pilgrim services. I find no evidence that Kedar had any involvement in the internal administrative affairs of the Puri temple. Throughout

India such management was always left to local Indian authorities.

On the devotional side Kedarnath did spend much time in the temple. Puri was the earthly home of Lord Jagannātha and the place where Caitanya Mahāprabhu spent His final years immersed in deep religious ecstasy. Kedarnath had only recently embraced Caitanya's teachings and now he needed time to study and assimilate his new faith. In his younger days Orissa had acted as a buffer against the secularizing influence of Calcutta, and now again it offered shelter and time to cultivate devotion.

Kedarnath spent whatever time he could studying Sanskrit and various devotional writings. He also met with numerous Vaiṣṇavas and *sādhus*. He was particularly impressed by one *vairāgī* known as Svarup Das Babaji with whom he spent much time. Kedar hired a pundit to help him study Sanskrit and he soon read all twelve cantos of the *Bhāgavata* with Śrīdhara Svāmī's commentary. He also read Jīva Gosvāmī's *Ṣaṭ-sandarbha*, Baladeva's *Vedānta-sūtra* commentary, and Rūpa Gosvāmī's *Bhakti-rasāmṛta-sindhu*. It was a time of intense religious study. He wrote and published the *Datta-kaustubha* (1873), which is a collection of 104 Sanskrit verses outlining Vaiṣṇava philosophy. He also composed most of the Sanskrit portion of the *Kṛṣṇa-saṁhitā*, which was later published in 1879. Near the Mukti-maṇḍapa[23] he regularly studied the *Bhāgavata* and soon formed a society called the Bhagavat Samsad. This brought him criticism from certain pundits within the Mukti-maṇḍapa who objected to his presumption to study and teach the *Bhāgavata* without proper *dīkṣā* (initiation). He later apologized for this. Summarizing his devotional life he writes:

> In Puri I made a lot of devotional advancement. I was becoming detached from worldly life and I no longer believed that material progress produced anything of last-

---

23. The Mukti-maṇḍapa is a place within the Jagannātha Temple where an assembly of sixteen *śāsana brāhmaṇas* sit as royal advisors. The *brāhmaṇas* who sit in the Mukti-maṇḍapa are elected from a group of villages known as *śāsana* villages (villages set aside for *brāhmaṇas'* residence). These *brāhmaṇas* are responsible to advise the king on matters of *dharma-śāstra* and temple affairs.

> ing value. . . . I spent my time in great happiness seeing the festivals, acquiring knowledge and cultivating devotion. There is no doubt that Śrī Puruṣottama Kṣetra [Puri] is directly Vaikuṇṭha [Viṣṇu's heaven] itself. . . . At this time I gave up all *karma-kāṇḍa* practices and depended solely on Vaiṣṇava *prasāda*.[24]

In the course of his studies Kedar discovered that many devotional writings could be found only as hand copied manuscripts in temple libraries or in the homes of private individuals. He undertook a search to collect many manuscripts and have them copied. Years later in Calcutta he started a society called Vishva Vaishnav Sabha to promote the preservation and publication of devotional writings.

In spite of the great opportunities for study and devotion that Puri offered, it also presented great political turmoil. In Orissa Kedarnath faced some of the most difficult trials of his government service involving conspiracy and terrorism. In one particular incident, there had been reports of a conspiracy against the government near Bhuvaneshwar from a religio-political group called the Atibaḍīs. According to Bhaktivinoda's record in his *Jīvanī,* their political objective was to overthrow the British. Such political agitation was not new. From the time the British took control of Orissa, numerous resistance movements like the Atibaḍīs had sprung up. The most serious rebellions had already taken place at Bhuvaneshwar in the 1840s.

Through intelligence reports Kedarnath learned that the Atibaḍīs were holding nightly meetings in the jungles near Bhuvaneshwar to commit terrorist acts against the British. They were headed by a man named Bishkishan, who subsequently claimed to be an incarnation of God. Reports had been made by local *brāhmaṇas* who charged that Bishkishan had attempted to seduce their wives, posing himself as Mahāviṣṇu. Kedarnath investigated the matter and eventually arrested Bishkishan for sedition

24. *Jīvanī,* 143, 145.

and conspiracy. During the trial Kedarnath and his family were repeatedly threatened. There were riots and other disturbances throughout the Cuttack district, and civic life in both Puri and Bhuvaneshwar came to a standstill. In the end Bishkishan was convicted of sedition and sentenced to jail where he later died. Many of his followers were also convicted and put into jail. This affair entailed great personal risk for Kedar and his family. Ultimately he emerged successfully and became greatly respected by the British for his brave loyalty. It is clear that any deficiencies that may have arisen from Kedar's inability to pass the law examination in Bengal were now overlooked in the light of his ability and his proven loyalty to the government.

Sometimes the story of Bishkishan is told as a religious story more than a political one. Bishkishan's crime is in presenting himself as an incarnation of God. Kedarnath writes of this story in a work called *Avatāra Viṣakiṣaṇa* using the pen name Nitya Sakha Mukhopadhyay. *Svalikhita-jīvanī* describes the Bishkishan story in political terms, while *Avatāra Viṣakiṣaṇa* describes it as a religious story. *Avatāra Viṣakiṣaṇa* was published serially in the *Sajjana-toṣaṇī*.[25]

The Atibaḍīs affair raises the issue of Kedarnath's regard for the British. It was not uncommon for many *bhadraloka* to feel great loyalty for the British, especially in the early half of the nineteenth century. Kedarnath was no exception.[26] In his *Kṛṣṇa-saṁhitā* he contrasts British and Islamic rule:

> In 1206 AD the Muslims established their empire in India, and then again in 1757 the English took control. Muslim rule in India was inauspicious because many temple

25. ST, Vol. 8, 161-167, 207 and 229.

26. There is a manuscript in the India Office Library entitled *British Māhātmyam*, [India Office Library in London, IOL: VT 2928b 1903] by a Kedarnath Datta in which British rule in India is glorified in the extreme. From a study of the title page it is fairly certain that the work is not from the pen of our Kedarnath Datta, but from another Kedarnath Datta. As proof to the existence of more than one Kedarnath Datta during the second half of the nineteenth century, there are two Kedarnath Dattas listed in the History of Services of Officers Holding Gazetted Appointments Under the Government of Bengal (Corrected to 1st July 1894)

> deities were destroyed and the blood of the Aryans became impure. In addition, *varṇāśrama-dharma* was degraded and the Aryan history became lost. Under rule from the great personalities of England things are now better. The ancient stories of the Aryans and their glory are again being discussed and there is no more destruction of the temple deities. In brief we have been released from a great danger.[27]

On the other hand, there were a growing number of *bhadraloka* who felt resentment over British rule. By the 1870s, disillusion with the British had set in and the Svaraj movement was beginning to grow. Men like Bankim Chandra Chatterjee were representative of a large number of *bhadraloka* who looked upon the British with distrust. By this time, Bankim Chandra was stirring up Hindu nationalism through his writings. By the close of the century, Kedar's feelings towards the British were in the minority. For Kedarnath, devotional culture took priority over all secular concerns. So long as the British did not interfere with spiritual pursuits and were reasonable in their dealings, they had his respect and loyalty.

In his *Sajjana-toṣaṇī* Kedarnath creates an interesting analogy to describe the relationship between the Indians and the British.[28] He compares the Indians and the English as two Aryan brothers who have a mutual interest in each others' welfare. The Indians are older brothers (*jyeṣṭha bhrātā*) and the British are younger brothers (*kaniṣṭha bhrātā*). The older brothers have now retired and turned the affairs of the world over to their younger brothers, the British, who are giving protection to the older brother. In the past the older brothers dominated, but now that they have retired they should give

found in the National Library in Calcutta. One Kedarnath is born in September 24, 1838 and joined the service on February 16, 1866 (listed on pp. 603-604) and the other is born October 5, 1840 and joined the service on September 28, 1877 (listed on pp. 604-605). The former Kedarnath Datta is Bhaktivinoda Thakur and the latter is unknown. There is no evidence that even the latter Kedarnath is the author of *British Māhātmyam* or any other work.

27. KS, *Upakramaṇikā*, 45.

28. ST, 1885, Vol. 2, p. 78: Appendix V, 1.

their blessing to the younger brothers and take to the feet of Hari. Kedar is content to let the British deal with the worldly affairs of India while letting the Indians focus on spiritual affairs. Such views even in 1885 must have raised the hair of Bankim Chandra and some of Kedarnath's other colleagues. Perhaps Kedar is being "tongue in cheek" in making such a comparison, but there is no doubt that he is quite serious about the spiritual focus of his views.[29]

If Kedar's lack of interest in political and national issues was a factor in his continued respect for the British, it was a source of frustration for many of his colleagues. In his *Kṛṣṇa-saṁhitā* Kedar addresses this criticism by saying that a Vaiṣṇava should not be preoccupied with worldly pursuits. Many of the *bhadraloka* maintained that God could not be pleased by one who did not do his best to improve society. This was the view of Bankim Chandra Chatterjee and Sisir Kumar Ghosh, who both held strong allegiance to Vaiṣṇava ideals but also felt that the fulfillment of their religious duties lay in social and political elevation. Both these men were frustrated by Kedarnath's neglect of political and social reforms and his continued respect for the British. In his defense Kedarnath repeated the view of the *Bhāgavata* that no amount of material endeavor will ultimately solve political and social problems. Instead he believed that the problems of society must be treated spiritually. Such a view led Kedar to a policy of minimal involvement in worldly affairs. So long as one can cultivate bhakti one should not be concerned with the conditions of the secular world. The following statement that appeared in his English essay "Sri Chaitanya Mahaprabhu, His Life and Precepts" reflects the "tone" of Kedar's devotional attitude:

> While located in the *mayik* world, man must live peacefully with the object to cultivate the Spirit. In his society he

29. The idea that the East and West, primarily India and Europe, should complement each other was a common idea during Bhaktivinoda's time. Keshub Chandra Sen also speaks of the Europeans teaching the Indians science, while learning in turn "ancient wisdom" from India. See Wilhelm Halbfass, *India and Europe* (Albany: State University of New York Press, 1988), 226.

> must lead a pure life, avoid sins and do as much good as he can to his brother man. He must be himself humble, bearing difficulties of life with heroism, must not brag of any goodness or grandeur he has, and must treat every one with the respect due to him. Marriage with a view to peaceful and virtuous life, and with an idea to procreate servants of the Lord, is a good institution for a *Vaishnav.* Spiritual cultivation is the main object of life. Do everything that helps it, and abstain from doing anything which thwarts the cultivation of the Spirit. Have a strong faith that *Krishna alone* protects you and *none else.* Admit Him as your only guardian. Do everything which you know that Krishna wishes you to, and never think that you do a thing independent of the holy wish of Krishna. Do all that you do with humility. Always remember that you are a sojourner in this world and you must be prepared for your own home. Do your duties and cultivate *Bhakti,* as a means, to obtain the great end of life, *Krishna priti.* Employ your body, mind and spirit in the service of the Deity. In all your actions, worship your Great Lord.[30]

During Kedar's residence in Puri two more sons arrived: Kamala Prasad, born in the winter of 1872, and Bimala Prasad, born in the winter of 1874. Bimala Prasad became famous as Bhaktisiddhanta Sarasvati, the founder of the Gaudiya Math and guru to A. C. Bhaktivedanta Swami. Soon time arrived for the marriage of his oldest daughter, ten-year-old Saudamani. This meant Kedar would have to return to Bengal. This was a hard decision for him because Puri was a place that he loved dearly. There he had access to the Jagannātha Temple and wonderful saintly association. But according to social customs Saudamani could only marry a *kāyastha* Bengali boy, something not easily found outside of Bengal. On 9 November, 1874, Kedar left Puri to find a suitable husband for her. For this purpose he took a three-month privilege leave and moved his family back to Bengal.

---

30. Kedarnath Datta, *Sri Chaitanya Mahaprabhu, His Life and Precepts* (Calcutta: Gaudiya Mission, 1933), 45.

Family Portrait *circa* 1900.

From left to right:
Back row: Bimala Prasad, Barada Prasad, Bhaktivinoda, Krishna Vinodani, Kadambani and Bhagavati Devi.
Second row: Kamala Prasad, Shailaja Prasad, unknown grandchild, and Hari Pramodini.
Front row: two unknown grandchildren.

Chapter Four

The Literary Years

1874 – 1914

Ranaghat to Serampore 1874 – 1887

Once back in Bengal, Kedarnath began his search for a suitable boy for Saudamani. After three months, he still had not located the right boy and now the government wanted him back in Puri. He resisted. Caste restrictions demanded that he remain in Bengal while he conducted his search. In Orissa it would be virtually impossible to find a suitable Bengali boy for his daughter. After considerable pressure, the government finally relented and posted him at Arrareah in the northern Bengal district of Purneah. The date was 12 April 1875. He remained there for the next three years. There is no record of literary activity during this period, but it is reasonable to assume that he continued to study. Eventually Saudamani was married and one more child was born to Kedarnath and his wife. They now had seven children: five sons and two daughters.

Kedar and his wife, Bhagavati Devi, maintained a small garden at their home where they occasionally entertained some of their English friends. In his autobiography he hardly mentions the role of his wife in family and social affairs. When his family was small his wife would often accompany him as he transferred throughout Bengal and Orissa. As his family became large he established a home in Calcutta where his wife remained.

During the nineteenth century, one of the greatest complaints of the British was their inability to communicate with the *bhadraloka* wives due to purdah restrictions and language barriers. Women's education was a controversial issue and many women lacked a formal education. Only a few obtained literacy in Bengali, much less

English. The more westernized members of the *bhadraloka* set out to remove these barriers and their wives increasingly assumed the role of hostess to aid and complement their husbands' careers. There is no indication that Kedar's wife ever became an official hostess in a public event, but she did often accompany her husband on official business and sometimes privately entertained English friends at her home. It is likely that she did not speak English and did not have a formal education.

Kedarnath's attempts to socialize with the British were limited. The growing size of his family may have been one limiting factor, but also as he advanced in devotion he simply became less inclined to cultivate non-devotional relations.

On 27 November 1877, Kedarnath was transferred to Maheshrakh in the district of Howrah. In 1878, Biraja, his ninth child, was born. On 12 February 1878, he returned to Orissa at Bhadrak in the district of Balassore. He remained in Bhadrak for seven months. On 14 August 1878, he was given a fixed posting at Naral in the district of Jessore, east of Calcutta. He remained there for the next three years. In the Jessore district malaria was prevalent and Kedar often suffered bouts of fever which necessitated his wife's assistance while he traveled on his circuit court. Traveling from village to village, he and his wife met with the local people who would hold *kīrtana*, devotional songs. In the evenings the village ladies would bring them various kinds of *prasāda* as they relaxed for *kīrtana*. He writes, "I stayed in Naral for almost three years and the local people came to like me very much. Whenever I traveled from village to village the local residents would serenade me with *kīrtana*." I believe these experiences provided the seed for Kedarnath's later program of Vaiṣṇava evangelism, *nāma-haṭṭa*.[1]

In later years, Kedarnath organized a preaching program called *nāma-haṭṭa*[2] in which he sent parties of *kīrtana* singers and speakers from village to village. The idea for *nāma-haṭṭa* was modeled after

1. *Jīvanī*, 152.

2. In Bengal *nāma* means name and *haṭṭa* means market place. Therefore *nāma-haṭṭa* literally means "marketplace of the name." *Nāma-haṭṭa* was a system of preaching used by Bhaktivinoda to propagate the holy name of Kṛṣṇa.

these days as a circuit court judge traveling from village to village.

In Naral Kedarnath published his first major work, the *Kṛṣṇa-saṁhitā*. Shortly thereafter he wrote the *Kalyāna-kalpataru*. These two books were published in 1879 and 1880. The *Kalyāna-kalpataru* was a collection of devotional songs. It was well received. The *Kṛṣṇa-saṁhitā,* on the other hand, was an historical and philosophical essay which dealt with the character of Śrī Kṛṣṇa. This work created a storm throughout Bengal.

The *Kṛṣṇa-saṁhitā* was written in response to an important issue among the Hindu *bhadraloka.* In the face of slanderous propaganda against Kṛṣṇa by Christian missionaries and the Brahmo Samaj, many *bhadraloka* came to doubt the value of their religious beliefs. An attack on Kṛṣṇa amounted to an attack on the very foundations of Hinduism. The critics charged that the thieving and erotic pastimes of Kṛṣṇa made a mockery of God and so justified the Europeans' opinion that the Indian people lacked moral character. Christian missionaries used stories about Kṛṣṇa as a weapon against Hinduism, challenging its ethical basis. In response, the Western educated *bhadraloka* felt they had no choice but to sympathize with such views. It was impossible for them to adhere to mere tradition in the face of what appeared as sound arguments and reasoning put forward by the missionaries. Thus Vaiṣṇavism, if not all of Hinduism, found itself under attack during the nineteenth century. This crisis forced the *bhadraloka* into a frenzy of self-examination.

Such attacks even came from members of the *bhadraloka* themselves. In the 1820s a Bengali publication entitled *Brāhma Pauttalik Samvād* (*A Tract Against Idolatry*)[3] laid out a series of convincing arguments against the Hindu practice of image worship. The work was so powerful that it caught the attention of the Serampore missionaries who wrote: "It is a masterly expose, by a Native, on the absurdities of the present Hindoo system. . . . What European could have written a work equally delicate and equally

---

3. *A Tract Against Idolatry: Dialogue Between a Theist and an Idolater,* ed. Stephen N. Hay (Calcutta: Firma K. L. Mukhopadhyay, 1964). In this work Hay argues convincingly that Rammohun Roy is the actual author of the work.

severe in its application?"[4]

Kedarnath's *Kṛṣṇa-saṁhitā* was an attempt to rectify the situation using the same methods of rational analysis that were used to attack Hinduism. In his work Kedar traces the roots of ancient Indian history in the light of modern textual and archaeological methods. He then interprets the life of Śrī Kṛṣṇa according to modern theological thought. The *Kṛṣṇa-saṁhitā* is a prime example of Kedar's synthesis of tradition and modernity. However, it appears that the *Kṛṣṇa-saṁhitā* was not properly understood. Many orthodox Vaiṣṇavas were confused and offended by the work's modern approach, and it seems that the young *bhadraloka* failed to comprehend the work's subtleties. Kedar comments:

> Some thought the book was a new point of view. Some said it was good. The younger educated people said the book was nice, but no one fully understood the essence of the work, which was to show that Kṛṣṇa was transcendent (*aprākṛta*). Some thought that my interpretations were strictly psychological (*ādhyātmika*). But they were incorrect. There is a subtle difference between what is transcendent and what is psychological, which few understood. The reason behind this mistake is that no one had any understanding of transcendence (*aprākṛta*).[5]

A few years later, Bankim Chandra Chatterjee wrote a similar work entitled *Kṛṣṇa-caritra* (1884) in another attempt to explain the character of Kṛṣṇa against the attacks of the Christian missionaries. Bankim Chandra's position differed markedly from Kedarnath's. His solution was to discard everything which might be considered immoral or improper according to the standards of the nineteenth century. His work amounted to a wholesale jettisoning of the tradition. Kedar's approach, on the other hand, maintained the basic tradition, but in a way that was in accord with modern understanding. Bankim Chandra's work was flatly rejected by the orthodox

4. Ibid., 2-3.
5. *Jīvanī,* 155.

Vaiṣṇava community, but it did appeal to the young, who were touched by the work's patriotic undertones and less interested in maintaining the tradition intact.

Interestingly, Pundit Satkari Chattopadhyay mentions that before Bankim Chandra published his *Kṛṣṇa-caritra* he discussed his ideas with Kedarnath, who objected to the elimination of so much of the life of Kṛṣṇa. For Kedarnath, Bankim Chandra's approach negated the whole point of Kṛṣṇa *līlā*. There is no doubt that Kedarnath and Bankim Chandra differed greatly in their interpretation of Kṛṣṇa's personality and activities, and just how they understood Kṛṣṇa is an indication of how each reacted to the demands of modernity. One wanted to reinterpret the tradition and the other preferred to cut it away selectively. Bhaktivinoda's approach is modeled after what Paul Hacker calls "Traditionalism" while Bankim Chandra's approach is representative of Neo-Hinduism. Neo-Hinduism and Traditionalism describe the different ways the Hindu *bhadraloka* appealed to tradition under the pressures of modernity. Traditionalism tended to preserve the continuity of the past, and build upon this foundation by carrying on the traditions of the past with strategic additions and extrapolations. Neo-Hinduism, to be sure, also invoked tradition and tried to return to it, but did so as a result of a rupture and discontinuity with the past. It is clear that Bhaktivinoda wanted to maintain continuity with the past, while Bankim Chandra had no hesitation in making a break with the past.[6]

Kedarnath felt so convinced about his *Kṛṣṇa-saṁhitā* that he sent copies of it to prominent persons in America and Europe. There is little doubt that Bhaktivinoda must be credited with the first attempt to transfer Caitanya's teachings to the West. The following paragraph is a portion of a letter that Kedarnath received from Reinhold Rost, a well known Sanskrit scholar in London:

---

6. In spite of their differences it is interesting that Bankim Chandra acknowledged his indebtedness to Kedarnath for bringing out Viśvanātha Cakravartī's commentary on the *Bhagavad-gītā* as well as his own translation. From his *Bhagavad-gītā* introduction Bankim Chandra writes: *paṇḍita śrīyukta bābu kedāranātha datta nija-kṛta anuvāda, aneka samaye viśvanātha cakravartī praṇīta ṭīkāra samārtha diyāchena.*

India Office Library
S. W. April 16, 1880

My dear Sir,

A long and painful illness has prevented me from thanking you earlier for the kind present of your *Shri Krishna Samhita.* By representing Krishna's character and his worship in a more sublime and transcendent light than has hitherto been the custom to regard him in, you have rendered an essential service to your coreligionists and no one would have taken more delight in your work than my departed friend Goldstucker, the sincerest and most zealous advocate the Hindoos ever had in Europe.

Reinhold Rost

From America came a note from Ralph Waldo Emerson thanking Kedar for his gift.

May 10, 1886
Concord, Massachusetts

Dear Sir,

I have received with pleasure the book you so kindly sent me. I am sorry that I do not know the language and cannot read it and can only send my thanks.

R. Waldo Emerson

Kedarnath's contact with the West, as early as 1880, shows that he saw the teachings of Caitanya as a universal message of love addressed to the whole world and not just for the *bhadraloka* and masses in Bengal or India. In his *Saṁhitā* he writes:

> Through the mercy of God it is hoped that the Europeans and Americans will soon experience the wine of *mādhurya-rasa.* They have seen that whatever *rasa* develops in India

> eventually spreads to the West and there is no doubt that the *mādhurya-rasa*[7] is long overdue in the West. As the sun first rises in India and then gradually spreads its light West, so the unparalleled beams of spiritual truth rise first in India and then spread to the West.[8]

The obvious problem with Kedarnath's first attempt to reach the West was language. Few people in the West could read Sanskrit or Bengali, not to mention Sanskrit published with Bengali characters. Therefore, the *Saṁhitā* failed to find an adequate audience. It was not until 1896 that Kedar again reached out to the West, only this time in English and Sanskrit. He prepared a short collection of Sanskrit verses summarizing Caitanya's teachings entitled *Śrī-gaurāṅga-līlā-smaraṇa-stotram*, which included a forty-seven page English introduction called *Sri Chaitanya Mahaprabhu, His Life and Precepts.* The work was sent to various universities and intellectuals in different parts of the world and eventually found its way onto the book shelves of McGill University in Montreal, the University of Sydney in Australia and the Royal Asiatic Society of London. In the beginning of his work Kedar states his purpose:

> The object of this little book is to bring the holy life of Caitanya Mahaprabhu and his precepts to the notice of the educated and the religious people. Most of the books treating these subjects have hitherto been printed in Bengali characters. Hence the life and precepts of Caitanya have scarcely passed beyond the boundaries of Bengal. This book has therefore been printed in Sanskrit type for circulation all over India. Our educated brethren of Europe and America have taken, of late, to the study of the Sanskrit language, and it is our belief that this *brochure* will go to their hands in a very short time. . . . With a view to help our English knowing readers in going through the

7. *Mādhurya-rasa* is one of the aesthetic mellows (*rasas*) of divine love described by Rūpa Gosvāmī in his *Bhakti-rasāmṛta-sindhu.*
8. KS, *Upakramaṇikā*, 77.

> book, we have here summarized in English the contents of the work.[9]

The work was favorably reviewed in the *Journal of the Royal Asiatic Society* of London.

Initiation

In 1880 while living in Naral, Kedarnath and his wife finally received initiation (*dīkṣā*) into the *Caitanya-sampradāya.* Since his days in Puri, when he had been criticized by the Vaiṣṇava community for teaching the *Bhāgavata* without initiation, he had a strong desire for initiation. He recalls his feelings:

> I had been searching for a suitable guru for a long time, but had not found one, so I was feeling disturbed. Whenever I met someone who inspired my devotion, when I studied his character, I became disappointed and lost faith. I was anxious to find a guru and so I prayed to God. One night in a dream the Lord indicated that soon I would receive initiation. The next morning I felt relieved. In a few days Gurudeva finally wrote a letter saying, "I will come soon and give you initiation." When Gurudeva finally came both my wife and I received initiation and we were pleased. From that day on I felt compassion towards all beings and the sin of meat eating vanished from my heart and compassion arose towards living beings.[10]

Kedarnath and Bhagavati were initiated by Shri Bipin Bihari Goswami, (1848-1919) a *jātī gosāñi*[11] and direct family descendant of Vaṁśīvadana Ṭhākura. Bipin Bihari Goswami was a disciplic

---

9. Kedarnath Datta Bhaktivinoda, *Sri Chaitanya Mahaprabhu, His Life and Precepts,* ed. Bhaktisiddhanta Sarasvati (Nadiya: Shree Caitanya Math, 1932, 4th edition), 1.
10. *Jīvanī,* 155-6: See Appendix V, 87.
11. The *jātī gosāñis,* otherwise known as Caste *Gosvāmīs,* are the hereditary descendants from the original followers of Caitanya, who control most of the temples and shrines, provide *dīkṣā,* or initiation, and much of the intellectual and community

descendant of the Jāhnavā-vaṁśa and eleventh in line from Rāmāi Gosvāmī, the founder of the Bāghnāpāḍā Vaiṣṇavas. Rāmāi Gosvāmī moved north of Calcutta to the Baghnapara area towards the end of the sixteenth century to set up his own *śrīpāṭa* or religious seat. The center developed a distinct theology based on the *rasa-rāja* concept, which some argue has been influenced by tantric *sahajiyā* ideas. Rāmāi was a foster-child of Jāhnavā Devī, the wife of Nityānanda Prabhu, and grandson of Vaṁśīvadana Ṭhākura, the earliest proponent of the *rasa-rāja* concept.[12] The history and theology of the Bāghnāpāḍā group is given in two works entitled *Muralī-vilāsa* and *Vaṁśī-śikṣā*.[13]

According to the *rasa-rāja* idea the activities of Kṛṣṇa and his followers are viewed exclusively in terms of *rasa*. The concept of *rasa* is very prominent throughout Kedarnath's writings. Caitanya is thought to have introduced two forms of bhakti, one exoteric and the other esoteric. Exoteric bhakti is "external" Vaiṣṇavism consisting of *kīrtana*, temple worship, *prasāda*, chanting, and so on. Esoteric bhakti consists of the secret worship of Kṛṣṇa as *rasa-rāja*. This involves *siddha-praṇālī, aṣṭa-kāliya-līlā-smaraṇa,* and so on. That Kedarnath was clearly involved with the *rasa-rāja* approach to *sādhana-bhakti* is evident from his discussion of the process of *siddha-praṇālī* found in his *Jaiva-dharma* and *Hari-nāma-cintāmaṇi*. This matter is discussed in detail in chapter eight.

Kedarnath was age forty-two when he received initiation from

---

leadership for the Caitanya Vaiṣṇava orthodoxy.

12. There are conflicting opinions concerning Vaṁśīvadana. According to the *Prema-vilāsa,* Vaṁśīvadana looked after Śrīnivāsa Ācārya in Navadwip. Others say that he was adopted by Caitanya's wife, Viṣṇupriyā, as her son and looked after Śacī Devī, Caitanya's mother, and Viṣṇupriyā after Caitanya moved to Puri.

13. The *Muralī-vilāsa* by Rājavallabha Gosvāmī was written towards the beginning of the seventeenth century and the *Vaṁśī-śikṣā* was written by Premadāsa Miśra in 1716. Biman Bihari Majumdar rejects these works as forgeries and *sahajiyā* texts. Bhaktivinoda seems to accept them because they are advertised in the *Sajjana-toṣaṇī* vol. 5, no. 5, 1894. For more information on the Baghnapara Vaiṣṇavas and the *rasa-rāja* concept see R. Chakrabarty, *Bengal Vaiṣṇavism,* chapter XVI.

Bipin Bihari Goswami. The question of Kedarnath's guru lineage is an interesting issue that relates to the form of *sādhana* that he practiced, namely the *rasa-rāja* approach of the Bāghnāpāḍā Vaiṣṇavas.

Although the name of Bipin Bihari Goswami is not mentioned in Bhaktivinoda's autobiography, presumably because he was writing to his son Lalita Prasad—the matter was obvious—the name of Bipin Bihari Goswami appears in three places in Bhaktivinoda's writings: the *Siddhi-lālasā* section of his *Gītā-mālā* (1893), the *Caitanyāmṛta-pravāha-bhāṣya* (1895) and the *Bhāgavatārka-marīci-mālā* (1901). In the *Siddhi-lālasā* he writes:

> When will **Vilāsa Mañjarī** and Anaṅga Mañjarī see me and, being very merciful, speak the following essential words?

Then in the same work:

> O **Vilāsa Mañjarī**, Anaṅga Mañjarī and Rūpa Mañjarī, please notice me and accept me at your feet, bestowing on me the essence of all perfection.[14]

Vilāsa Mañjarī is the name of the *mañjarī-svarūpa* (internal spiritual persona)of Bipin Bihari Goswami. So when Bhaktivinoda refers to Vilāsa Mañjarī he is in fact referring to his guru, Shri Bipin Bihari Goswami. Anaṅga Mañjarī is the *mañjarī* name of Jāhnavā Mā, wife of Śrī Nityānanda Prabhu. Rūpa Mañjarī is the name of Rūpa Gosvāmī.

In the *Amṛta-pravāha-bhāṣya* (1895) he writes:

> Bipin Bihari Goswami, the excellent Prabhu, is the *śakti avatāra* of Vipina-vihari-hari [Kṛṣṇa]. Seeing that his servant had fallen into the well of material life, he assumed

14. Kedarnath Datta Bhaktivinoda, *Gītā-mālā,* ed. Srila Bhaktikusuma Sramana (Shridham Mayapur, Nadiya: Sree Caitanya Math), 498 Śri-gaurābda: Appendix V, 105 and 106.

> the form of a *gosvāmī-guru* and rescued me.[15]

And finally in his *Bhāgavatārka-marīci-mālā* (1901):

> My exalted master, Bipin Bihari Goswami Prabhu, is the moon in the family of Śrī Vaṁśī Vadanānanda. I hold his order on my head.[16]

We also find reference to Bipin Bihari Goswami when the honorific title *bhaktivinoda* was bestowed on Kedarnath Datta by the Bāghnāpāḍā Vaiṣṇavas headed by Bipin Bihari Goswami during January of 1886. We find letters of conferral in Bhaktivinoda's autobiography that include the name of Bipin Bihari Goswami at the head of the list.[17] In addition we find articles by Bipin Bihari Goswami in Bhaktivinoda's journal, *Sajjana Toṣaṇī* (1885)[18] and we find that Bipin Bihari Goswami was an active participant in Bhaktivinoda's *nāma-haṭṭa* program. In 1893 Bipin Bihari Goswami, along with other Bāghnāpāḍā Vaiṣṇavas, is listed among the dignitaries at the meeting in the A. B. School at Krishnanagar to establish the project at Shri Dhama Mayapur.[19]

Finally, the most interesting reference to Bipin Bihari Goswami comes from my field research in India. There I traced the life of one of Bhaktivinoda's disciples, Bhaktitirtha Ṭhākura (1865–1922).[20] Bhaktitirtha lived near Khargpur in southern Bengal at the Shauri Prapanna Ashram. Here I found photographs of Kedarnath Datta

---

15. *Amṛta-pravāha-bhāṣya*, p. 1687: *vipina-vihārī hari, tāṅra śakti avatari', vipina-vihārī prabhu-vara/ śrī-guru-gosvāmi-rūpe, dekhi' more bhava-kūpe, uddhārila āpana kiṅkara//*
16. Bhaktivinoda Ṭhākura, *Bhāgavatārka-marīci-māla*, ed. Bhaktivilāsa Tīrtha (Śrīdhāma Māyāpura: Śrī Caitanya Maṭha, 470 Gaurābdīya (Bengali)), 436: Appendix III, 107.
17. *Jīvanī*, 176-177*:* Appendix V, 108.
18. ST, Vol 2, (1885) *śrī kṛṣṇa bhaktera pāpa kothāya?* p. 27, *Gururūpā Sakhī Stotram*, p. 166; and *Kṛpaṇa Praṇāma Stotram*, p. 165.
19. ST, Vol 5 (1893), 204.
20. This is not the Bhaktitirtha associated with the Gaudiya Math, but a gentleman who was originally named Sitanath before he was initiated by Bhaktivinoda.

Bhaktivinoda and Bipin Bihari Goswami together on the Shauri Prapanna temple altar.[21]

It is interesting that Kedarnath had not completely given up meat eating until the time of his initiation at age forty-two. This was a full ten years since his famed speech on the *Bhāgavata*, the composition of the *Datta-kaustubha*, the *Kṛṣṇa-saṁhitā*, the *Kalyāna-kalpataru* and some other smaller devotional writings. In the context of the *kāyastha bhadraloka* in Bengal, Kedar's non-vegetarian diet is not unusual, but in the context of Caitanya Vaiṣṇavism, considering that he had written so many works and been so active as a Vaiṣṇava, it is unusual.

Soon after his initiation Kedar made a second trip to Vrindavan. This time he took his wife, mother-in-law, youngest child, and two servants. At Triveni (Allahabad) he was struck by fever, which threatened to jeopardize the whole trip. He tells how he prayed to God asking Him to postpone the fever until a later time. Vrindavan was just too important to miss. Remarkably Kedar's fever abated, and he and his family were able to enjoy the remainder of their pilgrimage. During this trip he visited all the major temples in Vrindavan and met many Vaiṣṇava *sādhus*. This was when he first met Jagannath Das Babaji, a Vaiṣṇava ascetic who regularly moved between Navadwip and Vrindavan. Later on, in Navadwip, Kedar would often visit Jagannath Das.

Before Kedarnath left Naral in 1881 he was able to publish the first volume of his journal *Sajjana-toṣaṇī*. The *Toṣaṇī* included reviews of Vaiṣṇava publications, topical announcements and serialized publications of Kedar's writings. In July 1881 Kedarnath received a three-month privilege leave which he used to find a house in Calcutta. He now had ten children and it was necessary to

21. I obtained a book written in Bengali entitled *Prabhupāda Śrila Bhaktitīrtha–ṭhākurer Saṅkṣipta-jīvanī* from the Shauri Prapanna Ashram. This book describes the life of Bhaktitirtha and details his relationship with Bhaktivinoda. It was compiled by Vasu Bhaktisagar in 1959 and includes many letters written by Bhaktivinoda to his disciple Bhaktitirtha. We find the Shauri Prapanna Ashram following the same form of *sādhana,* based on the *rasa-rāja* concept as Bhaktivinoda followed.

establish a permanent home. He preferred to live in Calcutta because the city offered better educational and job opportunities. Malaria was also a fact of village life that he wanted to avoid. After much searching he finally bought the house at 181 Maniktala Street (now Ramesh Datta Street) for 6,000 rupees. The house needed some repair which he did himself, and when everything was ready he performed the *gārhya-praveśa-pūjā* (house consecration ceremony) and named the house Bhakti Bhavan. Not only did Bhakti Bhavan become a base for his family; it also became an important center of Kedar's preaching activities. He set up the Depository Press and the Vishva Vaishnav Sabha at this location.

Once Kedarnath was established in Calcutta, Sisir Kumar Ghosh (1840–1911), a fellow Vaiṣṇava and editor of the *Amṛta Bazaar Patrikā* (a prominent English language daily), invited him to attend the opening performance of Girish Chandra's new play *Caitanya-līlā* at the Star Theater. Sisir Kumar Ghosh had been deeply impressed by Kedarnath's Dinajpur speech. He recognized Kedar's growing importance as a Vaiṣṇava leader and wanted him to come as guest of honor. Kedarnath, however, declined to attend, saying that it was improper to hear a performance of Caitanya's pastimes in the presence of worldly-minded people.

The Star Theater incident is characteristic of Kedar's puritanical outlook. During the nineteenth century, Victorian influence had fostered the growth of Puritanism amongst the *bhadraloka,* some of whom uncompromisingly condemned smoking, gambling, drinking, and theater attendance. Kedar's Vaiṣṇava perspective also shunned all worldly dealings. Sisir Kumar Ghosh and Bankim Chandra Chatterjee, on the other hand, were deeply involved in the social and political affairs of the day. In another incident Kedar jointly edited the journal, *Viṣṇupriyā Patrikā,* with Sisir Kumar Ghosh, but later, when he felt that Sisir Kumar was introducing too much social intercourse into the publication, he stopped co-editing the paper. From Kedar's perspective worldly involvement was incompatible with bhakti.

On 30 September 1881, Kedar was transferred from Naral to Jessore. The moment he arrived the fever he had postponed in

Vrindavan struck with a vengeance. Jessore became the home of fever personified. By January 1882 he was forced to take a three-month medical leave. The doctors told him that he had no choice but to eat fish and meat to improve his condition. Even his mother pressured him to at least eat fish again. But Kedar had given up non-vegetarian food at the time of his initiation and now he was determined to avoid these things at all cost. He writes, "They said that eating fish heads would be good for my eyes, but the thought of eating fish after so much time was just too painful."[22] As an alternative he found a homeopathic approach that eventually proved successful. His condition improved and on 9 April 1882, he moved out of Jessore for good and went to Barasat near Calcutta, where he took over from Bankim Chandra Chatterjee. He remained in Barasat for the next two years.

Life in Barasat was mixed. Some of the local people were fighting in the courts and Kedar constantly had to intervene. Each side gave him trouble. In March 1883, he received a promotion to fourth grade Deputy Magistrate, which improved his salary. His wife lived in Calcutta while he and his two sons, Radhika Prasad and Kamala Prasad, lived together in a lovely rented house with a garden and a pond. A close friend and colleague, Sharad Charan Mitra, made sure that Kedar was well supplied with devotional books. Sharad Charan sent him copies of Viśvanātha Cakravartī's *Gītā* and *Bhāgavata* commentaries and other works including the *Narottama-vilāsa.* Wherever Kedar lived he constantly studied *bhakti-śāstra,* and was gradually becoming very knowledgeable. His position as a spokesperson for the Caitanya tradition was also increasing.

In the fall of 1884, Kedar's eleventh child, Krishnavinodini, was born. Later that year, for an unknown reason Annada Prasad, Kedar's eldest son, began to experience bouts of depression. Kedar had to care for him. For the remainder of Annada's life, his psychological condition never satisfactorily improved and so Annada was unable to work. This understandably caused much grief to Kedar and his family. Soon there was more bad news. Kedar's moth-

22. *Jīvanī,* 165.

er, who had been living with him since the end of his student days in Calcutta, passed away. In order to take care of her funeral rites, Kedar received a month's privilege leave to go to Gaya. There he saw the famous steps up Pretshila Hill that had been built by his great grandfather and renowned Vaiṣṇava, Madan Mohan Datta. Kedarnath was impressed by Madan Mohan's accomplishment and recorded the words of the dedication stone at Gaya in his *Jīvanī*.

On 1 April 1884, Kedarnath was transferred to Serampore. Originally Serampore was a Danish colony lying in the midst of British controlled India. It had become famous as a base for European missionaries in Bengal even though the British had banned missionary activities in British India. Under Reverend William Carey, Serampore had acquired a reputation for vigorous evangelism and religious publication. In the spirit of William Carey, Kedar began to preach and print devotional books in earnest.

With the help of some friends he established the Shri Vishva Vaishnav Sabha for preaching *hari-bhakti*. Later he produced volumes two and three of *Sajjana-toṣaṇī*. Volume three was a smaller edition dedicated to the newly established Vishva Vaishnav Sabha.[23] While Kedar was in Serampore, the first and only English edition of the *Sajjana-toṣaṇī* was published with the help of Shri Upendra Goswami. In that issue Kedar reviewed Upendra Goswami's new work, *Nitya-rūpa-saṁsthāpanam*.

Unfortunately, Kedarnath could not publish the *Toṣaṇī* regularly. It was not until 1892, with the editorial help of his son, Radhika Prasad, that the *Toṣaṇī* was published regularly. Radhika Prasad was twenty-two years of age when he began editing his father's journal. From volume four the journal appeared without interruption until volume seventeen in 1905 when it was discontinued. Years later the journal resumed publication under the auspices of Bhaktisiddhanta Sarasvati.

Before Kedarnath left Serampore, Sundarananda Vidyavinoda

23. Volume three of the *Sajjana-toṣaṇī* is not mentioned in Kedar's *Jīvanī* nor is it catalogued at the Bangiya Sahitya Parishat in Calcutta with the other volumes of *Sajjana-toṣaṇī*. Instead it can be found at the National Library in Calcutta.

reports that Kedar met with the famous Ramakrishna Paramahamsa, but nothing apparently came of this meeting.

At his home in Calcutta, Kedar established the Vaishnav Depository[24] for the purpose of distributing devotional literature. Later he established the Caitanya Press with the help of Bipin Bihari Goswami, who became its manager. On that press Kedar published many of his own works as well as others' writings. In 1886 he wrote and published the *Caitanya-śikṣāmṛta,* his own Bengali translation of the *Bhagavad-gītā* with Viśvanātha Cakravartī's commentary, the *Āmnāya Sūtras* and the *Vaiṣṇava-siddhānta-mālā,* the *Prema-pradīpa,* the *Manaḥ-śikṣā,* the *Kṛṣṇa-vijaya* by Maladhar Basu, the *Śikṣāṣṭakam,* the *Caitanyopaniṣad* and two *khaṇḍas* of *Caitanya-caritāmṛta.* He also began the annual publication of a Vaiṣṇava calendar called the *Caitanya-pañjikā.*

Unfortunately, such a rigorous publication schedule was too great a strain and his health began to fail. His eyes and head gave him trouble. Kedar laments that he could not read or write anymore due to severe dizzy spells. In 1886 his twelfth child was born and later that year he took a month's medical leave. After a month's rest his condition improved. He writes in his *Jīvanī:*

> Gradually I recovered from my head ailment and I was able to resume my studies. In the association of so many bhaktas I was becoming more renounced and so I began to think, "I am wasting my life and I have accomplished nothing because I have been unable to obtain even a small taste of service to Śrī Rādhā Kṛṣṇa. So while I am still able, let me retire from government work, draw my pension, and find some place on the banks of the Yamuna near Vrindavan or Mathura to perform *bhajana* in peace."[25]

Driven by these devotional sentiments, Kedar decided to retire from government service and move to Vrindavan. He even tried to persuade his close friend Ramsevak Chattopadhyay to accompany

24. Also known as the Depository Press.
25. *Jīvanī,* 174.

him. However, Kedar tells how Caitanyadeva appeared in a dream one night and asked, "Why do you want to go to Vrindavan when you live so close to Navadwip *dhāma*? Have you done what there is to do in Navadwip first?"[26] Kedar was astonished and for a time he did not know what to do. Ramsevak's advice was to remain at work and try to transfer to Navadwip instead of going to Vrindavan. Soon afterwards Kedarnath requested a transfer to Krishnanagar, close to Navadwip, but his supervisor Mr. Peacock rejected the idea, saying that Kedar should postpone his plans to study archeology until after his retirement.

In spite of Peacock's objections Kedar continued to push for a transfer, even declining the post of personal assistant to the chief Commissioner of Assam. When this failed he applied for an early pension, wishing to retire altogether. But the application was denied. Disappointed, he remained in Serampore waiting for his opportunity to move to Nadiya. During this time there was a glimmer of hope as the Bāghnāpāḍā Vaiṣṇavas headed by Bipin Bihari Goswami presented a letter to Kedarnath conferring the title "Bhaktivinoda" on him in recognition of his tremendous preaching and literary output. I have included a translation of the letter taken from Kedarnath's autobiography:

> Glory to Śrī Śrī Rāma and Kṛṣṇa.
>
> With great respect the title "Bhaktivinoda" is hereby given to the disciple and devotee named Shri Kedarnath Datta by the *gosvāmīs* who reside at the village Baghnapara.
>
> May that saintly disciple, Shri Kedarnath Datta, who strives for the feet of Govinda, be always victorious. O beloved of the Vaiṣṇavas, who in this world is not liberated seeing your devotion to Śrī Śrī Rādhā and Kṛṣṇa, and seeing your writings which always follow the teachings of Caitanyadeva? Those who are beloved of God always desire that coveted bhakti, which they see in your heart. O beloved servant, you are most fortunate. That intense bhakti alone is the life for every soul. Please therefore,

26. Ibid., 175.

accept the title "Bhaktivinoda."

In the four-hundredth year of our Caitanyadeva, in the month of Magh, the following *gosvāmīs* bestow this title: Shri Bipin Bihari Goswami, Shri Tinkari Goswami, Shri Gopalandra Goswami, Shri Gaurachandra Goswami, Shri Ramchandra Goswami, Shri Yajneshwar Goswami, Shri Binod Bihari Goswami, Shri Yadunath Goswami, Shri Binod Bihari Goswami, Shri Yogendra Chandra Goswami, Shri Gopalchandra Goswami, Shri Hemchandra Goswami, Shri Chandrabhushan Goswami, Shri Kanailal Goswami, and Shri Haradhan Goswami.

It was January 1886, and from this time on Kedarnath Datta was known as Kedarnath Datta Bhaktivinoda. The letter was signed by fifteen of the leading *gosvāmīs* from Baghnapara and it was a great honor. Still, in frustration, Kedar comments, "My masters had given me the title 'Bhaktivinoda' and I accepted this as the desire of Mahāprabhu. Yet in spite of this honor my transfer to Shri Dham Navadwip was obstructed and my heart was very anxious."[27]

Krishnanagar 1887

Kedar was convinced that Mahāprabhu wanted him to go to Navadwip instead of Vrindavan, so he focused his attention on getting to Krishnanagar near Navadwip. Two things blocked the way: his superior officer and his health. As luck would have it, Peacock Sahib was himself transferred to another posting, leaving Kedar free to move to Krishnanagar. He found a colleague in Krishnanagar who was willing to transfer to Serampore if Kedar would transfer to Krishnanagar. They arranged the deal and soon the order to transfer to Krishnanagar arrived dated 15 November 1887. But now fever blocked the way. Kedar's fever was relentless. He was hardly eating and his strength was decreasing rapidly. At the time to move he writes:

I was overjoyed, but at the same time I was worried about

27. *Jīvanī,* 177.

> my fever. It never went away. Collector Toynbee suggested that I postpone the move, but I thought, "I will live or I will die, but I will go to Krishnanagar." I returned home and the fever seemed to lessen, but the cough and weakness persisted. I had not eaten for twenty days. Bholanath Babu and Mahendra Mama requested that I take a short vacation, but I knew that if I took time off I might lose the opportunity. In my bedridden condition I chose to go. My wife and Mahendra Mama went with me. There were many difficulties on the way, but the joy of going to Navadwip diminished them.[28]

In Krishnanagar Kedar was ravaged by fever. He had not eaten anything but milk in forty-five days. Somehow he held court in the mornings, but by noon he would collapse. At night the fever increased and by day it lessened. This went on for weeks. The doctors told him that he would die if he did not take rest. He felt great frustration. Even though he had come to Krishnanagar still he could not go to Navadwip, just twenty-five kilometers away. Finally he met a physician, Doctor Russell, who forced him to take quinine and eat some solid food. By Christmas of 1888 he was gaining strength. He writes, "During the Christmas break I was well enough to take a train to Navadwip with my wife. Going there and seeing the land made the hairs on my body stand on end. Crossing the Ganges I came to Navadwip. For weeks I had not eaten a full meal. Now I took rice and jack-fruit soup, banana flower *sabaji* and other preparations. The meal was nectar. Since my birth I had not tasted such delight."[29]

Gradually Kedarnath became strong enough to assume a full work routine. On the weekends he took the train from Krishnanagar to the Ganges twenty kilometers to the west, where he caught a boat to Navadwip. As he always did when he moved to a new locality, he studied the local geography and history. Only this time he was searching for the places of Caitanya's *līlā* in Navadwip.

---

28. Ibid., 178.
29. Ibid., 180.

The local people told him that Caitanya's birth site was in Navadwip, but after some inquiry he began to suspect that the town was barely a hundred years old. It was common for the Ganges to shift its course so the towns along the river tended to shift as well. This meant that he could not positively confirm that any of the sites from Śrī Caitanya's life in Navadwip were genuine. He concluded that Navadwip was not the likely site of Caitanya's *līlā*, although the local people were adamant that it was. He felt a sense of deep regret and frustration. He writes: "At the present time the people of Navadwip pay more attention to their stomach than they do for the places of Caitanya's life."[30]

Then one evening something mystical occurred. Kedarnath, his son Kamala Prasad, and a friend were on the roof of the Rani Dharmashala in Navadwip. The day had been scorching hot and they wanted to feel the cool breezes coming off the Ganges. Kedar saw something unusual across the river. He describes:

> By 10 o'clock the night was very dark and cloudy. Across the Ganges in a northern direction I suddenly saw a large building flooded with golden light. I asked Kamala if he could see the building and he said that he could, but my friend Kerani Babu could see nothing. I was amazed. What could it be? In the morning I went back to the roof and looked carefully back across the Ganges. I saw that in the place where I had seen the building was a stand of palm trees. Inquiring about this area I was told that it was the remains of Lakshman Sen's fort at Ballaldighi.[31]

On Sunday afternoon Kedarnath returned to his government duties at Krishnanagar. On the following weekend he returned to Navadwip to pursue the sight he had seen previously. That Saturday he again saw the building across the Ganges. On Sunday he crossed the river to Ballaldighi to inquire about the area from the local people. They told him that Ballaldighi was the birth site of Śrīmān

30. Ibid.
31. Ibid., 181.

Mahāprabhu. Of course, that was not unusual; most everyone in Nadiya claimed that their village was the actual birth site of Mahāprabhu. Kedar investigated further.

Kedar decided that the best way to prove or disprove the matter was to find textual and geographic evidence. Investigating local history was easy because he had made this kind of study many times in the past. Immediately he went to the Krishnanagar Collectory where he studied the maps of the Nadiya district. He also checked some old manuscripts of the *Caitanya-bhāgavata, Bhakti-ratnākara* and *Navadvīpa-parikramā-paddhati,* which gave geographic references associated with Caitanya's birth. He also interviewed many elderly people throughout the Navadwip area. Using these maps, manuscripts and verbal reports, he learned a great deal about the villages of Nadiya. He soon discovered that his earlier suspicion that Navadwip was a village of less than 100 years was true. He even found people living who could remember moving there in their childhood. From the manuscripts he confirmed that Caitanyadeva appeared on the eastern banks of the Ganges.[32] Navadwip was on the western bank. Elderly villagers in Ballaldighi called the area Myeyapur, and one eighteenth century map listed the region as Mayapur. In the *Bhakti-ratnākara,* he found the following reference:

navadvīpa madhye māyāpura nāme sthāna/
yathā janmilena gauracandra bhagavān//

In the land of Navadwip there is a place called Mayapur,
where Bhagavān Gaurachandra was born.[33]

Kedarnath was convinced that Ballaldighi was indeed the site of Caitanya's original home. In his *Jīvanī* he states that he consulted an engineer in Krishnanagar who drew an area map that he published in a work entitled, *Navadvīpa-dhāma-māhātmyam* (1890). Kedarnath's discovery of Caitanya's birth site became a landmark in the history

32. ST vol. 5 no. 11, 221 (1894): Appendix V, 2.
33. Quoted from the *Bhakti-ratnākara* in *Sajjana-toṣaṇī* vol. 5 no. 11, 221 (1894) in an article entitled *Śrī-dhāma-māyāpura*: Appendix V, 3.

of Caitanya Vaiṣṇavism. It also became a source of great division within the community.

Meanwhile, in Navadwip tension was mounting. Controversy centered around a letter from Sisir Kumar Ghosh written to Kedar encouraging him to proceed with his discovery of Caitanya's birth site. In his letter Ghosh calls Kedar the seventh *gosvāmī*, comparing him to the six *gosvāmīs* of Vrindavan. He writes, "Just as the six *gosvāmīs* of Vrindavan had reclaimed the places of Śrī Kṛṣṇa's pastimes in Vraja, so your mission is to recover the places of Caitanya's *līlā* in Nadiya." I include a translation of Sisir Kumar's letter because it shows the support and respect that Sisir Kumar Ghosh and other members of the *bhadraloka* held for Kedar.[34] Ghosh writes:

> Deoghar
> Vai Baidyanath E. I. Ry
> November 23, 1888
>
> Dear Bhaktivinoda,
>
> I received your new book. The great devotees endure much difficulty, and we who are very low and fallen take the benefit of that trouble. Many call you "Bhaktivinoda," but I consider you the "seventh *gosvāmī*." When they were present, there were six *gosvāmīs*, now that they are gone you are the *gosvāmī*. You are blessed and by your mercy I will become blessed. You are sent by the Lord and in these barren times you are rejuvenating the eternal dharma. Even though I have not yet read your book (*Śrī-dhāma-parikramā*), just by touching it I am soothed. Someone else established another Navadwip, but where is the real goddess of Navadwip? Without the goddess, Navadwip is empty. Please bring her and by doing so make tens of millions of beings like me eternally indebted.
>
> All the rest banded together have obscured the

34. This letter is from a Bengali publication called *Ṭhākura Bhaktivinoda* by Sundarananda Vidyavinoda, 1937, 56-57. Edited by Bhakti Pradipa Tirtha. Appendix V, 4.

presence of Viṣṇupriyā Devī as the goddess of Navadwip and this has disturbed Śrī Navadvīpa Candra. For this reason Gaurāṅga and Viṣṇupriyā appeared in a vision before the most beloved servant Śrī Narottama Ṭhākura. The details of this are seen in the *Narottama-vilāsa* and the *Bhakti-ratnākara*. Even today that form exists in Shri Kheturi. O Ṭhākura, only you have the vision and are qualified to carry out the direct order of Bhagavān Gaurāṅga. For this reason, with deep feeling we take shelter of your feet. There are many stories about Devī in the *Caitanya-maṅgala* and also a few in the *Bhakti-ratnākara*. Viśvanātha Cakravartī has written about meditating upon that dual form of Viṣṇupriyā-Gaurāṅga. Besides this there is more information in other past stories. What more have I to say? I always take shelter of you.

Yours sincerely,
Sisir Kumar Ghosh Das

Sisir Kumar's acknowledgment of Kedar as the seventh *gosvāmī* was a direct recognition of his growing importance as a spiritual leader, not just within his own group by the Bāghnāpāḍā Gosvāmīs, but by the Hindu *bhadraloka* in general. To the residents of Navadwip, Ghosh's involvement meant that Kedar's claim was taking hold. Ghosh even suggested that Kedar arrange to install the *mūrtis* of Śrī Viṣṇupriyā and Gaurāṅga at Mayapur.

Sisir Kumar's suggestion to build a temple and install the *mūrtis* of Śrī Viṣṇupriyā and Caitanya at Mayapur created great anger amongst the residents of Navadwip. They flatly rejected Kedarnath's claims and soon formed a group headed by Kanticandra Radi to oppose him. In a published work, *Navadvīpa-tattva*,[35] they tried to show that Navadwip was the true location of Caitanya's birth and not Mayapur.[36] Kedar's only known response to the whole matter is

35. I have been unable to procure a copy of Kanticandra's work and so I am reporting information recorded by Ramakanta Chakrabarty in his book, *Vaiṣṇavism in Bengal*, 396.

blunt. He writes in his *Jīvanī:*

> Much envy arose from the people of Navadwip over the finding of old Navadwip near Ballaldighi. There was much talk and a storm of abuse against the worshippers of Gaurāṅga (Caitanya), but those who have offered their life to the feet of Gaurāṅga do not retreat simply from the talk of wicked people. Ignoring such envious people, the followers of Gaurāṅga arranged to build a temple and worship God.[37]

Kedarnath was convinced by his vision and subsequent research that the place he had seen from the roof of the Rani Dharmashala that dark evening was the actual site of Śrī Caitanya's birth. He was determined to proceed.

There is good evidence that Kedar's site near Ballaldighi may indeed be the location for Caitanya's birth and childhood. K. N. Mukherjee's research confirms Kedar's pick. However, the matter is still hotly contested. Even as recently a 1931 another site, north of the present day Navadwip, called Ramchandrapur, was suggested as the birth place of Caitanya. This new site was chosen by an ascetic called Brajamohan Das Baba who moved to Navadwip in 1916.[38]

In the autumn of 1889 Kedar purchased a piece of property near Mayapur which he called Shri Surabhikunj. There he planned to retire and oversee the temple construction. Later on his discov-

---

36. Charges were made against Bhaktivinoda that he forged certain texts in order to substantiate his claim for Mayapur as the birth site of Mahāprabhu. For instance, Prabodhānanda's *Navadvīpa-śataka* and Jagadānanda's *Prema-vivarta* were alleged to have been written by Bhaktivinoda himself and not the supposed authors. Similarly, the course of the Ganges has been contested. It appears that the movement of the Ganges has been eastward constantly for hundreds of years and that the old riverbed can be found on the western side of the current town. This would throw doubt on Bhaktivinoda's claim. Whatever the case, Bhaktivinoda certainly pushed his views with vigor and the support of 'newly discovered' documents.

37. *Jīvanī,* 201.

38. See K. N. Mukherjee, "A Historico-Geographical Study for Sri Chaitanya's Birthsite," *Indian Journal of Landscape System and Ecological Studies,* Vol. 7, No. II (Calcutta, 1984), 33-56.

ery of Mayapur led to the discovery of many of the other sites associated with Caitanya's pastimes. For the time being that was as far as his discovery of Mayapur could go; his health was again deteriorating. The doctors told him to transfer immediately from Krishnanagar to a place that was less damp and better for his health. After all the trouble in coming to Nadiya his health was again taking him away. The residents of Navadwip were naturally delighted.

During his stay in Krishnanagar he had fared well in government service. He had received a promotion to third grade of deputy magistrate and his family continued to grow with the birth of his thirteenth child, Hari Pramodini. On his doctor's advice, in the spring of 1889 he moved to Netrakona in the district of Mymensing to work under R. C. Datta, one of the few Indian members of the Indian Civil Service. By September of 1889, he was stationed at Burdwan and in the last months of 1890 he again spent time in Dinajpur overseeing the government census of 1891. On 4 August 1891, he received a two year furlough and the last of his fourteen children, Shailaja Prasad, was born in Calcutta during the summer. He was now fifty-three years old.

During Kedar's furlough he began his famous *nāma-haṭṭa* program styled after his circuit court. It was a great success. During *nāma-haṭṭa* he traveled all over Bengal holding *kīrtana*, distributing Kṛṣṇa *prasāda* and lecturing. His group even made a trip to Vrindavan. He writes, "We did *nāma-pracāra* (preaching) in many places and we were delighted. When we spoke, many *bhaktas*, *brāhmaṇas* and pundits were present. After finishing in one place we would go to the next. We did *nāma-saṅkīrtana* everywhere. In Krishnanagar there were many *sabhās* and when we lectured even Englishmen came."[39] For most of his two year furlough Kedar traveled and preached to his heart's content. On one occasion he met with Jagannath Das Babaji and helped him organize a large festival

---

39. *Jīvanī,* 191. For example, the *Sajjana-toṣaṇī* Vol. 4 p. 117 notes that Reverend Butler and Munro Sahib were present on Tuesday afternoon on the 12th day of *Śravaṇa-māsa* for Bhaktivinoda's lecture entitled, *Śrīman Mahāprabhu Krishna-caitanya o tāṅhāra śikṣā.*

in Mayapur. Until the turn of the century Kedarnath actively organized *nāma-haṭṭa*. In his *Jīvanī* he lists the numerous tours he made throughout Bengal. Whatever spare time he could find was spent with *nāma-haṭṭa*.

On 2 April 1893, Kedar resumed his government work with a promotion to second-grade deputy magistrate. This was his highest level of government service, but by now his coveted government job was interfering with his true heart's desire. He wanted to devote his full time to *nāma-haṭṭa* and to Mayapur. Instead he was sent to the sub-district of Sasaram, where Hindus and Muslims were fighting. In one incident a Hindu *sannyāsī* wanted to build a temple on the site of a Muslim tomb. In another incident a *brāhmaṇa's* bull was butchered by a group of Muslims, resulting in a riot that killed many people. Kedar had to preside over many cases of this nature. It was exhausting work.

In October of 1893 he again returned to Krishnanagar. He writes, "I wrote to Cotton Sahib and he gave me a transfer to Nadiya from Sasaram. The days of my troubles were over. I did not delay, but went directly to Krishnanagar where I purchased a carriage and a pair of horses."[40] Regularly he traveled between Krishnanagar and Mayapur. Being urged by Sisir Kumar Ghosh and others, he began to execute his plan for a temple at Shri Mayapur. He arranged a meeting at the A. B. School in Krishnanagar where he spoke before a large public assembly concerning his investigation and research into the birth site of Śrī Caitanya at Mayapur. He was applauded for this work. A review of the meeting can be found in Kedar's *Toṣaṇī* along with an impressive list of *bhadraloka* participants.[41]

In the meeting a committee called the Navadwip Dham Pracarini, headed by Naphor Chandra Pal Chaudhuri was formed to purchase land and oversee temple construction. During the meeting a decision was also made to install the deities of Śrī Viṣṇupriyā and Śrī Caitanya as soon as possible. In his *Jīvanī* Kedar

40. *Jīvanī,* 199.
41. "Śrī Śrī Navadvīpa Dhāma Pracāriṇī Sabhā," *Sajjana-toṣaṇī,* 1894 vol. 5 no. 11, 201-207.

summarizes the events:

> One society named Shri Shri Navadwip Dham Pracarini was established. Naphor Babu was named the chairmen of that *sabhā*. Funds were collected in the public meeting and approval was given for the installation of *śrī-mūrti*. . . . Land at Shri Mayapur was purchased and a thatched building was built and the *mūrtis* of Śrī Viṣṇupriyā–Gaurāṅga were established. On the eighth of Caitra (1894) there was a huge installation festival of *śrī-mūrti*. Countless people came. There were *kīrtana*, folk plays, and *nāma-saṅkīrtana* all performed in great bliss.[42]

Reviewing the pages of *Sajjana-toṣaṇī* month by month after the installation of the *mūrtis* in Mayapur, it is evident that a large campaign was underway to collect funds for a temple at the site. Now that Kedarnath had overseen the installation of Śrī Caitanyadeva he had to proceed with temple construction. Unfortunately, it was impossible to properly raise funds for this project while he still held a government position. Therefore, in the same year that he installed the *mūrtis*, Kedarnath Datta retired from government service. At first the government tried to persuade him to stay, but this time he was determined. He writes, "The government sent some people to Krishnanagar to advise me to remain working a little longer, but I gave them thanks. I no longer had any taste to continue working, so on the fourth of October, 1894, I took retirement and moved my things to the house at Surabhikunj near Mayapur."[43] Kedarnath retired with a pension of 300 rupees per month.

Now Kedar's plans for Mayapur could proceed without interruption. With the help of Ramsevak, his close friend and supporter, he began full-scale fund-raising. An article published in the *Amṛta Bazaar Patrikā* on 6 December 1894 describes his endeavors:

> Babu Kedarnath Datta, the distinguished Deputy

42. *Jīvanī*, 200-201.
43. Ibid., 202.

> Magistrate who has just retired from the service, is one of the most active members [of the committee]. Indeed, Babu Kedarnath Datta has been deputed by his committee to raise subscriptions in Calcutta and elsewhere and is determined to go from house to house if necessary and beg a rupee from each Hindu gentleman for the noble purpose. If Babu Kedarnath Datta, therefore, really sticks to his resolution of going around with a bag in hand, we hope no Hindu gentleman whose home may be honored by the presence of such a devout bhakta as Babu Kedarnath will send him away without contributing his mite, however humble it may be, to the Gaura Viṣṇupriyā Temple Fund.[44]

His efforts were successful, and a magnificent temple was soon constructed in Mayapur. The installation of Śrī Śrī Viṣṇupriyā Gaurāṅga and the construction of the temple was an important accomplishment for Kedarnath and the committee. Unfortunately criticism and opposition from Navadwip never ended. In Mayapur, after the *mūrti* installation, most of the other important sites associated with Śrī Caitanya's early life were also established, which further aggravated the matter. To this day a battle still quietly rages between Navadwip and Mayapur and on both sides of the river you will find duplicate pastime locations.[45]

Much less is known about Kedarnath's life after 1886 because he ends his autobiography on June 21 of that year. Unfortunately, much of what is reported by the various Bengali and English biographers about his remaining years is unsubstantiated information. It does not appear that Kedar had any more children. We know that he remained in Bengal until 1900, at which time he went to Puri. Most of the time between 1886 and 1900 was spent collecting funds, overseeing temple construction, publishing books, and participat-

44. Quoted from Satkari Chattopadhyay *A Glimpse into the Life of Thakur Bhakti-vinode* (Calcutta: Bhaktivinoda Memorial Committee, 1916), 20.
45. During the 1920s the Nitāi Gaura Rādhe Śyāma group from Navadwip enlisted the help of an engineer who did a number of digs on the western bank of the Bhagirathi river and founded the Navadwip version of Caitanya's birth site. There were harsh words and threats between both sides of the river.

ing in *nāma-haṭṭa* throughout Bengal. What documented information we do have about this period comes from *Sajjana-toṣaṇī* and mostly concerns the *nāma-haṭṭa* program.

Reading through the pages of *Sajjana-toṣaṇī,* one is impressed by Kedarnath's intense evangelizing spirit. In the years between 1885 and 1900, there are numerous articles describing his various preaching activities.[46] A typical *nāma-haṭṭa* report was a monthly review. A segment of one such report reads as follows:

> On Saturday afternoon of the 26th of Āṣāḍh [1892] a *nāma-haṭṭa* festival was hosted by Shriyuta Ray Yatindranath Chaudhuri Mahashay of Barahanagar. Many learned and inquisitive gentlemen were in attendance. At the request of the organizers of the *nāma-haṭṭa,* everyone took turns singing. Afterwards the sweeper of the market,[47] Shriyuta Kedarnath Datta Bhaktivinoda, gave a long discourse entitled "Mahashay Śrī Kṛṣṇa and Śrī Kṛṣṇa Caitanya" that lasted over three hours. Afterwards the *mahājanī*[48] Shriyuta Advaita Das Babaji Mahashay sang two songs ending with Haribol. At the conclusion, all the assembled guests gave a great cry of Hari and the meeting ended.[49]

Kedar regularly held *nāma-haṭṭa* throughout Bengal. His *Svalikhita-jīvanī* is replete with elaborate lists of *nāma-haṭṭa* programs that occurred just before and after his retirement. We mentioned that the scheme for *nāma-haṭṭa* developed during his days as a circuit court magistrate traveling from village to village in the *mofussil* (rural environs). As he moved from one place to another to hold court, the local villagers would hold *bhajana* and *kīrtana* with him.

---

46. The *nāma-haṭṭa* reports can be found mostly in volumes four and five (1892-93) of the *Sajjana-toṣaṇī.*
47. *Parimārjaka,* or the sweeper, was the term used to describe Bhaktivinoda's humble place in the *nāma-haṭṭa* scheme of preaching.
48. *Mahājanī* or money lender is another term describing a position in the *nāma-haṭṭa* program. In this case he refers to one ascetic, Advaita Das, as the bestower of the treasure of bhakti.
49. ST, vol. 4 (1892), 117.

Specifically the *nāma-haṭṭa* was a scheme of preaching conceived after the image of a commodities market. According to this idea, the *Bhāgavata* and its related literature were considered the storehouses (*bhāṇḍāra*). The principle trader (*mūla-mahājana*) was Nityānanda Prabhu and the share traders (*aṁśī mahājana*) were Advaitācārya in Bengal, Rūpa and Sanātana Gosvāmīs in Vrindavan, and Svarūpa Dāmodara and Rāya Rāmānanda in Jagannath Puri. The chief commodity was the holy name and the main currency was faith (*śraddhā*). The customers (*kretā*) were all the people of the world. In this market there were shopkeepers (*vipaṇī*), who distributed the holy name locally, and traveling salespeople (*vrajaka-vipaṇī*), who distributed the holy name abroad. There was also a treasurer (*kośādhyakṣa*), sales agents (*dālāla*), guards (*caukidāra*) and other members—all complete with job descriptions and responsibilities. *Nāma-haṭṭa* even included various policies to deal with the behavior of shopkeepers, sales agents, traveling salespeople (i.e., preachers and distributors), and any disturbances that may occur from the public. Kedarnath regularly refers to himself as the lowly sweeper (*parimārjaka*), whose job it was to keep the marketplace clean. He also describes how it was the sweeper's responsibility to send all kinds of notes and correspondence to the market reporter to publish as he cleaned the market. Repeatedly the market sweeper invites all persons, locally and from foreign countries, to become shopkeepers in their own localities or to become traveling sales people abroad.

Sometimes a hall or school was rented for the *nāma-haṭṭa* meetings.[50] At other times they were held in the open under a large canopy or *pāṇḍāla*. Most often they were simply held in the homes of private individuals. On many occasions prominent Europeans, including Christian missionaries and government officials, would be in attendance.[51] Judging by the reports listed in the *Sajjana-toṣaṇī*, the meetings attracted a high class of patrons.[52] It seems that the

50. The A. B. School in Krishnanagar was a popular location for area meetings.
51. ST vol. 4 (1892), 117.

nāma-haṭṭa was a successful and important part of Kedar's life from the years before his retirement until the turn of the century. During that time Kedarnath established over five hundred *nāma-haṭṭa saṅgas* (associations) throughout Bengal.

In 1896 he made a trip to the state of Tripura at the request of the Maharaja of Tripura and there spent time preaching in Darjeeling and Kurseong. In 1896, as we have already noted, Kedarnath again contacted the West by broadcasting the teachings of Caitanya in the form of the small booklet entitled *Gaurāṅga-smaraṇa-maṅgala-stotram.* The following review of his work appears in the *Journal of the Royal Asiatic Society.*

> Under the title of *Śrī-gaurāṅga-līlā-smaraṇa-maṅgala-stotram,* the well-known Vaishnava Shri Kedarnath Bhaktivinoda, M. R. A. S., has published a poem in Sanskrit on the life and teachings of Caitanya. It is accompanied by a commentary, also in Sanskrit, in which the subject, further elucidated, is preceded by an introduction of sixty-three pages in English, in which the doctrines taught by Chaitanya are set out in somewhat full detail. The little volume will add to our knowledge of this remarkable reformer, and we express our thanks to Bhaktivinoda for giving it to us in English and Sanskrit, rather than in Bengali, in which language it must necessarily have remained a closed book to the European students of the religious life of India.[53]

In 1897 Kedar traveled and preached in many villages and towns throughout southern Bengal near Midnapore. During the years 1898 to 1900 he edited and published many important devotional works including Bilvamaṅgala's *Kṛṣṇa-karṇāmṛta,* Rūpa Gosvāmī's

52. Generally speaking, Bhaktivinoda directed his preaching efforts toward the *bhadraloka* and not toward the lower classes of Bengalis. Of course, the *kīrtana* parties that traveled from village to village included everyone, but the literary record shows that his was a movement of educated and well-stationed Bengalis almost exclusively.

53. Quoted from Chattopadhyay, *Glimpse into the Life,* 21.

Upadeśāmṛta, Madhvācārya's *Bhagavad-gītā* commentary, the second *khaṇḍa* of Sanātana Gosvāmī's *Bṛhad-bhāgavatāmṛta* and Narahari Sarakāra's *Bhajanāmṛta*. In addition, he published his own works, entitled *Navadvīpa-bhāva-taraṅga*, and *Harināma-cintāmaṇi*.

In 1900 Kedarnath moved to Puri. This time he was not a representative of the government but was there for his own personal *bhajana* or worship at the site of Caitanyadeva's final pastimes. He constructed a simple shelter near the seashore and the *samādhi* (tomb) of Hari Dāsa Ṭhākura, which he called Bhaktikutir. There, he performed his *bhajana* in solitude. One disciple, a young man named Krishna Das Baba, stayed with him as an assistant. On the beach front at Puri, guests often visited Kedarnath to discuss devotional matters. In 1901 he published his *Bhāgavatārka-marīci-mālā*, a large compendium of *Bhāgavata* verses arranged according to philosophical subject. In the same year he published an edition of the *Padma-purāṇa* and the *Saṅkalpa-kalpadruma* of Viśvanātha Cakravartī with his own Bengali translations. In 1902 he brought out a supplement to his *Hari-nāma-cintāmaṇi* entitled *Bhajana-rahasya*.

By late 1903, poor health forced him to return to Mayapur in Bengal. There he lived quietly performing *bhajana* while he reedited many of his older writings. In 1904 he edited and published an edition of Gopāla Bhaṭṭa Gosvāmī's Sanskrit work *Sat-kriyā-sāra-dīpikā*, outlining Vaiṣṇava *saṁskāras* (life cycle rituals). The last known work composed by Kedarnath was entitled *Śrī-sva-niyama-dvādaśakam*. It was written in 1907 when Kedarnath was sixty-nine years old, but it was left unfinished due to his poor health. This work appears to be modeled after Raghunātha Dāsa's *Sva-niyama-daśakam*. It is a series of twelve final statements to himself regarding preparations to leave his earthly life and reminders not to budge from the path of devotion established by Rūpa Gosvāmī.

We are also told how in 1908, just three months before Kedarnath became a recluse, Sir William Duke, the Chief Secretary of Bengal, came to visit him in Calcutta. Kedar had previously worked for this gentleman as a magistrate. Sir William met him at the Writers' Building and is reported to have said, "My dear Kedarnath, when you were District Magistrate, I wanted to take you out of office. I thought that if there were many men as qualified as you in Bengal, then the English would have to leave. I apologize for the trouble I caused you."

In 1908 Kedarnath took *veśa* and adopted the lifestyle of a Vaiṣṇava recluse. By 1910 he spent most of his time in Calcutta living quietly at his home at 181 Maniktala Street. Kedar's health was so poor that he could hardly travel. He suffered from severe rheumatism that partially paralyzed him. In these final years he remained at Bhakti Bhavan in Calcutta performing *bhajana* until his passing away on 23 June 1914. Later that same year his wife, Bhagavati Devi, also passed away. Kedar's *samādhi* ceremony was delayed until January when the sun began its northern course. At that time, his last remains were taken from Bhakti Bhavan and brought to his home in Surabhikunj, where they were buried in a silver urn amidst a large *kīrtana* held by his family and friends.

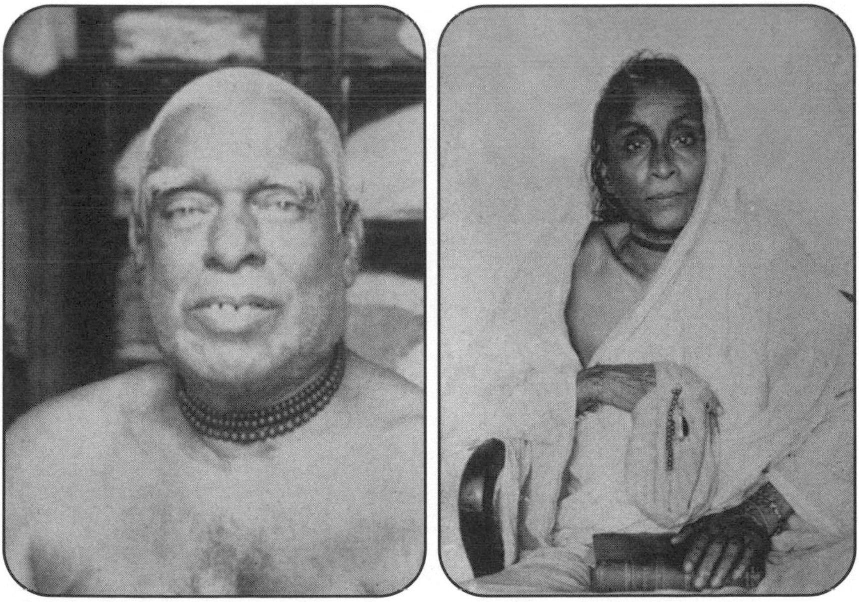

Bhaktivinoda and Bhagavati Devi in their later years.

Kedarnath Datta Bhaktivinoda
(1838–1914)

Bankim Chandra Chatterjee
(1838–1894)

Chapter Five

Reason and Religious Faith

> When we were in college, reading the philosophical works of the West and exchanging thoughts with the thinkers of the day, we had a real hatred towards the *Bhagavat.* That great work looked like a repository of wicked and stupid ideas, scarcely adapted to the nineteenth century, and we hated to hear any argument in its favor. With us a volume of Channing, Parker, Emerson or Newman had more weight than the whole lot of the *Vaishnav* works. Greedily we poured over the various commentaries of the holy Bible and of the labors of the Tattwa Bodhini Sabha,[1] containing extracts from the *Upanishads* and the *Vedanta,* but no works of the *Vaishnavs* had any favor with us.[2]

These words of Bhaktivinoda echo the sentiments of the *bhadraloka,* alienated from their traditional Hindu roots. No doubt, they are words of cynicism, but as the *bhadraloka* matured, their thinking gave way to a re-examination and often a selective acceptance of their once rejected religious culture. Here we explore how Kedarnath Datta Bhaktivinoda dealt with the colliding forces of traditional Bengali religious culture and nineteenth century modernity, and how he created a new understanding of Caitanya Vaiṣṇavism. In particular we focus on the broad foundational issues of his theological and historical perspective and its relationship with

1. The *Tattva-bodhinī-sabhā* refers to the Brahmo Samaj.
2. Kedarnath Datta, *The Bhagavat, Its Philosophy, Ethics and Theology,* ed. Bhaktivilas Tirtha, 2d ed. (Madras: Madras Gaudiya Math, 1959), 6.

rationalism, reason, and religious faith.

A Crisis of Faith

Bhaktivinoda's early life in the village of Ula was time spent in a religious environment that supported traditional Hindu faith. From the wealthy zamindars, who held the grand public *pūjās*, to the door keepers and domestic servants, who recited the stories from the *Rāmāyaṇa* and the *Mahābhārata*, all were a part of the Hindu matrix that nurtured the ancestral Hindu religious faith found throughout rural Bengal.

Calcutta, on the other hand, presented a radically different situation. Here the *bhadraloka* found themselves at the beginning of the modern era, in a time when religio-cultural pluralism on a global scale and foreign dominated technologies were unavoidable facts of life. Their skepticism and loss of faith in traditional Bengali culture, as Bhaktivinoda's opening comments illustrate, were not surprising. The ancestral religious culture that they turned to for support had been formulated in a traditional world innocent of global religious pluralism. Consequently, it could not provide the religious and cultural support that the *bhadraloka* so desperately needed.

Traditional Hindu theologians, regardless of their sectarian affiliations, had created a form of Hinduism from a perspective that did not account for Christian, Jewish, Darwinian, and the myriad of other foreign perspectives that the *bhadraloka* faced. Neither did it account for such technological advances as the printing press, steam locomotion, or the telegraph, all of which played a major role in the religious, cultural, and economic life of the *bhadraloka.* Even six centuries of Muslim domination had been largely ignored by mainline Hindu religious thought. In other words, traditional Hinduism had been formulated in terms of its own regional (subcontinental) and parochial context that was classically Hindu and Indian; it could not possibly foresee the global perspective that would emerge during the nineteenth century under the sway of European domination. Such a form of Hindu theology could not readily cope with the challenges of nineteenth century modernity.

Nor could the *bhadraloka*, who had become vulnerable through their British education, be expected to maintain confidence in a theological perspective that could not adequately address their religious and cultural needs.

In this situation the lives of many *bhadraloka* fragmented. Some, like the followers of Young Bengal, lost religious faith altogether; others, like Reverend Lal Behari De became Christian; an even larger group joined the Brahmo movement; and still others joined the ranks of the Positivists following Comte or became utilitarians working for non-denominational social reform. Bhaktivinoda recognizes this dilemma:

> It is regrettable that the intellectuals of Bengal have abandoned the religious traditions created by our great forefathers, and have wasted their time creating their own useless steps. Had there been a book on scriptural analysis (*śāstra-vicāra*) available to the intellectual class then the great waste of useless speculation in the formulation of lower religion (*upadharma*), cheating religion (*chala-dharma*), heresy (*vaidharma*), and other religions would not have entered India. The main purpose behind this book [*Kṛṣṇa-saṁhitā*] is to fill this need.[3]

The need for more sophisticated interpretations of Hindu *śāstra* is an apt recognition of the problem that existed in relating Bengali Hindu religious traditions to the modern situation. First we will examine the crisis of faith that led to the writing of Bhaktivinoda's *Kṛṣṇa-saṁhitā*.

During the nineteenth century one of the most crucial religious concerns was the status and character of Śrī Kṛṣṇa as a symbol of Hindu morality and spirituality. Kṛṣṇa embodies the very essence of religious life for many Hindus, and how the *bhadraloka* regarded the life of Kṛṣṇa revealed their religious and cultural identity. The impact of Kṛṣṇa upon the character of Hinduism has been

3. KS, *Upakramaṇikā*, 5: Appendix V, 5.

immense. It is not surprising that the character of Śrī Kṛṣṇa should have been a prime focus of both the problems and solutions to Hindu identity. Bhaktivinoda's religious and civil service colleague, Bankim Chandra Chatterjee, eloquently sums up the concerns of the *bhadraloka* in this regard:

> Kṛishṇa is God incarnate, but how do people look upon God? They take Him as a thief in His childhood, stealing butter; as an adulterer in his youth, leading innumerable milkmaids away from the path of chastity; and as a rogue in his maturity, taking the lives of Drona and others by deceit. Is this the character of God? Is it reasonable that one who is purity itself and who is the repository of all that is true, whose name dispels all impurity and impiety would indulge in sin while in human incarnation?[4]

The doubts that Bankim Chandra expresses about the life of Kṛṣṇa reflect the crisis of religious faith that was prevalent among the *bhadraloka.* Consequently, there was a need to understand the historical and spiritual nature of Śrī Kṛṣṇa upon which the *bhadraloka* could build their emerging religious and cultural identity. With this purpose in mind, Bhaktivinoda, Bankim Chandra, and other members of the *bhadraloka*[5] set out to re-interpret their ancestral religious traditions in a way that could dispel their doubts and provide a basis for a religious and cultural revival suited to modern life.

In the cases of both Bhaktivinoda and Bankim Chandra, the

4. R. C. Majumdar, *History of Modern Bengal* (Calcutta: G. Bharadwaj and Co., 1978), 181.

5. Other names that may be added to this list include: Navin Chandra Sen (1847–1909), who wrote three poems, *Raivataka* (1887), *Kurukṣetra* (1893) and *Prabhāsa* (1896), each reinterpreting the myths associated with Kṛṣṇa's life; Premananda Bharati, who came to America in 1905 and wrote a work, *Shree Krishna*; Bipin Chandra Pal, who interpreted Kṛṣṇa as a national hero along the same lines as Bankim Chandra; and Bhudev Mukhopadhyay (1827-1894), who was a strict follower of traditional Bengali *brāhmaṇism.* For more details see B. B. Majumdar's *Krishna in History and Legend*, pp. 250- 265, or Tapan Raychaudhuri's *Europe Reconsidered.*

idea that traditional learning could be combined with modern historical and comparative methods of critical scholarship is prevalent throughout their writings. However, the two differ radically over the use of rationalism in religion. Bhaktivinoda rejects the exclusive use of rationalism. Instead he builds an approach that involves a combination of both reason and religious faith. Bankim Chandra, on the other hand, is a strict rationalist who makes exclusive use of rational analysis, to the exclusion, it would seem, of religious faith.

Although rationalism, which was brought to the *bhadraloka* through such vehicles as British Orientalism, was a major component of early nineteenth century thought, Bhaktivinoda felt it had great limitations when applied to the field of religious studies. Reason is a great attribute of the human mind that could be used to achieve high levels of religious understanding. But there are limitations. To follow the rationalist's approach and to limit religious understanding to the strict use of reason alone is a great mistake. The key to religious understanding is to know the limits of human reason. Let us compare Bhaktivinoda's use of logical analysis with that of his respected colleague Bankim Chandra.

The Rationalism of Bankim Chandra

Like Kedarnath Bhaktivinoda, Bankim Chandra Chatterjee (1838–1894) worked as a magistrate in the Collectorate Service under the British Government in India. Although their careers ran in parallel, the two men were very different. Bhaktivinoda was deeply religious whereas Bankim Chandra was a patriot and social commentator. In presenting the life of Śrī Kṛṣṇa, Bankim Chandra wanted to create a hero to serve as a model for Hindu national revival. He was more interested in Kṛṣṇa's moral and cultural value than in Kṛṣṇa's spiritual significance. Although the details of Kṛṣṇa's life are found mostly in the *Mahābhārata* and the *Purāṇas,* Bankim Chandra felt that any scriptural passage that was to be held as genuine had to be rationally and morally acceptable. Consequently, he uses no hesitation to declare as spurious or as interpolated any passage of *śāstra* that did not meet these criteria.

According to Bankim Chandra, Hindu *śāstra* depicted two forms of Kṛṣṇa: one, the Kṛṣṇa of the *Bhagavad-gītā,* and the other the Kṛṣṇa of the *Purāṇas.* Bankim Chandra felt that the Kṛṣṇa of the *Bhagavad-gītā* was the real historical Kṛṣṇa, whereas the Puranic Kṛṣṇa, described as the lover of the *gopīs,* was the product of sensual imagination. The Kṛṣṇa of the *Bhagavad-gītā* was rational and moral, whereas the Kṛṣṇa of the *Purāṇas* was irrational, immoral, and a source of embarrassment. As far as Bankim Chandra was concerned, there was an obvious need to extricate the historical Kṛṣṇa from the imaginary and mythological Kṛṣṇa for the sake of developing personal character and national integrity. To accomplish this he adopted a system of textual analysis based on what seemed logical and reasonable. On this basis, Bankim Chandra attempted to reconstruct the authentic life of Śrī Kṛṣṇa according to a rationalist's approach.

Bankim writes that the *Mahābhārata* is the oldest and most authentic record of Kṛṣṇa's life and so those incidents which are not mentioned in the *Bhārata* may be discarded as mere poetic fancy. He rejects the Puranic Kṛṣṇa, including the life of Kṛṣṇa as told in the *Bhāgavata,* considered by many Vaiṣṇavas to be the most important presentation of Kṛṣṇa's life. As for those stories and passages found in the *Mahābhārata* that allude to the Puranic Kṛṣṇa, Bankim also rejects them as spurious. In fact, all passages referring to Kṛṣṇa's life at Vrindavan as reported in the *Mahābhārata* are considered interpolations. Bankim Chandra emphatically states that the allegations of Kṛṣṇa's love affairs with the *gopīs* are baseless – that they are the products of sensual imagination by the Puranic authors.[6] He says that the story of Kṛṣṇa's transfer to the house of Nanda and all the incidents relating to Kṛṣṇa's boyhood and adolescence at Vraja are false and baseless. He even denies that Kaṁsa was the maternal uncle of Kṛṣṇa. Bankim concludes:

6. In later editions of his *Kṛṣṇa-caritra,* Bankim Chandra modified his views somewhat. He later considered the love between Kṛṣṇa and the Gopīs to be an allegory of the relation between *puruṣa* and *prakṛti* as outlined in Sāṅkhya philosophy.

> I have studied the Purāṇas and historical materials to the best of my ability, with the purpose of ascertaining the real character of Śrīkṛishṇa [*sic*] as described in the Purāṇas and history, and I have come to the conclusion that the current sinful anecdotes about Śrīkṛishṇa [*sic*] are without any foundation and if these are discarded, what we are left with is of the utmost purity, sanctity, and grandeur.[7]

Bankim Chandra's work is thorough and precise, and there is no doubt that in his own mind, he had successfully extricated the historical Kṛṣṇa from the mythological Kṛṣṇa. His approach was nothing less than a complete disregard for Hindu tradition because he had to dismiss a major part of Hindu religious culture as imagination. The problem, however, is that it is the Puranic Kṛṣṇa, as butter thief and as lover of Śrī Rādhā, who has ignited the religious and poetic imagination of India for centuries. The Puranic Kṛṣṇa embodies the very heart and soul of Hindu faith at least as much as the Kṛṣṇa of the *Bhagavad-gītā*. To deny this is to reduce the religious tradition to a cold and lifeless mass stripped of its emotive and spiritual value. Herein lie the deficiencies of exclusive rationalism when applied to the field of religious studies.

According to Bhaktivinoda, the rational approach inspired by British Orientalism, when taken to its logical extreme, was severely lacking because it was incapable of penetrating the realm of religious faith that had created the religious tradition in the first place. Bankim Chandra's *Kṛṣṇa-caritra* was a perfect example of the excesses and misuse of the rationalist's approach in the area of religious studies. His rationalist's approach failed to embrace the spiritual side of religious faith, so his work could not comprehend the inspirational and mystical aspects of religious culture. Bankim Chandra's *Kṛṣṇa-caritra* did not, therefore, constitute a viable synthesis of tradition and modernity.

It was evident to Bhaktivinoda that he had to go beyond both the parochial nature of traditional religious culture and the pure

7. Majumdar, *History of Modern Bengal*, 181.

rationalism of modernity in his quest for an adequate theological perspective. Growing up in Ula, he lived in an atmosphere of religious faith participating in the grand Durgā *pūjās* and other religious festivals celebrated at his grandfather's home. At school in Calcutta he met a constant stream of Calcutta's cultural elite, most of whom had been students of Hindu College and had been deeply influenced by the rationalism of British Orientalism. That Bhaktivinoda grew up in a time permeated by the approach of traditional Hinduism and the emerging rationalistic and objective approach of modernity inspired by British Orientalism profoundly affected his theological perspective and his approach to the problems of modernity and tradition.

Bhaktivinoda and British Orientalism

As the comparative and rational techniques of British Orientalism formed the basis of Bankim Chandra's study of the life of Kṛṣṇa, similarly these techniques formed a major component of Bhaktivinoda's interpretation of the life of Kṛṣṇa. The discovery and appreciation of traditional learning that Orientalism fostered, combined with the methodology of modern comparative scholarship, was a prime element that inspired Bhaktivinoda's *Kṛṣṇa-saṁhitā*.[8]

The influence of British Orientalism is obvious in the *Kṛṣṇa-saṁhitā* from the outset. In his preface Bhaktivinoda writes:

> History and chronology are natural sciences *(artha-śāstra)*.[9] When they are judged according to sound reasoning India can benefit greatly. Eventually we hope

8. Bhaktivinoda's *Kṛṣṇa-saṁhitā,* published in 1879, appeared a full five years before Bankim Chandra's *Kṛṣṇa-caritra,* published in 1884. Biman Bihari Majumdar gives credit to Bankim Chandra for being the first Indian scholar to undertake a critical study of the life of Kṛṣṇa, but this credit should be given to Bhaktivinoda.

9. There are two terms used by Bhaktivinoda in this regard. They are *artha-śāstra* and *paramārtha-śāstra. Artha-śāstra* refers to the phenomenal sciences such as mathematics, history, medicine, architecture and so on. *Paramārtha-śāstra* refers to the

> there will be much progress in regard to the Transcendent. When the stream of logic meets the river of traditional faith, the moss of illusion is washed away. In the course of time when the stench of discredit is thoroughly exhausted, the scientific knowledge of India will become healthy.[10]

Compare this statement with that of H. H. Wilson, the famed British Orientalist. Through the use of modern research Wilson hoped to:

> preserve from decay and degradation a system of science and literature held in pious veneration by the great body of its subjects, deeply interwoven in their domestic habits and religious faith . . . but . . . to combine with this the still more important one of opening new sources of intellectual and moral improvements by the gradual admission of European science and learning.[11]

Bhaktivinoda's *Kṛṣṇa-saṁhitā,* like Bankim Chandra's *Kṛṣṇa-caritra,* was a reassessment of the life of Kṛṣṇa in light of modernity. Unlike Bankim Chandra, who felt that the existing Hindu tradition was filled with much illusion and superstition, Bhaktivinoda thought the tradition was simply misunderstood. What was really needed was a change in the popular understanding of the tradition and not a rejection of the tradition itself. Whereas Bankim Chandra used rational criticism to *eliminate* the mythology surrounding the life of Kṛṣṇa, Bhaktivinoda proposed the use of critical analysis to *interpret* the life of Kṛṣṇa instead of rejecting it. Bhaktivinoda was not prepared to dismiss whole segments of the life of Kṛṣṇa just because they did not immediately tally with nineteenth century man's sense of what was reasonable. Instead, he wanted to apply the tools of

---

spiritual sciences such as are found in works like the *Upaniṣads* and *Bhagavad-gītā* and so on.

10. KS, *Vijñāpana,* ii: Appendix V, 6.

11. C. Lushington, *The History, Design and Present State of the Religious, Benevolent, and Charitable Institutions* (Calcutta, Hindoostanee Press, 1884), 133.

modern rational analysis to those parts of the tradition that were within the realm of logical analysis. Bhaktivinoda's approach is clearly representative of Hindu Traditionalism, while Bankim Chandra's approach is representative of Neo-Hinduism. Bhaktivinoda wanted to maintain continuity with the past, whereas Bankim Chandra expressed a break with the past.

In Bhaktivinoda's opinion, the methods of British Orientalism were useful in developing a sound perspective suited to the needs of the modern intellectual. Whenever possible he employed rational means to make the tradition comprehensible to the modern minds of the *bhadraloka.* However, he was not prepared to treat with such crude tools as rational analysis those areas of the tradition that transcended human reason, even though they might seem irrational or incomprehensible to the human intellect. Neither was he prepared to dismiss them as the product of sensual imagination as did Bankim Chandra. Instead, he synthesized the rational and historical Kṛṣṇa with the traditional Puranic Kṛṣṇa, within one system of theological understanding. Let us examine Bhaktivinoda's approach.

The *Kṛṣṇa-saṁhitā* and the *Ādhunika-vāda*

Bhaktivinoda begins his *Kṛṣṇa-saṁhitā* with an *Upakramaṇikā,* or Bengali introduction that was specifically written according to what he calls the *ādhunika-vāda* or the "modern approach."

The *Upakramaṇikā* first establishes the date of many important events of Indian history. The coming of the Aryans into Brahmavarta (India), their progressive migration from north to south, and the date of the *Mahābhārata* war were all presented according to the methodology of what was then modern scholarship. It divided history into eight periods spanning 6341 years starting with the rule of the *Prājāpatyas* and ending with British rule.

In preparing Table One, Bhaktivinoda cites the works of Archdeacon Pratt, Major Wilford, Professor John Playfair, and Mr. Samuel Davis—all British military officers or civil administrative officials who undertook historical research in India just prior to the

Table One

Vedic History

	Period Name	Period Rulers	Period in Years	Beginning Date
1	Prājāpatyas	Rule by the sages	50	4463 B.C.
2	Mānavas	Rule by Svāyambhu-manu and his dynasty	50	4413 B.C.
3	Daivas	Rule by Aindras	100	4363 B.C.
4	Vaivasvatya	Rule by Dynasty of Vaivasvana	3,465	4263 B.C.
5	Antyajas	Rule by Ābhīras, Śakas, Yavanas, Khasas, Andhras and others	1,233	798 B.C.
6	Brātyas	Rule by the new Aryan Castes	771	435 A.D.
7	Muslims	Rule by the Pāthāns and Moghuls	551	1206 A.D.
8	British	British Rule	121	1757 A.D.
		Total	6,341	

time of Bhaktivinoda.

The *Upakramaṇikā* further divides India's philosophic development into eight periods as in Table Two. The important feature of Bhaktivinoda's view of history is not his particular categorization of Vedic history into eight time periods or even the particular dating scheme that he suggests. Instead it is his evolutionary view of history. The idea that history is evolutionary—that it leads to higher and higher levels of cultural and spiritual development is characteristic of nineteenth century modernity. During the nineteenth century

Table Two
Philosophical History

	Śastra Name	Patrons
1	Pranava (Om) *Sānketika Śruti*	Prājāpatyas
2	*Sampūrṇa Śrutis,* Gāyatrī hymn and others	Mānavas, Daivas and some families of Vaivasvata
3	*Sautra Śrutis*	First half of Vaivasvata's Dynasty
4	*Manu Smṛti* and others	Second half of Vaivasvata's Dynasty
5	*Itihāsa*	Second half of Vaivasvata's Dynasty
6	Philosophic Texts	Antyajas
7	*Purāṇas* and *Sātvata Tantras*	Brātyas
8	*Tantra*	Muslims

the influence of Darwin and Comte greatly supported the notion of history as an evolutionary process. This perspective is reflected throughout Bhaktivinoda's work. In the *Saṁhitā* portion of his *Kṛṣṇa-saṁhitā* he interprets the ten incarnations (*avatāras*) of Viṣṇu in a way that illustrates an evolutionary view of history. He writes:

Text

5. To whatever form of life the *jīva* goes, Śrī Hari manifests through His inconceivable energy and plays with him in that way.
6. Śrī Hari assumes the form of the Matysa *avatāra* among fish, the form of Kūrma among turtles, and the form of Varāha among *jīvas* who possess a spine.

Commentary

When the *jīva* takes the form of a fish, Bhagavān becomes the Matysa *avatāra*. A fish is spineless, but when the spineless state gradually becomes the hard shell state, the Kūrma *avatāra* appears. When the hard-shell state gradually becomes a spine, the Boar (Varāha) incarnation appears.

Text

7. Midway (between man and animal) Nṛsiṁha appears. Among dwarfs Vāmana appears. Among uncivilized tribes Bhārgava (Paraśurāma) appears. Among the civilized tribes the son of Daśaratha (Rāma) appears.
8. When man attains full consciousness (*sarva-vijñāna*), Bhagavān Kṛṣṇa Himself appears.
9. According to the advancement in the heart of the *jīva*, the *avatāras* of Hari appear. Their appearance in this world is never dependent on birth and action.
10. Analyzing the successive characteristics of the *jīva*, time in the *śāstras* has been divided by the *ṛṣis* into ten stages.[12]

Here the *Saṁhitā* describes how each incarnation of God successively assumes a physical like form to match the evolutionary development of the embodied soul (*jīvātmā*) from its most primitive invertebrate state to its highest vertebrate and intelligent state. Not only do these passages suggest the evolutionary theories of Darwin, they also reflect the view that the passage of time is synonymous with progress.

In a similar manner Bhaktivinoda analyzes history in terms of *rasa* or spiritual mood. He describes how there are five primary *rasas* (*śānta, dāsya, sakhya, vātsalya,* and *mādhurya*—peace, servitude, friendship, parental and amorous) and how the various stages of Indian history exhibit each of these *rasas*. He suggests that the dawn of Vedic civilization embodied *śānta-rasa*, the peaceful mood. Later on, in successive ages, higher and higher stages of *rasika* development occurred. The Rāmāyaṇa exhibits the *dāsya-rasa* (servitude) through Hanumān. Later on Uddhava and Arjuna

12. KS, *Saṁhitā*, 3/5-10.

manifest the *sakhya-rasa,* the friendly mood, and so on. He even describes how non-Vedic religions exhibit different *rasas.* Mohammed and Moses express *dāsya-rasa,* servitude, while Jesus embodies *vātsalya-rasa,* the parental mood. Finally, with the advent of Caitanya comes *mādhurya-rasa,* the quintessential amorous *rasika* mood. He compares the development of *rasa* in the world to the sun which first rises in the East and then follows its course to the West. So the flood of *rasa* first rises in the East and then flows to the West.

It is interesting that Bhaktivinoda never suggests a return to Vedic times although he shows a great respect and reverence for the past. He views Vedic culture as the foundation of Hindu culture but not something that India or the *bhadraloka* should return to. Life is dynamic and progressive and just as the *śānta-rasa* formed the foundations of Vedic civilization, so successive stages of spiritual and cultural development have occurred since that time. Today something higher, *mādhurya-rasa,* has arisen, so it would be regressive to return to *śānta-rasa.* The ideas of Vedic culture are important in Bhaktivinoda's thinking, indeed they are foundational, but they are not an absolute paradigm for modern emulation. Later on during a discussion of social development, we will see how Bhaktivinoda's ideas of social evolution reflect similar theories of human evolution prevalent during the nineteenth century.

Three Kinds of Spiritual Seekers

The *ādhunika-vāda* was Bhaktivinoda's attempt to approach the study of Vedic history and geography from the perspective of the modern historian. He wanted to use the tools of modern comparative scholarship to show the antiquity of Vedic thought and thereby draw attention to the spiritual significance of Śrī Kṛṣṇa and Vaiṣṇava culture. The *ādhunika-vāda* was based on the premise that the existing religious traditions within Bengal had neglected the needs of the modern intellectual. Bhaktivinoda identified three types of spiritual seekers (*adhikārīs*): *komala-śraddhas, madhyamādhikārīs,* and *uttamādhikārīs.*[13] Such a classification of spiritual seekers was based

13. A more standard use of these three terms comes from the *Bhāgavata,* where

on their ability to comprehend spiritual truth.

Komala-śraddhas are those persons in the first stages of spiritual growth. They have simple faith. The expression *komala-śraddhas* literally means persons of "tender faith."[14] Their most common characteristic is their inability to see beyond their own subjective and parochial religious perspective. Next are the *madhyamādhikārīs,* or persons of middle faith. They are also known as *yukty-adhikārīs,* or persons capable of independent reasoning. Perhaps their most common characteristic is that they are plagued by profound religious doubt. Skepticism is the hallmark of the *madhyamādhikārīs.* They are the intellectuals of society, who in Bhaktivinoda's time included many of the *bhadraloka.* Above them are the *uttamādhikārīs,* or the enlightened *sāragrāhīs.* Such persons are naturally the rarest of all.[15] Bhaktivinoda's classification of spiritual seekers is analogous to Paul Tillich's three types of believers: primitive believers, doubting believers, and enlightened believers.

Komala-śraddhas and *madhyamādhikārīs* differ widely in their ability to understand spiritual truths and consequently in the way they must be approached for spiritual elevation. Bhaktivinoda writes:

> Men have different rights according to their knowledge and tendencies. Only one with pure spiritual understanding can worship the pure spiritual form of God. To the extent that one is below this stage, one understands God accordingly. One at a low stage cannot realize the higher spiritual aspects of God.[16]

Unfortunately, pre-nineteenth century Hindu tradition had addressed the needs of *komala-śraddhas* more than those of

---

they apply to three grades of *bhaktas* (*Bhāg* 11.2.45-47). In the *Kṛṣṇa-saṁhitā* however, Bhaktivinoda uses these terms in a slightly different way, applying them to people in general and not exclusively to *bhaktas.*

14. KS, *Upakramaṇikā,* 3: *yāhādera svādhīna vicāra-śaktir udaya haya nāi, tāṅhārā komala-śraddha nāme prathama-bhāge avasthāna karena/ viśvāsa vyatīta tāṅhādera gati nāi/*

15. Ibid., 3: Appendix V, 7.

16. JD, 197-8: Appendix V, 8.

madhyamādhikārīs.[17] Bhaktivinoda suggests that traditional forms of religious exegesis, the *ṭīkās* and *ṭippanīs* (commentaries), failed to address the modern concerns of the *bhadraloka* and therefore his *Kṛṣṇa-saṁhitā* was an attempt to fulfill that need. The problem, however, was even more complex. Not only did the *bhadraloka* lack sophisticated religious texts or commentaries, they also lacked access to the intellectual side of their Hindu tradition, which was largely preserved in Sanskrit. Consequently, they were apt to reject the popular religious tradition as superstitious or irrelevant.

In fact most Hindu texts were meant to be read with elaborate commentaries and living gurus to interpret the texts in more sophisticated ways, but in the absence of such textual and human aids, the *bhadraloka* were inclined to reject their traditions outright. The problem was further exacerbated by traditional commentaries that did not deal with modern critical issues. It was, therefore, the task of individuals like Bhaktivinoda to bridge the gap between tradition and modernity and create a relevant link between the past and the present.

In his *Kṛṣṇa-saṁhitā* Bhaktivinoda tells us that texts like the *Mahābhārata, Rāmāyaṇa* and *Purāṇas* present spiritual teachings to *komala-śraddhas* through entertaining and superhuman stories, fantastic time calculations, and awesome descriptions of heavens and hells in order to inspire faith and regulate the activities of *komala-śraddhas* for their ultimate progress.[18] This is what the *Bhāgavata* calls *parokṣa-vāda* or the presentation of spiritual teachings through indirect means.[19] *Parokṣa-vāda* often involves the placing of spiritual truths within historical or fictional narratives with the threat of punishment for failure or the promise of reward for compliant activities. In the *Tattva-sūtra* (1893), Bhaktivinoda describes this:

> Due to their instinctual nature, common people engage in worldly enjoyments. Their nature is generally inclined

17. KS, *Upakramaṇikā,* 4: Appendix V, 9.
18. Datta, *The Bhagavat,* 28; KS, *Upakramaṇikā,* 16; TS., 199.
19. *Bhāg.*, vs. 11/3/44: *parokṣa-vādo vedo 'yaṁ bālānām anuśāsanam/ karma-mokṣāya karmāṇi vidhatte hy agadaṁ yathā*

> towards the gratification of their senses, but the scriptures try to reform them through various types of tricks, coercion or other strategies. Often the scriptures threaten the ignorant with the punishment of hell, or with the temptations of heaven. At other times they are purified by engagements suited to their nature.[20]

According to Bhaktivinoda, the popular approach of orthodox Hinduism, that which most of the *bhadraloka* grew up hearing, was the approach of Vedic culture presented for the benefit of *komala-śraddhas.* It is a kind of religious literalism that involved only the most basic narrative level of *śāstric* interpretation. In most cases literal interpretations of this type do not appeal to the logical and rational minds of *madhyamādhikārīs.* In fact, they are intellectually and spiritually alienated by such an approach. As a result, the Bengali *madhyamādhikārīs* (the typical *bhadraloka*), when faced with rational alternatives, rejected their ancestral traditions and followed foreign philosophies or created their own rational systems of thought.[21] According to Bhaktivinoda, however, the *bhadraloka* need not restrict themselves to the perspective of *komala-śraddhas,* but have the right and the obligation to examine their religious traditions from their own perspective. Spiritual truth is eternal, but how it is understood varies according to the capacity and the perspective of the individual.[22]

An approach suited to the *komala-śraddhas* is often inappropriate for *madhyamādhikārīs.* In a similar manner, a perspective tailored to the intellectual needs of *madhyamādhikārīs* is inappropriate for *komala-śraddhas.* The *Kṛṣṇa-saṁhitā* and the *Tattva-sūtra,* to cite two examples, were not written for *komala-śraddhas. Śāstra* can and should be presented in various ways to suit the intellectual and spiritual qualifications of a diverse audience, including all categories of *adhikārīs.* But Bhaktivinoda warns that it is not always appropriate

20. ST, Vol. 8 (1896), Appendix V, 10.
21. KS, *Upakramaṇikā,* 4.
22. KS, *Saṁhitā,* 7.2: *jīve sāmbandhikī seyaṁ deśa-kāla-vicārataḥ/ pravarttate dvidhā sāpi pātra-bheda-kramād iha/*

for *komala-śraddhas* to hear what is written for *madhyamādhikārīs* as it may confuse and damage their tender faith,[23] as much as *madhyamādhikārīs* feel alienated when subjected to the literal perspective of *komala-śraddhas.*[24] In presenting his work, Bhaktivinoda states that the whole point of his presentation is to show the antiquity of the Vedic tradition and the development of Vaiṣṇava culture within that tradition. He writes:

> Just when this pure Vaiṣṇava dharma arose and how it developed in our country has to be determined, but before we discuss this we must discuss many other topics. Therefore, we will begin with the dates of the most important historical events of Indian history according to modern opinion. Then we will determine the dates of the many respected books. As we fix the date of these texts we will determine the history of Vaiṣṇava dharma. Whatever seems clear according to modern opinion we will discuss. We examine time according to the ancient method, but for the benefit of people today we will rely upon the modern conventions.[25]

In other words, Bhaktivinoda is saying: My fellow *bhadraloka,* your minds are trained to accept the conclusions of rational analysis fashioned with the tools of modern scholarship, so we shall employ these tools to examine our religious traditions. Let us apply the techniques of modern textual criticism and historiography to the geographic and historical information of the *Purāṇas* and *Itihāsas* to achieve a renewed understanding of our Hindu traditions. This was the *ādhunika-vāda.*

His use of the *ādhunika-vāda* was a means to appeal to the Western educated *bhadraloka.* In doing so he was attempting to give them the confidence to follow their ancestral religious traditions by

---

23. KS, *Upakramaṇikā,* 56: *komala-śraddha mahodaya-gaṇa āmādera vākya-tātparya nā buddhiyā evam vidha śāstrake ādhunika baliyā hata-śraddha haite pārena, ataeva ei vicāra tāṅhādera pakṣe pāṭhya naya/*
24. Ibid., 4.
25. Ibid., 11: Appendix V, 11.

showing how those traditions could plausibly be redefined and re-appropriated according to the culture of the modern world.

By employing the approach of the *ādhunika-vāda,* Bhaktivinoda extends himself beyond the parochial position of the traditional theologian and places himself in a position to peer back at his tradition through the cyes of the critical observer. This is the role of what Bhaktivinoda calls the true critic.

He describes the true critic as one who:

> should be of the same disposition of mind as that of the author, whose merit he is required to judge. Thoughts have different ways. One who is trained up in the thoughts of the Unitarian Society or of the Vedant [*sic*] of the Benares School, will scarcely find piety in the faith of the Vaishnav. An ignorant Vaishnav, on the other hand. . . . will find no piety in the Christian. This is because the Vaishnav does not think in the way in which the Christian thinks of his own religion. . . . In a similar manner the Christian needs to adopt the way of thought which the Vedantist pursued, before he can love the conclusions of the philosopher. The critic, therefore, should have a comprehensive, good, generous, candid, impartial, and sympathetic soul.[26]

The religious perspective that Bhaktivinoda describes here encompasses the perspective of the religious believer as well as the critical observer. The perspective of the true critic is what eventually evolves into what Bhaktivinoda calls the *sāragrāhī,* or essence seeker.

Paul Tillich proffers a model of theology—which he calls the theological circle—that illustrates Bhaktivinoda's perspective. The area within the circle is the perspective of the religious insider and the area outside is the perspective of the religious outsider. Tillich suggests that it is the unique ability of the theologian to move on both sides of the theological circle. In the contemporary global context, the theologian must have the ability to step beyond the

26. Datta, *The Bhagavat,* 8 and 11.

parochial perspective of the religious insider and critically examine that perspective from a position shared with the religious outsider.

Bhaktivinoda's use of the *ādhunika-vāda* entails this ability. To take the approach of the *ādhunika-vāda* meant that he had to step beyond his own position—in this case the traditional perspective of the Caitanya theologian—and move into the world of the religious outsider (to the Caitanya Vaiṣṇava tradition). The ability to step beyond one's own theological and philosophic perspective and appreciate the views of others without losing one's faith is the perspective of the *sāragrāhi.* He describes this as follows:

> Subjects of philosophy and theology are like the peaks of large towering and inaccessible mountains standing in the midst of our planet inviting attention and investigation. Thinkers and men of deep speculation take their observations through the instruments of reason and consciousness. But they take different points when they carry on their work. These points are positions chalked out by the circumstances of their social and philosophical life, different as they are in the different parts of the world . . . but the conclusion is all the same in as much as the object of observation was one and the same. They all hunted after the Great Spirit, the unconditioned Soul of the universe.[27]

Bhaktivinoda explains that the *sāragrāhī* is not attached to a particular theory or religious doctrine.[28] Even when an opposing

27. Datta, *The Bhagavat*, 9-10.

28. According to Bhaktivinoda a religious sect (*sampradāya*) is characterized by three traits: physical (*ālocaka*), cultic (*ālocanā*), and doctrinal (*ālocya*). Physical traits refers to the external cultural differences that exist between the various religions such as type and color of dress, sectarian marks (*tilaka*), the wearing of sacred articles, and so on. Cultic traits refers to differences of worship, which include the honor of different rivers and places of geography, fasting times, dietary restrictions, etc. Doctrinal traits are differences based on interpretation of sacred texts which conclude that God is immanent or transcendent, male or female, and so on. He points out that such differences are external and do not constitute the true essence of religious understanding. A *sāragrāhī* is able to see beyond these externals.

opinion is offered, if it is presented according to sound reasoning, it can be worthy of respect and consideration. *Sāragrāhīs* can perceive the essential truth in other religious perspectives because they are not limited to their own formulation of the truth. The irenic perspective of the *sāragrāhī* relates well to the religious pluralism and cosmopolitanism of modernity.[29] The historical perspective of the *Kṛṣṇa-saṁhitā* is in the spirit of the *sāragrāhī.* This was Bhaktivinoda's rationale for sending his *Kṛṣṇa-saṁhitā* to America and Europe at such an early time. He was reaching out to fellow *sāragrāhīs.*

The fruits of this endeavor were impressive. Not only did he reformulate the theology of the Caitanya *sampradāya* in terms of modernity, but he also initiated religious communication with members of the international community. In his *Kṛṣṇa-saṁhitā* he expresses a profound sense of collegiality with his fellow truth-seekers throughout the world. He writes:

> Those who are endowed with spiritual vision can recognize foreign *sāragrāhīs* as fellow *yogīs. Komala-śraddhas* and those who are inexperienced think of them as worldly or sometimes even against God. But *sāragrāhīs* can easily recognize their fellow spiritualists, who are endowed with all good qualities, whether of their own country or foreign. Even though their customs, symbols, worship, language, and dress are different, they easily address one another as "brother."[30]

We know from Bhaktivinoda's autobiography that some of the foreign *sāragrāhīs* that he was referring to were Ralph Waldo Emerson and Reinhold Rost.

Theologically speaking, the ability to step beyond one's parochial position is a requirement of modern theological scholarship. The globalization that Bhaktivinoda faced in the melting pot

29. KS, *Upakramaṇikā,* 61: *sāragrāhī janagaṇa vāda-niṣṭha nahena, ataeva sad-yukti dvārā ihāra viparīta kona viṣaya sthira haileo tāhā āmādera ādaraṇīya/*
30. Ibid., 79-80: Appendix V, 12.

of Calcutta—and that religious traditions still face—demanded self-criticism and comparative scholarship. What we need to understand, however, is how Bhaktivinoda was able to operate on both sides of the theological circle without loss to his religious faith. As we shall see, it is not so easy.

Two Modes of Religious Understanding

Bhaktivinoda's *Kṛṣṇa-saṁhitā* was indeed a radical departure from orthodox understanding of Vedic history, although by today's standards his Indian historiography is completely out of date. The fact that he employs the *ādhunika-vāda* is a major innovation for the Caitanya religious tradition. It is not difficult to understand how the British Orientalists, who were outsiders to Hindu tradition, could employ the tools of modern analysis to the Vedic traditions, but it is remarkable to find Bhaktivinoda, a Vaiṣṇava insider, employing those same techniques. We might expect that a historical study of the life of Kṛṣṇa using modern methodology would diminish or even deny the divine aspects of Kṛṣṇa's existence. So the question arises: How could Bhaktivinoda justify the use of the *ādhunika-vāda* and at the same time maintain his faith in the spiritual integrity of the Vaiṣṇava tradition? What was Bhaktivinoda's theological basis for employing modern methods of critical analysis.

Let me give an example that shows how the problem was not just a concern for the nineteenth century, but is still a real challenge for Caitanya Vaiṣṇavas today. I once presented a paper that summarized Bhaktivinoda's analysis of Vedic history from his *Upakramaṇikā* to an audience of Caitanya Vaiṣṇavas. During my presentation, I stated Bhaktivinoda's view that the *Bhāgavata-purāṇa* might not be a work compiled by *the* Vedavyāsa 5,000 years ago, as orthodox Vaiṣṇava tradition teaches, but may be a work not older than a 1,000 years, compiled by a southerner writing in the name of Vedavyāsa. Bhaktivinoda had reached this conclusion by analyzing certain geographic and cultural aspects of the *Bhāgavata*.[31] In other words, he was voicing an opinion arrived at through the use of the techniques

31. Ibid., 57-59.

of the *ādhunika-vāda.*

A suggestion such as this coming from a secular scholar steeped in Western criticism would not be unusual and could be easily deflected by my audience, but coming from Bhaktivinoda, a teacher from within the tradition, cast a spell of disbelief over my audience. All sorts of doubts arose: Perhaps Bhaktivinoda did not actually believe these things but used these ideas as a "preaching tactic" to attract the *bhadraloka;* perhaps he wrote his work when he was young and still learning but later came to reject these views, or perhaps my understanding of his perspective was incorrect.

Afterwards I was approached by one respected participant who was greatly disturbed and perplexed. He mentioned that he was upset by the mere suggestion that Bhaktivinoda may have said that the *Bhāgavata* was only 1,000 years old or that it was not written by *the* Vedavyāsa. This individual even questioned how I could make such a presentation. In fact, *I* was being accused of disturbing the spiritual peace.

Reflecting on this, I realized that this individual was upset because I had challenged one of his most sacred beliefs, namely, the spiritual authority of the *Bhāgavata.* And what is more, by questioning his beliefs concerning certain historical details about the *Bhāgavata,* I had challenged his basic faith as a whole. This is the perspective of the *komala-śraddha.* I also realized that so long as he maintained this theological perspective he would be incapable of performing modern critical research. The internal and subjective perspective of the *komala-śraddha* will not give credence to material facts that do not support and nurture religious faith.

I too wondered how Bhaktivinoda, a champion of Caitanya Vaiṣṇavism, could go to such lengths and question so many traditional beliefs yet maintain a strong and abiding faith in the authority of the *Bhāgavata* and the Vedic tradition as a whole. Whereas so many of my respected colleagues were put on the spiritual defensive by even a small amount of such a discussion, the whole matter seemed insignificant to Bhaktivinoda. In fact, on two separate occasions he encourages subsequent intellectuals to continue the study of Vedic history and geography using the *ādhunika-vāda.*[32]

The reason Bhaktivinoda could afford to employ the *ādhunika-vāda* lay rooted in his theological perspective, a perspective that enabled him to differentiate between the various aspects of a religious tradition. Simply put, the perspective of the *sāragrāhī* views religion in two dimensions: one relating to this world and the other relating to transcendence. At the beginning of the *Upakramaṇikā,* Bhaktivinoda writes:

> Scripture is of two types: that which relates to phenomenal matters (*artha-prada*) and that which relates to transcendent matters (*paramārtha-prada*). Geography, history, astrology, philosophy, psychology, medicine, entomology, mathematics, linguistics, prosody, music, logic, yoga, law, dentistry, architecture, and the military arts, are all sciences which are *artha-prada*. . . . [On the other hand] that scripture which discusses the supreme goal of life is *paramārtha-prada,* or transcendent.[33]

The religious equation comprises two parts: the reality of this phenomenal world and the reality of a transcendent world. According to Bhaktivinoda, knowledge relating to this world, even if it is derived from scripture, is subject to human analysis and logical scrutiny, whereas knowledge pertaining to transcendence is not subject to the logic and reasoning of this world. Responding to criticism from religious colleagues, Bhaktivinoda states:

> With folded hands I humbly submit to my respected readers who hold traditional views, that where my analysis opposes their long held beliefs, they should understand that my conclusions have been made for persons possessing appropriate qualifications. What I have said about dharma applies to everyone, but with regard to matters

---

32. Ibid., 40: *hauka, bhaviṣyat sāragrāhī paṇḍitera e viṣaya adhikatara anu..āna-sahakāre sthira karite pāribena/* p. 61: *bhaviṣyat paramārtha-vādī vā buddhimāna artha-vādīdigera nikaṭe haite aneka āśā karā yāya/*
33. Ibid., 1: Appendix V, 13.

> which are secondary to dharma, my conclusions are meant to produce benefits in the form of intellectual clarification only for qualified specialists. All the subjects which I have outlined in the Introduction concerning time and history are based on the logical analysis of *śāstra*, and whether one accepts them or not does not affect the final spiritual conclusions. History and time are phenomenal subject matters (*artha-śāstra*) and when they are analyzed according to sound reasoning much good can be done for India.[34]

Here Bhaktivinoda answers the charge that the *ādhunika-vāda* is necessarily incompatible with sacred tradition. In response he states that matters which are secondary to dharma, and by this he means phenomenal knowledge, is subject to human analysis. Knowledge relating to this world, even if it is derived from *śāstra*, can be subject to human scrutiny.

To illustrate how a sacred text may be scrutinized Bhaktivinoda shows how a specific verse of the *Bhāgavata* is incorrect. *Bhāgavata* verse 12/1/19 states that the kings of the Kāṇva dynasty will rule for 345 years.[35] Through logical analysis and in conjunction with other Puranic texts, Bhaktivinoda concludes that the correct figure is 45 years and not 345 years. Bhaktivinoda even says that Śrīdhara Svāmī, the original commentator of the *Bhāgavata*, is mistaken in accepting the defective reading of 345 years.[36] A more traditional way to reconcile a discrepancy of this type would have been to show how the number of years given in the *Bhāgavata* is actually correct and not to state outright that the *Bhāgavata's* text is corrupt or that the original commentator was in error. For Bhaktivinoda those parts of *śāstra* that are *artha-prada*, i.e. in relation to this world, are subject to human scrutiny.

In another example he points out how the *Bhāgavata* contains

---

34. KS, *Vijñāpana,* i-ii: Appendix V, 14.

35. *Bhāg.* 12/1/19: *kāṇvāyanā ime bhūmiṁ catvāriṁśac ca pañca ca śatāni trīṇi bhokṣyanti varṣāṇāṁ ca kalau yuge//*

36. KS, *Upakramaṇikā,* 41: *bhāgavatera pāṭha aśuddha thākā bodha haya/ durbhāgya-krame śrīdhara-svāmīo ai aśuddha pāṭha svīkāra kariyāchena*

both phenomenal knowledge (*artha-prada*) and transcendent (*paramārtha-prada*) knowledge. During his descriptions of the heavens and hells in the *Bhāgavata* he writes:

> The *Bhagavat* certainly tells us of a state of reward and punishment in the future according to our deeds in the present situation. All poetic inventions [the various descriptions of heaven and hell], besides this spiritual fact, have been described as statements borrowed from other works in the way of preservation of old traditions in the book which superseded them and put an end to the necessity of their storage. If the whole stock of Hindu theological works which preceded the *Bhagavat* were burnt like the Alexandrian library and the sacred *Bhagavat* preserved as it is, not a part of the philosophy of the Hindus, except that of the atheistic sects, would be lost. The *Bhagavat* therefore, may be styled both as a religious work and a compendium of all Hindu history and philosophy.[37]

By contrast those parts of *śāstra* that are strictly *paramārtha-prada* —in relation to transcendence—are not subject to rational analysis or human scrutiny. Bhaktivinoda writes, "What is Divine is beyond human reasoning."[38] He is adamant in stating that the spiritual aspects of *śāstra* are not open to rational analysis. Again he writes, "According to our *śāstra,* analysis of fundamental principles of theology and mystic insights are not subject to revision."[39] Such things cannot be approached through human reason, but only by direct perception of the soul, mystic insight.[40]

The subject matter of the *Upakramaṇikā* is mainly history and

---

37. Datta, *The Bhagavat,* 28-29.
38. ST, vol 7 (1895), *Tattva-sūtra* p. 186: *bhagavad-viṣayaṭī yuktir atīta.*
39. KS, *Upakramaṇikā,* p. 62: *āmādera śāstra-mate kalpa-vicāra o yoga-vicāra e prakāra naya.*
40. DK, vs. 10: *svaṁ paraṁ dvi-vidhaṁ proktaṁ pratyakṣaṁ cendriyātmanoḥ/ anumānaṁ dvidhā tadvat pramāṇaṁ dvi-vidhaṁ matam//* "Direct perception is said to be obtained by either the material senses or the spirit soul directly. Similarly, inference may be performed in these two ways."

geography in the form of data gleaned from the *Purāṇas* and *Itihāsas*. Therefore, it can legitimately be scrutinized by human reason. By contrast, what is *paramārtha* knowledge is not subject to human revision. This means that the fundamental spiritual truths of *śāstra* are not the subject of human speculation and interpretation. In accordance with this understanding, Bhaktivinoda has accepted two general categories of knowledge: temporal knowledge and eternal spiritual knowledge.

It is possible that Bhaktivinoda derived these ideas from the Unitarian influence of Theodore Parker, who expressed these ideas in his famous speech, "The Transient and Permanent in Christianity."[41] Parker writes:

> In actual Christianity—that is, in that portion of Christianity which is preached and believed—there seem to have been, ever since the time of its earthly founder, two elements, the one transient, the other permanent. The one is the thought, the folly, the uncertain wisdom, the theological notions, the impiety of man; the other, the eternal truth of God.[42]

The temporal level of scripture serves as the carrier for the spiritual level, just as a jewel is placed within a particular setting. Similarly the spiritual essence of the *Purāṇas* has been placed within a particular temporal setting, namely, the Puranic narratives. This is why Bhaktivinoda could afford to take some liberty in terms of the historical interpretation of the *Purāṇas* and other *śāstras*. Bhaktivinoda's *ādhunika-vāda* simply becomes another setting for the eternal spiritual truths of the *Purāṇas*.[43] He also freely admits

41. Theodore Parker's essay, "The Transient and Permanent in Christianity" was delivered in Boston in 1841.

42. Conrad Wright, *Three Prophets of Religious Liberalism: Channing Emerson Parker* (Boston: Unitarian Universalist Association, 1980), 118.

43. This could also be extended to include empirical history as a carrier or medium of spiritual knowledge. In other words, both conservative and liberal interpretations of *śāstra* may be carriers or mediators of transcendent meaning.

that if someone can document a better interpretation, he will accept it.[44]

Bhaktivinoda's assertion that matters secondary to dharma need have no effect on the understanding of eternal truth was a challenging new concept. His separation of scriptural knowledge into phenomenal and transcendent components had profound ramifications.[45] Inevitably his approach was threatening to much of Hindu orthodoxy. His free use of the *ādhunika-vāda* opened new doors to scriptural understanding that resulted in many independent conclusions,[46] but at the same time prepared the way for comparative and historical religious scholarship—in the spirit of modernity—by the religious insider.

The *Kṛṣṇa-saṁhitā* is as much a statement about the relationship between reason and religious faith as it is a study of the life of Śrī Kṛṣṇa and a summary of India's religious history. It is Bhaktivinoda's unique blend of these components that gives his synthesis of modernity and tradition its extraordinary utility even today, perhaps also beyond the realm of Caitanya Vaiṣṇavism.

Bhaktivinoda's division of a religious tradition into two dimensions allowed him to combine the best of modernity, namely, the rational approach of British Orientalism, with the best of Hindu mysticism, *Kṛṣṇa-līlā*. He combines both the Kṛṣṇa of the *Bhagavad-gītā* and the Kṛṣṇa of the *Purāṇas*. Indeed, the union of these two forms of Kṛṣṇa embodies the very essence of his synthesis of modernity and tradition.

The extent to which Bhaktivinoda employed the methodology of modern religious scholarship can be appreciated when we compare his work with that of Wilfred Cantwell Smith. Smith points out that one of the greatest stumbling blocks to the study of religion, for

44. KS, *Upakramaṇikā,* 61: Appendix V, 15.

45. It can be questioned whether or not it is even possible to separate the historic and geographic content of *śāstra* from its spiritual principles without challenging the validity of those absolute principles. The answer to this question depends on one's understanding of how ultimate reality manifests Itself in human terms. This important question is basic to the next chapter.

46. KS, *Vijñāpana,* ii: *Upakramaṇikāra svādhīna siddhānta dekhiyā...*

both the religious insider and the outsider, is the very concept of religion itself. Smith suggests that historically "religion" is a vague and misleading term. To the insider, religion denotes religious faith, but to the outsider it denotes the hard data of a tradition. Smith proposes that we conceive of religion as two complementary categories, one, the historical cumulative tradition and the other, the personal faith of the individuals who take part in that tradition. Both tradition and faith exist in their own right, and together they form what we call religion.

This is similar to the distinction that Bhaktivinoda makes. What Bhaktivinoda calls *artha-prada*—the phenomenal side of a religious tradition—is nothing less than the cumulative religious tradition. What he calls *paramārtha-prada*—the transcendent side of religion, although not directly faith as Smith describes it—is an experiential reality that must be approached through faith. What Smith calls religious faith ultimately leads to what Bhaktivinoda terms *sahaja-samādhi*, or a state of innate spiritual insight or intuition. For Bhaktivinoda pure religious faith is the means by which an inner awareness of spiritual reality arises, and when that inner spiritual reality is expressed in physical terms the cumulative religious traditions of the world arise.

Perhaps the most important feature of the cumulative tradition is that it lies within the realm of empirical history accessible to the rational mind and therefore can be the object of logic and comparative study. There is significant value in making the distinction between what lies within the realm of empirical observation and what lies beyond that realm because it allows the religious insider to differentiate between the two dimensions of the religious experience. This allows him to treat each area separately and thus keep the door open for higher perceptions. Bankim Chandra's mistake lay in that fact that he failed to differentiate between that part of a religious tradition that lies within the realm of empirical observation, and the part that does not. He felt that if one part could be rationally scrutinized then all parts could be treated in the same way. Consequently, his approach excluded the possibility of higher spiritual perceptions.

Bhaktivinoda, on the other hand, felt that the phenomenal could be the object of logical scrutiny, but that which transcended logic should only be approached by the innate seeing ability of the soul called *sahaja-samādhi*.[47] Religious faith, unfettered by rational processes, is the key to unlock that ability. *Sahaja-samādhi* is the soul's natural faculty which everyone possesses, except that in most people the ability has been diminished due to occlusion by the rational mind. Religious mystics and saints are individuals who have reawakened this natural seeing ability of the soul. Bhaktivinoda's discussion of *sahaja-samādhi* is a fascinating topic and one that is reminiscent of the nineteenth century American Transcendentalists' and Unitarians' ideas of natural intuition. I will discuss this in the following chapter.

Faith and Belief

One important implication that arises from the differentiation of the phenomenal and the transcendent is the distinction between faith and belief.[48] Returning to our previous discussion about the date of the *Bhāgavata*, the reaction of my audience, who became upset on hearing my summary of Bhaktivinoda's historical conclusions, was natural for those whose faith is rigidly tied to their belief system. There is little doubt that the relationship between religious faith and belief that Bhaktivinoda experienced was radically differ-

47. Bhaktivinoda himself never gives an English translation for this term, but he does describe it as a natural function of the soul that everyone potentially has access to. *Sahaja-samādhi* is a state of cognition that is totally free of any kind of rational or conceptual processes (*vikalpa*). Elsewhere he describes it as *nirvikalpa-samādhi*. See KS, *Saṁhitā* 9/2e. I discuss *sahaja-samādhi* in the following chapter.
48. W. C. Smith points out that many people, especially in the West, equate religious faith with belief because in Christianity the two have been made inseparable. Church theology, expressed in terms of doctrinal belief, is often set forth as a formal qualification for church membership. Smith writes: "Doctrine has been a central expression of faith, has seemed often a criterion of it; the community has divided over differences in belief, and has set forth belief as a formal qualification of membership." (*Faith and Belief*, p. 13) The faithful have been distinguished by what doctrines they believe. Belief has even been translated into salvation—that all one

ent from what many in my audience experienced. The latter experienced faith in terms of their belief systems, considering faith and belief as virtually the same thing. They felt that faith was inseparable from certain historical conceptions. To tinker with one's belief system or revise one's view of history was to tinker with the foundations of religious faith itself. Bhaktivinoda, however, made a significant distinction between his religious faith and his belief.

When the person of religious faith becomes aware of the distinction between belief and faith, fully understanding that beliefs are a part of the cumulative (and changing) religious tradition he is able to relax intellectually and spiritually, so to speak, and take a critical look at his religious tradition from a perspective that is not tied to vested intellectual and emotional interests. In other words, religious faith becomes somewhat insulated from changes that may occur in the belief system as a result of critical research. This is why Bhaktivinoda could afford to make his presentation of Vedic history according to the *ādhunika-vāda* or modern approach. His conclusion that the *Bhāgavata* may be a work of only a 1,000 years had no effect on his faith in the spiritual truths of that great work. Regardless of the *Bhāgavata's* historicity, it remained an authoritative spiritual text. Bhaktivinoda clearly points out that the value of the *Bhāgavata* is in its expression of eternal spiritual principles:[49] in its capacity to elicit a response of faith, and not in who wrote it or when it was written. The spiritual truths which it embodies are its real value.[50]

---

has to do is believe certain creeds in order to obtain salvation. There is little doubt that in the West with its long history of Church influence, faith and belief have been made synonymous or at least so tightly intertwined as to be indistinguishable.

49. KS, *Upakramaṇikā,* 56: Appendix V, 16.

50. The distinction between religious faith and belief can also be shown to exist outside the religious field. In philosophy, for example, it is not what a philosopher believes that makes him a philosopher, but rather the individual's faith in philosophy, out of which the beliefs, the particular philosophies, are produced and sustained. The same can be said about science. A person is a scientist because of his faith in science, in the spirit of science, and not because of his beliefs in the particular theorems, which unquestionably come and go.

For Bhaktivinoda, faith is a living quality of the soul and therefore faith in God is a natural condition of life.[51] Belief, on the other hand, is primarily a mental act that involves the holding of certain ideas in the mind. Belief is an expression of faith just as religious architecture and dance are expressions of faith. Belief is a part of the cumulative religious tradition. It is *artha-prada* and, like all aspects of the cumulative tradition, it has the capacity to induce and nurture faith. And because belief is part of the cumulative tradition, it is also the object of reason and logic by which it can be inspected, shaped, and molded. This explains why beliefs change so often and why those who fail to make the distinction between faith and belief often experience a crisis of faith when their beliefs are challenged.

In his *Upakramaṇikā,* Bhaktivinoda could afford to show empirically how the Vedic historical and literary traditions may have developed. He knew that whatever he might believe about that development and however his beliefs may change as a result of his research, would not necessarily affect his confidence in the spiritual essence of the Vedic/Vaiṣṇava tradition. History and time are simply various aspects of the cumulative religious tradition.[52] Bhaktivinoda is able to conclude his critical assessment of Indian history by honestly saying that he has done his best and that future historians should attempt to do better. He writes:

> As far as possible, I have determined the chronology of the major events and important books according to the modern perspective. A *sāragrāhī,* however, is not attached to a particular view, so if, in the future, any of my conclusions are refuted by better reasoning, then those new conclusions are worthy of my respect and consideration. Indeed, there is much hope that future spiritual seekers and intellectuals will improve upon this matter.[53]

51. Bhaktivinoda, *Tattva-viveka, Tattva-sūtra, Āmnāya-sūtra,* trans. Narasimha Brahmachari (Madras: Sree Gaudiya Math, 1979), 18.
52. KS, *Vijñāpana,* p. i.
53. KS, *Upakramaṇikā,* 61.

Since Bhaktivinoda makes the subtle but important distinction between the cumulative tradition and faith, he is able to keep the door open for continued empirical study of the cumulative tradition. The distinction he draws between the two, along with the separation of faith and belief, is basic to much of modern critical scholarship in religious theology. Moreover, it is possible that Bhaktivinoda derived his ideas, at least in part, from Theodore Parker, whom we have noted earlier. Parker makes a similar distinction between faith and belief in his sermon, "The Transient and Permanent in Christianity." Speaking of one who builds his faith solely upon human beliefs, Parker writes, "You will be afraid of every new opinion, lest it shake down your church; you will fear 'lest if a fox go up, he will break down your stone wall.' The smallest contradiction in the New Testament or Old Testament; the least disagreement between the Law and the Gospel; any mistake of the Apostles, will weaken your faith."[54]

54. Conrad Wright, *Three Prophets of Religious Liberalism: Channing Emerson Parker* (Boston: Unitarian Universalist Association, 1980), 147.

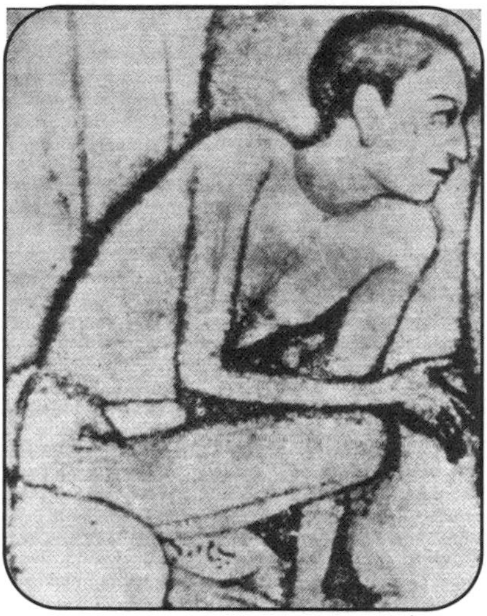

Rūpa Gosvāmī
(1489–1564)

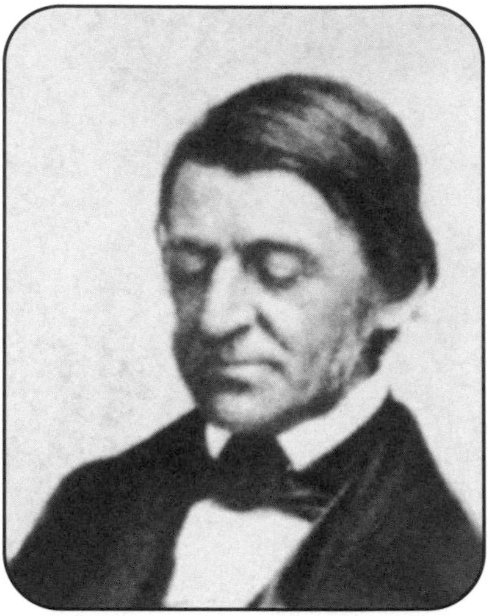

Ralph Waldo Emerson
(1803–1882)

Theodore Parker
(1810–1860)

Kedarnath Datta Bhaktivinoda
(1838–1914)

Chapter Six

Systematic Theology

Sahaja-samādhi and the Symbolic Process

> He is the best critic who can show the further development of an old idea; but a mere denouncer is the enemy of progress and consequently of Nature. "Begin anew," says the critic, "because the old masonry does not answer at present. Let the old author be buried because his time is gone." These are shallow expressions. Progress certainly is the law of nature and there must be corrections and developments with the progress of time, but progress means going further or rising higher. . . . The true critic advises us to preserve what we have already obtained and to adjust our race from that point where we have arrived in the heat of our progress. He will never advise us to go back to the point whence we started.[1]

This passage captures the probing nature of Bhaktivinoda's theological inquiry and his willingness to make change, yet it also reveals his unwillingness to destroy what has preceded. In the spirit of modernity Bhaktivinoda perceives religious development as an evolution—an ongoing dynamic process. He never advises that we invalidate the past, yet neither does he recommend that we block the way of progress. Instead we are asked to reinterpret and build on what has preceded.

In the next two chapters we examine Bhaktivinoda's role as a systematic theologian discussing how human beings comprehend

1. Kedarnath Datta, *The Bhagavat, Its Philosophy, Ethics and Theology*, ed. Bhaktivilas Tirtha, 2d ed. (Madras: Madras Gaudiya Math, 1959), 1–2.

divine reality and how transcendence manifests itself in human terms. Specifically, we focus on Bhaktivinoda's understanding of the role of the theologian, the means of divine comprehension known as *sahaja-samādhi,* and his use of the symbolic process. In the second part we examine three categories of divine manifestation namely: divine sport *(līlā),* sacred image (*śrī-mūrti*), and holy name (*nāma*) in the light of Bhaktivinoda's theological perspective.

Bhaktivinoda states, "Essential truth is of two types: original form (*svarūpam*) and in relation to the people who will receive it (*sāmbandikam*)."[2] Paul Tillich suggests a similar idea when he describes theology as "a statement of the truth of the Christian message and the interpretation of this truth for every new generation."[3] Theology, thus understood, has two poles: a statement of what is held to be eternal truth and an interpretation of that statement in terms of the temporal or historical situation in which the eternal truth must be understood. Satisfying the demands of both these poles is, of course, the role of the theologian.

Amongst the Caitanya Vaiṣṇavas this function of theology and the role of the theologian can readily be illustrated from the following verse of the *Bhāgavata:*

vadanti tat tattva-vidas tattvaṁ yaj jñānam advayam/
brahmeti paramātmeti bhagavān iti śabdyate//

"Those who know the Absolute Truth speak of this Truth
(tattva) as undifferentiated knowledge categorized as
Brahman, Paramātmā and *Bhagavān.*"[4]

This verse defines *tattva* or the "Absolute Truth" as

2. Kedarnath Datta Bhaktivinoda, *Datta-kaustubha,* (Bengali edition), ed. by Bhakti-pradipa-tirtha Goswami (Mayapur: The Gaudiya Mission, 1942), vs. 4. Herein noted as DK.: *sarva-śāstrāt svayaṁ vidvān gṛhṇīyāt sāram uttamam/ sāmbandhikaṁ svarūpaṁ ca pātra-bheda-vicārataḥ//*

3. Paul Tillich, *Systematic Theology* (Chicago: University of Chicago Press, 1967), 3.

4. *Bhāg.* 1/2/11.

undifferentiated knowledge. Literally, however, *tattva* is *tat-tva,*[5] or "that-ness." But "that-ness" is so abstract an idea that it can never remain unqualified. So immediately the *Bhāgavata* qualifies the concept of "that-ness" by stating that *tattva* is *jñānam advayam,* undifferentiated knowledge. One pole of the theological statement is complete: "Thatness is undifferentiated knowledge."

The other side of the theological pole is fulfilled by the last word of the verse, *śabdyate,* meaning "is expressed." In this case the Absolute Truth is expressed as: *brahman, paramātmā,* and *bhagavān.* In other words, "Thatness" is expressed in human terms according to three possible categories: all pervading consciousness (*brahman),* indwelling soul (*paramātmā),* and transcendent personality (*bhagavān).* Thus the two poles of the theological statement are complete: "Thatness is undifferentiated knowledge, which is expressed (in human terms) as *brahman, paramātmā* and *bhagavān.*" Since the time of the *Bhāgavata* it has been the business of generations of Vaiṣṇava theologians to explain the import of this verse. In the case of Bhaktivinoda as theologian, it was his task to mediate the meaning of this profound theological statement for the nineteenth century Bengali *bhadraloka.* Bhaktivinoda begins that task as follows.

Sahaja-samādhi

As sense perception and human reason are the means of acquiring knowledge of the phenomenal world, so *sahaja-samādhi* is the means of knowing about what is transcendent. The term *sahaja-samādhi* is not an expression commonly used within Caitanya Vaiṣṇava theology or in Hindu theology in general.[6] Haridas Das does not mention the term in his *Gauḍīya Vaiṣṇava Abhidhāna* nor is it used by the Gaudiya Math or by ISKCON. I believe the term is

---

5. *Tattva* is a combination of two grammatical components: the neuter pronoun *tat,* meaning "that," and the abstract suffix *tva,* meaning "ness," or "the state of being."
6. Interestingly, the term is used within Sikh theology to refer to constant devotion. See: J. S. Grewal, *The New Cambridge History of India II. 3 The Sikhs of the Punjab* (Cambridge: Cambridge University Press, 1990), 32.

Bhaktivinoda's translation of Emerson's idea of natural intuition that appears throughout American Transcendentalism and nineteenth century Unitarianism. Theodore Parker similarly speaks of the "instinctive intuition of the divine."[7] We have noted Reverend Charles Dall's efforts to spread the works of his Unitarian brethren among the *bhadraloka,* and Bhaktivinoda freely acknowledges his reading Channing, Parker, Emerson, and Newman as a student in Calcutta. Spencer Lavan quotes the comments of C. N. Banerji concerning the popularity of natural intuition among the *bhadraloka.* Banerji writes, "The writings of Francis Newman and of the late Theodore Parker have done much for intuition or *intertuition* in Calcutta. For a time, Keshub Babu's success was remarkable—for every Brahmo talked of intuition."[8] Here the Keshub Babu referred to is Keshub Chandra Sen, Bhaktivinoda's classmate. Keshub regularly referred to "instinctive belief," "common sense," "a priori truths," and "primitive cognitions."[9] Bhaktivinoda's *sahaja-samādhi* is likely the result of Dall's Unitarian efforts in Calcutta.

In his *Upasaṁhāra*[10] Bhaktivinoda describes the theological basis behind *sahaja-samādhi* by describing the relationship between God, soul, and matter. Pure soul is a "particle" of *cit* "substance." *Cit* is pure spiritual consciousness. The primary difference between the soul and God is that God is an unlimited reservoir of *cit* consciousness, whereas the soul is a limited particle of *cit*—like a spark compared to the whole fire. Even though the soul is just a particle of *cit,* it is still extremely brilliant and powerful. The soul, therefore, has its own natural inner light or seeing ability that it uses to apprehend reality. Unfettered by matter, the soul is highly conscious. However, when the soul becomes enmeshed in the phenomenal world, its nat-

7. Theodore Parker uses this expression in his essay, "The Previous Question Between Mr. Andrews Norton and His Alumni Moved and Handled." See Appendix to John Edwards Dirks, *The Critical Theology of Theodore Parker* (New York: Columbia University Press, 1948), 140.

8. Spencer Lavan, *Unitarians and India* (Chicago: Exploration Press, 1991), 108.

9. Quoted in Wilhelm Halbfass, *India and Europe* (Albany: State University of New York Press, 1988), 225.

10. KS, *Upasaṁhāra,* 176-179.

ural consciousness becomes filtered and dimmed by matter, much like white light passing through a dark lens. The projection of *cit* consciousness through matter is called *cit-ābhāsa* (*ābhāsa* means semblance or reflection).[11] *Cit-ābhāsa* is a mere reflection or semblance of pure consciousness, and, depending on the density of the material covering, the soul will exhibit higher or lower levels of consciousness, as reflected in various species of life and in different grades of human beings. From *cit-ābhāsa,* ego (*ahaṅkāra*), intelligence (*buddhi*), and mind (*manas*) develop. Thus, the physical and mental being of the living entity arises from the combination of matter and spiritual consciousness.

In his *Datta-kaustubha* Bhaktivinoda tell us that the soul, whether enmeshed in matter or not, has two basic tools for gathering knowledge: direct perception (*pratyakṣa*) and inference (*anumāna*). He writes:

> Knowledge is acquired by direct perception or by inference. Direct perception may be performed by either the material senses or the soul directly. Inference may also be performed in these two ways.[12]

According to this statement, direct perception and inference can occur at two levels: in pure *cit* consciousness or in materially obscured *cit-ābhāsa* consciousness. What in this world is called empirical observation and rational analysis is nothing less than sense perception (*pratyakṣa)* and inference (*anumāna)* produced at the level of *cit-ābhāsa. Sahaja-samādhi* is precisely the same thing, only produced at the level of pure *cit* consciousness. In standard *pramāṇa-vāda* (epistemology) what is normally called *śabda* or *śruti* (scriptural knowledge) is nothing less than the direct perception and inference of great sages performed at the level of *cit* conscious-

11. In order to simplify the language, I am not employing the phonetic modifications called *sandhi,* according to which the more correct form of *cit-ābhāsa* would be *cid-ābhāsa.*

12. DK, vs. 10: *svaṁ paraṁ dvi vidhaṁ proktaṁ pratyakṣaṁ cendriyātmanoḥ/ anumānaṁ dvidhā tadvat pramāṇaṁ dvi-vidhaṁ matam//*

ness and then recorded in the form of *śāstra* or scripture.[13] However, such spiritual perception and inference may also be mixed with material perception and inference. To the degree that the writers of *śāstra* are not wholly pure, their observation and inferences will be mixed with the direct perception and inference produced at the level of *cit-ābhāsa.*

At the level of *cit-ābhāsa,* the mind obscures the real *cit* consciousness of the soul. In this case the soul's natural seeing ability is blocked by the functioning of the living entity's mental state. Seeing by means of *sahaja-samādhi* therefore involves stopping the functions of thc material mind and allowing the soul's natural cognitive ability to shine through. Bhaktivinoda describes this:

> Thought arises from *cit-ābhāsa* and therefore it cannot be independent of the material elements. However, by stopping the functioning of the mind, a state of *ātma-samādhi* can be induced in which the soul can be perceived. In other words, when we examine the soul through introspection, a direct spiritual perception of the soul can be obtained.[14]

Therefore, *sahaja-samādhi* is the process of allowing the natural abilities of the soul to shine forth. This is what saints and mystics are able to do. On another occasion Bhaktivinoda describes the process of *sahaja-samādhi* in a slightly different way. He writes:

> *Samādhi* is of two kinds: *savikalpa* and *nirvikalpa.* . . . The *sātvatas* refer to *nirvikalpa-samādhi* as the real *sahaja-samādhi* and *savikalpa-samādhi* as *kūṭa-samādhi* (false *samādhi*). The soul (*ātmā*) is made of conscious (*cit*) substance, therefore, it has an innate ability to illuminate itself and other objects. By self-illumination the soul is able to perceive itself. By its nature of other-illumination, it is able to cognize all things other than itself. *Nirvikalpa-samādhi* is natural because it is an inherent quality of the

13. DK, vs. 12, commentary: Appendix V, 17.
14. KS, *Upasaṁhāra,* 179: Appendix V, 18.

> soul. *Nirvikalpa* means that the process is free of conceptualization (*vikalpa*) because the soul does not utilize the mind and intellect for cognizing sense objects. When, however, conceptualization becomes part of *samādhi*, the process becomes analytical and is called *savikalpa-samādhi*.[15]

What Bhaktivinoda calls *kūṭa-samādhi* (false intuition) in this passage is just another way of describing direct perception and inference performed at the level of *cit-ābhāsa*. In other words, ordinary sense perception and inference.

The *Datta-kaustubha* provides an overview of the whole cognitive process including *sahaja-samādhi* in the following table:[16]

Table One – The Cognitive Process

sādhana (the means)	***āśraya*** (the goal)	***sādhya*** (the result)
***Gauṇa-samādhi* (Indirect Cognition)**		
1. *sāṅkhya-jñāna-samādhi*	*brahman*	*prapañca-nivṛtti*
2. *ātma-jñāna-samādhi*	*paramātmā*	*ātma-gata-kṣudrānanda*
3. *jñāna-miśra-sahaja-samādhi*	*bhagavān*	*kiñcid-dvaitānanda*
***Sākṣāt-samādhi* (Direct Cognition)**		
4. *sahaja-samādhi*	*nārāyaṇa*	*aiśvarya-svarūpānanda*
5. *nitānta-sahaja-samādhi*	*kṛṣṇa*	*mādhurya-svarūpānanda*

According to this table the cognitive process has two basic forms, one indirect (*gauṇa-samādhi*) and the other direct (*sākṣāt-*

15. KS, *Saṁhitā*, 9/2e: Appendix V, 19.
16. DK, texts 75 through 78.

samādhi). Indirect cognition is *cit-ābhāsa* cognition, and direct cognition is *cit* cognition. Indirect cognition is further divided into three stages: *sāṅkhya-**jñāna**-samādhi, ātma-**jñāna**-samādhi,* and ***jñāna**-miśra-sahaja-samādhi.* I have highlighted the word *jñāna* to indicate that each level is characterized by a degree of conceptualization. In the first case, *sāṅkhya-**jñāna**-samādhi,* the cognitive process is characterized by the accumulation of analytical knowledge (*sāṅkhya-jñāna*) of the physical universe. This eventually leads to a perception of ultimate reality called *brahman.* The fruit of such realization is worldly detachment (*prapañca-nivṛtti*). The next mode, *ātma-**jñāna**-samādhi,* involves the cultivation of self-knowledge (*ātma-jñāna*). This ultimately leads to a perception of the *paramātmā* or the Soul of God within all things. The result of this experience is a sense of limited self-satisfaction (*ātma-gata-kṣudrānanda*). The final level of indirect cognition, called ***jñāna**-miśra-sahaja-samādhi,* is a form of mystic intuition (*sahaja-samādhi*) that is mixed with material perceptions. This eventually leads to an understanding of God in personal form as *bhagavān.*

Direct cognition (*sākṣāt-samādhi*), on the other hand, differs from indirect cognition in that it is free from any degree of material conceptualization. Direct cognition has two modes both qualified by the term *sahaja,* meaning that it is natural or innate to the soul. S*ahaja-samādhi* proper focuses on a transcendent and personal form of God known as Nārāyaṇa. This mode creates a form of spiritual bliss known as *aiśvarya-bhāva,* or the adoration of the majestic form of the Lord. The second mode, *nitānta-sahaja-samādhi,* is the highest form of *sākṣāt-samādhi,* which culminates in the adoration of Śrī Kṛṣṇa in sweetness (*mādhurya-bhāva*). The distinction between *aiśvarya-bhāva* and *mādhurya-bhāva* is a subtle distinction of great salience for Caitanya Vaiṣṇavas but not something that we need to discuss here. The main point is that cognition takes place at two levels, one indirect—under the influence of matter, and the other direct—at the level of soul.[17]

The prime qualification for accessing direct *sahaja-samādhi* is a

17. DK, vs. 10 commentary: Appendix V, 20.

level of faith that is free from doubt. Doubt is said to be a product of the rational mind and something that obstructs the natural light of the soul. *Madhyamādhikārīs* (typically intellectuals) have the greatest difficulty attaining *sākṣāt-samādhi* because of their inability to let go of their materially dominated cognitive processes that ultimately create doubt. Bhaktivinoda writes:

> It is difficult for *madhyamādhikārīs* to know these truths because they are always affected by doubts. . . . Men generally place more faith in logic, which arises when *saṁvit* contacts *māyā,* than in *sahaja-samādhi,* which they dismiss as superstition.[18]

In another instance he asserts: "The wise say that *samādhi* is self-illuminating, but because it is extremely subtle, it is easily destroyed by doubt."[19] And again, "subtle spiritual truths cannot be approached by logic or even *śāstra.*"[20] Consequently, *madhyamādhikārīs* are more or less condemned to remain at the various levels of indirect cognition (*gauṇa-samādhi*). It is pure faith alone that provides the gateway to direct cognition (*sākṣāt-samādhi*).

In this sense Bhaktivinoda often praises the virtues of *komala-śraddhas* for their simple and undoubting minds. The story of the wives of the *karma-kāṇḍī brāhmaṇas* from the *Bhāgavata* illustrates this point. The *brāhmaṇas'* wives are *komala-śraddhas* who have a natural faith in Śrī Kṛṣṇa that easily leads them to liberation. On the other hand, their husbands, who are *madhyamādhikārīs*, fail to achieve Kṛṣṇa because of their pride and arrogant belief in their intellectual abilities.[21] It is the *komala-śraddhas'* pure faith, which is free from doubt, that opens the door to spiritual reality. For this reason, *komala-śraddhas,* under proper guidance, can often advance more easily than *madhyamādhikārīs,* who are afflicted by doubts in

18. KS, *Saṁhitā* 4/2e: Appendix V, 21.
19. Ibid., 9/5: *sva-prakāśa-svabhāvo 'yaṁ samādhiḥ kathyate budhaiḥ/ ati-sūkṣma-svarūpatvāt saṁśayāt sa vilupyate/*
20. Ibid., 1/34e: *śāstra vā yukti-dvārā eta-tattva gamya haya nā*
21. Ibid., 5/7e.

spite of their greater intellectual abilities.

Bhaktivinoda's reliance on *sahaja-samādhi* as a genuine process of spiritual knowledge is a distinctive feature of his theological system. To him, direct spiritual cognition was not something remote or reserved only for the sages of old, but something of personal utility and immediate relevance that you or I may experience if we have the right faith. In other words, direct spiritual insight is the ultimate measure of spiritual understanding—above empiricism, human reason, and even *śāstra.* He concludes:

> Although I am incapable of clearly describing these truths using language, I have tried to give an idea of the truth. First practicing *samādhi,* I have described some details about God, but words are crude and so we are unable to fully realize the Supreme through descriptions. Therefore, I pray that our readers will realize these truths through *samādhi* themselves . . . as I have done this before I made my description, our readers should do the same.[22]

Holy Scripture

Unfortunately, most human beings are unable to directly experience the benefits of *sahaja-samādhi*; consequently, the primary means by which spiritual truth appears to human beings is in the form of holy scripture or *śāstra.* Bhaktivinoda writes:

> Essential truth is like the sun, and the scriptures are like the rays of the sun. Therefore, no scripture can contain the full extent of divine knowledge. The source of the scriptures is self-validating knowledge (*svataḥ-siddha-jñāna)* which arises in the heart of the living being and must be considered as God-given. The sages, endowed with compassion, have received this self-validating knowledge from the Supreme Lord and recorded it in the Vedas for the benefit of the souls of this world.[23]

22. Ibid., 1/33e: Appendix V, 22.
23. ST, Vol. 8 (1896), TS 143: Appendix V, 23.

The "data" of divine revelation first appear in the hearts of great sages and saints, who are then confronted with the problem of how to describe, in human terms, what they have "seen" in direct *samādhi*. Eventually such descriptions and stories (*kathā*) become *śāstra* or holy scripture. In the case of Vyāsadeva and Vālmīki (or whoever may have written in their names), their insights have been recorded in the most popular of Hindu scriptures, the *Rāmāyaṇa, Mahābhārata,* and *Purāṇas.* Holy scripture, therefore, is one of the most important modes of divine manifestation in human terms.

But, the question arises: How reliable are such descriptions? According to Bhaktivinoda, direct *samādhi* is rarely achieved and even when it is there are many problems that inevitably interfere with its transmission. He describes three basic problems that distort the purity of divine revelation: 1) problems associated with the recipients of essential truth, 2) the personal bias of the writers of *śāstra,* and 3) the limitations of human language itself.

The first and most critical problem associated with the transmission of spiritual knowledge is the limitation imposed by the human psychology of the *various* recipients of essential truth. In his *Datta-kaustubha* he writes:

> The original form of truth has no reference to the particulars of time or place. It is understood by a soul who is pure in heart and it is rarely seen. Relative truth is that which pertains to the varying competencies of living beings from the very lowest state to the most highly elevated. That will be clarified in the analysis of competence (*adhikāra*).[24]

Essential truth is constant, but the manner in which it is understood varies according to the qualifications of the persons who receive it. The word used to describe the various grades of people who receive essential truth is *adhikāra.* People have different grades of *adhikāra,* or competence, to understand truth. Bhaktivinoda categorizes people according to three levels of *adhikāra*: *komala-śraddha, madhyamādhikārī,* and *uttamādhikārī.*

24. DK, vs. 4: Appendix V, 24.

Essential truth is understood differently by these various *adhikārīs*. The concept of *adhikāra* is an important aspect of Bhaktivinoda's theological understanding.

Specifically human beings understand and interpret all events, including spiritual revelation, in a way that is conditioned by three environmental factors: place (*deśa*), time (*kāla*), and recipient personality (*pātra*). Everything that we perceive around us, including what we read in *śāstra* or hear from realized souls, is conditioned by our own unique set of social, psychological, and cultural factors. Bhaktivinoda writes:

> The pastimes of Kṛṣṇa exist in their actual form in *Goloka-dhāma*, but from the perspective of the conditioned soul they are understood in relation to this physical world. The conditioned souls have attained a specific nature distinguished according to the particulars of place, time and personality. Consequently, their perception of *līlā* is differentiated according to those particulars of place, time, and personality. *Līlā*, however, is never materially contaminated, but in the contaminated understanding of the observers these distinctions are seen.[25]

In other words it is the perspective of the beholder that determines how the information of *śāstra* is received. Those whose *adhikāra* is high perceive the truth of *śāstra* in a subtle way, those whose *adhikāra* is middling perceive truth in a middle way, and those whose *adhikāra* is low interpret truth in a more basic way.

The second problem associated with the descriptions of essential truth is the personal bias of the authors of *śāstra*. Bhaktivinoda frankly admits that even the best of *śāstra* is naturally affected by the bias of its author(s). Bhaktivinoda cites an instance from the *Viṣṇu-purāṇa* as follows:

> There is no doubt that the *Viṣṇu-purāṇa* was written by a southern pundit because there it is stated that a man

25. KS, *Saṁhitā* 7/2e: Appendix V, 25.

> should eat bitter things at the end of a meal. This is a southern practice which shows that the author has inserted the flavor of his own country into the text. There is no doubt. . . . It is an obvious fact that a man is greatly devoted to his homeland and even the great sages were somewhat influenced by this tendency.[26]

Clearly *śāstra* contains an element of personal bias from its authors. Bhaktivinoda, therefore, advises that we take this into consideration and ultimately strive for direct cognition or *sahaja-samādhi*. In his *Tattva-sūtra* he writes:

> For the purpose of determining the true meanings of the Vedic statements, sages like Manu, Yājñavalkya, Śātātapa, Vaśiṣṭha, and Vāmadeva have composed many treatises called *dharma-śāstras*. Other sages, like Veda Vyāsa, have also introduced many Puranic scriptures, and Lord Mahādeva has explained many types of *Tantric* scriptures. It is the duty of human beings to study the meanings of the Vedas in the light of all these explanations, but even after the implementation of all these things, the individual study of divine knowledge with the help of one's own self-validating knowledge is an essential requirement because the writers and commentators are not always absolutely clear. In various places even the commentators are seen to have doubts. . . . Therefore, the independent cultivation of self-validating knowledge is always necessary along with the study of the scriptures.[27]

Bhaktivinoda's suggestion that we understand *śāstra* according to its historical context reflects the influence of nineteenth century Unitarian thought among the *bhadraloka*. Channing's famous Baltimore sermon emphasizing that "the Bible is a book written for men, in the language of men"[28] is a common theme within

---

26. KS, *Upakramaṇikā* p. 55-56: Appendix V, 27.
27. ST, Vol 8 (1896), TS, 144: Appendix V, 26.
28. William Ellery Channing, "Unitarian Christianity," in *Three Prophets of Religious*

Bhaktivinoda's writing. Channing stressed that God's revelation in the Bible was refracted through human language and the circumstances of human history. To understand God's will, we must make allowance for that refraction; and to that end, all the resources of philology, of history, and of philosophy, must be brought to bear on the sacred text.

The final problem associated with the transmission of spiritual knowledge is the inherent limitations of language. Human language is the principle means by which *śāstra* is conveyed, but as language is a human instrument, it cannot escape the constraints of the physical world including time. By its very nature, language is incapable of accurately conveying the true content of a spiritual perception. What is Absolute must appear as mundane when expressed in human terms. In his *Jaiva-dharma* Bhaktivinoda writes, "The eternal truth is beyond human description. Purified souls see Kṛṣṇa's form and pastimes as part of the all conscious *cit* "world," but when they express these things in human terms it can only be described as mundane history."[29] Elsewhere he writes, "Although I am incapable of clearly describing these truths using language, I have tried to give an idea of the truth. First practicing *samādhi*, I have described some details about the Lord as far as possible, but words are crude, and so we cannot actually realize the Supreme Truth in the highest form through descriptions."[30]

Regarding the problem of time, he writes, "In our descriptions of *jīva* (soul) and *cit* (spiritual consciousness), we cannot remove the influence of mundane time. The past and future are automatically there."[31] Human language is a crude tool when used to describe spiritual affairs, but because we cannot avoid the use of language we must take the limitations of language into consideration as we approach scriptural knowledge.

All these problems affecting the transmission of essential truth

---

Liberalism: Channing, Emerson, Parker, ed. Conrad Wright (Boston: Unitarian Universalist Association, 1980), 49.

29. JD, 51: Appendix V, 28.

30. KS, *Saṁhitā* vs. 1/33e: Appendix V, 29.

31. JD, 264: Appendix V, 30.

mean that even Vyāsadeva's pure descriptions of *Kṛṣṇa-līlā* are conditioned by the limitations of human psychology, *adhikāra,* personal bias, and the constraints of language, including the influence of time and place. For Bhaktivinoda even the authority of *śāstra* is secondary to personal realization. In the end, *śāstra* assumes the role of a spiritual guide while primary importance is given to direct experience obtained through *sahaja-samādhi.* In the *Datta-kaustubha* he affirms, "Scripture is like a friend who helps with what is to be done."[32]

However, there is one important condition: people in general are not qualified to know the provisional character of *śāstra.* In fact the provisional character of *śāstra* is never directly stated within *śāstra.* The reverse is true. For the sake of those *adhikārīs* who are not qualified to know this aspect of *śāstra* the absolute authority of *śāstra* is stated. He writes:

> The provisional character of scriptural texts is evident, but the authors of the scriptures do not explicitly indicate this because those qualified to discard the scriptural bindings naturally become independent of scripture with the help of the hidden indications of the scriptural authors and also by their own purified knowledge. Such persons carry on sinless activities with the help of their own intellect as well as by the advice of the scriptures. In that stage the scriptures do not have any binding power over them, but only serve as their guides.
>
> On the other hand, those who are unable to understand their own spiritual path for want of self-evident knowledge may not be able to ascertain their duties and so may fall into misery due to sensuality; for such people the scriptural rules are imperative. Such persons should not know that there is any way for them apart from the bindings of the scriptures. When they become authorized due to their advancement, they will be able to know this secret by the

32. DK, vs. 12: *tasmāc chāstraṁ pramāṇaṁ syān mitravat kārya-sādhane/*

suggestions of the scriptures.[33]

For this reason the influence of *śāstra* in religious life varies according to the *adhikāra* of the recipient. Let us now examine Bhaktivinoda's theory of religious symbolism.

The Symbolic Process

As the *ādhunika-vāda* was presented to the *bhadraloka* for their historical understanding, so an interpretation of religious symbolism is presented for their theological understanding. That Bhaktivinoda even discusses religious symbolism is indicative of his involvement with modernity. Indeed, one of the most important roles of the modern Vaiṣṇava theologian was to provide a conceptual understanding of religious symbolism. In this regard Bhaktivinoda chose to explain the character and functioning of the tradition's religious symbols in reference to *Kṛṣṇa-līlā*.

In the course of his discussion of religious symbolism Bhaktivinoda employs the words *praticchāyā*, *nidarśana*, and *udāharaṇa*. He points out that the spiritual descriptions found in *śāstra* are not direct perceptions of spiritual reality, but rather are "facsimiles" (*praticchāyā*) of spiritual reality. Similarly, the specific details of *līlā* (cows, peacocks, flutes, and so on) are indicators (*nidarśana*) of spiritual truths. In his *Kṛṣṇa-saṁhitā* he writes:

> We have said that the activities of the spiritual "world" are not visible in their actual form to the conditioned soul. They can be felt through *samādhi* to a certain extent, but even that realization is achieved by visualizing a material facsimile (*māyika praticchāyā*) of the actual form. This is because all the indicators (*nidarśana*) of place, time, and persons[34] found in the Vraja pastimes are just that —indicators (*nidarśanas*).[35]

33. ST, Vol. 8 (1896), TS p 149: Appendix 3 Sanskrit and Bengali Passages 31.
34. Places on earth such as Vrindavan and Mathura. Times such as *Dvāpara-yuga*. Personalities such as those born in the family of cowherds and Yadus.
35. KS, *Saṁhitā* 7/2e: Appendix V, 32.

Here he states that the affairs of the spiritual "world" (*cit-jagat*) cannot actually be understood in human terms because they transcend human comprehension, so they must be expressed using the things of this world as indicators or *nidarśanas*. He defines a *nidarśana* as that which points to or suggests a situation or an object that cannot be described in words.[36] This is the symbolic process. Consequently, the places (*deśa*), times (*kāla*) and personalities (*pātra*) of *Kṛṣṇa-līlā* are all things of this world used to indicate what is transcendent.

Similarly Bhaktivinoda employs the term *udāharaṇa* (example) in a way that also suggests a symbolic process. In the *Jaiva-dharma* Vrajanath, one of the characters in the novel, asks his teacher, "Why are material things employed as examples (*udāharaṇa*) to indicate spiritual truth?" Babaji, the teacher, replies, "I have told you that whenever we speak about a spiritual subject the dirt of matter must be there because words are material. So it is under compulsion that such examples (*udāharaṇa*) must be used. . . . Examples only explain the character of a particular thing and not the whole matter."[37] Thus, the terms *praticchāyā*, *nidarśana*, and *udāharaṇa* suggest a form of religious symbolism that forms one of the most distinctive features of Bhaktivinoda's theology.

But what is the precise nature of the symbolic process that Bhaktivinoda refers to? How does a symbolic process relate to traditional Caitanya Vaiṣṇava theology? What are the implications of such an idea? Bhaktivinoda highlights the paradox of symbolism when he says that the activities of Kṛṣṇa are "not historical events like the activities of men who live in matter. . . . but neither are they events imagined (or projected) from the life of a man."[38] His refusal to reject the Kṛṣṇa of the *Bhāgavata-purāṇa* is predicated on his faith that the descriptions of the *Purāṇas* are real and not mere fantasies as Bankim Chandra supposes. But still Bhaktivinoda's use of the

36. KS, *Saṁhitā*, 7/2e ft.: *ye sattā vā kārya kona anirvacanīya sattā vā kāryake lakṣya kariyā dekhāya, tāhāra nāma nidarśana/*

37. JD, 226.

38. KS, *Saṁhitā* 3/16e: *jaḍāśrita mānava-caritrera nyāya uhā aitihāsika naya . . . athavā nara-carita haite kona kona ghaṭana saṁyoga-pūrvaka uhā kalpita haya nāi/*

terms *praticchāyā, nidarśana,* and *udāharaṇa* leaves open the question as to the exact nature of divine *līlā.*

If it is the business of the theologian to form the concepts of theology consonant with the symbols of religious expression, it is appropriate to discuss what theologians generally mean by religious symbols and, in particular, how Bhaktivinoda applies the concept of religious symbolism. Literally, the words that Bhaktivinoda uses —*praticchāyā, nidarśana* and *udāharaṇa*—mean reflection, indicator, and example respectively.[39] These terms do not mean symbol directly. They have distinct connotations that are not preserved in the single world symbol. Instead a more precise Bengali term for *symbol* would have been *pratīka,*[40] a word that Bhaktivinoda seems not to use. His use of the words *praticchāyā, nidarśana,* and *udāharaṇa* does, however, suggest something akin to the symbolic process. Traditionally, of course, Vaiṣṇavas do not use the terms *symbol* or *myth* to describe divine *līlā.* These are Western concepts that have no exact equivalents in Vaiṣṇava theology. In fact they suggest something less historically and literally real than *līlā* is conceived to be. In addition, they imply a form of materialist illusionism called *māyāvāda* that is adamantly refuted by Caitanya Vaiṣṇavas.[41]

The general understanding is that *līlā* is a divine occurrence that takes place not only as a literal event within human history, but also as a transcendent event outside of human history. Yet unlike

39. The word *praticchāyā* is cited by Haridas Das in his *Gauḍīya Vaiṣṇava Abhidhāna* in three senses: *ābhāsa* (faint presence or shadow), *pratibimba* (a reflected image) and *sādṛśya* (likeness or resemblance). He renders *nidarśana* as *dṛṣṭānta* (example or instance), and as *cihna-viśeṣa* (sign). He similarly renders *udāharaṇa* as *dṛṣṭānta* (example or instance). Surendranath Dasgupta in his *History of Indian Philosophy* points out that the terms *udāharaṇa* and *nidarśana* are commonly used in Indian syllogism (*anumāna*) to refer to the various elements of the logical premise. Typically *udāharaṇa* is the instance or example, which is usually the third element in the logical premise. The word *praticchāyā* is not listed by either Dasgupta, B. K. Matilal, nor by Potter in his *Indian Metaphysics and Epistemology.*

40. For a short discussion of *pratīka* see: B. N. K. Sharma, *Philosophy of Sri Madhvacarya* (Bombay: Bharatiya Vidya Bhavan, 1962).

41. *Māyāvāda* is the word used by many Vaiṣṇavas to describe the theology of the

ordinary historical events, *līlā* has no material form or material substance. It consists of real action by real actors, but their reality is of *cit* form and substance, though this appears as if it were material. Moreover, the apparent ("as if") material bodies and personalities of *līlā* may do wondrous and miraculous things beyond what material nature is capable of. The devotee–philosopher O. B. L. Kapoor describes *līlā*:

> The place on earth known as Vraja-maṇḍala, wherein Vṛndāvana and Mathurā exist, has a spiritual counterpart known as Goloka situated in the spiritual "sky" (*cit-jagat*). In other words, there is a spiritual Vṛndāvana that has its replica on earth in the form of the geographic Vṛndāvana. However, the geographic Vṛndāvana appears as a part of the phenomenal world only due to our clouded vision; in fact it is identical with its spiritual counterpart in Goloka. *Līlā,* therefore, has two modes: unmanifest (*aprakaṭa*) and manifest (*prakaṭa*). Unmanifest *līlā* is what takes place in Goloka, the spiritual "sky"; it is completely transcendent and it has no contact with the phenomenal world. (Even today Kṛṣṇa is said to be eternally present in Vraja-maṇḍala where He performs *līlā* that can be seen by those who are blessed with the divine vision of *līlā* while in their present bodies.) Manifest *līlā,* on the other hand, is what takes place in Vraja-maṇḍala at certain times in human history; it is a mixture of both the phenomenal and the non-phenomenal. In manifest *līlā* a particular manifestation of Goloka descends on earth to create a congruence of the material and the spiritual—but it is not mixing in the ordinary sense, for the touch of spirit makes the particular part of the phenomenal world, where it descends,

---

advaita-vedānta school of Śaṅkara. According to the *advaita* school ultimate reality is non-dual. However, the fact that we perceive reality as variegated is explained by postulating the theory of *māyā* or material illusion that covers our vision of that ultimate non-dual reality known as Brahman. This means, for example, that the various incarnations or *avatāras* of Viṣṇu are covered or influenced by *māyā* when they appear in this material world. Such a view is adamantly rejected by the Vaiṣṇavas. God is never subject to the influence of *māyā*.

> also spiritual. Consequently the place on earth where the spiritual "sky" touches the phenomenal world is known as a divine abode (*dhāman*).[42]

However, to view *līlā* as fictional or to ascribe an allegorical interpretation to it is to diminish or deny its historical and ontological reality. The following statements describe the Caitanya Vaiṣṇava understanding of *Kṛṣṇa-līlā.* A. C. Bhaktivedanta Swami writes:

> The Supreme Lord Śrī Kṛṣṇa cannot be seen by our present conditional vision. In order to see Him, one has to change his present vision by developing a different condition of life full of spontaneous love of Godhead. When Śrī Kṛṣṇa was personally present on the face of the globe, not everyone could see Him as the Supreme Personality of Godhead. Materialists like Rāvaṇa, Hiraṇyakaśipu, Kaṁsa, Jarāsandha and Śiśupāla were highly qualified personalities by acquisition of material assets, but they were unable to appreciate the presence of the Lord. Therefore, even though the Lord may be present before our eyes, it is not possible to see Him unless we have the necessary vision. The necessary qualification is developed by the process of devotional service only . . . "[43]

This passage means that Kṛṣṇa actually walked on the earth as an historical personality, but only those with a devotional mentality could appreciate Kṛṣṇa's divine presence. Others without such "necessary vision" saw him as an ordinary person with various degrees of human power.

Another commentator, not a professed devotee, S. K. De, writes:

> It is important to note that the *Vṛndāvana-līlā* is not a

42. O. B. L. Kapoor, *The Philosophy and Religion of Śrī Caitanya* (Delhi: Munshiram Manoharlal, 1977), 115.

43. A. C. Bhaktivedanta Swami's comments on Bhāg. 1/8/36. Vyāsadeva, *Śrīmad Bhāgavatam,* trans. and ed. A. C. Bhaktivedanta Swami, First Canto, vol. 1 (Los Angeles: Bhaktivedanta Book Trust, 1987), 444-445.

> mere symbol or divine allegory, but a literal fact of religious history. The Rādhā-Kṛṣṇa myth, as depicted in the *Purāṇas* and elaborated in the *kāvyas, nāṭakas,* and *campūs,* as well as in the *rasa-śāstra* . . . is taken as a vivid historical, as well as super historical reality; and there is no suggestion of its being an allegory. The pressure of modern thought has, no doubt, induced some modern writers on the subject to the desperate method of allegorical interpretation; but the theologians and poets of the sect never think it necessary to spiritualize the myth as a symbolism of religious truth, for the Purāṇic world to them is manifestly a matter of religious history.[44]

Here again *līlā* is viewed as an historic reality that is meant to be accepted literally. O. B. L. Kapoor describes *Kṛṣṇa-līlā* as follows:

> When . . . Kṛṣṇa descends on these *dhāmans* [divine abodes] at the time of manifest *līlā* [*prakaṭa-līlā*], even those who are not devoted can see him and his *parikaras* [divine associates] in their true form. Such is the effect of the divine touch of Kṛṣṇa on these *dhāmans*, which otherwise appear to be phenomenal.[45]

Finally Daniel Sheridan writes, "The Vṛndāvana play is not a mere allegory or symbol but literally history."[46] These passages all point to an historical and literal understanding of *līlā*. The underlying idea in all of these passages is that *Kṛṣṇa-līlā* was in fact a divine event that appeared at some point in human history.

Divine *līlā* becomes manifest as an historical fact of human history, and anyone fortunate enough to have been present could have witnessed it as an event within human history, though not all may

---

44. S. K. De, *Early History of the Vaishnava Faith and Movement in Bengal* (Calcutta: Firma K. L. Mukhopadhyay, 1961), 223.
45. Kapoor, *Religion of Śrī Caitanya,* 110.
46. Daniel P. Sheridan, *The Advaitic Theism of The Bhāgavata Purāṇa* (Delhi, Motilal Banarsidass, 1986), 132.

have realized its further transcendent reality.

For Bhaktivinoda such a literal understanding of *līlā* is only the first level of interpretation. Certainly he does not reject this point of view, but neither does he leave the matter at this level. Instead, he offers two further levels of interpretation, one symbolic and the other *rasika*.[47] Here we are concerned with Bhaktivinoda's second level of interpretation, the symbolic level. Later we will discuss the *rasika* level.

Religious Symbolism

The symbolic process is simply the bringing together of the concrete and the abstract. The symbol is something concrete and specific that points to what is abstract and generalized, which then becomes a focal point for thoughts and emotions. A nation's flag, for example, symbolizes nationhood. The flag is a piece of cloth, a concrete thing, whereas nationhood is an abstract idea. In the course of the symbolic process they are fused.

In a similar manner, the religious symbol points to the ultimate level of reality. The religious symbol takes its concrete form from the things of this world to point to what is beyond ordinary human comprehension. In short, the religious symbol is part of a process of what I would like to call *ascending* symbolism, namely, a process that uses the finite things of this world to point beyond itself to the basis of all reality and thereby form a bridge between phenomenal reality and ultimate reality.

If we apply the idea of ascending religious symbolism to our original theological statement[48] the human-like form of Kṛṣṇa, as

---

47. *Rasika* means "in relation to *rasa.*" *Rasa* is "relishable flavor or sentiment." When something is pleasurable or enjoyable it possesses *rasa.* That which accounts for an object's pleasurableness is its *rasa.* According to the *Bhāgavata* the source of all *rasa* is *bhagavān* Śrī Kṛṣṇa. But not only is Kṛṣṇa the source of all *rasa,* He is also the supreme enjoyer of *rasa.* The Vṛndāvana *līlā* is, therefore, the play of Kṛṣṇa wherein an endless number of *rasas* are tasted by both Kṛṣṇa and His followers.

48. *vadanti tat tattva-vidas tattvaṁ yaj jñānam advayam/ brahmeti paramātmeti bhagavān iti śabdyate* "Those who know the Absolute Truth speak of this Truth *(tattva)* as undifferentiated knowledge categorized as *Brahman, Paramātmā* and *Bhagavān.*"

bhagavān, who stands in a threefold bending form holding a flute and who is adorned with a peacock feather, is concrete and tangible, whereas *tattva*, described as undifferentiated knowledge (*jñānam advayam*), is abstract and general. The form of *bhagavān* Śrī Kṛṣṇa easily becomes the focal point for human thoughts and emotions, which are actually intended for the higher and more abstract principle, *tattva*. The finite and human-like form of Kṛṣṇa points to the ultimate level of reality, *tattva*.

However, Vaiṣṇava theology never views *bhagavān* as a mere symbol pointing towards the Absolute Truth. *Bhagavān* is the Absolute Truth. And to ascribe a process of religious symbolism to *bhagavān*, whereby *bhagavān* is merely perceived as a complex of human ideas pointing to an abstract transcendent reality beyond itself, would be to impute material attributes to what is inherently spiritual. This type of ascending symbolic process was no doubt the easiest way to solve the problem of religious literalism and, of course, many members of the *bhadraloka* did in fact interpret *līlā* in this way.[49] But, according to Vaiṣṇava theology *bhagavān* is not a mere symbol of the Divine; it is the Divine—literally. Therefore, Bhaktivinoda never accepts such a process of ascending religious symbolism; instead he proposes another process of religious symbolism that I call *descending* symbolism.[50]

In ascending symbolism a nation's flag reaches out to symbolize nationhood, and even though the flag may participate in the feeling of nationhood, still the flag is something different from that

49. As we have seen, Bankim Chandra's first alternative was to remove the so-called irrational aspects of *līlā* outright. When he realized that this was not possible, he admitted an allegorical symbolic interpretation. For example, Kṛṣṇa's *rāsa-līlā* dance becomes symbolic of the interaction between *puruṣa* and *prakṛti* in Sāṅkhya philosophy. Similarly, he interpreted incidents like the turning over of the cart, the destruction of Tṛṇāvarta, Vatsāsura, Bakāsura and Aghāsura and the suppression of the serpent Kāliya as mere allegory. Other commentators, such as Navin Chandra Sen (1847–1909) and Bipin Chandra Pal, similarly interpret *Kṛṣṇa-līlā* allegorically.

50. The terms *ascending symbolism* and *descending symbolism* are not used by either modern theologians or by Bhaktivinoda. These are terms that I use to distinguish

which it symbolizes. In the same way, if we interpret *līlā* according to the ascending process, then Kṛṣṇa is a personality of this world who enables those who participate in Hindu faith to reach out and grasp what is Absolute (*tattva*). This means that Kṛṣṇa is qualitatively different from that which He symbolizes, and like the cloth of the flag or the paper of the Bible, Kṛṣṇa is flesh and blood. In other words, Kṛṣṇa is a product of this world. However, this is decidedly *not* the theology of the *Caitanya-sampradāya*, which adamantly asserts that Kṛṣṇa is not a product of matter.

A conclusion of this type conflicts with the very essence of Vaiṣṇava theology. By drawing a distinction between Kṛṣṇa and the Absolute, we are attributing materialism to Kṛṣṇa's body and committing the error of ascribing material qualities to what is spiritual. This is known among Caitanya Vaiṣṇavas as the theory of *māyā* (*māyāvāda*), according to which Kṛṣṇa's body, Kṛṣṇa's name, and Kṛṣṇa's activities are all transient phenomenal products of matter. Describing this fault, Bhaktivinoda writes:

> *Māyāvādīs* say that when *bhagavān* descends to this world He has to seek help from *māyā*. He cannot appear in the phenomenal world unless He accepts a form fit for the region of *māyā* because He has no form as *brahman*. In the form of Īśvara He gets a body of matter and when His incarnations descend to this world they also have material bodies and perform great deeds. When they return to their own region they leave these bodies here. . . . All these are the wrong conclusions of the *māyāvādīs*.[51]

Contrary to this, Vaiṣṇava theology teaches that Kṛṣṇa's name, form, and activities are never even tinged with matter, what to speak of being a product of matter. Kṛṣṇa's appearance in this world is a pure spiritual event, one in which His appearance and activities are not different from His divine form. To think of Kṛṣṇa is to have

---

the more common understanding of religious symbolism from the distinctive approach to religious symbolism that Bhaktivinoda is employing.

51. JD, 318: Appendix V, 33.

Kṛṣṇa directly, for He is Absolute.[52] Consequently, Bhaktivinoda never accepts an interpretation of *Kṛṣṇa-līlā* that involves an ascending symbolic process.[53]

The challenge for Bhaktivinoda was how to move beyond the problem of religious literalism without falling into the trap of *māyāvāda,* ascribing transient phenomenal characteristics to essential elements of Vaiṣṇava faith.

Descending Symbolism and The Theory of *Vikāra*

In the didactic novel *Jaiva-dharma,* Vijaya Kumar poses an important question: "If what is transcendent and what is mundane are so generically different, how can one be used as a proper example (*udāharaṇa)* of the other?"[54] In other words, what is the relationship between matter and spirit and how can one be used to symbolize the other? The answer is found in Bhaktivinoda's theory of modification (*vikāra*), wherein the material shapes and forms of this world are said to be imperfect modifications, known as *vikāras,* of eternally existing spiritual "forms." Bhaktivinoda writes:

> I have already said that only *cit* (spiritual substance) has true reality; matter is its *vikāra* or imperfect modification. There are many similarities between a pure thing and its

52. The notion that *bhagavān* is Absolute and therefore his form, name, and activities are all non-different from his actual spiritual being is a form of spiritual absolutism and a cardinal point of Vaiṣṇava theology. That Kṛṣṇa's name is seen to be non-different from Kṛṣṇa himself is a prime example of this theology.

53. Even Paul Tillich's statement that God is a symbol for God is the same as saying that *bhagavān* is a symbol for *tattva* according to an ascending process of religious symbolism. From the Vaiṣṇava perspective this is a statement of the *māyāvāda,* because it implies that *bhagavān* is a concept of this world used to symbolize what transcends this phenomenal world. The process of ascending symbolism, therefore, goes hand in hand with the theory of *māyā,* which is diametrically opposed to the very essence of Vaiṣṇava theology. Paul Tillich, *The Dynamics of Faith* (New York: Harper and Row, 1958), 46.

54. JD, 268: *cid-vastu o jaḍa-vastu ubhayai yadi jātite bhinna haya, tāhā haile udāharaṇa ki rūpe suṣṭhu haite pāre?*

> *vikāra* and although a *vikāra* is different from its pure counterpart, similarity lingers in many respects. For example, ice is a *vikāra* of water and although it differs from water, still, similarity exists in respect to some of its properties like coldness, and so on. . . . Thus a *vikāra* continues to hold some common properties of its pure counterpart. Therefore, as this mundane world is the *vikāra* of the world of *cit*, a *cit* subject may be discussed with the help of an example from matter.[55]

He goes on to say:

> The variegated world of *māyā* is the distorted reflection of the variegated spiritual world. [56] For example, as a human body, when reflected on a plain glass mirror appears to be similar to the real body, but on closer inspection is seen to be reversed—such that the right arm appears to be the left one and vice versa—so the diversities of the *cit* world and those of the world of *māyā* appear to be similar from the perspective of our crude vision. However, in reality, they are inverse when seen with subtle vision. . . . [57] As such there is resemblance in description, but dissimilarity in reality.[58]

According to this idea the whole world of matter is an imperfect modification of a transcendent realm. Sometimes it is said that this world of *māyā* is a shadow or reflection (*praticchāyā*) of the world of *cit.* The depictions of *līlā* in the *Bhāgavata* that enact transcendence, such as the form of Kṛṣṇa holding peacock feather and flute, are not symbols in the way a modern theologian such as Paul Tillich or a mythologist such as Joseph Campbell would speak of them, but are indicators (*nidarśana*) or reflections (*praticchāyā)* because they bear a direct relationship to their real spiritual counterparts. The

55. Ibid., 268: Appendix V, 34.
56. Ibid., 244: *māyā-vaicitrya cid-vaicitryerai vikṛta pratiphalana/*
57. Ibid., 244: Appendix V, 35.
58. Ibid., 244: *ataeva tad-ubhayera varṇane sāmya, kintu vastute pārthakya āche/*

things of this world which are used "symbolically" in the *Bhāgavata* are not symbols in the typical modern sense, but are symbols in the sense of being indicators or reflections because of their direct relationship to their "more real" spiritual counterparts. I call this relationship between matter and spirit, where the material *vikāra* is used to indicate its spiritual counterpart, *descending* symbolism.

The form of Śrī Kṛṣṇa adorned with peacock feather and flute is one such example. According to this perspective, the peacock feather which is worn by Kṛṣṇa is not a mere symbolic pointer to His frolicsome and rustic nature devised from the collective consciousness of the Indian culture of 5,000 years ago, as an interpretation along the line of ascending symbolism would have it. Instead, the iconic peacock feather has indicatory value precisely because there exists a spiritually perfect peacock feather that is worn by Kṛṣṇa in the eternal world of *cit*. It is solely due to the reality of the spiritual (*cit*) feather that its imperfect modification (*vikāra*), the material peacock feather that we touch and see in this world, can be effectively used to indicate that spiritually perfect *cit* counterpart. In this world, we have no exposure to a spiritually perfect peacock feather, but at least the phenomenal peacock feather can serve as the most suitable indicator (*nidarśana*) to "symbolize" the spiritually perfect peacock feather worn by Śrī Kṛṣṇa.

Bhaktivinoda compares the correspondence of matter and spirit with the analogy of sighting *Arundhatī*,[59] a small star in the constellation *Ursa Major*. He writes, "Adopting the principle of sighting *Arundhatī*, the subtle properties of *cit* may be appreciated by extrapolation from the crude and perverted matter of this phenomenal world."[60] As one can get an indication where *Arundhatī* is by pointing to the constellation *Ursa Major*, so, in the same way, by using the things of this world we can indicate the general

59. *Arundhatī-darśana-nyāya:* The maxim of pointing out the star Arundhatī. This is a common Sanskrit illustration used in Indian epistemology. In Hindu mythology Arundhatī is the wife of Vasiṣṭha, whose star is the second in the constellation *sapta ṛṣi* (Ursa Major). The star Vasiṣṭha is known a Mizar in Western astronomy.

60. JD, 269: *ābara "arundhatī-darśana" nyāya avalambana karile cit-tattvera sukṣma-dharma-sakala jaḍa-tattvera sthula o viparyanta tattvālocanāya upalabdha haya/*

characteristics of the *cit* world.

As an artist in his creative genius paints a landscape and, through the artistic symbols, reveals levels of meaning that would otherwise be unknown, Bhaktivinoda sees mystics such as Vyāsadeva and Jayadeva as spiritual artists. In *sahaja-samādhi* (mystic trance), these mystics have a vision of the *cit* realm and then return to paint spiritual landscapes using the words and concepts of this world. The challenge they face is that the words they must use to describe what they have seen are material and cannot adequately describe their visions. In spite of this, it is out of material language, utilizing the closest material counterpart of the real *cit* form, that the mystic-poets describe what they have seen in *sahaja-samādhi.*

This semblance of relationship is dependent on the idea that the phenomenal world is a *vikāra* or imperfect modification of a spiritually perfect *cit* reality. To show how this is possible, Bhaktivinoda devotes the second chapter of his *Kṛṣṇa-saṁhitā* to explain the morphology of the spiritual and material worlds, showing how the two are built from the same building blocks.

The Morphology of Matter and Spirit

The fundamental energy that emanates from *bhagavān* is known as *parā-śakti,* which manifests Itself in three *bhāvas* or primary phases: *sandhinī, saṁvit,* and *hlādinī.*[61] *Sandhinī* is the principle of being or existence; *saṁvit* is the principle of cognition; and *hlādinī* is the principle of bliss.[62] Besides these *bhāvas* there are three secondary emanations from the *parā-śakti* known as *prabhāvas*: *cit, jīva,* and *māyā,* where the *cit-prabhāva* is spiritual substance, the *jīva-prabhāva* is soul substance, and the *māyā-prabhāva* is material substance. The *bhāvas* and the *prabhāvas* intermix resulting in the formation of three levels of existence: the divine or spiritual realm, individual souls, and the phenomenal world.

---

61. In the theology of the *Bhāgavata* these terms *sandhinī, saṁvit, and hlādinī* correspond to *sat, cit,* and *ānanda.*

62. KS, *Saṁhitā* 2/3e: *brahmera parā śaktir tinaṭi bhinna bhinna bhāvera upalabdhi haya arthāt sandhinī, saṁvit o hlādinī/*

The basic morphology of each realm is similar because each is constituted of the same elements: *sandhinī, saṁvit,* and *hlādinī.* In the case of the spiritual realm, *sandhinī, saṁvit,* and *hlādinī* interact with the *cit-prabhāva* to produce the reality of the spiritual "world" including all of its spiritual "forms," "relationships," and "activities." In the case of the soul, *sandhinī, saṁvit,* and *hlādinī* interact with the *jīva-prabhāva* to produce the reality of individual souls. Finally, in the case of the phenomenal world, *sandhinī, saṁvit,* and *hlādinī* interact with the *māyā-prabhāva* to produce the reality of this phenomenal world with all its forms, relationships and activities. Thus there is a parallel construction underlying each realm. Therefore the things of this world are related to the "things" of the spiritual "world" as a shadow is related to its source. For example, when *hlādinī* interacts with spiritual substance (*cit-prabhāva*), it produces spiritual bliss known as *ānanda,* but when the same interaction takes place with the *māyā-prabhāva, kāma* or material pleasure is produced. Spiritual bliss is said to be eternal and unlimited, whereas material pleasure is temporary and limited. In this way, material pleasure is a *vikāra* or modification of spiritual bliss.

I summarize the morphology of each realm in the following table found in the *Kṛṣṇa-saṁhitā*:

Table Two – The Morphology of Creation

Bhāva	***Prabhāva***	***Effect***
sandhinī	*cit*	spiritual existence
saṁvit	*cit*	spiritual awareness
hlādinī	*cit*	spiritual bliss
sandhinī	*jīva*	jīva's existence
saṁvit	*jīva*	jīva's awareness
hlādinī	*jīva*	jīva's satisfaction
sandhinī	*māyā*	material existence
saṁvit	*māyā*	material awareness
hlādinī	*māyā*	material pleasure

Many religions describe heaven as an idealized replica of an imperfect earth. Even Kṛṣṇa's land of Vraja (Vrindavan) or Viṣṇu's heaven of Vaikuṇṭha can easily be construed along these lines. Such an idea is consonant with an "ascending" process of religious symbolism. According to the Vaiṣṇavas, however, a reverse process is involved. Instead of heaven being a perfect replica of an imperfect earth, this earthly world is an imperfect replica of a perfect *cit* reality or heaven. The phenomenal world that we see is a *vikāra* or modification of an Absolute *cit* reality. This suggests that the things of this world have an innate potential to act as *nidarśanas* or indicators of that eternal *cit* reality of which they are modifications. The religious poets and mystics like Vyāsadeva have learned to use the things of this world to serve as *nidarśanas* to point to the *cit* reality. Likewise, Bhaktivinoda advances a process of religious symbolism that does not compromise the spiritual integrity of the *Bhāgavata,* but also overcomes the problem of religious literalism for the *bhadraloka.*

This reverse way of regarding the world in relation to transcendence creates a number of interesting possibilities. For example, Bhaktivinoda's theory of modification and its function in the symbolic process has a direct bearing on understanding what constitutes beauty in this world. If the totality of this phenomenal world is an imperfect reflection of the unseen *cit* world, then true beauty and real substance exist in the *cit* world alone. As the things of this world are seen in relation to their spiritual referents, they become symbolic and reflect more purely their actual *cit* form. Good art is possible in this world through the use of the symbolic process the artist uses to create a symbolic window into the real world of spiritual form. Good art is a more perfect characterization of pure form, and poor art is a less perfect representation of pure form.

Similarly, by studying what constitutes beauty in this world we can gain an appreciation and even participation in the beauty of the spiritual "world." Such beauty is experienced in terms of spiritual *rasa* or inexhaustible bliss. From the Vaiṣṇava perspective, *rasa* is generated though the interaction of spiritual relationships between friends, lovers, parents, children, and so on. By studying the relationships of this world we can gain insight into the relationships of the spiritual "world," because the relationships of this world exist as material reflections of their pure spiritual counterparts. Therefore, Bhaktivinoda writes, "We can describe the relationships of *Vaikuṇṭha* only by describing the illusory states of the material world, which are reflections of the real states in *Vaikuṇṭha.* There is no other way to do it."[63]

It is interesting that Bhaktivinoda's theory of modification is similar to Plato's theory of forms. According to Plato, just as the human mind comes into contact with the things and happenings of this world through sensory perception such as sight, hearing, and touch, so the soul gets into non-sensory contact with the ideal and eternal objects of a transcendent world.[64]

From Bhaktivinoda's early studies and later writings we know that he was aware of Plato,[65] but we cannot determine whether his theory of modification is actually derived from Plato's theory of form. He never specifically mentions Plato in any of his explanations of *vikāra.* Whatever may have been the origin of Bhaktivinoda's theory, what is important is that his theory implies a process of religious symbolism, albeit descending symbolism, such as might appeal to the modern intellectual needs of the *bhadraloka.*

---

63. KS, *Saṁhitā* 5/19e: *vāstavika vaikuṇṭhagata bhāvanicayera pratiphalana-rūpa māyika bhāvasakala varṇana-dvārā vaikuṇṭha-tattvera varṇane āmarā samartha hai/ tad-viṣaye anya upāya nāi/*

64. Plato explains the contrast between reality and imitation as,"A painter may produce a likeness of a real bed that a carpenter manufactures. But the carpenter, in manufacturing beds is in a supposedly analogous way "imitating" the concept of Bed. What he produces in wood is either a good or bad specimen of Bed. ... As the painter has to know things about the real bed if he is to try to produce a good likeness of it, so the carpenter has to know what a bed is if he is ever to try to make a good specimen of a bed. ... [In the same way], God, the cosmic artificer, is similarly described as modeling the things in his new world after eternal or timeless thing-patterns."(*The Encyclopedia of Philosophy*, 1972 ed., s. v. "Plato," by Gilbert Ryle.) What Plato describes in this passage corresponds to Bhaktivinoda's idea of *vikāra.*

65. Bhaktivinoda Thakur, *Tattva-viveka, Tattva-sūtra and Āmnāya-sūtra,* trans. and ed. Narasimha Brahmachari (Madras: Shree Gaudiya Math, 1979), 8. In his *Tattva-viveka* Bhaktivinoda mentions his reading of both Plato and Aristotle.

Nāma kīrtana.

Chapter Seven

Perceptions of Divine Manifestation

Kṛṣṇa-līlā, Śrī-mūrti* and *Nāma

At the beginning of this discussion we touched on the historicity of *Kṛṣṇa-līlā* by stating the opinions of various observers. We also mentioned that while Bhaktivinoda does not reject the literal understanding of *līlā*, neither does he limit his perspective solely to that understanding. Now we want to see how his perspective specifically applies to divine *līlā*.

Kṛṣṇa-līlā

For Bhaktivinoda, awareness of *līlā*, whether from the pages of the *Bhāgavata* or as *prakaṭa-līlā*,[1] is always a state of mind. Different levels of perceptive ability are fundamental to Bhaktivinoda's theology. From the perspective of God there is only one reality, but from the *jīva's* perspective, being conditioned according to time, space and personality, reality appears varied according to the perspective of the observer. What each individual sees of *prakaṭa-līlā* or understands from *śāstra* is determined according to the internal perspective of the observer. The *Caitanya-śikṣāmṛta* confirms this:

> When the living entity hears or reads about the character of Śrī Kṛṣṇa there are two possible realizations according to the level of spiritual qualification (*adhikāra*). The realization will be either of the nature of *vidvat-pratīti* or *avid-*

1. *Prakaṭa-līlā* refers to manifest *līlā*, namely, the time when the *avatāras* of Hari are manifest on earth.

> *vat-pratīti.* Even the activities of Śrī Kṛṣṇa that are visible during His existence in the world (*prakaṭa-līlā*) give rise to *vidvat-pratīti* in the truly learned men and *avidvat-pratīti* in men with material intellect. . . . The divine *līlā* that comes within the range of the senses during the period of *prakaṭa-līlā* does not give the the vision of God unless the observer sees with *vidvat-pratīti.*[2]

Here *vidvat-pratīti* and *avidvat-pratīti* are technical terms. *Pratīti* literally means seeing or cognizing, *vidvat* means possessed of knowledge, and *avidvat* means *not* possessed of knowledge. Thus *vidvat-pratīti* and *avidvat-pratīti* respectively refer to seeing spiritually and seeing materially.[3] Bhaktivinoda is saying that when the soul comes into contact with Kṛṣṇa, whether through the pages of the *Bhāgavata* or directly during the time of *prakaṭa-līlā,* what the person comprehends depends on how the person sees—whether spiritually or materially. Again he writes:

> Everything that you see in Vraja (Gokula) exists in Goloka. However, what is seen depends on the intensity of devotional practice. In reality there is no difference between Goloka and Gokula. The only difference lies in the eyes of the beholders. Very dull and disqualified people see all things in Gokula as spiritless and material. Active, energetic and intelligent persons see something very auspicious. But the people of loving devotion observe the living reality according to their respective power of sight. Each of these people have different perspectives and so they

2. CS, 15 and 17: Appendix V, 36.
3. Previously we noted that according to Bhaktivinoda *pratyakṣa* and *anumāna* may take place at one of two levels, namely, at the level of the soul or at the level of the body. Cognition at the level of the soul is *sahaja-samādhi,* whereas cognition at the level of the body is ordinary sense perception and reasoning. Here *vidvat-pratīti* is cognition at the level of the soul and *avidvat-pratīti* is cognition at the level of the body. In addition cognition may be mixed. To the degree that one is spiritually situated, one's perceptions are in terms of *vidvat-pratīti* and to the degree that one is *not* spiritually situated, one sees in terms of the *avidvat-pratīti.*

> observe the situation in different ways.[4] . . . Some see Goloka a little, others see a little more and still others see much more. Goloka is observed by the devotees in proportion to the grace bestowed upon them by Śrī Kṛṣṇa.[5]

Perception of *līlā* is not an either-or, all-or-nothing matter; it is a gradual process that is dependent on the internal perspective of the observer. If one considers whether or not the average observer would have seen the miraculous mountain lifting—the raising of Govardhana Hill by Kṛṣṇa to save the residents of Vrindavan from the wrath of Indra—he should know that it depends on the vision of the observer.[6] Describing the spiritual reality of Gokula on earth, he says:

> In Vraja (Gokula) everything is seen in tangible form by the influence of *yoga-māyā.* Yaśodā giving birth, Kṛṣṇa's maternity house, Abhimanyu, Govardhana and others getting married, and so on, are all seen in tangible material form. All these things are performed by the influence of *yoga-māyā* and are connected with their subtle original principle. Nothing is false and everything completely corresponds to what is in Goloka. Only what is seen varies according to the sensual obstruction of the observer. . . . The spiritual play of Kṛṣṇa is eternal. One who has acquired the capacity to observe spiritual reality sees Goloka even in Gokula. But one whose intelligence is affected by the external influence of worldly life cannot see Goloka. Although Gokula is Goloka, still such a per-

4. JD, 497-8: Appendix V, 37.
5. Ibid., 497: Appendix V, 38.
6. The *Caitanya-caritāmṛta* is full of incidents where spiritual events take place that cannot be seen by all who are present. For example, there is the incident of *choṭa* Haridāsa who committed suicide after rebuke from Caitanya and who then returns to sing nightly to Caitanya, but who is unseen by most of the *bhaktas.* (Antya 2/149–159) In another incident during a *kīrtana* and feeding festival Caitanya appears before Nityānanda Prabhu, but is unseen before all of the *bhaktas* of Nityānanda. (*Antya* 6/77–90)

> son will only see the material world of matter in Gokula due to a lack of spiritual vision.[7]

Although there are as many ways to perceive *līlā* as there are observers, Bhaktivinoda categorizes the perception of *līlā* according to the *adhikāra* of the observer. He writes:

> The pastimes of Vraja, as described in the *Bhāgavata*, are completely transcendental, and when they are read by a group of men, they produce an effect on them according to their respective competence (*adhikāra*). Those who are attached to mundane affairs hear these pastimes as if they involved an ordinary hero and heroine; those of intermediate competence (*madhyamādhikārīs*) experience them as manifestations of *cit* within mundane descriptions according to the principle of seeing Arundhatī; while those of the highest competence (*uttamādhikārīs*) immerse themselves in the *rasika* play of these divine sports beyond the scope of dull matter.[8]

Here three levels of perception are described: the literal, the symbolic, and the *rasika*. Those who hear *līlā* as if it were an ordinary dramatic activity experience *līlā* at its most basic level, the literal or narrative level. Those who understand *līlā* "according to the principle of seeing Arundhatī," which is to say as an indicator, perceive the symbolic level of *līlā;* and those who experience *līlā* as a pure relishable sentiment (*rasa*) beyond the scope of matter, perceive *līlā* in the most sublime way, the *rasika* level.

The literal level has two modes: with faith and without faith. Persons on the lowest level, who lack faith in God, see with the most blunt vision. Such persons are entirely attached to matter and only see with the *avidvat-pratīti*, materialistic vision. The story of Rādhā and Kṛṣṇa is perceived as an ordinary love affair, similar to that of Romeo and Juliet. By contrast, the *komala-śraddha* experiences *līlā* with an attitude of religious faith, which is vastly superior to those

7. JD, 498-499, 495: Appendix V, 39.
8. Ibid., 268: Appendix V, 40.

who observe *līlā* devoid of faith. Bhaktivinoda describes the position of *komala-śraddhas* as follows: "From the perspective of the *komala-śraddha* the *nidarśanas* of *līlā* are the location of complete faith. Apart from this basic understanding there is no other means for *komala-śraddhas* to advance."[9] Here Bhaktivinoda's expression, "the location of complete faith" means that *komala-śraddhas* accept the *nidarśanas* of *līlā* literally.

In this regard it is important to note the difference between theologians like Paul Tillich and Bhaktivinoda. According to Tillich one of the main functions of theological criticism is to prevent the reduction of symbols to the level of non-symbolic thinking. Tillich believes all religious thinking is symbolic and to take it literally is idolatrous. For Bhaktivinoda this is not the case. He never condemns the literal interpretation of *līlā*. According to him the fault is not with literalism *per se*, but with *madhyamādhikārīs* who mistakenly slip into the realm of the *komala-śraddha* when they should be seeking truth from a perspective suited to them. Spiritual truth can and must be approached according to the perspective of the recipient. Even the literal interpretation of *līlā* is beneficial because there is a direct link between the symbol as a *nidarśana* and its pure spiritual form. To meditate or to dwell on the indicators as the literal objects of the spirit, or in any other way to affix meaning to the *nidarśana*, even as symbols, has spiritual value. The indicator has the power to connect the practitioner to the real form.

We have already noted how Bhaktivinoda glorifies the wives of the *karma-kāṇḍī brāhmaṇas* for their literal understanding of *Kṛṣṇa-līlā*,[10] even above their *madhyamādhikārī* husbands. Although these ladies are described as *komala-śraddhas*, with only very simple faith in Kṛṣṇa, they far outshine their intellectual husbands, who lack even the most rudimentary elements of faith. Even though the literal understanding is preliminary,[11] it is full of spiritual merit and can

9. KS, *Saṁhitā* 7/2e: Appendix V, 41.

10. Ibid., 5/7e: Appendix V, 42.

11. Ibid.: *serūpa sthūla nirdeśa vyatīta tāṅhādera kramonnatira panthāntara nāi/* Bhaktivinoda uses the word *sthūla* to describe the vision of the *komala-śraddha*. I am taking the meaning as *preliminary* and not as *gross* or *coarse*.

lead to perfection. Failing the component of faith the literal level has little value.

Faith is paramount because faith leads to devotional feelings (*bhāva*), which are the key to advancement. The performance of religious practice without faith is compared to the pigeons that live in the temple towers or the fish that live in the Ganges. Although these creatures are in a favorable situation to take *prasāda* and hear the *kīrtana,* without devotional feelings they cannot take advantage of their holy habitations.[12] Incidentally, Bhaktivinoda's stress on religious sentiment as the means to spiritual advancement is reminiscent of Theodore Parker's assertion that religious sentiment provides a channel of direct communication to God.

Bhaktivinoda's only restriction to religious interpretation, whether it be from the *komala-śraddhas'* perspective or from the *madhyamādhikārīs'* perspective, is that it must not compromise the basic tenets of spiritual truth. Ascending religious symbolism is rejected whereas descending religious symbolism is accepted. The true understanding of *līlā* is not literal or even symbolic. The real point is *rasa*; whatever leads to *rasa* is accepted and whatever leads away from *rasa* is rejected. Religious literalism without faith is rejected whereas religious literalism with faith is accepted.

Śrī-mūrti

Let us look at another category of Vaiṣṇava theology, namely, the sacred image (*śrī-mūrti*) and see how Bhaktivinoda's religious approach affected this aspect of the tradition. As in the case of *Kṛṣṇa-līlā,* Bhaktivinoda argues that *śrī-mūrti* is also understood according to the competency (*adhikāra*) of the observer. Accordingly, he views *śrī-mūrti* in three basic ways: literally, symbolically and in terms of *rasa.*

During the nineteenth century many *bhadraloka* shunned image worship altogether. In the famous essay, "A Tract Against Idolatry," attributed to Raja Mohan Roy, image worship is rejected outright.

12. Kedarnath Datta Bhaktivinoda, *Tattva-viveka, Tattva-sūtra and Āmnāya-sūtra,* ed. Narasimha Brahmachari (Madras: Shree Gaudiya Math, 1979), 160.

The Christian missionaries of the day regarded image worship with the utmost degree of abhorrence. Similarly, both the Brahmo Samaj and the Arya Samaj rejected image worship. In general, there was a rejection of image worship among the *bhadraloka* during the nineteenth century. For those members of the *bhadraloka* who continued to follow the Hindu practice of image worship, many did so, not according to a traditional approach, but with a symbolic understanding. They felt the temple image was a man-made object —a focal point of worship—that was used by the worshipper to reach out to what is Divine. When the worshipper had achieved his goal, the image was discarded without further regard. Such a view is described in the following *āgama* text.

> Without a form, how can God be mediated upon? If (He is) without any form, where will the mind fix itself? When there is nothing for the mind to attach itself to, it will slip away from meditation or will glide into a state of slumber. Therefore, the wise meditate on some form, remembering, however, that the form is but a superimposition and not a reality.[13]

However, Bhaktivinoda rejects this view as *māyāvāda.* He writes:

> The worship of the Deity by the followers of the impersonal school is quite different from the Vaiṣṇava perspective. According to the impersonalist's school the Absolute is imagined in some material form and maintained during the time of worship, but afterwards the Deity is regarded as nothing more than a material object.[14]

Here the image is an object of this world used by a worshipper

13. *Viṣṇu-saṁhitā* XXIX 55-57. Cited in L. A. Ravi Varma, "Rituals of Worship" in H. Bhattacharya, ed. *The Cultural Heritage of India,* Vol. IV (Calcutta: Ramakrishna Mission Institute of Culture, 1956), 453.

14. JD, 74: *jñānavādīdigera pūjita-vigraha serūpa naya/ tāhādera mate ekaṭī pārthiva tattve brahmatā kalpita haiyā pūjā-kāla paryanta upasthita thāke/ pare se mūrti pārthiva vastu vai āra kichui naya/*

in an ascending symbolic process. This understanding, of course, is considered *māyāvāda* because it ascribes materialism to the form of God in the same way as it does to the understanding of divine *līlā.* If the nineteenth century *bhadraloka* could accept image worship at all, they did so in terms of this ascending symbolic process.

Faced with the challenge of explaining the rationale behind *śrī-mūrti* to the *bhadraloka,* Bhaktivinoda writes:

> Scriptural evidence for *śrī-mūrti* is well known. Therefore, only rational evidence will be shown here. The Supreme Lord does not have a material form, but is endowed with a transcendent spiritual form called *sat-cit-ānanda-vigraha.* The fullest manifestation of this transcendent form cannot be perceived by the conditioned *jīvas.* For this reason, in whatever fashion man conceives of God in this world, his conception must always assume a degree of idolatry. In language idolatry may be theoretically avoided, but not in practical worship. The supreme attractor, Śrī Kṛṣṇa, can be perceived in the heart to some extent through the help of divine love. When this form is perceived in the mind during meditation it assumes a greater degree of phenomenality. While being served through the body and senses in physical form *śrī-mūrti* assumes the greatest level of phenomenality. In reality the aspirants will eventually need to acquire transcendental sentiments toward all three forms of *śrī-mūrti. Śrī-mūrti* is the manifestation of God in the soul, in the mind, or in physical form.[15]

This passage declares that the spiritual existence of God is beyond anything that can be imagined in this world. But, in whatever way people conceive of God while in this world, their conception must be founded on the relations of this world. To Bhaktivinoda a mental image or even an intellectual conception of God is still a material image, albeit a subtle one. This is because mind (*manas*) is a material element as much as earth or water are.[16]

15. ST, Vol. 8 (1896), TV, 28-29: Appendix V, 43.

16. *Bhagavad-gītā* describes mind (*manas*) as one of the eight material elements:

The most subtle and sublime conception of God occurs in the soul (*ātmā*), next to this is the image that occurs in the mind (*manas*), and finally, at the most tangible level, is the form of God that one can physically touch at the level of the body (*deha*). The appearance of *śrī-mūrti* at the physical level is the form that is generally considered the sacred image, but according to Bhaktivinoda the form of God appearing at the level of the mind and soul is also the sacred image, *śrī-mūrti*.

In the *Jaiva-dharma* there is an interesting discussion in which a group of Muslim scholars approach the Vaiṣṇavas to discuss image worship. They ask: "Is it not better to meditate within the mind on God than to create a material image?" Bhaktivinoda answers, "There is no difference between the two because even mind and thought are material."[17] He points out that even if the physical image is rejected as idol worship, still the mental image that we conceptualize is also material, albeit more subtle. Due to human nature there is no other way to conceive of God except through a material image, be it subtle or gross. He writes:

> Even when one meditates on God in the mind, he imagines some image or idol that is composed of material qualities. To accept an earthen idol to be the divine image of God is as good as meditation on the gross material image in the heart. Therefore, however far one has advanced, it is best to conceive of God at that level. In fact, if there were no idol worship, human beings would have a great problem. When a common man becomes eager for God he loses hope if he cannot see an image of God before him. . . . Image worship is therefore the foundation of human religion.[18]

In the end Bhaktivinoda writes:

---

bhūmir āpo 'nalo vāyuḥ khaṁ mano buddhir eva ca/ ahaṅkāra itīyaṁ me bhinnā prakṛtir aṣṭadhā// BG 7/4

17. JD, 199: *dui samāna/ mana jaḍera angata, yāhā cintā karibe tāhāi jaḍa/*

18. Ibid., 197-8: Appendix V, 44.

> Everything depends on the sincerity of the heart of the one who worships. The more the heart is free from contact with matter, the more the person is able to worship the Divine Image of God[19] . . . For an elevated person the image is the all-conscious transcendent form of God. For a middle person, the image is formed of the mind, and for the lower person the image at first appears as gross matter, but when the thoughts gradually become purified, the spiritual image manifests Itself. Therefore the sacred image should be worshipped by all classes of *adhikārī*.[20]

Bhaktivinoda's explanation of *śrī-mūrti* affirms that the perception of divinity is a function of internal cognition. Seeing materially is simply seeing separate from the Divine. For one on the highest level, *śrī-mūrti* "is the all-conscious transcendent form of God." This is the *rasika* level of understanding, wherein the *sādhaka* may enter into a personal relationship with the Deity. For the second class person, *śrī-mūrti* "is formed of the mind," which is to say, the Deity appears in a symbolic fashion according to either a system of ascending or descending symbolism. And for the lowest person, *śrī-mūrti* "appears as inert matter," in other words, as a mere statue. Only by gradual spiritual advancement may the spiritual image of God be perceived.[21]

---

19. Ibid., 196: Appendix V, 45.
20. Ibid., 198: Appendix V, 46.
21. It would appear that according to Bhaktivinoda what *śāstra* describes as the transubstantiation of matter into spirit during the *prāṇa-pratiṣṭhā* ceremony is actually the installation or awakening of awareness of *śrī-mūrti* in the minds of the observers and not the installation of God in matter. The spirit of God already exists everywhere. From God's perspective both matter and spirit are His energies, but from the human perspective, matter is seen without relation to God. Therefore, during the *prāṇa-pratiṣṭhā* ceremony, what in the beginning is perceived as matter, in the end is perceived as spirit. Matter has not changed, but how matter is perceived has changed. Through the power of ritual, human consciousness is elevated, at least from the gross level to the symbolic level, if not beyond. Divine realization is divine seeing. This, of course, depends on the *adhikāra* of the individual.

Holy Name (Nāma)

Finally, we come to the matter of Holy Name. In the *Caitanya-sampradāya* there is no aspect of the tradition more important than Holy Name. The great dictum from the *Bṛhad-nāradīya-purāṇa* rules the day: *harer nāma harer nāma harer nāmaiva kevalam/ kalau nāsty eva nāsty eva nāsty eva gatir anyathā.* "In this age of Kali there is no other means of deliverance, no other means, no other means than the name of Hari, the name of Hari, just the name of Hari."[22]

As in the case of divine *līlā* and *śrī-mūrti*, Holy Name appears in three modes according to the *adhikāra* of the participants: divine name itself (*nāma*), semblance of the name (*nāmābhāsa*), and the name uttered with offense (*nāmāparādha*). We will review each of these modes successively.

In the section of *Jaiva-dharma* that deals specifically with Holy Name, Bhaktivinoda gives over twenty quotes that show the importance of Holy Name (*nāma*) in its various aspects, but to serve our purpose I will give only three of his citations and with just one of his comments. From the *Padma-purāṇa* he cites the following verse:

> The name of Kṛṣṇa is the crest jewel of all names; it is the embodiment of all consciousness and sentiments; it is complete; it is pure; it is ever free because the name and the possessor of the name are one and the same.[23]

From the *Brahmāṇḍa-purāṇa* he cites the verse: "The results that are gained by three times reciting one thousand names of Viṣṇu (*sahasra-nāma*) are obtained by uttering the name of Kṛṣṇa only once."[24] And in the *Bhāgavata* it is said:

> All that was gained in the Satya-yuga through the medita-

---

22. *Bṛhad-nāradīya-purāṇa* 3/8/126.

23. JD, 408: (*Padma-purāṇa*): *nāma cintāmaṇiḥ kṛṣṇaścaitanya-rasa-vigrahaḥ/ pūrṇaḥ śuddho nitya-mukto 'bhinnatvān nāmanāminoḥ//*

24. Ibid., 409: *sahasra-nāmāṁ puṇyānāṁ trirāvṛttyā tu yat phalam/ ekāvṛttyā tu kṛṣṇasya nāmaikaṁ tat prayacchati//*

> tion on Viṣṇu, in the Tretā-yuga through the performance of sacrifice, and in Dvāpara-yuga through service, is obtained in the Kali-yuga through the chanting of the name of Hari.[25]

Regarding these verses he comments:

> The name and the possessor of the name are inseparable, so all the transcendental qualities of Kṛṣṇa, who is the possessor of the name, exist in His name. The name is always a perfect thing, the name of Hari is never touched by matter, it is ever free because it is never bound by illusion. The name *is* Kṛṣṇa Himself, and so it is the embodiment of all consciousness and all sentiments. The name is like the *cintāmaṇi* gem, which is the fulfiller of all wishes."[26]

In fact there are dozens of such verses and comments recorded throughout the *Jaiva-dharma* and other works, and after hearing them the rational mind soon begins to wonder whether or not all this praise is to be taken literally or whether it is just poetic embellishment or exaggeration. Vaiṣṇava tradition, however, affirms the credibility of these statements and the efficacy of the divine name. It is no wonder that the *bhadraloka* were alienated by such literal interpretations of Holy Name. Anticipating the doubts of the *bhadraloka,* Bhaktivinoda, speaking through the words of Vijaya Kumāra, asks, "How can a mere name, which is nothing but a combination of letters, be more than mundane words?"[27] Bābājī answers as follows:

> The name of Hari is not born in this material world. A soul who is an infinitesimal part of the Infinite is only eligible to pronounce the name of God when he lives in his own pure transcendental body. Nobody of this world

25. Ibid., 407: (BP 12/ 3/52) *kṛte yad-vyāyato viṣṇuṁ tretāyāṁ yajato makhaiḥ/ dvāpare paricaryāyāṁ kalau tad hari-kīrtanāt//*
26. Ibid., 408: Appendix V, 47.
27. Ibid.: *nāmākṣara kirūpe māyika-śabdera atīta haite pāre?*

> who lies in the bondage of illusion is able to utter the pure name, but when the real self works through the grace of the *hlādinī-śakti*, it is then that the real name of God appears. With the appearance of the divine name, the pure name most kindly descends on the mind of the devotee and begins to dance on his tongue sanctified by devotion. The name is not just a combination of syllables; only when it dances on the material tongue does it assume the shape of letters. This is the mystery of the Name.[28]

In other words, when *śāstra* talks about the glory of Divine Name it is not referring to the material sound, but to the spiritual sound that is evoked through material sound by a qualified person at the time of the utterance of the Holy Name. Elsewhere he says that merely reciting the external syllables of the Holy Name is not the actual Holy Name.[29] He states that pure name is the result of a state of consciousness, which is completely devoid of other desires.[30] Finally he tells us that "the name of Kṛṣṇa that is uttered with wholehearted devotion and unalloyed love is the true name of Kṛṣṇa; anything else is but a semblance of the name (*nāmābhāsa*), or the name uttered with offense (*nāmāparādha*)."[31]

As in the case of *līlā* and *śrī-mūrti*, the internal competence (*adhikāra*) of the person who utters and hears the name is paramount. Only a person who has achieved the highest degree of devotional saturation can utter the actual Holy Name, and then, to what degree a hearer can perceive the actual name is dependent on the devotional attributes of the hearer. In other words, the appearance of divine name in this world is viewed in precisely the same way as *līlā* and *śrī-mūrti*. It is a matter of divine descent and internal personal perspective. When *śāstra* extols the glories of

28. Ibid.: Appendix V, 48.

29. *nāma-kara bahir haya, nāma nihi haya/ Hwi '74.12A/B.T.G. Handbook, 43.*

30. JD, 426: *anyābhilāṣitā-śūnya o jñāna-karmādidvārā anāvṛta, ānukūlya-bhāvera sahita nāma karile śuddha-nāma haya/*

31. Ibid., 411: *sampūrṇa-śraddhodita ananya-bhaktite ye kṛṣṇa-nāmera udaya haya, tāhākei "kṛṣṇa-nāma" bale, taditare ye kichu nāmera mata lakṣita haya tāhā haya nāmābhāsa, naya nāmāparādha haiyā thāke/*

divine name, there is no exaggeration because it is referring to the actual spiritual name of God, which is not different from God. *Śāstra* is not refering to the material sound composed of the various letters and phonemes.

For this reason Bhaktivinoda is deeply concerned with the mode of uttering the Holy Name. The actual utterance of the name is never a mechanical act that a skillful speaker with the correct intonation can evoke. The ability to utter the name is an act of divine grace bestowed upon those devotees who have saturated their minds and bodies with devotion in the same way as the ability to perceive the *rasika* level of divine *līlā* or *śrī-mūrti* is an act of divine grace. Until that time what is uttered is something less than the divine name, known as semblance of the name (*nāmābhāsa*) or the name uttered with offense (*nāmāparādha*). Bhaktivinoda writes, "Obstacles against the divine name are of two kinds: major and minor. If a minor obstacle stands in the way, the name uttered becomes a semblance of the name (*nāmābhāsa*), but if a major obstacle stands in the way, the name uttered becomes an offense against the name (*nāmāparādha*)."[32]

Nāmābhāsa is defined as, "That which appears like the divine name, but is not actually the Holy Name."[33] Semblance of the name is the result of ignorance, mistake, or confusion where the name of God is uttered without devotion or clear understanding. But even such a material utterance of *nāmābhāsa* has great spiritual value because it is directly related to the spiritual sound as a *nidarśana.* This is illustrated in the story of Ajāmila, who had become infatuated with an outcaste woman in his youth. When, at the moment of death, he called out the name of Nārāyaṇa, his favorite son, he was given protection by Viṣṇu and saved from hell because he had called out the name of God. Nārāyaṇa, of course, is one of the major names of Hari and even though Ajāmila was calling his son and not Hari directly, his utterance of the name of Nārāyaṇa

32. Ibid., 414: *ei pratibandhaka dui prakāra arthāt sāmānya o bṛhat—sāmānya pratibandhaka thākile uccārita nāma "nāmābhāsa" haya, ... bṛhat pratibandhaka thākile uccārita nāma "nāmāparādha" haya.*
33. Ibid., JD, Eng, 373.

was an *ābhāsa* or semblance of the real name of Nārāyaṇa. In this context the *Bhāgavata* describes *nāmābhāsa* as follows: "The wise know that taking the name of the Lord of Vaikuṇṭha (Nārāyaṇa) even indirectly to indicate something else, jokingly, for musical entertainment, or even neglectfully can destroy unlimited sins."[34] Ajāmila's utterance of "Nārāyaṇa" to indicate his son is technically called *sāṅketyam,* meaning "assigned to something else," but because the sound *nārāyaṇa* is a *nidarśana* of Nārāyaṇa, Ajāmila gained tremendous spiritual benefit and was saved from hell.

Nāmāparādha, on the other hand, is an utterance of Holy Name that is made consciously with malice in the heart. It is the grossest form of utterance. Quoting Rūpa Gosvāmī, Bhaktivinoda cites ten specific offenses against divine name that are considered to relegate *nāma* to the condition of *nāmāparādha:* 1) to slander the holy saints who propagate the divine name, 2) to consider the divine name as different from the owner of the name, 3) to consider one's preceptor who knows the underlying truth of the divine name to be an ordinary person, 4) to slander the holy scriptures that propagate the name, 5) to think that the glories of divine name are an exaggeration, 6) to think the names are imaginary, 7) to commit sin on the strength of the divine name, 8) to consider the utterance of the divine to be the same as worldly religious acts, 9) to instruct the faithless about the divine name, and 10) to not have faith in the name in spite of hearing instruction on the power of the name. [35] Bhaktivinoda cautions that any one of these offenses can constitute a major obstacle to the utterance of divine name and should be carefully guarded against.

Similar to divine *līlā* or *śrī-mūrti,* the manifestation of Holy Name is dependent on the spiritual competency (*adhikāra*) of both the transmitter and the receiver of *nāma.* Whether or not there is the manifestation of the divine through matter is dependent on the spiritual competency of the person uttering the name. Similarly,

34. *Bhāg.*, 6.2.14: *sāṅketyaṁ pārihāsyaṁ vā stobhaṁ helanam eva vā/ vaikuṇṭha-nāma-grahaṇam aśeṣāgha-haraṁ viduḥ//*

35. JD, Eng., 362.

whether or not that manifestation can be recognized and appreciated to its fullest extent is also dependent on the spiritual competency of the person who hears the name. The principle of spiritual competency is a most important feature of Bhaktivinoda's theology and the one which affects all aspects of his approach whether we are examining divine *līlā*, *śrī-mūrti*, or Divine Name.

Conclusion

Bhaktivinoda has pointed out that spiritual perception is ultimately more a function of internal perspective than of external reality. Reason is an important tool that human beings have to discern spiritual truths. However, reason has distinct limitations. Beyond reason is the innate "seeing" ability of the soul, known as *sahaja-samādhi*, that may be utilized to progress even further along the spiritual path. There are different levels of *adhikāra* or spiritual competence and accordingly the various *adhikārīs* interpret and understand spiritual truths in various ways.

In the past, great spiritual seekers and mystics, those of the highest *adhikāra*, have used the facility of *sahaja-samādhi* to perceive spiritual truths. Some of their experiences have been recorded as scripture or *śāstra*. Unfortunately, human language is a crude tool and can never completely describe spiritual truth. Nevertheless, because this phenomenal world is a *vikāra* or imperfect modification of an absolute spiritual reality, the things of this world can serve as significant indicators (*nidarśanas*) of spiritual reality. In this way *śāstra* often describes spiritual events in terms of the events of this phenomenal world, and according to the *adhikāra* of the individual these spiritual events will be understood in different ways.

What is perceived of *Kṛṣṇa-līlā* from the pages of the *Bhāgavata* depends on the *adhikāra* of the observer. Some will hear these stories as mere fiction, some will perceive them in a symbolic manner and others will perceive them according to a *rasika* mood. The activities of Kṛṣṇa that are recorded in the pages of the *Bhāgavata* are a record of the spiritual vision of Śukadeva, mediated by the revered Vyāsa. These great visionaries witnessed these events, but whether or not you and I can perceive these events as they did depends on our *adhikāra* or ability to perceive spiritual reality; and this, of course, is dependent on our faith. In a similar manner, other divine manifestations such as the sacred image or divine name will be perceived according to the level of faith and *adhikāra* of the observer or hearer.

Bhaktivinoda assumed the role of modern theologian, mediating the Vaiṣṇava tradition to the *bhadraloka* of his day. Convinced that religious faith, regardless of its cultural mode, was universal, and assuming the perspective of *sāragrāhī,* he sought to show the *bhadraloka* how traditional religious faith might legitimately be expressed in terms of contemporary nineteenth century Bengali culture.

Bhaktitirtha Ṭhākura (1865–1922), Kedarnath Datta Bhaktivinoda (1838–1914) and Bipin Bihari Goswami (1848–1919).

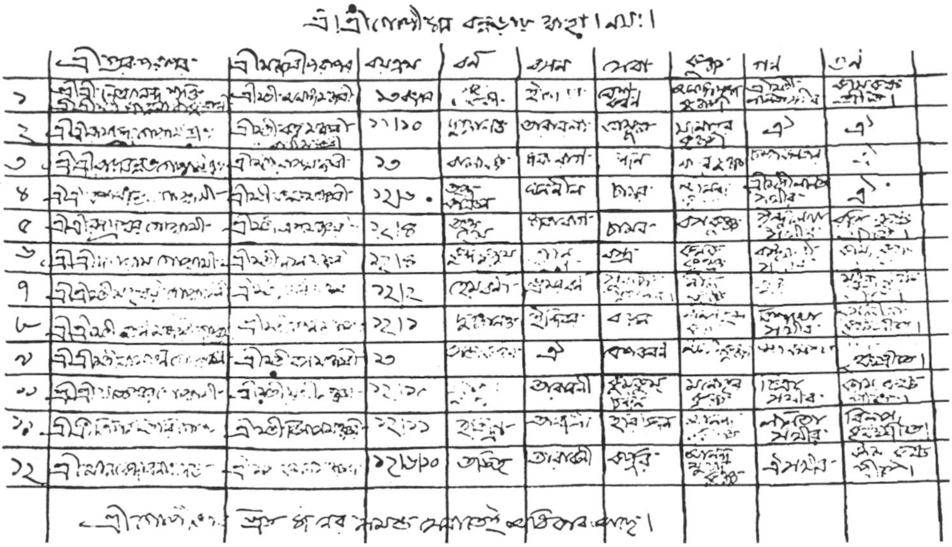

Kedarnath Datta Bhaktivinoda's handwritten *siddha-praṇālī* chart.

Chapter Eight

Sādhana

> The *Bhagavat* does not allow its followers to ask anything from God except eternal love towards Him. The kingdom of the world, the beauties of the local heavens, and the sovereignty over the material world are never the subjects of Vaishnav prayer. The Vaishnav meekly and humbly says, "Father, Master, God, Friend and Husband of my soul! . . . I have called You my God; let my soul be wrapped up in admiration at Your greatness! I have addressed You as my Master; let my soul be strongly devoted to your service. I have called You my friend; let my soul be in reverential love towards You and not in dread or fear! I have called You my husband; let my spiritual nature be in eternal union with You, forever loving and never dreading, or feeling disgust. Father! Let me have strength enough to go up to You as the consort of my soul, so that we may be one in eternal love!"[1]

These words admonish us to pass beyond the mere worship of God out of fear or obedience and to embrace one of the *rasika* modes of worship as admirer, servant, friend, father, or lover. If there is one word that best denotes the essence of this prayer and describes Bhaktivinoda's religious development, it is *rasa,* devotional sentiment. It is his desire for *rasa* that allows him to sort through the colliding speculations of nineteenth century philosophy and religion, and it is *rasa* that eventually leads him to embrace the reli-

1. Kedarnath Datta, *The Bhagavat, Its Philosophy, Ethics and Theology*, ed. Bhaktivilas Tirtha, 2d ed. (Madras: Madras Gaudiya Math, 1959), 29-30.

gion of the Caitanya Vaiṣṇavas.

Religion as *rasika* experience may at first seem strange, particularly in the West, where religion is judged typically in terms of morality. But for Bhaktivinoda the moral basis of religion is only the preliminary stage in religious development.[2] Beyond morality is the cultivation of devotion (*sādhana-bhakti*), and beyond the cultivation of devotion is the *rasika* experience itself. The *rasika* experience, however, assumes one's ability to taste that experience. Therefore Bhaktivinoda declares, "*Rasa* is not the subject of knowledge, but of taste (*āsvāda*). However, taste, which is the culmination of knowledge, does not arise until inquiry and attainment, the two preliminary aspects of knowledge are complete. . . . Without taste there can be no *rasa*."[3]

In this chapter we examine Bhaktivinoda's views on the religious practice (*sādhana-bhakti*), which is the principal means by which the embers of religious faith are fanned and nurtured into the full flame of *rasika*[4] experience. Most of Bhaktivinoda's writings include a major discussion on this topic. His autobiography (*Svalikhita-jīvanī*) and journal (*Sajjana-toṣaṇī*) show how religious practice was a major factor in his personal life. For Bhaktivinoda, life is the divine journey of the soul, an unfolding from one stage of development to successively higher stages. It is one that ultimately culminates in an unlimited expansion of eternal play and joy in communion with the Divine. This is the *rasika* experience.

Faith as the Natural Condition of the Soul

The journey of the soul begins with faith. Faith in God is the natural condition of the soul and something that manifests at

2. CS, pt. 1, 233-234: *nara-jīvana pañca-prakāra yathā:* 1. *nīta-śūnya jīvana/* 2. *kevala-naitika jīvana/* 3. *seśvara-naitika jīvana/* 4. *sādhana-bhakta jīvana/* 5. *bhāva-bhakta jīvana/*

3. CS, pt. 2, 6: Appendix V, 49.

4. For a good explanation of the concept of *rasa* as it is understood within the Caitanya Vaiṣṇava schools see: David L. Haberman, *Acting as a Way of Salvation* (New York: Oxford University Press, 1988), 23-39. Also see O. B. L. Kapoor, *The Philosophy and Religion of Śrī Caitanya* (Delhi: Munshiram Manoharlal, 1977), 213-230.

almost every stage of human development. Bhaktivinoda describes this condition:

> From a careful consideration of the historical records and traditions of the inhabitants of this land and foreign countries, it is evident that faith in God is a common characteristic of human life. Even uncivilized tribes that eat flesh like animals offer worship and salutations to the sun and the moon, large mountains, rivers and great trees, with the belief that these things control the necessities of their lives. Why is this? It is faith in God, which is a symptom of the religious quality of consciousness.[5]

For Bhaktivinoda, human consciousness has a natural religious component that is indicated by faith in God. Again the influence of the American Unitarian, Theodore Parker, seems evident. Parker insisted that man is by nature religious, "that he was made to be religious, as much as an ox was made to eat grass."[6] Hence the existence of God is not something that human beings must discover. It is, as Parker continues, "a truth fundamental in our nature; given outright by God; a truth which comes to light as soon as self-consciousness begins."[7] As human consciousness evolves, human religious development similarly evolves. Bhaktivinoda notes:

> All souls have the capability of worshipping the Divine, but how that Divinity is understood depends on the degree of impurity in the worshipper's heart. According to the internal condition (*saṁskāra)* of the worshipper the Divine is worshipped in five religious types: *śākta, saura, gāṇapatya, śaiva,* and *vaiṣṇava*. . . . From the doubtful stage, to those having full knowledge of the Absolute, every soul has the capacity to worship the Divine. The

5. CS, pt. 1, 8: Appendix V, 50.
6. Quoted from Conrad Wright, *Three Prophets of Religious Liberalism: Channing–Emerson–Parker* (Boston: Unitarian Universalist Association, fourth printing, 1980), 33.
7. Ibid.

> purity and elevation of love (*rāga)* are indications of the soul's development. All souls should worship the independent Supreme Divinity, who is *sat cit ānanda.*[8]

In this passage the terms *śākta, saura, gāṇapatya, śaiva,* and *vaiṣṇava* do not refer to the corresponding religious sects of India. Instead they are categories of religious typology or modes of personal religious consciousness. In his *Kṛṣṇa-saṁhitā* Bhaktivinoda points out, "In all countries and at all times these religious types are prevalent even though they may have different names. If we examine the religions that exist in this country as well as in foreign countries, we see that in one way or another they can be categorized according to these five religious types."[9] For example, Buddhism and Jainism are *śaiva* type religions because they recognize human consciousness as the highest developmental principle; Islam and Christianity are *vaiṣṇava* type religions because they recognize a Supreme Godhead as the highest principle.[10] As Bhaktivinoda views history as a progressive evolution, he regards religious development as an evolution to higher stages of spiritual growth. The idea of progressive development through various stages suggests the influence of European thinkers such as Auguste Comte, whose ideas on human development viewed man as evolving through numerous stages of social and technological development. The *bhadraloka* similarly viewed history, culture, and society as advancing through various phases.

Bhaktivinoda points out that as man passes through various stages of development certain impediments also arise. The rewards of civilization are not always supportive of religious faith. Consequently, the faithful yearnings of the soul are often thwarted. He writes:

> After coming to the civilized state the soul cultivates

8. ST, vol. 8 (1896), TS p. 176-177: Appendix V, 51.
9. 1. KS, *Upakramaṇikā,* 10: Appendix V, 52.
10. Ibid., 11: *khrīṣṭa o mahammadera dharma sāmpradāyika vaiṣṇava-dharmera sadṛśa/ bauddha o jaina-dharma śaiva-dharma sadṛśa/*

> various kinds of learning that often cover its natural faith with impure reasoning. This gives way to the state of atheism or the doctrine of *nirvāṇa,* which is a kind of "non-difference" doctrine. But we should realize that such ugly beliefs are the symptoms of an unhealthy condition of immature consciousness. In human life there are three intermediate stages between the base uncivilized stage and the beautiful stage of full faith in God. These stages are categorized as atheism, materialism, and agnosticism (or the *nirvāṇa* doctrine), which are diseases that block the soul's development and so lead one to assume some very low positions.[11]

In this way the soul's natural expression of religious faith is often subverted. However, even the atheistic and agnostic impositions of human civilization cannot endure forever. He cites the example of a Burmese Buddhist gentleman who talked of God as the creator who incarnates as the Buddha and who resides in heaven. "This man clearly knew nothing of the doctrine of the Buddha," Bhaktivinoda writes, "Instead he was describing, in the name of Buddhist philosophy, what is natural for human nature."[12] Even amidst the atheistic and agnostic tendencies of human civilization, faith in God ultimately prevails. And while a doctrine may initially be devoid of devotional qualities, human nature, being what it is, eventually adds the elements of faith and devotion. No form of human endeavor ever remains long separated from the soul's natural faith.

Bhaktivinoda concludes: "The universal affection of Comte, Jaimini's God in the form of *apūrva,* based on the atheistic doctrine of karma, and the Buddhist's doctrine of materialistic extinction (*nirvāṇa-vāda*) are gradually transformed by their followers into the natural religion of the human being."[13] Faith and devotion to God are the two essential qualities of the soul that manifest in terms of

11. CS, pt. 1, 8-9: Appendix V, 53.
12. ST, vol. 4 (1892), TV., 69: Appendix V, 54.
13. Ibid., TV, 70: Appendix V, 55.

the infinite varieties of human religious experience. Even though human culture is diverse, primary human nature is the same the world over.[14]

From another perspective, Bhaktivinoda categorizes human spiritual development in the following way: 1) life without morality, 2) moral life without God, 3) moral life with God, 4) regulated devotional life, and 5) spontaneous devotional life.[15] Immoral life and moral life without God have little regard for what is divine. The third stage, moral life with God, is of two types, one that imagines some form of God and the other that accepts a genuine form of God. Moral life that simply imagines a form of God does not focus on God directly but, for moral purposes, postulates a theoretical God. By contrast, moral life that accepts a genuine form of God recognizes the spiritual existence of a real God, Who is the foundation of all morality. The first three stages—immoral life, moral life without God, and moral life that simply imagines a form of God—all present a view of life that is limited to the realm of rational thought.[16] Such levels of development provide little spiritual satisfaction for want of divine vision and true religious faith. However, from the stage of moral life that accepts a genuine form of God, true devotional practice begins.[17]

The *Bhāgavata* and Religious Practice

The question arises, what then is the best means to cultivate devotion? Bhaktivinoda answers by stating that the main characteristics of devotional practice (*sādhana-bhakti*) are inherent in the acts of hearing, glorification, and remembrance (of God). This reply is consonant with the *Bhāgavata*'s observation that attraction and love for the things of this world develop naturally from the hearing and

14. CS, pt. 1, 10: *mānavera mukhya-prakṛti sarvatrai eka/ gauṇa-prakṛti pṛthak pṛthak/*
15. Ibid., 234: *nara-jīvana pañca-prakāra yathā:* 1. *nīta-śūnya jīvana/* 2. *kevala-naitika jīvana/* 3. *seśvara-naitika jīvana/* 4. *sādhana-bhakta jīvana/* 5. *bhāva-bhakta jīvana/*
16. Ibid., 234: *mukti paryanta manovṛtti tāhāte parilakṣita haya/*
17. Ibid., 235: *ataeva vāstavika seśvara-naitika jīvane sādhana-bhaktimaya jīvanei vikacita-cetana jīva parilakṣita hana/*

praising of an object.[18] In other words, the natural attributes of hearing, glorification, and remembrance form the basis of attraction and love in this world, and if these basic attributes can be turned in the direction of what is eternal and Supreme, instead of what is temporary and material, then absolute communion with the Supreme can result. Therefore, Bhaktivinoda writes, "The main characteristics of devotional practice are inherent in the acts of hearing, glorification and remembrance of the divine name, qualities, form and pastimes of Kṛṣṇa."[19]

We have seen how the *Bhāgavata* describes Absolute reality as undifferentiated knowledge and how that Absolute reality is differentiated according to three grades of reality, namely *brahman*, *paramātmā*, and *bhagavān*. According to the Caitanya Vaiṣṇavas, *bhagavān* is the highest reality and of all the various forms of *bhagavān* the form of Śrī Kṛṣṇa is the highest because it leads to the highest level of *rasika* experience. The narration of the *Bhāgavata*, therefore, culminates in its tenth canto with the *līlā* of Śrī Kṛṣṇa, who is described as the embodiment of all *rasa (akhila-rasa-mūrti)*. Bhaktivinoda writes, "The great Vyāsa, in his divine wisdom, delivered this ocean of *rasa* through the pages of the *Bhāgavata* with the aid of pictures from the material world."[20] We are repeatedly invited to dive into this ocean of spiritual happiness by following the path of devotional practice called *sādhana-bhakti*.

However, explanation of devotional practice is not the main purpose of the *Bhāgavata*. Instead, its business is to present the basic spiritual substance for hearing, glorification, and remembrance, as well as the theological framework with which to understand this material.[21] Few details of devotional practice beyond what is most

18. *Bhāg.*, 1/19/39: *yac chrotavyam atho japyaṁ yat kartavyaṁ nṛbhiḥ prabho/ smartavyaṁ bhajanīyaṁ vā brūhi yad vā viparyayam//*

19. CS, pt. 1, 62: *kṛṣṇera nāma, guṇa, rūpa, līlā-kathā śravaṇa, kīrtana, smaraṇa ityādi kāryai sādhana-bhaktir svarūpa-lakṣaṇa/*

20. Datta, *The Bhagavat*, 33.

21. For example, Bhakta Prahlāda describes the process of bhakti as a combination of nine devotional practices. He prays, "Hearing and glorifying Lord Viṣṇu, remembering and serving His lotus feet, offering worship and praying to Him,

natural are mentioned in the *Bhāgavata.* Over the progression of time, it was the task of later theologians to arrange these natural processes into a formal system of mental and physical training called *sādhana-bhakti.*

Sādhana-bhakti

For Bhaktivinoda three names stand out for their contributions to devotional practice: Rūpa Gosvāmī (1489–1564), Gopāla Guru (*ca.* 1550), and Dhyānacandra Gosvāmī (*ca.* 1600). Rūpa Gosvāmī is most famous for creating the very foundations of devotional practice amongst the Caitanya Vaiṣṇavas. Later Gopāla Guru and Dhyānacandra Gosvāmī added their thoughts to Rūpa's system of *rāgānugā-bhakti-sādhana.*

It is not necessary to describe the details of their system of devotional practice; suffice it to say that bhakti may be divided into three divisions: *vaidhī-bhakti-sādhana, rāgānugā-bhakti-sādhana* and *rāgātmikā-bhakti.*[22] *Vaidhī-bhakti-sādhana* entails the following of a specific set of devotional rules[23] and *rāgānugā-bhakti-sādhana* involves following the moods of those who possess *rāgātmikā-bhakti,* or spontaneous love for God.[24] What we want to focus on is how Bhaktivinoda reinterpreted and presented this system of devotion to the *bhadraloka* in the context of nineteenth century modernity.

For the most part, Bhaktivinoda's interpretation of Rūpa Gosvāmī's system of *sādhana-bhakti* is orthodox. He adds to the

---

serving Him, considering Him one's best friend, and surrendering everything to Him are the nine ways of pure devotion." (BP 7/5.23-24)

22. BRS, 1/2/5: *vaidhī rāgānugā ceti sā dvidhā sādhanābhidhā//* The simple distinction between the two is that *vaidhī-bhakti* is followed according to the commands or rules (*vidhis*) of *śāstra* and guru whereas *rāgānugā-bhakti* is followed out of a spontaneous longing (*lobha*) for devotion.

23. The word *vaidhī* is derived from "*vidhi*" meaning "rules." Specifically, *vidhi* refers to the sixty-four limbs (*aṅgas*) of bhakti that Rūpa Gosvāmī enumerates.

24. Rūpa Gosvāmī defines *rāgānugā-bhakti-sādhana* as, "that method of bhakti which follows the mood of the *rāgātmikā-bhakti* [that] clearly manifests itself in the residents of Vraja." Thus the term *rāgānugā* appropriately means "following the passion." Here the residents of Vraja, mother Yaśodā, Nanda Mahārāja, the various

discussion by commenting on the social side of *sādhana-bhakti*. Caitanya theologians such as Gopālaguru Gosvāmī, Narottama Dāsa (*ca.* 1600), Dhyānacandra Gosvāmī, and Viśvanātha Cakravartī (*ca.* 1700) give only limited attention to *sādhana-bhakti* and its relationship to society (*varṇāśrama*). Their focus was on *rāgānugā-bhakti-sādhana*. No doubt the changes that had occurred in the lives of the *bhadraloka* and the misuse of *sādhana-bhakti* by fringe groups of Vaiṣṇavas demanded Bhaktivinoda's commentary on *sādhana-bhakti* and society.

Bhaktivinoda begins his explanation of *sādhana-bhakti* by stating that devotional practice (*sādhana-bhakti*) best takes place within a supportive social and cultural environment—and the social and cultural environment that best supports that practice is *varṇāśrama-dharma*. He says, "*Vaidha-bhaktas* should always try to bring their hearts to the lotus feet of Kṛṣṇa while spending their lives situated in *varṇāśrama-dharma*. This is *bhakti-yoga*."[25]

Varṇāśrama-dharma is the organization of society into four *varṇas* and four *āśramas*[26] fashioned according to scientific principles. This is what Bhaktivinoda calls *vaijñānika-varṇāśrama*, or scientific *varṇāśrama*. He writes: "Truly, all sympathetic and scientific persons will agree that social rules reached their climax at the hands of the *ṛṣis*, who, with scientific understanding, divided the rules of society in a two-fold way: according to *varṇa* and according to *āśrama*."[27]

---

gopālas and *gopikās* and so on, become role models, who exhibit a perfect love for Kṛṣṇa that Rūpa Gosvāmī calls *rāgātmikā-bhakti*. The *rāgātmikā-bhakti* of the Vrajaloka, the residents of Vrindavan, is a spontaneous love that totally binds the worshipper and the worshipped. Thus the love of the Vrajaloka is a fit model for those engaged in *rāgānugā-bhakti-sādhana*. In this way the *sādhaka* studies the emotional status of the Vrajaloka and, by hearing the stories involving these individuals, learns to follow the mood of their *rāgātmikā-bhakti*.

25. CS, pt. 1, 140: Appendix V, 56.

26. The four *varṇas* are *brāhmaṇas* (the priestly class), *kṣatriyas* (the martial class), *vaiśyas* (the mercantile community) and *śudras* (the laborers). The four *āśramas* are *brahmacārīs* (student), *gṛhasthas* (householder), *vānaprasthas* (retired) and *sannyasīs* (renounced).

27. Ibid., 83: Appendix V, 57.

The *varṇas* were established in accordance with an individual's nature (*svabhāva*) and the *āśramas* were established with respect to an individual's relationship to society.[28] The system of *varṇas* and *āśramas* that Bhaktivinoda refers to is not the traditional caste system of his time. In his opinion the existing caste system was only a remnant of that ancient and scientific *vaijñānika-varṇāśrama* system.

Bhaktivinoda is critical of the prevailing caste system, particularly over the issue of birth as the selective criterion of *varṇa*. He equates this form of *varṇāśrama* with *smārta-dharma*.[29] He points out that originally the system of *varṇāśrama* was pure and based on scientific principles, but gradually from the time of Jamadagni and Paraśurāma, the system became corrupt and deviated from its original purpose. As a result, a quarrel broke out between the *brāhmaṇas* and *kṣatriyas* so the scientific system of *varṇāśrama-dharma* gradually degraded. Due to the selfish desires of the *brāhmaṇas,* birth as the criteria of *varṇa* was inscribed into the *Manu-saṁhitā* and other *dharma-śāstras*.[30] In frustration, the rebellious *kṣatriyas* created Buddhism and the *vaiśyas* created Jainism and both tried to bring the downfall of *brāhmaṇism*. This weakened Vedic culture and eventually allowed outside *mleccha* kings to take control of India. The present caste system is the corrupted remnant of that originally pure scientific *varṇāśrama-dharma*.

Bhaktivinoda notes that there is a natural system of *varṇāśrama* that functions within all human societies. He writes:

> When we consider the modern societies of Europe, whatever beauty exists in these societies depends upon the natural *varṇāśrama* that exists within them. In Europe those who have the nature of traders are fond of trading and thereby advance themselves by trade. Those who have the nature of *kṣatriyas* adopt the military life, and those who have the nature of *śūdras* love doing menial service.[31]

28. Ibid.: Appendix V, 58.
29. Ibid., 131: Appendix V, 59.
30. Ibid., 109-110: Appendix V, 60.
31. Ibid., 107: Appendix V, 61.

In its broadest sense *varṇāśrama* is the system of rules of civilized life that pertain to physical, intellectual, social, and religious development. Every culture and every society has a set of cultural rules to regulate its civic life and the personal lives of its participants. No society can function without adopting the system of *varṇāśrama* to some extent. Bhaktivinoda writes, "In reality, no society can smoothly carry on unless the *varṇa* system is more or less adopted."[32] In Bhaktivinoda's opinion the ancient Greek, Roman and even the modern nineteenth century European societies are examples of natural *varṇāśrama* societies. However, even though these societies all show a natural form of *varṇāśrama*, he stops short of calling them scientific (*vaijñānika*) *varṇāśrama*. He continues, "Though the nations of Europe follow the *varṇa* system to some extent, it is not scientific.[33] . . . In Europe, and for that matter in all countries except India, it is the nonscientific *varṇa* system that guides them."[34]

What Bhaktivinoda calls scientific (*vaijñānika*) *varṇāśrama* is the original Vedic *varṇāśrama-dharma*. The most distinguishing feature of Vedic *varṇāśrama* is that *varṇa* is not based on birth but on the psychological makeup and qualifications of the individual. In Vedic *varṇāśrama* the natural *varṇas* and *āśramas* are scientifically delineated to create a complex and highly specialized social system where the rules of society are directed not only towards the material advancement of society, but most importantly, towards its spiritual and ultimately its devotional development. In this way *vaijñānika-varṇāśrama* becomes a part of *sādhana-bhakti*.[35]

The express purpose of Vedic *varṇāśrama-dharma* is to raise human society from the lowest stages of material life to the highest stage of devotional fulfillment. This is accomplished by managing mankind's physical, mental, social, and spiritual life in accordance with devotional culture. The cultivation of devotion is the ultimate

32. Ibid., 107: Appendix V, 62.
33. Ibid., 107: Appendix V, 63.
34. Ibid., 108: *varṇa-vidhānera avaijñānika prāguvasthāyai iurope (saṁkṣepataḥ bhārata chāḍā sarvatrai) samājera cālaka haiyā āche/*
35. Ibid., 131: Appendix V, 64.

purpose of the *varṇāśrama-dharma*. He writes, "The main purpose of *varṇāśrama-dharma* is to obey the laws of health, to cultivate and improve the faculty of the mind, to cultivate the social good, and to learn spiritual truth in order to cultivate devotion.[36] . . . Therefore the observance of *varṇāśrama-dharma* is a necessity for the cultivation of devotion."[37] *Sādhana-bhakti* can best be undertaken within the culture of scientific or Vedic *varṇāśrama-dharma*.

The concern is raised that the practice of *varṇāśrama-dharma* can be overly elaborate and time consuming and often not in full harmony with the practice of devotion. It is asked: how much *varṇāśrama-dharma* should actually be undertaken by the *sādhaka*[38] and what should be the course of action when conflict arises between *varṇāśrama-dharma* and *sādhana-bhakti*?[39] Bhaktivinoda answers by saying that if the body, mind, society, and spiritual life are not protected and nourished, there is little possibility that devotion can be cultivated. "If death is premature, or if mental disease arises, or if social revolution occurs, or if there is a lack of spiritual education, how can the seeds of devotion take hold in the heart?"[40] When *varṇāśrama-dharma* is abandoned arbitrarily without devotional purity, the bodily and mental demands of life lead to moral degradation. He insists that the practice of *varṇāśrama-dharma* is necessary for the cultivation of devotion in spite of its time consuming and elaborate nature.[41] In the end, he suggests that the cultivation of devotion will shorten the course of *varṇāśrama-dharma*[42] and he advises the devotional practitioner to progress slowly, step by step, and gradually leave those portions of *varṇāśrama-dharma* that are contrary to devotion.[43]

---

36. Ibid., 174: Appendix V, 65.
37. Ibid.: *ataeva sei dharmera ānukūlye bhaktir anuśīlana karibe/ bhakty-anuśīlanera janyai varṇāśrama-dharmera pālana karā prayojana haiyāche/*
38. A *sādhaka* is a person who performs *sādhana*, religious practice.
39. CS, pt. 1, 174-175: Appendix V, 66.
40. Ibid.: Appendix V, 67.
41. Ibid.: Appendix V, 68.
42. Ibid.: Appendix V, 69.
43. Ibid.: Appendix V, 70.

Just how the rules of *varṇāśrama-dharma* become sanctified through the process of *vaidhī-bhakti-sādhana* is explained in the following way. *Vidhis* are of two kinds, primary rules (*mukhya-vidhi*) and secondary rules (*gauṇa-vidhi*).[44] Those rules which pertain directly to devotion, such as hearing divine *līlā*, chanting the holy name, seeing the sacred image, and surrendering to guru are *mukhya-vidhi* because "the direct fruit of the *vidhi* is God's worship (*upāsanā*)."[45] The sixty-four elements (*aṅgas*) of *vaidhī-bhakti-sādhana* that Rūpa Gosvāmī mentions fall within the category of *mukhya-vidhi.*

Secondary rules are those indirectly related to God's worship. For the most part these are the rules of *varṇāśrama-dharma.* Bhaktivinoda gives the following example: By taking a morning bath the mind becomes calm because the body is cool and free of disease. Although the direct result of bathing is mental calmness and physical cleanliness, and not devotion *per se,* it does happen that the worship of God is improved through bathing. Consequently, when bathing is done in relation to the worship of God, it becomes a secondary aspect or *gauṇa-vidhi* of *sādhana-bhakti.*[46] Similarly, the other rules of *varṇāśrama-dharma,* when undertaken in relation to devotion, benefit devotional life and thereby are converted into *gauṇa-vidhi.* This can only take place when the rules of *mukhya-vidhi* have first been firmly established in the life of the *sādhaka.* The rules of *mukhya-vidhi* work in conjunction with *varṇāśrama-dharma.* Through *vaidhī-bhakti* the heart of the *sādhaka* is cleansed and prepared for the next step along the path of devotion, *rāgānugā-bhakti-sādhana.* Until that time, however, Bhaktivinoda warns:

> So long as deep attachment (*rāga*) for Kṛṣṇa has not arisen, the *sādhaka* must be devoted to Kṛṣṇa out of a sense of duty by adopting the primary and secondary rules of devotion.[47]. . . *Rāga* is rare, but when it arises the *vidhis*

44. Ibid., 20: Appendix V, 72.
45. Ibid., 21: *mukhya-vidhira sākṣāt phalai bhagavad upāsanā/ vidhi o upāsanāra madhye avāntara phala nāi/ hari-kīrtana o hari-kathā śravaṇake mukhya-vidhi balā yāya/*
46. Ibid., 20: Appendix V, 73.
47. Ibid., 19: Appendix V, 75.

> no longer hold the *sādhaka*. However, until that time it is the main duty of a person to be guided by *vidhis*. . . . It is only the most fortunate and highly competent person who is able to walk the path of *rāga*.[48]

In the initial stages the effectiveness of *vidhis* is based on a sense of duty, a hope of a future reward, or a fear of sin. Duty, hope, and fear, however, do not constitute pure motives of worship.[49] Eventually the path of *vaidhī-bhakti-sādhana* matures and a state of internal desire called *rāga* arises as the practitioner wishes to practice devotion free of any sense of duty, hope, or fear. Bhaktivinoda further points out, "Fear and hope are contemptible. When the intelligence of the practitioner develops he gradually gives up fear and hope and begins to follow *śāstra* out of a sense of duty alone. That sense of duty cannot be abandoned until the state of *rāga* towards God develops."[50] This is how the path of devotion gradually transforms itself from a state of obligation to a state of spontaneous passion, called *rāga*. The manifestation of *rāga* is the ultimate goal of *vaidhī-bhakti*. When *rāga* springs forth in the heart of the *sādhaka*, devotional life takes on a new vibrancy as the door to *rāgānugā-bhakti-sādhana* opens wide.

Rāgānugā-bhakti-sādhana

As *rāga* arises in the heart of the *sādhaka* he is no longer content to follow the rules of *bhakti* in a passive state. Instead he intensely desires to experience *līlā* directly as a participant. In such a condition the *sādhaka* is ready to adopt the path of *rāgānugā-bhakti-sādhana*.[51] Bhaktivinoda describes this condition: "When *lobha* for the path of *rāgānugā* arises, the *sādhaka* should approach the proper guru with great humility. Examining the disciple's inclinations, the

---

48. Ibid.: Appendix V, 76.
49. Ibid., 7: *bhaya, āśā o kartavya-buddhi-dvārā ye sakala upāsaka īśvara-bhajane pravṛtta hana, tāṅhādera bhajana tata viśuddha naya/*
50. Ibid., 7: Appendix V, 77.
51. For an overview of *rāgānugā-bhakti-sādhana* see *Journal of Vaiṣṇava Studies* vol. 1, no. 3. This issue is dedicated to the topic.

guru should instruct the disciple and introduce his *bhajana* along with the details of the disciple's *siddha-deha*."[52]

The term *siddha-deha* is significant. Literally *siddha-deha* means "perfect body." In the context of *rāgānugā-bhakti-sādhana* the *siddha-deha* is the "spiritual body" that the *sādhaka* uses to participate within *līlā*. This is where the influence of Gopālaguru Gosvāmī and Dhyānacandra Gosvāmī and the post Rūpa tradition of *sādhana-bhakti* become clear in Bhaktivinoda's approach to *sādhana*.

There is no need to elaborate on the details of Rūpa Gosvāmī's system. Instead we will summarize by saying that unlike *vaidhī-bhakti*, *rāgānugā-bhakti* involves the transformation of identity. This change of identity is accomplished as the *sādhaka* patterns his internal feelings and activities after one of the exemplary characters among the residents of eternal Vrindavan. By approximating the internal feelings and activities of these eternal residents the *sādhaka* learns to develop a frame of mind and mood similar to those within *Vṛndāvana-līlā*. In fact, the *sādhaka* learns to participate within *līlā* through one of the five primary relationships: *śānta*, *dāsya*, *sakhya*, *vātsalya*, and *mādhurya*. Rūpa Gosvāmī, however, does not specifically mention the *siddha-deha* or "spiritual body" that the *sādhaka* uses to practice *rāgānugā-bhakti-sādhana*. This is a later development and one of the most prominent features of Bhaktivinoda's *sādhana*.

The following example, cited from the *Jaiva-dharma*, shows how the path of *rāga-bhakti* is initiated, how *siddha-deha* is adopted, and how transformation of identity actually occurs. Vijaya Kumāra and Vrajanātha, two fictional but typical sixteenth century Vaiṣṇavas, are disciples of Raghunātha Dāsa Bābājī in Navadwip. Vijaya is married with a family and Vrajanātha is about to get married. Raghunātha Dāsa is a *siddha-puruṣa* or a master of esoteric devotional practice. After learning the tenets of *vaidhī-bhakti* and becoming established in that *sādhana*, Vijaya and Vrajanātha approach their guru with the

52. CS, pt. 1., 315: *sādhakera yakhana rāgānuga-mārge lobha haya, takhana sad-gurura nikaṭa prārthanā karile tini sādhakera ruci parīkṣā kariyā tāṅhāra bhajana-nirṇayera saṅge saṅge siddha-dehera paricaya kariyā dibena/*

intention of requesting initiation into the path of *rāgānugā-bhakti.*

The scene opens as follows: "A wonderful feeling arose in the minds of Vijaya Kumāra and Vrajanātha, both unanimously decided to be initiated by Bābājī Mahārāja who was a master in the spiritual field. . . . The next morning they finished their bath in the Ganges, put on twelve marks of *tilaka,* and went to Raghunātha Dāsa Bābājī where they prostrated themselves at his feet."[53] Vrajanātha asks, "What is *rāga?*" Bābājī answers by explaining the many details of *rāgānugā-bhakti-sādhana.* Finally, Vrajanātha asks the most important question, "What kind of *rāgānugā-bhakti* are we qualified for?"[54] In other words: how is the *sādhaka* to know in which relationship he belongs and which *rāgātmikā-bhakta* he is to follow? Bābājī answers:

> My child, minutely study your nature (*svabhāva*), and according to your nature and feelings (*ruci*), cultivate the appropriate sentiment (*rasa*). Attend to one who is eternally perfected in respect to that *rasa.* You must examine your feelings exclusively. If you have feelings for the path of *rāga,* then act according to those feelings, but so long as you have no feelings for the path of *rāga,* you should have firm faith in the path of *vaidhī-bhakti.*"[55]

Accordingly, Vijaya Kumāra describes how he has been listening to the activities of Śrī Kṛṣṇa from the *Bhāgavata* for a long time and has become inclined to hear about the *līlā* of Rādhā and Kṛṣṇa in the mood of Śrīmatī Lalitā Devī.[56] To this Bābājī immediately replies, "You need say no more. You are a *mañjarī* following Lalitā Devī. What type of service do you like best?"[57] Vijaya responds, "I think I am ordered by Lalitā Devī to string garlands of flowers; I shall cut beautiful flowers and make garlands and hand them to

53. JD, 369: Appendix V, 78.
54. Ibid., 381: *āmādera ki prakāra rāgānugā-bhaktira adhikāra āche?*
55. Ibid.: Appendix V, 79.
56. Ibid., 381-2.
57. Ibid., 382: *tomāra āra balite haibe nā, tumi śrī-lalitādevīra anugatā mañjarī-viśeṣa/ tomāra kon sevā bhāla lāge?* (Lalitā Devī is one of the chief *gopīs.*)

her; she will smile on me out of infinite grace and put them round the neck of Rādhā and Kṛṣṇa."[58] Bābājī responds, "May your desire for service (*sevā*) be fulfilled, I bless you. . . . My son, go on practicing *rāgānugā-bhakti* in this way, but externally let the practice of the various limbs of *vaidhī-bhakti* continue."[59]

Vrajanātha then says, "My master, whenever I study the loving activities of Śrī Kṛṣṇa, I feel the urge to follow in the foot-steps of Subala."[60] Bābājī asks, "What things are you inclined to do?" Vrajanātha responds, "I would like to fetch the calves as a companion of Subala. Sitting nearby, Kṛṣṇa plays on His flute, and being favored by Subala, I let the calves drink water and bring them to Kṛṣṇa—this is my heart's desire." Bābājī says, "I bless you that you may serve Kṛṣṇa in obedience to Subala. You are eligible to cultivate the sentiment of friendship (*sakhya-rasa*)."[61]

Here both Vijaya and Vrajanātha are preparing to follow what Rūpa Gosvāmī has defined as, "that (method of bhakti) which follows the *rāgātmikā-bhakti* clearly manifest in the inhabitants of Vraja."[62] This, of course, is *rāgānugā bhakti-sādhana*. Vijaya will follow the mood of *rāgātmikā-bhakti* demonstrated by Lalitā Devī according to the *mādhurya-rasa*, and Vrajanātha will follow the mood of *rāgātmikā-bhakti* expressed by Subala as *sakhya-rasa*. They will respectively study the *līlā* activities of these *rāgātmikā-bhaktas* as they gradually internalize the feelings of these paradigmatic individuals.

There is just one more aspect to this story that reflects the further developments beyond Rūpa Gosvāmī's original definition of *rāgānugā-bhakti-sādhana*. Both Vijaya and Vrajanātha ask, "What more remains to be done in this respect?' To which Bābājī replies, "Nothing at all, except that you must know the name, appearance,

---

58. Ibid., Appendix V, 80.
59. Ibid.: Appendix V, 81.
60. Ibid.: *prabho, āmi yakhana yakhana kṛṣṇa-līlā anuśīlana kari, takhana takhana subalera anugata haiyā thākite vāsanā janmāya/* (Subala is one of Kṛṣṇa's cowherd friends.)
61. Ibid.: Appendix V, 82.
62. BRS, 1/2/168: *virājantīm abhivyaktāṁ vraja-vāsi-janādiṣu/ rāgātmikām anuśṛtā vā sā rāgānugocyate/*

garment, and so on, of your spiritual body (*siddha-deha*). Come later and I will tell you."[63] Bhaktivinoda concludes as follows:

> On that day Vrajanātha and Vijaya considered themselves blessed, and with great delight, set themselves to follow the path of *rāga*. Externally everything remained as before; all their manners were like those of a man, but internally Vijaya Kumāra was imbued with the nature of a woman and Vrajanātha assumed the nature of a cowherd boy.[64]

The final statement of Bābājī, "You must know the name, appearance, garment, and so on, of your spiritual body (*siddha-deha*)," is indicative of that part of the later tradition of *rāgānugā-bhakti-sādhana* that has to do with how transformation of identity takes place. This is a key element.

After Rūpa Gosvāmī, the tradition of *rāgānugā-bhakti-sādhana* is dominated by many important personalities, among whom are Gopālaguru Gosvāmī, Dhyānacandra Gosvāmī, Narottama Dāsa Ṭhākura, Viśvanātha Cakravartī and Siddha Kṛṣṇadāsa Bābā.[65] Gopālaguru Gosvāmī, Dhyānacandra Gosvāmī, and Siddha Kṛṣṇadāsa Bābā have each composed a *paddhati*, or manual, outlining the details of *rāgānugā-bhakti-sādhana*.[66] Collectively these

63. JD, 383: Appendix V, 83.
64. Ibid.: Appendix V, 84.
65. Gopālaguru Gosvāmī (*ca.* 1550) was a disciple of Vakreśvara Paṇḍita, a contemporary of Caitanya. Dhyānacandra Gosvāmī (*ca.* 1600) was a disciple of Gopālaguru Gosvāmī. Both were from Orissa. Narottama Dāsa (*ca.* 1600) was a disciple of Lokanātha Gosvāmī of Vrindavan. Viśvanātha Cakravartī (*ca.* 1700) lived in Vrindavan sometime between 1654 and 1754. He was one of the most prominent commentators of Rūpa Gosvāmī. Siddha Kṛṣṇadāsa Bābā (*ca.* 1800) was from Govardhan, near Vrindavan. Bhaktivinoda makes no mention of him, so considering that Kṛṣṇadāsa was so close to Bhaktivinoda's time it may be that Bhaktivinoda was unaware of Siddha Kṛṣṇadāsa's work. In his *Guṭikā* Kṛṣṇadāsa lists himself as the ninth from Narottama Dāsa. Therefore we place him *circa* 1800.
66. The compositions of both Gopālaguru and Dhyānacandra Gosvāmī bear the

works are known as the *paddhati-traya,* and they comprise the *bhajana-paddhatis* for the Caitanya Vaiṣṇavas.[67] We have mentioned that among these personalities, Gopālaguru Gosvāmī and Dhyānacandra Gosvāmī are prominent in Bhaktivinoda's writings.

None of these followers of Caitanya discusses the path of *vaidhī-bhakti-sādhana* to any extent; instead they focus their attention on *rāgānugā-bhakti-sādhana.* Under their influence three new developments are introduced. The first is the creation of a specialized form of spiritual practice called *mañjarī-sādhana* in which the *sādhaka* in meditation assumes the identity of a young maidservant (*mañjarī*) in *Kṛṣṇa-līlā.* The second development affects the manner in which spiritual identity is assumed, called *siddha-praṇālī-dīkṣā* or sometimes *ekādaśa-bhāva.* The third is a formalization of the process of remembrance *(līlā-smaraṇa)* called *aṣṭa-kāliya-līlā-smaraṇa.* Each of these developments is represented in the *sādhana* of Bhaktivinoda.

Gopālaguru and Dhyānacandra are specifically mentioned in Bhaktivinoda's *Jaiva-dharma* when Vijaya Kumāra and Vrajanātha travel to Puri to meet them for instruction.[68] Vijaya and Vrajanātha are told to find Gopālaguru, "in the house of Kāśī Miśra at Śrī Puruṣottama." There they hear that, "At the house of Kāśī Miśra in Puri, Śrī Gopālaguru Gosvāmī, the disciple of Śrī Vakreśvara, now occupies the honored seat of Śrīman Mahāprabhu."[69] They are told to have *darśana* of his lotus feet and take his instruction respectfully. Bhaktivinoda tells us that, "Śrī Dhyānacandra Gosvāmī was a past master in all subjects, and in the matter of worship of Hari espe-

same title, *Śrī Gaura-govindārcana-smaraṇa-paddhati.* The *Śrī Gaura-govindārcana-paddhati* is by Siddha Kṛṣṇadāsa Bābā.

67. Dhyānacandra's *paddhati* is identical to Gopālaguru's work except that he has added items about *gaura-līlā-smaraṇa,* including *siddha-deha-dhyāna* for *Gaura-līlā.* Siddha Kṛṣṇadāsa's *paddhati* shows more details of Kṛṣṇa's life in the *mādhurya-rasa.*

68. The narrative time setting of the *Jaiva-dharma* is about AD. 1600.

69. JD, 435: *śrī-puruṣottame kāśīmiśrera bhavane śrīman-mahāprabhura gadite ājakāla śrī-vakreśvarera śiṣya śrī-gopālāguru gosvāmī virājamāna/* Apart from this statement Bhaktivinoda does not appear to discuss anymore details concerning the *paramparā* or line of succession coming from Caitanya.

cially he was second to none. He was the first and foremost of all the disciples of Śrī Gopālaguru Gosvāmī. He gave instruction on all the principles of *bhajana* to Vijaya and Vrajanātha, considering them competent to learn the matter of worship."[70] There is no question that Bhaktivinoda held both Gopālaguru and Dhyānacandra Gosvāmīs in high esteem.[71]

When Bābājī says to Vijaya Kumāra and Vrajanātha, "You must know the name, appearance, garment, and so on, of your spiritual body," he is referring to the specific manner in which the transformation of identity takes place as described in the *paddhati-traya.* In these works a third level of initiation called *siddha-praṇālī-dīkṣā* is described where eleven aspects (*ekādaśa-bhāva*) of a spiritual identity are given to the *sādhaka* by the guru.[72] These eleven aspects characterize the internal spiritual persona, usually of a *mañjarī,* that allows the *sādhaka* to participate within *Kṛṣṇa-līlā.* The word *mañjarī* refers to a young maid who serves the needs of Rādhā and Kṛṣṇa in *mādhurya-rasa.*[73]

Siddha-praṇālī

In the final chapter of the *Hari-nāma-cintāmaṇi* (1900), Bhaktivinoda describes *siddha-praṇālī-dīkṣā* as follows: "In order to fulfill one's ambitions for attaining *ujjvala-rasa* [*mādhurya-rasa*] there are eleven items that form one's spiritual identity: relationship (*sambandha*), age (*vayasa*), name (*nāma*), form (*rūpa*), group

70. Ibid., 484: Appendix V, 85.

71. That Gopāla Guru and Dhyānacandra are intimately associated with the *siddha-praṇālī* process in Bhaktivinoda's writing is significant. It shows the connection between Bhaktivinoda's *sādhana* and the process of *siddha-praṇālī.*

72. The *Jaiva-dharma* describes *dīkṣā* (initiation). The first step is *hari-nāma* initiation or giving of the holy name wherein the initiate formally receives the *mahā-mantra: hare kṛṣṇa hare kṛṣṇa kṛṣṇa kṛṣṇa hare hare hare rāma hare rāma rāma rāma hare hare.*. After time, when the *dīkṣā-guru* feels that the disciple has matured, *mantra-dīkṣā* is offered. Here the disciple formally receives the 18-syllable *Kāma Gāyatrī mantra.* The final rite is *siddha-praṇālī-dīkṣā,* wherein the initiate receives eleven characteristics (*ekādaśa-bhāva*) of a spiritual persona known as the *siddha-deha.*

73. *Mañjarī-sādhana* is a unique form of *mādhurya-rasa* in which the *sādhaka* assumes

(*yūtha*), dress (*veśa*), assignment (*ājñā*), residence (*vāsa*), service (*sevā*), highest ambition (*parākāṣṭhā*), and feeling one's self protected and maintained (*pālyadāsī*)."[74] These eleven items are conferred on the disciple by the guru during initiation to define an internal spiritual identity that the *sādhaka* gradually uses to participate within *Kṛṣṇa-līlā*.

Just how such a spiritual identity is implemented is described as follows: "The *sādhana* is executed in five progressive stages: *śravaṇa-daśā* (the stage of hearing), *varaṇa-daśā* (the stage of accepting), *smaraṇa-daśā* (the stage of remembering), *āpana-daśā* (the stage of maturing), and *sampatti-daśā* (the stage of attainment)."[75]

Regarding the first stage, *śravaṇa-daśā*, Bhaktivinoda writes: "One should approach a guru who is considered more advanced than one's self and hear the principles of *bhāva* from him. This is the stage of hearing. There are two aspects of *bhāva-tattva* that you must consider: the eleven components of your own spiritual identity, and *Kṛṣṇa-līlā*."[76]

After this comes *varaṇa-daśā*, or the stage of accepting the eleven aspects of a spiritual persona. This is the most interesting stage. Bhaktivinoda writes: "When *lobha* arises upon hearing Rādhā's and Kṛṣṇa's *līlā*, the disciple may ask at the feet of his Guru, "O reverend sir, how is it possible to attain such *līlā*?' If pleased with the disciple, the guru will then mercifully explain the principles of *līlā* in relation to the *sādhaka's* internal identity saying, 'You may enter *līlā* in this way. After hearing with innocence about this sacred mood, you shall accept this within your own heart.' This is the stage of acceptance called *varaṇa-daśā*."[77]

---

the identity of a *mañjarī* or female servant. The *mañjarī* is a kind of *gopī* who serves as maidservant. Usually a *mañjarī* is between the ages of 12 and 16 years and is under the care of a main *sakhī* (female friend) such as Lalitā or Viśākhā. The *mañjarī* serves the needs of both Rādhā and Kṛṣṇa by serving betel nut, bringing water, fanning, combing and braiding hair, entertaining with music and dance, and so on.

74. HC, 15/27, p. 153: Appendix V, 88.
75. Ibid., 15/28, p. 154: Appendix V, 89.
76. Ibid., 15/ 29, p. 155: Appendix V, 90.
77. Ibid., Appendix V, 91.

Varaṇa-daśā is the stage when the *ekādaśa-bhāva* or the eleven aspects of internal identity are conferred: The first item is called *sambandha* or relationship. According to Bhaktivinoda *sambandha* means serving Kṛṣṇa through one of the five primary relationships known as *śānta, dāsya, sakhya, vātsalya,* and *mādhurya.* In the *Caitanya-sampradāya,* the main emphasis is on *mādhurya-rasa;* consequently, the *paddhatis* discuss *rāgānugā-bhakti-sādhana* only in relation to *mañjarī-sādhana.* In fact, Vrajanātha's adoption of *sakhya-rasa* is a rare instance and one that shows that the aspects of an internal spiritual identity may be applied to all of the major *rasas.* However, the later tradition does not accommodate any of the relationships other than *mādhurya-rasa,* and even within that relationship the focus is on a very specific form of *mādhurya-rasa* called *mañjarī-sādhana.* But according to Bhaktivinoda, the *ekādaśa-bhāva* could be applied to any of the relationships.

Bhaktivinoda builds on Rūpa Gosvāmī's original idea of *sambandha* as one of the five primary relationships and thereby broadens the meaning of *sambandha* to include all primary relationships. If the primary relationship is *vātsalya,* for example, then the nature of that relationship will determine the details of the other ten items of internal identity. This is an important innovation or perhaps restoration by Bhaktivinoda and it shows how the tradition of *rāgānugā-sādhana* can be expanded beyond just the *mādhurya-rasa.* Unfortunately, Bhaktivinoda does not discuss the specific details of attaining an internal persona within any of the relationships other than *mādhurya-rasa.* In the case of Vrajanātha, who chooses *sakhya-rasa,* Bābājī asks him to return later to hear the eleven items of his spiritual persona as a cowherd. But that is the last we hear of the matter. It would have been interesting to hear the details of Vrajanātha's spiritual persona within the *sakhya-rasa.* Because Bhaktivinoda does not elaborate on the matter the balance of our discussion is only in reference to the *mādhurya-rasa.*

The second aspect of persona is age (*vayasa*). Referring to the age of the *mañjarī* Bhaktivinoda writes, "The age of *kaiśora* is between ten and sixteen years. This is known as *vayasa-sandhi.*" In *mañjarī-sādhana* the *sādhaka* will have an internal identity as a young girl between ten and sixteen years.[78] In fact we will find that age becomes very specific. Bhaktivinoda, for instance, has an age of twelve years, six months and ten days in his *mañjarī-svarūpa.*

The third item is name (*nāma*). Bhaktivinoda writes, "If you are inclined to follow in the footsteps of a particular *sakhī* of Śrī Rādhā, your name will follow her name. Your guru knows your spiritual sentiments and accordingly he will select a suitable name as your eternal name."[79] Bhaktivinoda's *mañjarī* name is Kamalā Mañjarī.

The fourth item is bodily complexion or form (*rūpa*). This is described as follows: "When you have identified yourself as an adolescent damsel with beaming youth and beauty, then your guru will indicate your bodily complexion. Ah! Without brilliant effulgence and personal beauty how can you become a maid in the group of Śrī Rādhā?"[80] Bhaktivinoda's bodily complexion is that of lightning.

The fifth item is group (*yūtha*). This is described as follows: "Śrīmatī Rādhikā is the leader of the group. In Rādhārāṇī's group each of the eight chief *sakhīs* form subgroups called *gaṇas.*[81] According to your internal feelings, Śrī Gurudeva will place you under the protection of Śrī Lalitā's *gaṇa.*"[82] There are eight chief *gopī* friends of Śrī Rādhā known as *parama-preṣṭha-sakhīs,* and each *mañjarī* is a member of one of these groups. Bhaktivinoda is within Śrī Rādhikā's group (*yūtha*)and Lalitā's subgroup (*gaṇa*).[83]

The sixth item is dress (*veśa*). Bhaktivinoda describes this as follows: "According to the *sevā* that you are to perform you will be instructed in the appropriate fine arts. Your guru will instruct you in the most suitable qualities and dress."[84] Bhaktivinoda's dress is like

---

78. JD, 616: *kaiśora vayasai vayasa-daśa vatsara haite ṣola vatsara paryanta kaiśora/ ihākei vayaḥ-sandhi bale/*
79. Ibid.: *vraja-lalanādigera varṇanāte tomāra rucigata sevāra anurūpa ye rādhikā-sakhīra paricārikā, tāṅhāra nāmai tomāra nāma/*
80. Ibid.: Appendix V, 92.
81. Rādhā's eight closest friends (*aṣṭa-sakhīs*) are known as *parama-preṣṭha-sakhīs.*
82. JD, 616: Appendix V, 93.
83. The order and content of *ekādaśa-bhāva* varies slightly from one *paramparā* to another. In Bhaktivinoda's succession there is this extra category called *gaṇa.*
84. JD, 617: Appendix V, 94.

a cluster of stars.

The seventh item is assignment (*ājñā*). He writes, "Assignment is of two kinds, permanent and occasional. Whatever permanent *sevā* your most compassionate *sakhī* has requested of you, you should do in respect to *aṣṭa-kāliya-līlā* without hesitation; besides that, if she sometimes instructs you in some other service, that is occasional *sevā* which you should similarly attend to."[85] Bhaktivinoda's *siddha-praṇālī* chart[86] also includes the following statement regarding assignment: "My group leader is Lalitā, who is graceful and skilled in all arts. She is a constant companion of Śrī Rādhā. I always follow her orders and consider myself her *dāsī*."[87]

The eighth item is residence (*nivāsa*). Bhaktivinoda explains residence as follows: "To eternally reside in Vrindavan is the meaning of *nivāsa*. The *sādhaka* takes birth as a *gopī* in a particular village in Vraja. Then she will marry some *gopāla* from another village. But being attracted to the sound of Kṛṣṇa's flute, she will take up residence in a cottage near Rādhā-kuṇḍa in the grove of the *sakhī* to whom she is devoted. This is the perfect home for a *mañjarī*. *Parakīya-bhāva*[88] is her eternal mood."[89] Bhaktivinoda's residence is at Svānanda Sukhada Kuñja.

The ninth item is service (*sevā*). He writes, "You are a servant of Rādhikā; therefore to render pure service to Her is your permanent duty. When you go to meet Śrī Kṛṣṇa at a solitary place by Her command, if He expresses a desire to consort with you, you must not yield to Him, as you are a maid, confidante to Śrī Rādhā alone. Without Her permission you cannot independently serve Śrī Kṛṣṇa. Although you possess equal love for both Rādhā and Kṛṣṇa, your love for the service of Kṛṣṇa is subservient to your love for the service of Rādhā. This is the meaning of *sevā* and your *sevā* is to assist

85. Ibid.: Appendix V, 95.
86. The *siddha-praṇālī* chart is an initiation letter called *dīkṣā-patra* that describes the chain of gurus and the *mañjarī-svarūpa* of each guru.
87. Cited from the *siddha-praṇālī* chart.
88. *Parakīya-bhāva* is a particular *rasika* relationship that involves having a lover who is married to someone else.
89. JD, 617-618: Appendix V, 96.

the *aṣṭa-kāliya-līlā* of Śrī Rādhā."[90] In Bhaktivinoda's *mañjarī-svarūpa* as Kamalā Mañjarī, he brings camphor to be used in a variety of preparations that he may help prepare and offer. Camphor is used in sweet rice; it is mixed with *aguru* and burned (the fragrant smoke is used to dry Rādhā's hair); camphor is also mixed with sandalwood paste (*candana)* and applied to the bodies of Rādhā and Kṛṣṇa for a cooling effect.

The tenth item is divine cherished ambition (*parākāṣṭhā).* Bhaktivinoda describes this as follows: "Let me attain the *sevā,* form, and qualities of Śrī Rūpa Mañjarī.[91] By following in Her footsteps along with the other *sakhīs* and *mañjarīs,* let me begin Rādhā and Kṛṣṇa's *nitya-sevā* this very day. This mood is called divine cherished ambition."[92]

The eleventh and final item of one's *siddha-deha* is the feeling of being protected and maintained (*pālydāsī)* by one of the *aṣṭa-sakhīs* (group leaders–*gaṇeśvarīs*). Bhaktivinoda's *dīkṣā-patra* reads as follows: "I am looked after by Lalitā-devī, for she knows the essence of everything. I reside in her *Śrī kuñja mandira* and follow her every order, for by doing so, instantly Rādhā Kṛṣṇa's *sevā* will be available to me."[93] The *mañjarī-sādhaka* feels submission to a particular *gopī* who acts as her maintainer. This completes the eleven items of the *ekādaśa-bhāva* that form the basis of a spiritual persona within *Kṛṣṇa-līlā.* Through these eleven items the *sādhaka* is able to focus on an internal reality that is eventually meant to surpass the *sādhaka's* external physical reality.

To this description Bhaktivinoda adds one important qualification: the spiritual persona must match the natural feelings and psychology of the *sādhaka.* He writes, "At the time of acceptance, after discerning one's own *ruci* or taste for devotion you should humbly declare at the guru's feet: 'Lord, my full delight is in whatever identification you mercifully give. By nature my hankering

90. Ibid., 618: Appendix V, 97.
91. Śrī Rūpa Mañjarī is Rūpa Gosvāmī in his *siddha-deha.*
92. Cited from the *siddha-praṇālī* chart.
93. Taken from Bhaktivinoda's *siddha-praṇālī-dīkṣā-patra.*

is for this feeling, thus I am satisfied in accepting your command.'"[94] Bhaktivinoda explains that the *siddha-deha* is the soul's most precious possession so it must correspond in every way to the *sādhaka's* personal choice. If not, the required motivation to attain such a spiritual body will be lacking. He advises, "If there is no liking for the assignment of the spiritual body then one should candidly declare one's own liking at the feet of the guru. Upon reflection the guru will give a different persona. If there is liking for it, then one's proper persona will become manifest."[95] He continues, "At that time, the disciple must take full shelter of his guru and say, 'I accept this [*ekādaśa-bhāva*] which you have given me as my own, not only in this life, but also after death.'"[96]

The manner in which Bhaktivinoda regards the conferment of the *siddha-deha* is according to the emotional and psychological makeup of the *sādhaka*.[97] In contrast, David Haberman mentions two theories that illustrate how the *siddha-deha* is traditionally received. He calls one the "inherent theory" and the other the "assigned theory."[98] According to the "inherent theory" every *jīva* already has an existing eternal *siddha-deha*. During initiation, the guru "sees" the initiate's eternal identity in *līlā* by meditation and reveals this true identity to the *sādhaka*, who then begins the practice of *rāgānugā-bhakti* and eventually discovers for himself the reality of his eternal identity.

According to the "assigned theory" the guru assigns the appropriate *siddha-deha* to the initiate. The *siddha-dehas* are like "shiny new cars," as Haberman quotes one modern commentator,

94. HC, 15/30, p. 156: Appendix V, 98.

95. Ibid., 15/30, p. 157: Appendix V, 99.

96. Ibid., 15/31, p. 158: Appendix V, 100.

97. In fact the *paddhatis* do not describe how *siddha-praṇālī* is given. The only indications that Dhyānacandra makes in this regard occur when he uses the terms "*guru-prasāda-jananī*" (vs. 87, p. 28) "born from the mercy of Guru" and "*guru-dattam*" (vs. 108, p. 32) "given by the guru." It seems that the *paddhatis* only describe how the *sādhaka* meditates, not how he gets *siddha-praṇālī*.

98. David L. Haberman, *Acting as a Way of Salvation* (New York: Oxford University Press, 1988), 119-121.

that are assigned to the appropriate candidate according to the design of God through the mystic perception of the guru. In both theories, numerous inspiring stories abound to prove and illustrate how the *sādhaka* receives his actual inner form. While visiting Vrindavan, I, like David Haberman, heard many of these amazing and mystical anecdotes.

According to Bhaktivinoda, the act of receiving a *siddha-deha* is an attempt to match the psychological and emotional temperament of the *sādhaka* with the mood of the particular *rasika* relationship. It is less the result of a mystical intervention by the guru and more a mutual decision between the guru and disciple. At the time of *siddha-praṇālī-dīkṣā,* the candidate approaches the guru and together they decide on the appropriate spiritual persona for the disciple according to the internal *ruci* or feelings of the *sādhaka.*

Bhaktivinoda's approach seems to include more psychological and empirical input than what traditionally may be the case. As one becomes more and more purified through devotional practice one's natural (*sahaja*) spiritual condition develops. Such an emotional and psychological condition may be taken as a reflection or indication of one's inherent spiritual condition. The devotional feeling that one experiences in the phenomenal body is used to help decide the appropriate spiritual identity.

And, most important of all, if after some time the *sādhaka* feels that his identity is not suited to his internal disposition he may again approach the guru for an adjustment or a new identity altogether.[99] Thus the disciple receives an appropriate *siddha-deha* through a cooperative effort between the guru and disciple rather than by a flash of spiritual revelation by the guru alone.

For Bhaktivinoda the *ekādaśa-bhāva* is a meditative system, perhaps we could even suggest a technical device, used to lead the disciple to a realization of his or her true inner identity. What the guru bestows on the disciple is not the *siddha-deha* directly, but a working model of a *siddha-deha.* This seems to be a significant empirical innovation, and certainly it is one that fits well with Bhaktivinoda's

---

99. HC, 115.

task of interpreting the process of *rāgānugā-bhakti-sādhana* in the context of modernity.

The final stages of the *siddha-praṇālī* process, *smaraṇa-daśā*, *āpana-daśā*, and *sampatti-daśā* simply involve the practice, maturing, and fulfillment of *līlā-smaraṇa* in one's *mañjarī-svarūpa*. These final stages describe a gradual strengthening of the meditative process as the *sādhaka* becomes increasingly adept in the use of *siddha-deha* during meditation.

Interestingly, Bhaktivinoda provides a letter of initiation (*dīkṣā-patra*) that outlines the details of his *siddha-deha*. I include a reproduction of a handwritten copy of the *dīkṣā-patra* in Bengali (p. 202) along with its transcription and translation (p. 232-233) that I originally obtained from Bhaktivinoda's maternal family home. The *dīkṣā-patra* gives both the *siddha-praṇālī* and the *ekādaśa-bhāva* for Bhaktivinoda's entire *dīkṣā* line running back to Śrī Jāhnavā Mā, the wife of Nityānanda Prabhu.

To substantiate the information found in the *dīkṣā-patra*, we find that in the *Siddhi-lālasā* section of the *Gītā-mālā*, one of Bhaktivinoda's song books, he includes a selection of verses where he describes his *mañjarī-svarūpa* as follows:[100]

> My bodily complexion is like lightning and the color of my dress is like a cluster of stars. My name is Kamalā Mañjarī, I am eternally 12 1/2 years old, and my residence is called Svānanda Sukhada Kuñja. My *sevā* is to bring camphor and I am in Lalitā's group. Our party leader is Śrī Rādhā, and the Lord of my Goddess is Śrī Nandanandana [Kṛṣṇa]. They are the treasure of my life. My greatest hope is to attain *yugala-sevā* like that of Śrī Rūpa and the other *mañjarīs*. Certainly I shall reach that goal because I have strong faith. When will this *dāsī* attain perfection and make her residence at Rādhā-kuṇḍa? Always serving Rādhā and Kṛṣṇa, she will give up the memories of the past. While serving the lotus feet of the

100. We should also note Narottama Dāsa's warning that, "One should be careful not to mention the details of one's *bhajana* in public." In spite of this, knowledge of Bhaktivinoda's personal *siddha-deha* appears throughout his songs.

> daughter of Vṛṣabhānu [Śrī Rādhā], I shall be protected and maintained by Her. I shall always try to make Śrī Rādhikā happy. I know that Kṛṣṇa's happiness lies in seeing Rādhā happy. I shall never desire to give up the lotus feet of Rādhā to mix personally with Kṛṣṇa. The *sakhīs* in my group are my best friends, as well as my teachers in the art of loving Rādhā and Kṛṣṇa. Following them, I shall serve Rādhikā's lotus feet, which are like wish-fulfilling trees."[101]

If we compare this description with the information found in Bhaktivinoda's *dīkṣā-patra* we find that they match perfectly. All this evidence shows that Bhaktivinoda personally participated in and promoted the path of *rāgānugā-bhakti-sādhana* that included the process of *siddha-praṇālī* as defined by Gopālaguru and Dhyānacandra Gosvāmīs.

Aṣṭa-kāliya-līlā-smaraṇa

The adoption of the *siddha-deha* and *mañjarī-sādhana* are still not complete unless there is a setting in which to activate one's spiritual identity. This is accomplished by the use of *aṣṭa-kāliya-līlā-smaraṇa.* We have seen how the *Bhāgavata* recommends the hearing, glorification and remembrance of the name and activities of *bhagavān* Śrī Kṛṣṇa, called *līlā-smaraṇa.* In its most basic form *līlā-smaraṇa* involves meditating on the worship and activities of Kṛṣṇa as described in the *Bhāgavata* and related texts.

The system of *aṣṭa-kāliya-līlā-smaraṇa* is a formalization and extension of *līlā-smaraṇa* whereby Kṛṣṇa's day in Vrindavan is divided into eight time periods—night's end, early morning, forenoon, midday, afternoon, sunset, late evening and night—and where each period includes a particular pastime activity that the practitioner learns to visualize and meditate upon.[102]

---

101. Kedarnath Datta Bhaktivinoda, *Gītā-mālā,* ed. Śrila Bhaktikusuma Sramana (Sridham Mayapur, Nadiya: Shri Caitanya Math), 498 Śri-gaurābda: *Siddhi lālasā* VIII/1-4; IX/1–3. (Translations by Haridhāma Dāsa.) Appendix V, 104.

102. JD, 598: *arthāt niśānta, prātaḥ, purvāhna, madhyāhna, aparāhna, svāyaṁ, pradoṣa o rātri-līlā-bede līlā aṣṭa-kālīna/*

শ্রীশ্রীগোদ্রুমচন্দ্রায় নমঃ।

শ্রীমতী জাহ্নবা ঠাকুরাণীর ধারা

হরে কৃষ্ণ হরে কৃষ্ণ কৃষ্ণ কৃষ্ণ হরে হরে। হরে রাম হরে রাম রাম রাম হরে হরে॥

শ্রীগোপাল গুরু গোস্বামী এবং শ্রীধ্যানচন্দ্র গোস্বামীর অর্চনা পদ্ধতিদ্বয় নির্ণয় অনুসারে শ্রীসিদ্ধ প্রণালী নির্ণীত হয়।

	শ্রীগুরু পরম্পরা	শ্রীমঞ্জরী পরম্পরা	বয়স	বর্ণ (রূপ)	বসন (বেশ)	সেবা	আবাস কুঞ্জ	শ্রীরাধার যূথে গণ	গুণ
১	শ্রীনিত্যানন্দ শক্তি শ্রীজাহ্নবা ঠাকুরাণী	শ্রীমতী অনঙ্গ মঞ্জরী	১৩ বৎসর	বসন্ত কেতকী	ইন্দিবর	বেশ করণ	অনঙ্গাম্বুদ	শ্রীমতী ললিতারগণ	কৃষ্ণ প্রীতে কাম
২	শ্রীরামচন্দ্র গোস্বামী প্রভু	শ্রীমতী রত্ন মঞ্জরী	১২।১০	তুগ্ধালক্ত	তারাবলী	তাম্বুল	মনোহর	ঐ	ঐ
৩	শ্রীরাজবল্লভ গোস্বামী প্রভু	শ্রীমতী রাস মঞ্জরী	১৩	বালার্ক	জবারাগ	চন্দন	মোহন	চম্পকলতার	ঐ
৪	শ্রীকেশব চন্দ্র গোস্বামী প্রভু	শ্রীমতী কনক মঞ্জরী	১২।৬	তপ্ত কাঞ্চন	ঘন নীল	চামর	আনন্দ	ললিতার	ঐ
৫	শ্রীরুদ্রেশ্বর গোস্বামী প্রভু	শ্রীমতী রতি মঞ্জরী	১২।৪	তপ্ত হেম	জবারাগ	চামর	রস	ইন্দুরেখার	রতি কৃষ্ণ প্রীতে
৬	শ্রীদয়ারাম গোস্বামী প্রভু	শ্রীমতী দান মঞ্জরী	১২।৪	কুন্দ কুসুম	শোন পুষ্প	বস্ত্র	কনক	রঙ্গদেবীর	কাম কৃষ্ণ প্রীতে
৭	শ্রীমহেশ্বরী গোস্বামিনী	শ্রীমতী মধু মঞ্জরী	১২।২	হেমবর্ণা	ভ্রমর বর্ণা	স্নিগ্ধ জল	নীল	তুঙ্গবিদ্যার	মধুরে কৃষ্ণ প্রীতে
৮	শ্রীগুণ মঞ্জরী গোস্বামিনী	শ্রীমতী গুণ মঞ্জরী	১২।১	তুগ্ধালক্ত	ইন্দিবর	ব্যজন	মানস হরণ	বিশাখার	রাসলীলা কৃষ্ণ প্রীতে
৯	শ্রীরামমণি গোস্বামিনী	শ্রীমতী রস মঞ্জরী	১৩	বসন্ত কেতকী	ইন্দিবর	বেশ করণ	অনঙ্গ	চম্পকলতার	প্রীতি কৃষ্ণ প্রীতে
১০	শ্রীযজ্ঞেশ্বর গোস্বামী প্রভু	শ্রীমতী যূথী মঞ্জরী	১২।১০	প্রাতঃ অরুণ	তারাবলী	কুঙ্কুম চন্দন	মনোহর	চিত্রার	কাম কৃষ্ণ প্রীতে
১১	শ্রীবিপিন বিহারী গোস্বামী প্রভু	শ্রীমতী বিলাস মঞ্জরী	১২।১১	হরিদ্রা	তারাবলী	হরি চন্দন	আনন্দ	ললিতার	বিলাসে কৃষ্ণ প্রীতে
১২	শ্রীভক্তিবিনোদ ঠাকুর প্রভু •	শ্রীমতী কমল মঞ্জরী	১২।৬।১০	তড়িৎ	তারাবলী	কর্পূর	স্বানন্দ সুখদ	ললিতার	কৃষ্ণে কাম

সম্বন্ধ

"মম সিদ্ধ ভাব যাহা গুরু আজ্ঞা কৈল তাহা সেব্য সেবা সম্বন্ধ আমার
রাধাকৃষ্ণ কুঞ্জবনে সেব্য তত্ত্ব এক মনে নিত্য সেবা আমার আচার।
নিত্য দেহ সিদ্ধ সদা হ্রাস বৃদ্ধি নহে কদা। সদা তাহে কাল বর্ত্তমান
সিদ্ধ দেহে আমি যেই ব্রজে নিত্য দাসী সেই মঞ্জরীর ভাবে অবস্থান।"

আজ্ঞা

"যূথেশ্বরী শ্রীললিতা সর্ব্বগুণে সুললিতা শ্রীরাধার নিত্য সহচরী
আমি নিত্য তার গুণে তদাজ্ঞা প্রতিপালনে আমি থাকি তাঁহার কিঙ্করী॥"

পরাকাষ্ঠাশ্বাস

"সেবা বলে যেই রূপ রাধাকৃষ্ণ সখীরূপ পেল রূপ মঞ্জরী প্রভৃতি
হ'য়ে সখী অনুগামী অদ্যই লভিব আমি রাধাকৃষ্ণ নিত্য সেবা রীতি।
এই মত ভাব ল'য়ে পরাকাষ্ঠা বলি তাহে ভাব জানি যুগল সেবনে
সেই পরাকাষ্ঠা বলে, সখীর অনুগ হ'লে যুগল ভজিব ব্রজবনে॥"

পাল্যাদাসী

"পাল্যাদাসী ললিতার আপনাকে জানি সার বসি তাঁর শ্রীকুঞ্জ মন্দিরে
তাঁহার আদেশ মত সেবা কার্য্যে রহিয়াত পরিচর্য্যা পাইব সত্বরে।
শ্রীগোপীভাবাশ্রিত জীবের সমস্ত সেবাতেই অধিকার আছে।

Bhaktivinoda's *siddha-praṇālī* chart in Bengali.

Sri Sri Godruma Candraya Namah.

Srimati Jahnava Thakurani's Dhara (Parampara)

Hare Krsna Hare Krsna Krsna Krsna Hare Hare Hare Rama Hare Rama Rama Rama Hare Hare

Siddha Pranali is determined in accordance with Sri Gopal Guru Goswami, and Dhyan Candra Goswami's Archana Paddhati's.

	Sri Guru Parampara	Sri Manjari Parampara	Age	Bodily Color	Color of Dress	Seva	Kunja of Residence	Group	Quality	Relationship	Order	Divine Cherished Ambition	Maintainer
1	Sri Nityananda Sakti Sri Jahnava Thakurani	Srimati Ananga Maniari	13	Basanta Ketaki	Blue Lotus	Dressing and Decorating	Anangambuda	Lalita's	Krsna Priti Kama	As far as who is to be served and what is the seva, that has been given by my Guru : The worshipable object is Sri Sri Radha Krishna within the forest kunjes of Vrindaban, and my eternal occupation is rendering seva to them. The siddha deha is always trancendental, unchangeable, and unaffected by time, and that is my real self. For I am an eternal maidservant of Sri Radha.	My group leader is..................who is graceful and skilled in all the arts, she is a constant companion of Sri Radha. I always follow her order and consider myself her dasi.	Let me attain the seva, form, and qualies, like that of Sri Rupa Manjari. And by following in her footsteps along with the other sakhis and manjaris, let me begin Radha Krishna's nitya seva this very day. This mood is called 'Parakastha', by the strength of this firm conviction one will come to know all of the moods and mellows of jugal seva, if one is submissive to following in the foot steps of the sakhis.	I am looked after by......................for she knows the essence of everything. I reside in her Sri Kunja Mandira and follow her every order, for by doing so, instantly Radha Krishna's seva will be available to me.
2	Sri Ramacandra Goswami Prabhu	Srimati Ratna Manjari	12/10	Milkish color	Star Cluster	Pan	Manohar	Lalita's	Krsna Priti Kama				
3	Sri Rajaballabha Goswami Prabhu	Srimati Rasa Manjari	13	Morning sun	Jaba Flower Red	Candan	Mohana	Campak-lata's	Krsna Priti Kama				
4	Sri Keshavacandra Goswami Prabhu	Srimati Kanaka Manjari	12/6	Molten Gold	Deep Blue	Camara	Ananda	Lalita's	Krsna Priti Kama				
5	Sri Rudresvara Goswami Prabhu	Srimati Rati Manjari	12/4	Molten Gold	Jaba Flower (Red)	Camara	Rasa	Indulekha's	Rati Krsna Priti				
6	Sri Dayarama Goswami Prabhu	Srimati Dana Manjari	12/4	Kunda Flower (white)	Golden Flower	Dress	Kanaka	Rangadevi's	Kama Krsna Priti				
7	Sri Mahesvari Goswamini	Srimati Madhu Manjari	12/2	Golden color	Bumble Bce	Freshened Water	Nila	Tungavidya's	Madhure Krsna Priti				
8	Sri Guna Manjari Goswamini	Srimati Guna Manjari	12/1	Milkish color	Blue Lotus	Fanning	Manas Harana	Vishaka's	Rasa Lila Krsna Priti				
9	Sri Ramamani Goswamini	Srimati Rasa Maniari	13	Basanta Ketaki Flower	Blue Lotus	Dressing and Decorating	Ananga	Campak-lata's	Priti Krsna Priti				
10	Sri Jogesvara Goswami Prabhu	Srimati Juthi Manjari	12/10	Morning Sun	Star Cluster	Kunkuma Candan	Manohara	Citra's	Kama Krsna Priti				
11	Sri Vipina Bihari Goswami Prabhu	Srimati Vilasa Manjari	12/11	Tumeric	Star Cluster	Hari Candan	Ananda	Lalita's	Vilase Krsna Priti				
12	Sri Bhaktivinoda Thakura	Srimati Kamala Manjari	12/6/10	Lighting	Star Cluster	Camphor	Svananda Sukhada	Lalita's	Krsna Kama				

Bhaktivinoda's *siddha-praṇālī* chart in English.

Here is one example of morning (*prātaḥ*) *līlā.* Vijaya asks Gopālaguru Gosvāmī, "What are Kṛṣṇa's morning activities?" Gosvāmī answers:

> In the morning Śrī Kṛṣṇa is awakened by Mother Yaśodā, and after quickly rising from bed, He brushes His teeth along with Śrī Baladeva. Then, with His mother's permission, He eagerly goes to the *gośālā* to milk the cows.
>
> Śrī Rādhā is awakened by some of the older *sakhīs* and rises from bed. Then She brushes Her teeth, and after being massaged with oil, etc., She goes to the *snāna-vedī* (bathing platform). She is bathed by Lalitā and the other *sakhīs,* and then enters the dressing room, where She is adorned with a beautiful dress and ornaments, delightful perfume, garlands and ointments.
>
> After that, Mother Yaśodā sends one of her maidservants to ask Rādhā's mother-in-law to allow Śrīmatī and Her *sakhīs* to come quickly and cook.
>
> Śrī Nārada said, "O Devī, why does Mother Yaśodā call for Śrī Rādhā when Śrī Rohiṇī is known as the foremost of all cooks?"
>
> Śrī Vṛndā replied, "Maharṣi Durvāsā has personally given a boon to Śrī Rādhā. I previously heard this from the mouth of Śrī Kātyāyanī. Durvāsā has said, 'O Devī (Rādhe), by my grace, whatever food You cook shall be very delicious and challenge the taste of nectar. Whoever eats this food will have his longevity increased.' For this reason, Mother Yaśodā always calls Śrī Rādhikā for cooking. She considers, 'By my son eagerly eating the delicious and pure food prepared by the hand of Śrī Rādhā, He shall have a long life.'"
>
> After receiving the permission of Her mother-in-law, Śrī Rādhā and Her *sakhī-gaṇa* proceed in ecstasy to the home of Nanda Mahārāja to do the cooking.
>
> Kṛṣṇa and the others milk all the cows, and then, by the request of Nanda Mahārāja, Kṛṣṇa returns to His home surrounded by His *sakhas.* There, some of the servants blissfully massage Him with oil, etc., and assist Him with His bath. Then, after the bath, they offer Him clean

clothing, a fresh garland, and sandalwood paste. In this way, He looks very beautiful. Then, the hair above His forehead and neck is tied into a topknot, and on His forehead *tilaka* in the shape of a glowing moon is painted. His beautiful hands and arms are adorned with bangles, bracelets, armlets, and a jeweled seal ring. He wears an attractive necklace on His chest, and *makara* shaped earrings on His ears. After being called repeatedly by His mother, He takes her hand and enters the dining hall along with Śrī Baladeva and the *sakhas.*

Surrounded by His mother and the *sakhas,* Kṛṣṇa eats various kinds of food preparations. At this time, Kṛṣṇa and the *sakhas* crack funny jokes and make each other laugh. Submerged in this *hāsya-rasa,* they gradually finish their meals. After rinsing His mouth, Kṛṣṇa rests for a short while, lying comfortably on a soft bed. Then He and the *sakhas* divide and eat the *tāmbūla* offered by the servants. Śrī Rādhā secretly watches while Kṛṣṇa blissfully eats His meal, and then, when called by Mother Yaśodā, She shyly takes Her meal while surrounded by Śrī Lalitā and the other *sakhīs.* In this way, *prātaḥ-sevā* is performed.[103]

The system of *Aṣṭa-kāliya-līlā-smaraṇa* provides a structured framework around which the *sādhaka* learns to meditate. It becomes the setting for the *sādhaka's* participation within *līlā.* The eight time periods of *aṣṭa-kāliya-līlā-smaraṇa* form a meditative cycle that allows the *sādhaka* to track the activities of Rādhā and Kṛṣṇa throughout their entire day and night, and thereby include himself within these activities. The goal is to perfect the *smaraṇa* process until it can be performed without interruption and raised to the intensity of *samādhi. Mañjarī-sādhana, ekādaśa-bhāva,* and *aṣṭa-kāliya-līlā-smaraṇa* combine to form a meditative system that alters one's identity and allows entry into a *rasika* level of reality known as *Kṛṣṇa-līlā.*

The *sādhaka,* however, is not restricted solely to these activities described in received texts. Once the basic framework is learned, the *sādhaka* is free to create activities as long as they do not conflict

103. Translation by Haridhāma Dāsa. See: Dhyānacandra Gosvāmī, *Śrī Gaura-govindārcana-smaraṇa-paddhati.* Translated and edited by Haridhāma Dāsa (Los Angeles: SRI, 1993.), 96–98.

with each other in terms of *rasa*. Understanding the relationships between the various *rasas* and knowing what can be mixed with what is extremely important. The Caitanya theologians have discussed in great detail the particulars of combining the numerous *rasas*.

What I have described in the form of *mañjarī-sādhana*, *siddha-praṇālī-dīkṣā*, and *aṣṭa-kāliya-līlā-smaraṇa* are highly specialized and technical approaches to Kṛṣṇa bhakti that are solely based on the cultivation of *rasa*. From Narottama Dāsa and the discussions of *siddha-praṇālī* and *aṣṭa-kāliya-līlā-smaraṇa* as taught by Gopālaguru and Dhyānacandra Gosvāmīs till the time of Viśvanātha Cakravartī in the eighteenth century, this type of *rāgānugā-bhakti-sādhana* became the main form of *sādhana-bhakti* in the Caitanya-sampradāya. It was this kind of *sādhana*, developed in this early period of the Caitanya-sampradāya, that was actively practiced and promoted by Bhaktivinoda.

In Bhaktivinoda's middle and later writings, he regularly refers to *mañjarī-sādhana*, *ekādaśa-bhāva*, and *aṣṭa-kāliya-līlā-smaraṇa*.[104] Considering that these practices are standard for those following *rāgānugā-bhakti-sādhana* within the Caitanya-sampradāya, we conclude that Bhaktivinoda's *sādhana* is entirely orthodox, but with two important differences: First, the manner in which he interprets the awarding of the *siddha-deha* by the guru; and second, his expansion of the system of *ekādaśa-bhāva* to the *rasas* other than *mādhurya-rasa*.

If we return briefly to the incident that is described in the *Jaiva-dharma* where Vijaya and Vrajanātha receive their *siddha-deha* there are some important conclusions about Bhaktivinoda's interpretation of *rāgānugā-bhakti-sādhana* that we can learn. It appears that the path of *rāgānugā-bhakti-sādhana* is not beyond the reach of the so-called ordinary *sādhaka*, but is a path of devotion any serious *sādhaka* may hope to enter upon. Recall that Vijaya Kumāra is a married man and Vrajanātha is a young man about to become married. In fact, immediately after Vrajanātha's acceptance of

104. For examples see: CS, Eng., pp. 211, 213, 214, JD, Eng., pp. 562, 548, HC, p. 114.

siddha-deha, Vijaya begins to arrange for Vrajanātha's marriage. At first Vrajanātha expresses his desire not to marry, but after consulting their guru, he agrees.[105] Speaking to Vrajanātha, Bābājī Mahāśaya says, "You are the subject of Kṛṣṇa's mercy; you may serve Kṛṣṇa by making your household the household of Kṛṣṇa. Let the world carry on according to the teachings of Mahāprabhu. . . . Do not think that while living as a householder one cannot attain the supreme state of the love of Kṛṣṇa. Most of the recipients of Mahāprabhu's mercy are householders."[106] It is clear from this incident that marriage is no bar to *rāgānugā-bhakti-sādhana* if one has the aptitude. Bhaktivinoda's own life as a householder with fourteen children is a prime example of a married devotee practicing *rāgānugā-bhakti-sādhana.*

In this respect Vrajanātha is typical. He is a young man with a mother who is concerned about his marriage. Yet he is a serious *sādhaka* who has been practicing *vaidhī-bhakti-sādhana* for some time and now has become ready to take the next step into *rāgānugā-bhakti.* This shows that *rāgānugā-bhakti-sādhana* is not a path exclusively for devotees of the caliber of the six *gosvāmīs* of Vrindavan, but is a path within the reach of all serious *sādhakas* when and if they reach the point of *rāga.* The main criterion for adopting this path is *rāga.* The moment *rāga* arises in the heart of the *sādhaka,* the path of *rāgānugā-bhakti-sādhana* may be adopted.

This story also shows how *vaidhī-bhakti-sādhana* and *rāgānugā-bhakti-sādhana* are sequential. One path naturally flows into the other. At the same time, they are concurrent, in the sense that *vaidhī-bhakti* becomes subsumed and transformed as a part of *rāgānugā-bhakti-sādhana.* Bhaktivinoda points out:

> The practice of *rāgānugā* has two sides, one external and the other internal. Externally the *sādhaka* performs *śravaṇa* and *kīrtana* as an exoteric practitioner, whereas internally, in the mind, he possesses the body of an

105. JD, Eng., 349.
106. JD, 397-8: Appendix V, 109.

> accomplished devotee, who serves Kṛṣṇa in Vraja day and night. Following always the dearest servitor of his choice, he performs the service in his innermost mind.[107]

Thus the practice of *vaidhī-bhakti* is incorporated into the practice of *rāga* as its external aspect.

To Bhaktivinoda, *vaidhī-bhakti* embodies what is preliminary. Its course is slow. *Rāgānugā-bhakti*, on the other hand, is the easiest means to attain *bhāva* and *prema-bhakti*—the very essence of devotional life.[108] Comparing the two paths, Bhaktivinoda writes:

> The difference between *vaidhī* and *rāgānugā* is that the former reaches the stage of *bhāva* after some delay, whereas in *rāgānugā*, the delay in attaining the stage of *bhāva-bhakti* is very short. This is because from within the hearts of those *bhaktas* who practice *rāgānugā-bhakti* firm faith arises and takes the form of *ruci*, extreme hankering. Therefore, *bhāva* is never delayed."[109]

Indeed the path of *rāgānugā-bhakti-sādhana* has found the greatest prominence in the writings of Bhaktivinoda, even more than the path of *vaidhī-bhakti*. Virtually all of his middle and later works, including the *Caitanya-śikṣāmṛta* (1886), *Jaiva-dharma* (1893), *Hari-nāma-cintāmaṇi* (1900) and many of his songs deal with the details of *rāgānugā-bhakti-sādhana.*

In one of my conversations with Shrivatsa Goswami in Vrindavan,[110] he summed up the relationship between all these forms of bhakti as follows: *Vaidhī-bhakti-sādhana* is the grammar of love, *rāgānugā-bhakti-sādhana* is the poetry of love, and *rāgātmikā-bhakti* is the poetic experience itself. One process flows into the other. Both *vaidhī-bhakti* and *rāgānugā-bhakti* prepare the way for the fulfillment of the *rasika* experience, *rāgātmikā-bhakti.*

---

107. CS, pt. 1, 67: Appendix V, 110.
108. JD, 374: Appendix V, 111.
109. CS, pt. 1, 70: Appendix V, 112.
110. Conversations with Shrivatsa Goswami in Vrindavan in 1987.

Chapter Nine

Deviation in *Rāgānugā-bhakti-sādhana*

As with most behavioral models, there is a down side to the practice of *rāgānugā-bhakti-sādhana.* As the natural faith of the soul often becomes obstructed by the temptations of civilization, so the pure ideas of *mañjarī-sādhana* may become sullied by those unqualified to understand its subtleties or sustain its discipline. The idea of males assuming internal female identities in order to contemplate what appear as erotic episodes is a matter begging to create problems and public controversy. It is not hard to imagine the dangers of *mañjarī-sādhana* in the hands of immature or unscrupulous individuals and groups. Signs of trouble appeared early in the *sampradāya* when Rūpa Kavirāja was ousted[1] for his doctrine that allowed male *sādhakas* to wear female dress as an outward manifestation of their internal female *mañjarī-svarūpa.*[2]

Along with the inherently problematic nature of *mañjarī-sādhana* there has also been the prevalence of the so-called *sahajiyā* practices that have pervaded Caitanya Vaiṣṇavism since the time of Caitanya himself.[3] An example has been cited from Bhaktivinoda's own experience while he was in Orissa working as a magistrate. There he had to deal with the leader of the Atibaḍīs, a man named

1. In 1727 a council was held in Jaipur to condemn Rūpa Kavirāja's interpretation of *mañjarī-sādhana* and expel him from the Caitanya-sampradāya. See: Haberman, *Way of Salvation*, 98.

2. David L. Haberman, *Acting as a Way of Salvation* (New York: Oxford University Press, 1988), 98-104.

3. The term *sahajiyā* is not a word that identifies a particular group. Instead it is used to identify a particular idea. In general the term *sahajiyā* describes the idea that men and women have within themselves the divine essence of Rādhā and

Bishkishan, who claimed to be Mahāviṣṇu. Apart from his political activities, Bishkishan had a practice of inviting local villagers, both male and female, to meet with him for a ritual dance of the *rāsa-līlā*. This created a great scandal when some of the local ladies from respectable families became involved independently of their husbands.[4] It was common for many groups, such as the Kartābhajā and Bāuls to engage in various sexual-religious practices in the name of Caitanya Vaiṣṇavism. On the basis of many small manuscripts claiming to be Vaiṣṇava, but employing various sexual yogic practices, it is evident that many such heterodox and heteroprax groups were in existence by the end of the seventeen century.

In general, Bhaktivinoda's published books do not provide much information as to the extent of this problem. There is, in fact, only one major reference where he warns:

> The dharma promoted by such groups as the Neḍās, Bāuls, Kartābhajās, Daraveśas, Kumbhapaṭiyās, Atibāḍīs, Svecchācārīs, Bhāktas, and Brahmavādīs,[5] is very injurious and against the principles of *varṇāśrama-dharma*. In this way they introduce sin which prepares the way for world destruction. Similarly, the illicit cohabitation with females by Sahajiyās, Neḍās, Bāuls, and Kartābhajās, and the rest, which is commonly practiced, is utterly against the principles of religion.[6]

Bhaktivinoda's *Sajjana-toṣaṇī,* on the other hand, is replete with discussion and questions concerning the various groups that

---

Kṛṣṇa. A man is male because he is partly Kṛṣṇa and a woman is female because she has an element of Rādhā within her. Love between man and woman, therefore, reflects the cosmic and divine love between Rādhā and Kṛṣṇa. By experiencing the love between man and woman a person can understand the divine love between Rādhā and Kṛṣṇa.

4. ST, vol. 8 (1896), 205.

5. It is not clear precisely whom Bhaktivinoda is referring to by the use of this term. Perhaps some factions of the Brahmo Samaj.

6. CS, pt. 1, p. 127- 128: Appendix V, 113.

claimed connection to the Caitanya movement and engaged in these practices. Bhaktivinoda unhesitatingly deems such activities as extremely irreligious and antisocial. Here is some of the discussion.

In one article, a reader questions the legitimacy and practices of the Bāuls. Bhaktivinoda states that the activities of the Bāuls are not in accordance with Vaiṣṇava *śāstra*.[7] He categorically denies that they have anything to do with either *vaidhī-bhakti* or *rāgānugā-bhakti*.[8] When asked if such individuals as Rāya Rāmānanda[9] had any connection with the Bāuls, he denies any possible relationship and states that the stories that link him to such groups are false. He repeatedly defends the position of Rūpa Gosvāmī, Jayadeva, Vidyāpati, Caṇḍī Dāsa, and Mirābai.[10] Apparently the various groups had circulated stories and produced manuscripts that attempted to connect these traditional Vaiṣṇavas to themselves.[11]

Bhaktivinoda repeatedly states that the erotic aspects of *rāgānugā-bhakti* should never be understood in gross physical terms. The true practices of *rāga* bhaktas have nothing to do with this material world.[12] It is the mistake of the Bāuls to have brought the spiritual love expressed in the *Bhāgavata* and related texts to the gross level of the body. Bhaktivinoda asserts that the *sahajiyā* ideas that pervade such groups are absolutely opposed to Vaiṣṇavism and

---

7. ST, vol. 4 (1892), 64: *bāula-dharma ye ākākāre varttamāna samaye dṛṣṭa haya tāhā sarva śāstra viruddha*

8. Ibid.: Appendix V, 114.

9. Ibid.: *bāulerā nānā chale tāhādera sambandhe katakaguli mithyā ākhyāyikā racanā karata tāṅhādera nikaṭa aparādhī haiyā thāke/* I must further add that although Bhaktivinoda denied the linkage of Rāmānanda Rāya with *sahajiyā* ideas, a few recent scholars do accept the connection. Edward Dimock, for example, refers to Rāmānanda Rāya, Nityānanda, Jāhnavā Mā, etc., as Sahajiyā Vaiṣṇavas. However, others including Joseph T. O'Connell and Ramakanta Chakrabarty reject this claim and agree with Bhaktivinoda's point of view. See Edward Dimock's, *The Place of the Hidden Moon* p. 52-55 and 148-149, and Joseph T. O'Connell's "Rāmānanda Rāya: A Sahajiyā or a Rāgānugā Bhakta?" (JVS vol. 1. No. 3, p. 36-58.)

10. ST, vol. 4 (1892), 192.

11. Ibid., 65.

12. Ibid., 192-3: Appendix V, 115.

he denounces all sexual practices based on *sahajiyā* ideas.[13] The love that is expressed between Kṛṣṇa and the *gopīs* has nothing to do with physical love between man and woman. The use of language which is derived from physical love is symbolic and should not be taken literally. He writes:

> The condition of being male and female in the material world is a distorted reflection of the state of enjoyer and enjoyed found in the spiritual world. Searching through all the dictionaries we are not able to find the proper words to explain this non-material pastime of *saṁyoga* with the Supreme living force. On account of this, all the words concerning the contact between man and woman in the material world are used figuratively to express this relationship. However, there should be no cause for obscene thinking. If out of fear of being obscene we stop, then there can be no discussion of the Supreme Truth. In fact we are only able to describe the principles of Vaikuṇṭha by describing the phenomenal states in the material world that are reflections of all the authentic experiences of Vaikuṇṭha. There is no other way to describe this subject.[14]

In one instance, a reader asks whether it is even possible to make spiritual advancement without the sexual help of a woman. Here again the reference is to the various tantric ideas that involve sexual *sādhana.* According to Bhaktivinoda the Kartābhajā ascribed to the view that the sexual relations between husband and wife could serve as a model for the pure relationship between Rādhā and Kṛṣṇa.[15] Bhaktivinoda rejects such ideas and states that household-

---

13. Ibid., 115: Appendix V, 116.
14. KS *Saṁhitā* 5/19e: Appendix V, 117.
15. Recent scholarship by Sumanta Banerjee on the Kartābhajā suggests that the group was not generally involved in religio-sexual practices. In his *Jīvanī* Bhaktivinoda mentions how certain elements within the Kartābhajā became involved in illicit activities and thereby brought a bad name on the group. He tells how twenty-two fakirs were given the mission to spread the Kartābhajā dharma

ers should never consider their conjugal relations to have any relationship with spiritual *sādhana*. He emphatically states that all such ideas and practices are not Vaiṣṇava. Instead they are illicit practices performed in the name of Vaiṣṇavism[16] and whenever possible they should be actively rooted out.

Reading through this discussion in his journal, one is struck by two things: first, the pervasive nature of the problem, and second, the controversial nature of *rāgānugā-bhakti-sādhana* as practiced in the form of *mañjarī-sādhana*. Regarding the first problem we note that Akshay Kumāra Datta listed over fifty-six heterodox Vaiṣṇava or pseudo-Vaiṣṇava sects that existed between 1870 and 1880.[17] While some of them centered around a particular individual, others "floated" as ill-defined groups that shared common beliefs and rituals drawn from both the orthodox Vaiṣṇavas and the various tantric sects.

So far as the controversial nature of *rāgānugā-bhakti-sādhana* was concerned, there is little doubt that such problems and misunderstandings existed, since *rāga-bhakti* stood at the forefront of the Caitanya-sampradāya. We might surmise that Bhaktivinoda's inclusion of *sakhya-rasa* within the framework of the *ekādaśa-bhāva* was part of his effort to restore respectability to the Caitanya Vaiṣṇava system of *rāgānugā-sādhana-bhakti*. The adoption of a spiritual identity other than one that has strong erotic overtones like *mañjarī-bhāva* would be less problematic and controversial than an identity within *mādhurya-rasa*. Bhaktivinoda's innovative inclusion of the *rasas* other than *mādhurya* might tend to take the focus off *mañjarī-sādhana* and thereby diminish the controversial nature of *rāgānugā-bhakti-sādhana*. This, however, is *not* the case. Nowhere in his writings does he reject *mañjarī-sādhana, siddha-praṇālī*, or any other aspects of *rāgānugā-bhakti-sādhana*. The great emphasis continued to be on *mādhurya-rasa* and *mañjarī-sādhana*.

---

throughout Bengal, but that the work of Ramsharan Pal at Ghoshpara was not good and so spoiled the teachings. See *Jīvanī*, 63-64.

16. ST, vol. 4 (1892), 115-116: Appendix V, 118.

17. Cited in Chakrabarty, *Vaiṣṇavism in Bengal*, 348.

The problems associated with *rāgānugā-bhakti-sādhana* and its influence from various *sahajiyā* sources never seem to have diminished the prominence of *rāgānugā-bhakti* in Bhaktivinoda's eyes. For Bhaktivinoda the problems associated with *rāga-bhakti* are to be solved through the adoption of a strong system of *varṇāśrama-dharma* and a strict *sādhana* discipline, rather than by rejecting or underplaying *mañjarī-sādhana* or *rāgānugā-bhakti-sādhana.*

There is no denying that *rāgānugā-bhakti-sādhana,* particularly in the form of *mañjarī-sādhana,* left itself open to be tapped into and used to legitimize the various practices that were unacceptable to Vaiṣṇavas and to large sections of contemporary society. As a result the Caitanya movement had acquired a reputation as a religion of deviant sexuality.

Another problem that contributed to the difficult reputation of the Caitanya-sampradāya, and which also received considerable attention in the *Sajjana-toṣaṇī,* was the condition of mainstream Vaiṣṇava society in the nineteenth century. Bhaktivinoda notes that the community was organized into four distinct groups:[18]

1. the initiating gurus (*mantrācāryas*)
2. the renounced order of ascetics (*bhikṣāśramīs*)
3. initiated householders
4. the Vaiṣṇavas by caste (*jātī-vaiṣṇavas*)

The *mantrācāryas* primarily were the initiating *brāhmaṇa* gurus who were the hereditary successors of the original followers of Caitanya. They were the caste *gosvāmīs* or *jātī gosāñis.*[19] The *bhikṣāśramīs* were the mendicant Vaiṣṇavas, more commonly known as *vairāgīs,* who had left their social position within *varṇāśrama-dharma* to cultivate devotion exclusively. The third group, the initiated householders, were those, like Bhaktivinoda, who had taken *dīkṣā* from the *mantrācāryas* in order to cultivate devotion

18. ST, vol. 4 (1892), 3: Appendix V, 119.

19. The *mantrācāryas* held the primary right to award *dīkṣā* or initiation, but this did not mean that they were the only ones who gave initiation. Bhaktivinoda himself had disciples and so assumed the position of a *mantrācārya.*

according to their station as householders within the *varṇāśrama-dharma.*[20] These three groups formed the mainstream of Vaiṣṇava society. The final group, the *jāti-vaiṣṇavas,* were a growing group of individuals who had lost or rejected—or never had—caste status in regular Hindu society for any number of reasons but claimed status within Hindu society as an endogamous group (*jāti*) of Vaiṣṇavas.[21]

Bhaktivinoda has some harsh words for each of these divisions. He criticizes the initiating gurus for not maintaining high standards of spiritual conduct and thereby allowing the other groups to fall. It is interesting that Bhaktivinoda does not challenge the *mantrācāryas'* hereditary right to oversee the workings of the *sampradāya,* maintain the temples and shrines, award *dīkṣā,* and so on. He does not challenge the status quo. In fact, his own guru, Shri Bipin Bihari Goswami, was a member of this group of leading Vaiṣṇavas. Bhaktivinoda does, however, charge this group with negligence in fulfilling its spiritual and social responsibilities. He notes that one of the main problems within Vaiṣṇava society is that the guru-disciple relationship had not been properly maintained. The personal standards of the gurus were not being scrutinized by the prospective disciples before initiation, and similarly, the guru did not test the sincerity of the disciple before initiation.[22] This problem is specifically addressed in an article entitled *Pañca-saṁskāra,* in which he suggests there should be at least a one year observation period between the guru and disciple prior to initiation.[23]

Aparna Bhattacharya's work, *Religious Movements of Bengal,* summarizes the condition of some of the *gosvāmīs* in Bengal that I

20. This group could also include those householders who had not taken *dīkṣā,* but who nonetheless subscribed to many Vaiṣṇava practices.
21. For example, a householder who becomes a *vairāgī,* but who then later remarries would not then be allowed to reassume his former caste position. Such an individual would fall into the *jāti-vaiṣṇavas* category as would his children, and so on. For a good discussion of the *jāti-vaiṣṇavas* see: Joseph T. O'Connell, "Jāti-Vaiṣṇavas of Bengal: 'Subcaste' (*Jāti*) without 'Caste' (*Varṇa*)," *Journal of Asian and African Studies* XVII, 3–4 (1982),189-207.
22. ST, vol. 4 (1892), 3: Appendix V, 120.
23. Ibid., 6.

believe Bhaktivinoda would agree with:[24]

> . . . in the first half of the nineteenth century, guruship became greatly debased. The spiritual value of the movement greatly waned; it became largely materialistic. Formerly the guru was the wisest and the most learned person in the group and the head of the *akhra* but after some time, guruship became hereditary and became confined to one family. The son of a gosvāmī must be a gosvāmī even if he was licentious. The guru cared very little for the spiritual condition of the *śiṣya* (disciple) which was usually enjoined as the most noble task of the preceptor. He initiated a large number of disciples not with a view to imparting them religious teaching, but only to extract money, which served to meet his family expenses. Many of the temples previously donated by the Zamindars were used by them as their personal property.[25]

Bhaktivinoda similarly criticized the mendicant order of Vaiṣṇavas for their lack of understanding and spiritual sincerity[26] and the initiated householders for their lack of adherence to even the minimal practices of bhakti and for a total absence of understanding on how to act as Vaiṣṇavas.[27]

The so-called *jātī-vaiṣṇavas* present a separate problem altogether. Bhaktivinoda says they are Vaiṣṇavas in name only and it is the responsibility of the *mantrācāryas* for allowing them to take the title of Vaiṣṇava without consideration of the meaning of pure

24. Initially I was hesitant to use Aparna Bhattacharya's description of the situation because it seemed to lack substantiation, but after reviewing the discussion in the *Sajjana-toṣaṇī* I have to concede that it corresponds to Bhaktivinoda's feelings.

25. Aparna Bhattacharya, *Religious Movements of Bengal and Their Socio-economic Ideas 1800 - 1850* (Calcutta: Vidyasagar Pustak Mandir, 1981), 38-39.

26. ST, vol. 4 (1892), 3-4: Appendix V, 121. Melville Kennedy is similarly critical of Vaiṣṇava practices during the nineteenth century. See Melville T Kennedy, *The Caitanya Movement; A Study of the Vaishnavism of Bengal* (Calcutta: Association Press (Y.M.C.A.) 1925). For Ramakanta Chakrabarty's views on this matter see: Chakrabarty, *Vaiṣṇavism in Bengal,* 332-335.

27. Ibid., 4: Appendix V, 122.

bhakti.[28] He devotes a separate article to the problem of the *jāti-vaiṣṇavas,* and cites the 1881 census report which gives the demographic breakdown of the number of *jāti-vaiṣṇavas* in each district.[29] Their numbers had apparently risen sharply over the previous decade.

In Bhaktivinoda's opinion the solution for many of these problems, whether deviant groups such as the Bāuls or Kartābhajā or laxity in terms of the spiritual and social standards of mainstream society of Vaiṣṇavas, was the establishment of a strong social order in the form of *varṇāśrama-dharma.* By *varṇāśrama* he does not mean the natural *varṇāśrama* that he says exists in all human societies nor the prevailing system based on *smārta-dharma,* as we mentioned earlier, but the pure "scientific" *vaijñānika varṇāśrama* with its formal delineation of society according to the *varṇas* and *āśramas* in accordance with the principles of devotion.[30] To solve the problems of mainstream Vaiṣṇava society, he suggests that committees be formed to sort out and clean up the problems associated with each group according to the principles of *vaijñānika varṇāśrama.*[31] He further suggests that the *jāti-vaiṣṇavas* set up their own *varṇāśrama* system,[32] that they be encouraged to give up tantric rituals, practice monogamy, give up mendicancy, and cultivate various cottage industries for maintenance.[33]

The need for a formal *varṇāśrama* as a support for *sādhana-bhakti* is a recurrent theme within Bhaktivinoda's writings. This idea brings us back to our earlier point that bhakti develops best within a strong social system. He considered the current system, however, to be in decline and faltering. Its main failing was its acceptance of birth as the determining criterion for caste status. Alternatively he suggests

28. Ibid., 4: Appendix V, 123.
29. The census was taken once each decade.
30. It seems that the major difference between Bhaktivinoda's *vaijñānika varṇāśrama* and the common *smārta-dharma* is that according to Bhaktivinoda *vaijñānika varṇāśrama* rejects the idea of birth as the main criterion of *varṇa.*
31. ST, vol. 4 (1892), 4: Appendix V, 124.
32. ST, vol. 2 (1885), 142.
33. Ibid.

that *varṇa* should be determined on the basis of individual qualification and predilection.[34] Accordingly, he suggests how *varṇa* might be determined:

1. *Varṇa* should be determined by studying the nature of a child after examining a child's associations and tendency towards learning during childhood.
2. At the time of selecting *varṇa* there should also be some consideration of the *varṇa* of the mother and the father.
3. *Varṇa* should be determined at the time of education by the family priest, father, respectable seniors, and village headman.[35]
4. In case of dispute, there should be a two year trial period and a review committee to examine the case after that time.[36]

Bhaktivinoda sees assigning status by birth as the prime failure of modern Hindu society. In *vaijñānika varṇāśrama* there is no question of untouchability or outcasting since every individual naturally has a *varṇa*. It is just a matter of testing the individual to determine the proper *varṇa*.[37]

Apart from his disagreement on this key point of birth, he does not seem to disagree with nineteenth century Hindu society in general.[38] Although the early volumes of the *Sajjana-toṣaṇī* include many articles that are critical of contemporary society over this issue of birth, this is as far as he ever took the matter. He personally

34. Ibid.: Appendix V, 126.

35. CS, pt. 1, 113: *kon vyaktira kon varṇa-dharme adhikāra, tad-viṣaye pitā, kula-purohita, ārya-samāja, bhū-svāmī ihārā adhyayana-kāla upasthita hailei/* Presumably such committees to determine *varṇa* would be set up by local authorities.

36. ST, vol. 2 (1885), 123.

37. Interestingly, *varṇa* selection appears to be similar to the selection of the *siddha-deha* that we discussed previously. Just as the guru is to assign a spiritual body to the disciple that matches his or her internal *ruci*, so the village elders, etc. are to choose the *varṇa* of the child according to his social and psychological makeup.

38. This one issue alone, however, would in effect completely overturn the existing social system of caste.

participated within the system and he took great pains to see that his children were properly married according to the current (nineteenth century) social conditions.

Reading through Bhaktivinoda's writing, especially from the middle period onward (1885+), the reader finds that he tends to start out "down to earth," discussing the rudiments of bhakti and society, but quickly shifts to an esoteric level describing the details of *mañjarī-sādhana*.[39] Perhaps Bhaktivinoda's predisposition towards *mañjarī-sādhana* made it difficult for him to seriously address the failings of society. The more he advanced in years the more seriously he became involved in *rāga-bhakti*. This constantly pulled him away from the mundane to the mystical. Bhaktivinoda never became a social reformer within Bengal. It appears that he remained, for all practical purposes, a man of the status quo. We find, instead, that his fourth son, Bhaktisiddhanta Sarasvati, actively tried to put into practice many of the reforms that his father had talked about.[40]

39. In general we find that the journal *Sajjana-toṣaṇī* includes more "down to earth" discussion than his books. After volume 8 (1896) even the journal ceases to be a place for the topical discussion. Instead it becomes a place for the serialization of Bhaktivinoda's books.

40. It may also be the case that Bhaktivinoda's social status as a magistrate and a married man with many children to marry may have been a factor in his unwillingness to effect many of his reforms of Hindu society. By contrast, Bhaktivinoda's son, Bhaktisiddhanta Sarasvati, as a *sannyāsī* and therefore unmarried and detached from Hindu society, did actively try to carry out his father's reforms.

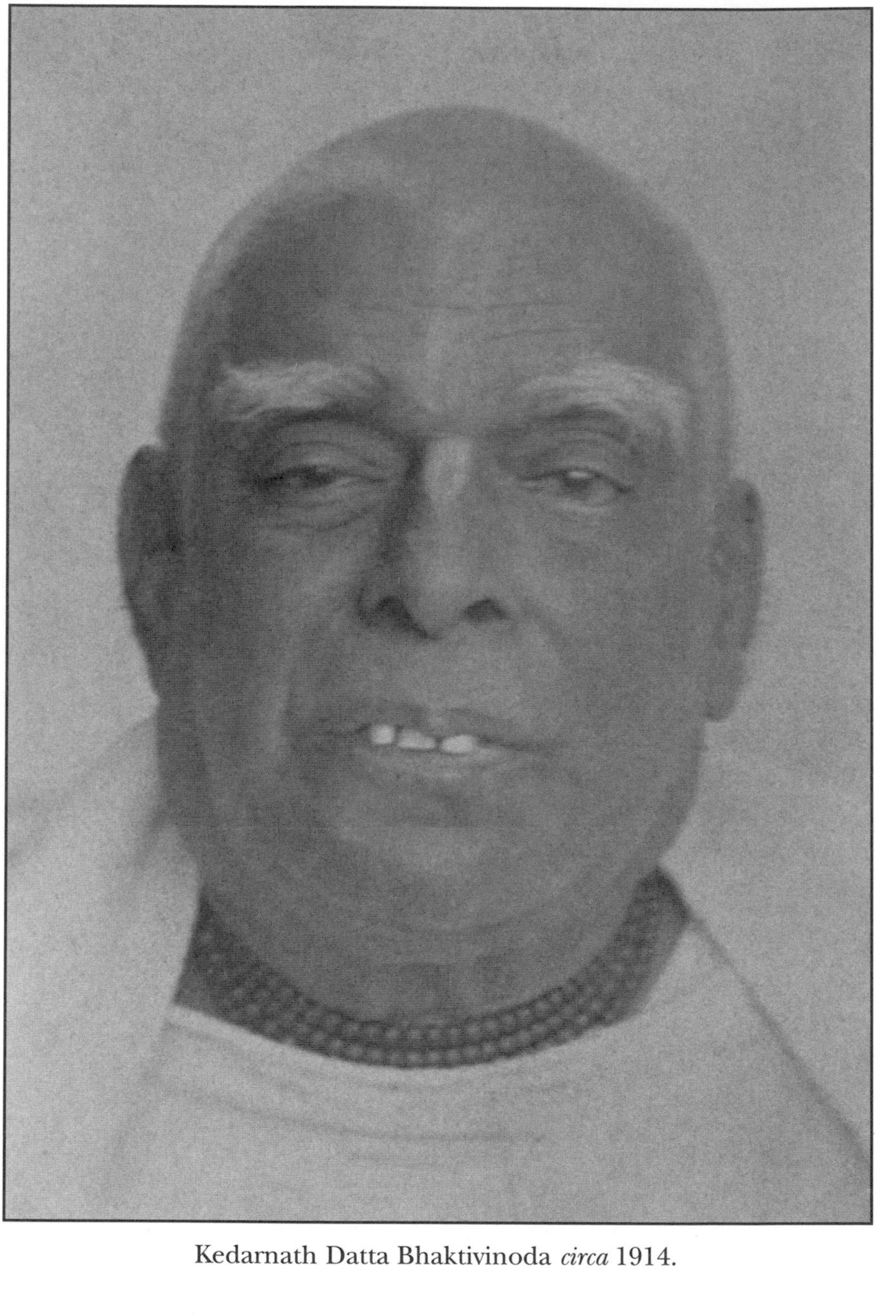

Kedarnath Datta Bhaktivinoda *circa* 1914.

Chapter Ten

Conclusion

We have noted the challenge to traditional culture and the impetus for change within Bengali society that occurred as a result of British penetration into Bengal. We have examined various aspects of Bhaktivinoda's life relative to that process of change and we have also seen how his historical and theological perspectives were radically expanded to suit the emerging global perspective. We have discussed Bhaktivinoda's analysis of religion into its constituent parts or dimensions—the phenomenal and the transcendent—and his ability to differentiate between and yet reconcile the two. We have seen how he applied the rules of human logic and reason to the phenomenal and how he approached the transcendent through religious faith rooted in *sahaja-samādhi*, innate religious intuition. We have also noted the implicit distinction he makes between religious belief and faith and how this allowed him to revise his beliefs without upsetting his religious faith.

Bhaktivinoda's all-important concept of *adhikāra,* an individual's capacity to understand spiritual knowledge, was perhaps the most crucial element of his theology. That the various aspects of divine manifestation—holy *śāstra,* divine *līlā,* sacred image (*śrī-mūrti*), and holy name (*nāma*)—can legitimately be understood in different ways according to the *adhikāra* of the individual, opened the door to multiple levels of religious interpretation.

According to Bhaktivinoda the quintessential religious experience lies in the development of *rasa,* or devotional sentiment. Faith in God is a natural condition of the soul and, if properly directed, it can lead to a *rasika* relationship with the divine. Unfortunately, faith is a fragile thing and sometimes, due to the distortions of civilization, faith becomes subverted by the various philosophies of atheism and nihilism. Consequently, faith must be protected, cultivated and nurtured through its many stages of development before it can reach the stage of *rasa*.

An effective means to nurture the soul's natural faith is through *sādhana-bhakti*, or devotional practice. Rūpa Gosvāmī has described a system of *sādhana-bhakti* in two phases: *vaidhī-bhakti-sādhana* and *rāgānugā-bhakti-sādhana*. Of the two, *rāgānugā-bhakti*, which involves the adoption of an internal spiritual identity that matches one's emotional and psychological temperament, is the most effective means to reach the stage of *rasa*. However, only the most fortunate and rare soul is qualified to follow the path of *rāgānugā-bhakti-sādhana*. Most *sādhakas* must follow the path of *vaidhī-bhakti* until such a time as the stage of *rāga* arises.

The path of *vaidhī-bhakti* is most effectively followed in conjunction with the Vedic social system called *varṇāśrama-dharma*. *Varṇāśrama-dharma* is a scientific social system meant to lead to material and spiritual prosperity in society. Strict adherence to *varṇāśrama* is also the best means to solve the various social problems of society, including those that may arise from *rāgānugā-sādhana-bhakti*. In general, Bhaktivinoda's approach to *sādhana-bhakti* is founded on rational and psychological principles. In *rāgānugā-bhakti* internal identity is determined in terms of one's emotional and psychological temperament. Similarly, in *varṇāśrama-dharma*, *varṇa* is selected in terms of one's physical and psychological temperament.

Bhaktivinoda's approach widened the limits of human reason and rational analysis within Caitanya Vaiṣṇavism. It changed the balance between traditional faith and human reason by allowing a greater degree of rational and symbolic understanding than might otherwise be permitted in Vaiṣṇava religious life. Bhaktivinoda's employment of the *ādhunika-vāda* allowed the *bhadraloka* to experiment with new historical perspectives that were better suited to life in the nineteenth century.

Bhaktivinoda envisioned the modern religious thinker as a *sāra-grāhī*, one able to transcend the limitations of his own religious culture and appreciate the spiritual essence of other religious traditions. There is no question that he viewed the teachings of Caitanya as universal, or that he regarded the *Bhāgavata* as the supreme scripture for all *sāragrāhīs*, whether they lived in India or abroad. But even though the spirit of *nāma-haṭṭa* was global and the perspective of the *sāragrāhī* universal, Bhaktivinoda's personal outreach to the world at large was relatively limited. He sent his writings to Europe and America on only two occasions. Virtually none of his major works were published in English during his lifetime. He never ventured beyond the shores of India as did his distinguished predecessor, Rammohun Roy, or his contemporaries, Keshub Chandra Sen, or Protap C. Mazumdar.[1] Bhaktivinoda remained exclusively within Bengal, Bihar and Orissa with only occasional trips to Vrindavan. Had Bhaktivinoda lived twenty years later, perhaps he might have come to the West as did his junior contemporaries, Swami Vivekananda or Premananda Bharati.

During Bhaktivinoda's own lifetime, however, the European historian and member of the Madras Civil Service R. W. Frazer did feel the touch of Bhaktivinoda's universal spirit when he wrote:

> This exponent [Bhaktivinoda] of the hopes of the present followers of the teachings of Caitanya declares his firm faith, that from a devoted love to Krishna like that of a girl to a loved one, shown by constant repetition of his name, by ecstatic raptures, singing, calm contemplation and fervor, a movement will yet take place to draw to the future church of the world "all classes of men without distinction of caste or clan to the highest cultivation of the spirit." This church, it appears, will extend all over the world, and take the place of all sectarian churches, which exclude outsiders from the precincts of the mosque, church or temple.[2]

1. Protap C. Mazumdar (1840-1905) was the cousin of Keshub Chandra Sen. Mazumdar came to America four times. The first trip was in 1874. Even though Bhaktivinoda never mentions Mazumdar by name, it is almost inconceivable that he did not know of him.
2. R. W. Frazer, *A Literary History of India* (New York: C. Scribner's sons, 1898), 349.

Today we are even seeing, as R. W. Frazer anticipated, that Bhaktivinoda's movement of *nāma-haṭṭa* has begun to appear in the "marketplaces" of the world. We have noted that during the early decades of this century, the Gaudiya Math worked to spread that movement throughout India, and more recently, in the form of the International Society for Krishna Consciousness (ISKCON), that the movement has begun to spread to the major cities of the world. There is little doubt that Bhaktivinoda's long-range vision was fixed on the future generations of *sāragrāhīs* throughout the world who might one day hear his message. But on a day-to-day basis, he had to communicate his message to the *bhadraloka* of his day in the context of nineteenth century Bengal. We have spent much time examining the details of this situation and have tried to discern the underlying theological basis behind Bhaktivinoda's presentation to the *bhadraloka.*

In the remaining pages I want to offer some provisional comments on how I believe Bhaktivinoda's "future church of the world," as Frazer referred to it, may benefit from Bhaktivinoda's work. Admittedly, a discussion of Caitanya Vaiṣṇavism outside of Bengal could easily involve a separate work and more. Instead, I want to address this topic only as it relates to the various aspects of Bhaktivinoda's approach that we have discussed in this work. It is hoped that others will soon take up this important topic in a more elaborate way.

I suggest that Bhaktivinoda's work during the nineteenth century can provide the intellectual and theological basis for the development of a tradition of critical scholarship among the Caitanya Vaiṣṇavas in the West. Specifically, there is a great need for an academic and intellectual tradition to develop among Vaiṣṇavas that is attuned to the intellectual and scholarly traditions of the West.

In this regard I am reminded of Reverend Lal Bihari De's comments during Bhaktivinoda's time concerning the establishment of Christianity in Bengal. Reverend De suggested, "If you wish to see Bengali Christianity develop itself freely and naturally, you must free it from its European trammels, you must remove it from the hot-house of European Church organization and plant it in the genial soil of Bengali modes of thought and feeling; or in other words, you must make Christianity indigenous in Bengal."[3] By this De meant that the religious rituals, the modes of organization, and the doctrines of Christianity, which in his day were European in form, must change to suit Bengali modes of culture and, in fact, must become Bengali. In a similar manner, concerning the adoption of *hari-nāma* by foreign *bhaktas,* Bhaktivinoda writes, "Foreign *sāragrāhīs* whose language and secular institutions are different may have recourse to symbolic forms of worship in their respective languages that are the equivalent of the name."[4] In other words, Bhaktivinoda recognized the need for spiritual and cultural adaptation during his time.

I make the same comment about Caitanya Vaiṣṇavism in the West today. If Caitanya Vaiṣṇavism is to become indigenous to the modern and even Western world, then it must similarly adapt to the conditions of modernity and to the West. I suggest that if Caitanya Vaiṣṇavism is going to have a lasting position and a positive impact on the West, then it must intellectually move beyond the literalism by which it entered the West and begin to develop new forms of intellectual expressions and perspectives that are a part of the Western intellectual and academic traditions. Bhaktivinoda's work provides the basis for such a development.

Bhaktivinoda's use of the concept of *adhikāra* separates the *madhyamādhikārī* from the perspective of the *komala-śraddha.* Critical scholarship cannot develop within the intellectual framework of the *komala-śraddha.* Bhaktivinoda's approach allows the different religious perspectives associated with the various *adhikārīs* to co-exist legitimately. This frees the intellectual from the literal and narrative perspective of the *komala-śraddha* and allows him to legitimately seek a level of understanding that is better suited to his own needs. Bhaktivinoda's conception of religious symbolism and

---

3. Narendra Krishna Sinha, *The History of Bengal (1757-1905)* (Calcutta: University of Calcutta, 1967), 605. Taken from a lecture entitled "The Desirableness and Practicability of Organizing a National Church in Bengal" delivered at the Bengal Christian Association in 1869.
4. KS. 79.

metaphoric interpretation of divine *līlā* are prime examples of this new approach.

Similarly, Bhaktivinoda's separation of the phenomenal and the transcendent, along with his implicit distinction between religious faith and belief, frees the religious insider from having to pursue religious scholarship with a vested emotional interest. We saw the reaction of some of my religious colleagues when I stated Bhaktivinoda's conclusion that the *Bhāgavata* may be a work of only a thousand years. The need to be rigorous and to discern rationally the evidence of the cumulative religious tradition—the phenomenal world—must be made distinct and separate from the deep emotions of religious faith if genuine critical scholarship is to be undertaken. Without this separation, the needs of religious faith will inevitably force the religious participant to distort the findings of the cumulative tradition. To approach what is inherently divine and transcendent with these same tools of human reason creates another kind of distortion—a spiritual subversion of divine truth in which the divine is minimized and made trivial. Bankim Chandra's presentation of the life of Kṛṣṇa was a prime example of this distortion. When religious faith is no longer inextricably connected to belief and we begin to recognize that religious faith ultimately lies within the realm of the transcendent and belief within the realm of the phenomenal, true religious scholarship can proceed free from the need to express the data of the cumulative tradition solely in terms of what nurtures faith.

I also suggest that Bhaktivinoda's theological approach may be of value to religious participants who belong to traditions other than Caitanya Vaiṣṇavism. The problems of religious scholarship are universal. Religious participants from other traditions may benefit from applying Bhaktivinoda's approach to their own situations. Bhaktivinoda's work may also benefit religious scholars who stand not as religious participants but as critical though sensitive observers to a particular religious tradition. Awareness that religion is composed of two distinct elements, the cumulative tradition and realm of religious faith, has immense potential for increased understanding of religion. Wilfred Cantwell Smith has developed this point at length.

Bhaktivinoda's idea that religion can be expressed in terms of *rasika* experience is another important contribution to religious studies. It is Bhaktivinoda's view that the religious experience understood mainly in terms of morality is limited because it fails to satisfy the ultimate spiritual yearnings of the soul. He contends that the soul ultimately hungers for spiritual taste, which can be satisfied through the *rasika* experience alone. The idea that religious experience can be interpreted as a development from a special kind of aesthetic or *rasika* experience is an idea that can add new depth to Western perceptions of the religious experience. By explaining the perspective of the *uttamādhikārī*, which is essentially a *rasika* perspective, Bhaktivinoda has gone a long way to frame this idea in terms that we in the West can begin to appreciate.

There is no doubt that the life and teachings of Bhaktivinoda apply specifically to those of us who are participating directly within the Caitanya movement that is developing in the West. The form of Caitanya Vaiṣṇavism that has emerged here in the West is largely a *vaidhī-bhakti* tradition in which the approach of *rāgānugā-bhakti-sādhana* has largely been excluded as a viable path. While the emphasis on *vaidhī-bhakti* may avoid many of the problems associated with the tradition of *rāgānugā-bhakti-sādhana,* it also has denied the tradition of much of its spiritual depth. Bhaktivinoda's emphasis on *rāgānugā-bhakti-sādhana* should be carefully considered. After all, it is one of the principle means by which the *rasika* religious experience may be accessed.

As in the case of many religious traditions, Caitanya Vaiṣṇavism operates in two modes: an exoteric mode that is tailored to the needs of its general followers and those entering upon the path, and an esoteric mode that embodies the mystical aspects of the tradition and which ignites its spiritual inspiration. Bhaktivinoda clearly taught the importance of the exoteric mode in his discussions on *varṇāśrama-dharma* and *vaidhī-bhakti-sādhana,* but ultimately it was the esoteric tradition of *rāgānugā-bhakti-sādhana* that commanded the attention of his heart and soul. It may be that Caitanya Vaiṣṇavism as it now exists in the West is largely disconnected from the tradition of *rāgānugā-bhakti-sādhana,* and for this reason is somewhat alienated from the esoteric depths and spiritual inspiration of its parent movement. I have no doubt that for most followers the path of *vaidhī-bhakti-sādhana* is the appropriate path. However, for those devotees who may one day feel the passion of *rāga* pulling at the heartstrings of their soul, I think the work of Bhaktivinoda has ever so carefully opened the door once again to the path of *rāgānugā-bhakti-sādhana.* Bhaktivinoda's suggestion that internal spiritual identity can be discerned in terms of one's personal feelings and psychology, in consultation with a competent spiritual guide, should be seriously considered.

Finally we must consider Bhaktivinoda's position as a Vaiṣṇava role model. His position as a family man with his Western education and high governmental office, combined with his coming to Caitanya Vaiṣṇavism at a mature age after long and careful study, provides an essential role model for those who are endeavoring to combine the best of what modernity has to offer with the sacred traditions and practices of Caitanya Vaiṣṇavism.

It is an undeniable fact that since Caitanya Vaiṣṇavism is so new to the West there is naturally a scarcity of viable role models. What role models do exist tend to be of the *tyāgī,* or renounced type, tending to be aloof from the needs of the young Vaiṣṇava householder. Bhaktivinoda's life, especially as told in his autobiography, provides an excellent example of responsible worldly engagement and Vaiṣṇava practice. For these reasons—intellectual, spiritual, and social—we are forever indebted to this great *sāragrāhī* Vaiṣṇava, Shri Kedarnath Datta Bhaktivinoda.

Reading Supplement

The *Bhāgavata*

Its Philosophy, Ethics, and Theology

by

Kedarnath Datta Bhaktivinoda*

> "O Ye, who are deeply merged in the knowledge of the love of God and also in deep thought about it, constantly drink, even after your emancipation, the most tasteful juice of the *Srīmad-Bhāgavatam,* come on earth through Śrī Śukadeva Gosvāmī's mouth carrying the liquid nectar out of the fallen and, as such, very ripe fruit of the Vedic tree which supplies all with their desired objects." (*Śrīmad-Bhāgavatam,* 1/1/3)

We love to read a book which we never read before. We are anxious to gather whatever information is contained in it and with such acquirement our curiosity stops. This mode of study prevails amongst a great number of readers, who are great men in their own estimation as well as in the estimation of those, who are of their own stamp. In fact, most readers are mere repositories of facts and statements made by other people. But this is not study. The student is to read the facts with a view to create, and not with the object of fruitless retention. Students like satellites should reflect whatever light they receive from authors and not imprison the facts and thoughts just as the magistrates imprison the convicts in the jail! Thought is

* Editor's note: This is the text of the famous Dinajpur speech repeatedly quoted throughout this book. It is one of the few extant samples of English writing that came from the pen of Bhaktivinoda.

progressive. The author's thought must have progress in the reader in the shape of correction or development. He is the best critic, who can show the further development of an old thought; but a mere denouncer is the enemy of progress and consequently of Nature. "Begin anew," says the critic, because the old masonry does not answer at present. Let the old author be buried because his time is gone. These are shallow expressions. Progress certainly is the law of nature and there must be correction and developments with the progress of time. But progress means going further or rising higher. Now, if we are to follow our foolish critic, we are to go back to our former terminus and make a new race, and when we have run half the race, another critic of his stamp will cry out: "Begin anew, because the wrong road has been taken!" In this way our stupid critics will never allow us to go over the whole road and see what is in the other terminus. Thus the shallow critic and the fruitless reader are the two great enemies of progress. We must shun them.

The true critic, on the other hand, advises us to preserve what we have already obtained, and to adjust our race from that point where we have arrived in the heat of our progress. He will never advise us to go back to the point whence we started, as he fully knows that in that case there will be a fruitless loss of our valuable time and labor. He will direct the adjustment of the angle of the race at the point where we are. This is also the characteristic of the useful student. He will read an old author and will find out his exact position in the progress of thought. He will never propose to burn the book on the grounds that it contains thoughts which are useless. No thought is useless. Thoughts are means by which we attain our objects. The reader who denounces a bad thought does not know that a bad road is even capable of improvement and conversion into a good one. One thought is a road leading to another. Thus the reader will find that one thought which is the object today will be the means of a further object tomorrow. Thoughts will necessarily continue to be an endless series of means and objects in the progresses of humanity. The great reformers will always assert that they have come out not to *destroy* the old law, but to *fulfill* it. Vālmīki,

Vyāsa, Plato, Jesus, Mohammed, Confucius and Caitanya Mahāprabhu assert the fact either expressly or by their conduct.

The *Bhāgavata* like all religious works and philosophical performances and writings of great men has suffered from the imprudent conduct of useless readers and stupid critics. The former have done so much injury to the work that they have surpassed the latter in their evil consequence. Men of brilliant thought have passed by the work in quest of truth and philosophy, but the prejudice which they imbibed from its useless readers and their conduct, prevented them from making a candid investigation. Not to say of other people, the great genius of Raja Rammohun Roy, the founder of the sect of Brahmoism, did not think it worth his while to study this ornament of the religious library. He crossed the gate of the *Vedānta*, as set up by the *māyāvāda* construction of the designing Śaṅkarācārya, the chosen enemy of the Jains, and chalked his way out to the Unitarian form of the Christian faith, converted into an Indian appearance. Rammohun Roy was an able man. He could not be satisfied with the theory of illusion contained in the *māyāvāda* philosophy of Śaṅkara. His heart was full of love to Nature. He saw through the eye of his mind that he could not believe in his identity with God. He ran furious from the bounds of Śaṅkara to those of the *Koran*. There even he was not satisfied. He then studied the pre-eminently beautiful precepts and history of Jesus, first in the English translation and at last in the original Greek, and took shelter under the holy banners of the Jewish reformer. But Rammohun Roy was also a patriot. He wanted to reform his country in the same way as he reformed himself. He knew it fully that truth does not belong exclusively to any individual man or to any nation or particular race. It belongs to God, and man whether at the poles or on the equator, has a right to claim it as the property of his Father. On these grounds he claimed the truths inculcated by the Western Savior as also the property of himself and his countrymen, and thus he established the *samāja* of the Brahmos independently of what was in his own country in the beautiful *Bhāgavata*. His noble deeds will certainly procure him a high position in the history of reformers. But then, to speak the truth, he would have done more if he had commenced his work of reformation from the point where the last reformer in India left it. It is not our business to go further on this subject. Suffice it to say, that the *Bhāgavata* did not attract the genius of Rammohun Roy. His thought, mighty though it was, unfortunately branched like the Ranigunj line of the railway, from the barren station of Śaṅkarācārya, and did not attempt to be an extension from the Delhi Terminus of the great *Bhāgavata* expounder of Nadia. We do not doubt that the progress of time will correct the error, and by a further extension the branch line will lose itself somewhere in the main line of progress. We expect these attempts in an abler reformer of the followers of Rammohun Roy.

The *Bhāgavata* has suffered alike from shallow critics both Indian and outlandish. That book has been accursed and denounced by a great number of our young countrymen, who have scarcely read its contents and pondered over the philosophy on which it is founded. It is owing mostly to their imbibing an unfounded prejudice against it when they were in school. The *Bhāgavata*, as a matter of course, has been held in derision by those teachers, who are generally of an inferior mind and intellect. This prejudice is not easily shaken when the student grows up unless he candidly studies the book and ruminates on the doctrines of Vaiṣṇavism. We are ourselves witness to the fact. When we were in college, reading the philosophical works of the West and exchanging thoughts with the thinkers of the day, we had a real hatred towards the *Bhāgavata*. That great work looked like a repository of wicked and stupid ideas, scarcely adapted to the nineteenth century, and we hated to hear any arguments in its favor. With us then a volume of Channing, Parker, Emerson or Newman had more weight than the whole lot of Vaiṣṇava works. Greedily we poured over the various commentaries of the Holy Bible and of the labors of the Tattwa Bodhini Sabha, containing extracts from the *Upaniṣads* and the *Vedānta*, but no work of the Vaiṣṇavas had any favor with us. But when we advanced in age and our religious sentiment received development, we turned out in a manner Unitarian in our belief and prayed as Jesus prayed in the garden. Accidentally, we fell in with a work about the great Caitanya, and on reading it with some attention in order to settle the historical position of that Mighty Genius of Nadia, we had the opportunity of gathering His explanations of *Bhāgavata*, given to the wrangling Vedantist of the Benares School. The accidental study created in us a love for all the works which we find about our Eastern Savior. We gathered with difficulties the famous *karcās* in Sanskrit, written by the disciples of Caitanya. The explanations that we got of the *Bhāgavata* from these sources, were of such a charming character that we procured a copy of the *Bhāgavata* complete and studied its texts (difficult of course to those who are not trained up in philosophical thoughts) with the assistance of the famous commentaries of Śrīdhara Svāmī. From such study it is that we have at least gathered the real doctrines of the Vaiṣṇavas. Oh! What a trouble to get rid of prejudices gathered in unripe years!

As far as we can understand, no enemy of Vaiṣṇavism will find any beauty in the *Bhāgavata*. The true critic is a generous judge, void of prejudices and party-spirit. One, who is at heart the follower of Mohammed will certainly find the doctrines of the New Testament to be a forgery by the fallen angel. A Trinitarian Christian, on the other hand, will denounce the precepts of Mohammed as those of an ambitious reformer. The reason simply is, that the critic should be of the same disposition of mind as that of the author, whose merit he is required to judge. Thoughts have different ways. One, who is trained up in the thoughts of the Unitarian Society or of the *Vedānta* of the Benares School, will scarcely find piety in the faith of the Vaiṣṇavas. An ignorant Vaiṣṇava, on the other hand, whose business it is to beg from door to door in the name of Nityānanda will find no piety in the Christian. This is because, the Vaiṣṇava does not think in the way which the Christian thinks of his own religion. It may be, that both the Christian and the Vaiṣṇava will utter the same sentiment, but they will never stop their fight with each other only because they have arrived at their common conclusion by different ways of thoughts. Thus it is, that a great deal of ungenerousness enters into the arguments of the pious Christians when they pass their imperfect opinion on the religion of the Vaiṣṇavas.

Subjects of philosophy and theology are like the peaks of large towering and inaccessible mountains standing in the midst of our planet inviting attention and investigation. Thinkers and men of deep speculation take their observations through the instruments of reason and consciousness. But they take different points when they carry on their work. These points are positions chalked out by the circumstances of their social and philosophical life, different as they are in the different parts of the world. Plato looked at the peak of the Spiritual question from the West and Vyāsa made the observation from the East; so Confucius did it from further East, and Schlegel, Spinoza, Kant, Goethe from further West. These observations were made at different times and by different means, but the conclusion is all the same in as much as the object of observation was one and the same. They all hunted after the Great Spirit, the unconditioned Soul of the Universe. They could not but get an insight into it. Their words and expressions are different, but their import is the same. They tried to find out the absolute religion and their labors were crowned with success, for God gives all that He has to His children if they want to have it. It requires a candid, generous, pious and holy heart to feel the beauties of their conclusions. Party-spirit—that great enemy of truth—will always baffle the attempt of the inquirer, who tries to gather truth from religious works of other nations, and will make him believe that absolute truth is nowhere except in his old religious book. What better example could be adduced than the fact that the great philosopher of Benares will find no truth in the universal brotherhood of man and the common fatherhood of God? The philosopher, thinking in his own way of thought, can never see the beauty of the Christian faith. The way, in which Christ thought of his own father, was love absolute and so long as the philosopher will not adopt that way of thinking he will ever remain deprived of the absolute faith preached by the western Savior. In a similar manner, the Christian needs adopt the way of thought which the Vedantist pursued, before he can love the conclusions of the philosopher. The critic, therefore, should have a comprehensive, good, generous, candid, impartial and a sympathetic soul.

What sort of a thing is the *Bhāgavata,* asks the European gentleman newly arrived in India. His companion tells him with a serene look, that the *Bhāgavata* is a book, which his Oriya bearer daily reads in the evening to a number of hearers. It contains a jargon of unintelligible and savage literature of those men who paint their noses with some sort of earth or sandal, and wear beads all over their bodies in order to procure salvation for themselves. Another of his companions, who has traveled a little in the interior, would immediately contradict him and say that the *Bhāgavata* is a Sanskrit work claimed by a sect of men, the Goswamis, who give *mantras,* like the Popes of Italy, to the common people of Bengal, and pardon their sins on payment of gold enough to defray their social expenses. A third gentlemen will repeat a third explanation. Young Bengal, chained up in English thoughts and ideas, and wholly ignorant of the Pre-Mohammed history of his own country, will add one more explanation by saying that the *Bhāgavata* is a book, containing an account of the life of Kṛṣṇa, who was an ambitious and an immoral man! This is all that he could gather from his grandmother while yet he did not go to school! Thus the great *Bhāgavata* ever remains unknown to the foreigners like the elephant of the six blind men who caught hold of the several parts of the body of the beast! But Truth is eternal and is never injured but for *a while* by ignorance.

The *Bhāgavata* itself tells us what it is:

nigama-kalpa-taror galitaṁ phalaṁ
śuka-mukhād amṛta-drava-saṁyutam/
pibata bhāgavataṁ rasam ālayaṁ
muhur aho rasikā bhuvi bhāvukāḥ//
(Bhāg. 1/1/3)

"It is the fruit of the tree of thought (*Vedas*) mixed with the nectar of the speech of Śukadeva. It is the temple of

> spiritual love! O! Men of Piety! Drink deep this nectar of the *Bhāgavata* repeatedly till *you* are taken from this mortal frame."

The *Garuḍa-purāṇa* says, again:

> *grantho 'ṣṭādaśa-sahasra-śrīmad-bhāgavatābhidhā*
> *sarva-vedetihāsānāṁ sāraṁ sāraṁ samuddhṛtaṁ/*
> *sarva-vedānta-sāraṁ hi śrī-bhāgavatam iśyate*
> *tad rasāmṛta-tṛptasya nānyatra syād rati-kvacit//*

> "The *Bhāgavata* is composed of 18,000 *ślokas*. It contains the best parts of the *Vedas* and the *Vedānta*. Whoever has tasted its sweet nectar, will never like to read any other religious book."

Every thoughtful reader will certainly repeat this eulogy. The *Bhāgavata* is preeminently the Book in India. Once enter into it, and you are transplanted, as it were, into the spiritual world where gross matter has no existence. The true follower of the *Bhāgavata* is a spiritual man who has already cut his temporary connection with phenomenal nature, and has made himself the inhabitant of that region where God eternally exists and loves. This mighty work is founded upon inspiration and its superstructure is upon reflection. To the common reader it has no charms and is full of difficulty. We are, therefore, obliged to study it deeply through the assistance of such great commentators as Śrīdhara Svāmī and the divine Caitanya and His contemporary followers.

Now the great preacher of Nadia, who has been deified by His talented followers, tells us that the *Bhāgavata* is founded upon the four *ślokas* which Vyāsa received from Nārada, the most learned of the created beings. He tells us further that Brahmā pierced through the whole universe of matter for years and years in quest of the final cause of the world but when he failed to find it abroad, he looked into the construction of his own spiritual nature, and there he heard the Universal Spirit speaking unto him, the following words:

jñānaṁ parama-guhyaṁ me yad vijñāna-samanvitam/
sarahasyaṁ tad-aṅgaṁ ca gṛhāṇa gaditaṁ mayā//

yāvān ahaṁ yathā-bhāvo yad-rūpa-guṇa-karmakaḥ/
tathaiva tattva-vijñānam astu te mad-anugrahāt//

aham evāsam evāgre nānyad yat sad-asat param/
paścād ahaṁ yad etac ca yo 'vaśiṣyeta so 'smy aham//

ṛte 'rthaṁ yat pratīyeta na pratīyeta cātmani/
tad vidyād ātmano māyāṁ yathābhāso yathā tamaḥ//
(*Bhāg*. 2/9/31-34)

"Take, O Brahmā! I am giving you the knowledge of my own self and of my relations and phases which is in itself difficult of access. You are a created being, so it is not easy for you to accept what I give you, but then I kindly give you the power to accept, so you are at liberty to understand my essence, my ideas, my form, my property and my action together with their various relations with imperfect knowledge. I was in the beginning before all spiritual and temporal things were created, and after they have been created I am in them all in the shape of their existence and truthfulness, and when they will be all gone I shall remain full as I was and as I am. Whatever appears to be true without being a real fact itself, and whatever is not perceived though it is true in itself are subjects of my illusory energy of creation, such as, light and darkness in the material world."

It is difficult to explain the above in a short compass. You must read the whole *Bhāgavata* for its explanation. When the great Vyāsa had effected the arrangements of the *Vedas* and the *Upaniṣads*, the completion of the eighteen *Purāṇas* with facts gathered from the recorded and unrecorded tradition of ages, and the composition of the *Vedānta* and the large *Mahābharata*, an epic poem of great celebrity, he began to ruminate over his own theories and precepts, and found like Fauste of Goethe that he had up to that time gathered no real truth. He fell back into his own self and searched his own spiritual nature and then it was that the above truth was communicated to him for his own good and the good of the world. The sage immediately perceived that his former works required supercession in as much as they did not contain the whole truth and nothing but the truth. In his new idea he got the development of his former idea of religion. He commenced the *Bhāgavata* in pursuance of this change. From this fact, our readers are expected to find out the position which the *Bhāgavata* enjoys in the library of Hindu theological works.

The whole of this incomparable work teaches us, according to our Great Caitanya, the three great truths which compose the absolute religion of man. Our Nadia preacher calls them *sambandha, abhidheya* and *prayojana, i.e.*, the relation between the Creator and the created, the duty of man to God and the prospects of humanity. In these three words is summed up the whole ocean of human knowledge as far as it has been explored up to this era of human progress. These are the cardinal points of religion and the whole *Bhāgavata* is, as we are taught by Caitanya, an explanation both by precepts and example, of these three great points.

In all its twelve *skandhas* or divisions the *Bhāgavata* teaches us that there is only one God without a second, Who was full in Himself and is and will remain the same. Time and space, which prescribe conditions to created objects are much below His Supreme Spiritual nature, which is unconditioned and absolute. Created objects are subject to the influence of time and space, which form the chief ingredients of that principle in creation which passes by the name of *māyā*. *Māyā* is a thing which is not easily understood by us who are subject to it, but God explains, as much as we can understand in our present constitution, this principle through our spiritual perception. The hasty critic starts like an unbroken horse at the name of *māyā* and denounces it as a theory identical with that of Bishop Berkeley. "Be patient in your inquiry," is our immediate reply. In the mind of God there were ideas of all that we perceive in eternal existence with Him, or else God loses the epithet of omniscient so learnedly applied to Him. The imperfect part of nature implying want proceeded also from certain of those ideas, and what, but a principle of *māyā*, eternally existing in God subject to His Omnipotence, could have a hand in the creation of the world as it is? This is styled as the *māyā-śakti* of the omnipresent God. Cavil as much as you can. This is a *truth* in relation to the created universe.

This *māyā* intervenes between us and God as long as we are not spiritual, and when we are able to break off her bonds, we, even in this mortal frame, learn to commune in our spiritual nature with the unconditioned and the absolute. No, *māyā* does not mean a false thing only, but it means concealment of eternal truth as well. The creation is not *māyā* itself but is subject to that principle. Certainly, the theory is idealistic but it has been degraded into foolishness by wrong explanations. The materialist laughs at the ideal theory saying, how could his body, water, air and earth be mere ideas without entity, and he laughs rightly when he takes Śaṅkarācārya's book in his hand at the butt end of his ridicule. The true idealist must be a dualist also. He must believe all that he perceives as nature created by God full of spiritual essence and relations, but he must not believe that the outward appearance is the truth. The *Bhāgavata* teaches that all that we healthily perceive is true, but its material appearance is transient and illusory. The scandal of the ideal theory consists in its tendency to falsify nature, but the theory as explained in the *Bhāgavata* makes nature true, if not eternally true as God and His ideas. What harm there can be if man believes in nature as spiritually true and that the physical relations and phases of society are purely spiritual?

No, it is not merely changing a name but it is a change in nature also. Nature is eternally spiritual but the intervention of *māyā* makes her gross and material. Man, in his progress attempts to shake off this gross idea, childish and foolish in its nature and by subduing the intervening principle of *māyā*, lives in continual union with God in his spiritual nature. The shaking off this bond is salvation of the human nature. The man who has got salvation will freely tell his brother that "If you want to see God, see me, and if you want to be one with God, you must follow me." The *Bhāgavata* teaches us this relation between man and God, and we must all attain this knowledge. This sublime truth is the point where the materialist and the idealist must meet like brothers of the same school and this is the point to which all philosophy tends.

This is called *sambandha-jñāna* of the *Bhāgavata*, or, in other words, the knowledge of relations between the conditioned and the Absolute. We must now attempt to explain the second great principle inculcated by the *Bhāgavata*, i.e., the principle of duty. Man must spiritually worship his God. There are three ways, in which the Creator is worshipped by the created.

vadanti tat tattva-vidas tattvaṁ yaj jñānam advyayam/
brahmeti paramātmeti bhagavān iti śabdyate//
(*Bhāg.* 1/2/11)

All theologists agree in maintaining that there is only one God without a second, but they disagree in giving a name to that God owing to the different modes of worship, which they adopt according to the constitution of their mind. Some call Him by the name of *brahman*, some by the name of *paramātmā* and others by the name of *bhagavān*. Those who worship God as infinitely great in the principle of admiration call Him by the name of *brahman*. This mode is called *jñāna* or knowledge. Those who worship God as the Universal Soul in the principle of spiritual union with Him give Him the name of *paramātmā*. This is *yoga*. Those who worship God as all in all with all their heart, body and strength style Him as *bhagavān*. This last principle is *bhakti*. The book that prescribes the relation and worship of *bhagavān*, procures for itself the name of *Bhāgavata* and the worshipper is also called by the same name.

Such is *Bhāgavata* which is decidedly *the* book for all classes of theists. If we worship God spiritually as *all* in all with our heart, mind, body and strength, we are all *Bhāgavatas* and we lead a life of spiritualism, which neither the worshipper of *brahman*, nor the *yogī* uniting his soul with (*paramātmā*) the universal soul can obtain. The superiority of the *Bhāgavata* consists in the uniting of all sorts of theistic worship into one excellent principle in human nature, which passes by the name of *bhakti*. This word has no equivalent in the English language. Piety, devotion, resignation and spiritual love unalloyed with any sort of petition except in the way of repentance, compose the highest principle of *bhakti*. The *Bhāgavata* tells us to worship God in that great and invaluable principle, which is infinitely superior to human knowledge and the principle of *yoga*.

Our short compass will not admit of an explanation of the principle of *bhakti* beautifully rising from its first stage of application in the form of *Brahmic* worship in the shape of admiration which is styled the *śānta-rasa*, to the fifth or the highest stage of absolute union in love with God, sweetly styled the *mādhurya-rasa* of *prema-bhakti*. A full explanation will take a big volume which is not our object here to compose. Suffice it to say that the principle of *bhakti* passes five distinct stages in the course of its development into its highest and purest form. Then again when it reaches the last form, it is susceptible of further progress from the stage of *prema* (love) to that of *mahā-bhāva* which is in fact a complete transition into the spiritual universe where God alone is the bride-groom of our soul.

The voluminous *Bhāgavata* is nothing more than a full illustration of this principle of continual development and progress of the soul from gross matter to the all-perfect Universal Spirit who is distinguished as personal, eternal, absolutely free, all powerful and all intelligent. There is nothing gross or material in it. The whole affair is spiritual. In order to impress this spiritual picture upon the student who attempts to learn it, comparisons have been made with the material world, which cannot but convince the ignorant and the impractical. Material examples are absolutely necessary for the explanation of spiritual ideas. The *Bhāgavata* believes that the spirit of nature is the truth in nature and is the only practical part of it.

The phenomenal appearance of nature is truly theoretical, although it has had the greatest claim upon our belief from the days of our infancy. The outward appearance of nature is nothing more than a sure index of its spiritual face. Comparisons are therefore necessary. Nature as it is before our eyes, must explain the spirit, or else the truth will ever remain concealed, and man will never rise from his boyhood though his whiskers and beard grow white as the snows of the Himalayas. The whole intellectual and moral philosophy is explained by matter itself. Emerson beautifully shows how all the words in moral philosophy originally came from the names of material objects. The words heart, head, spirit, thought, courage, bravery, were originally the common names of some corresponding objects in the material world. All spiritual ideas are similarly pictures from the material world, because matter is the dictionary of spirit, and material pictures are but the shadows of the spiritual affairs which our material eye carries back to our spiritual perception. God in His infinite goodness and kindness has established this unfailing connection between the truth and the shadow in order to impress upon us the eternal truth which He has reserved for us. The clock explains the time, the alphabet points to the gathered store of knowledge, the beautiful song of a harmonium gives the idea of eternal harmony in the spirit world, to-day and to-morrow and day-after-to-morrow thrust into us the ungrasped idea of eternity and similarly material pictures impress upon our spiritual nature the truly spiritual idea of religion. It is on these reasonable grounds that Vyāsa adopted the mode of explaining our spiritual worship with some sort of material phenomena, which correspond with the spiritual truth. Our object is not to go into details, so we are unable to quote some of the illustrations within this short compass.

We have also the practical part of the question in the 11th book of *Bhāgavata.* All the modes by which a man can train himself up to *prema-bhakti* as explained above, have been described at great length. We have been advised first of all, to convert ourselves into most grateful servants of God as regards to our relations to our fellow brethren. Our nature has been described as bearing three different phases in all our bearings of the world. Those phases are named *sattva, rajas,* and *tamas. Sattva-guṇa* is that property in our nature, which is purely good as far as it can be pure in our present state. *Rajo-guṇa* is neither good nor bad. *Tamo-guṇa* is evil. Our *pravṛttis* or tendencies and affections are described as the mainspring of all our actions, and it is our object to train up those affections and tendencies to the standard of *sattva-guṇa,* as decided by the moral principle. This is not easily done. All the springs of our actions should be carefully protected from *tamo-guṇa,* the evil principle, by adopting the *rajo-guṇa* at first, and when that is effected, man should subdue his *rajo-guṇa* by means of the natural *sattva-guṇa* which is the most powerful of them cultivated. Lust, idleness, wicked deeds and degradation of human nature by intoxicating principles are described as exclusively belonging to *tamo-guṇa,* the evil phase of nature. These are to be checked by marriage, useful work and abstinence from intoxication and trouble to our neighbors and inferior animals. Thus when *rajo-guṇa* has obtained supremacy in the heart, it is our duty to convert that *rajo-guṇa* into *sattva-guṇa* which is pre-eminently good. That married love, which is first cultivated, must now be sublimated into holy, good and spiritual love, i.e., love between soul and soul. Useful work will now be converted into work of love and not of disgust or obligation. Abstinence from wicked work will be made to lose its negative appearance and converted into positive good work. Then we are to look to all living beings in the same light in which we look to ourselves, i.e., we must convert our selfishness into all *possible disinterested* activity towards all around us. Love, charity, good deeds and devotion to God will be our only aim. We then become the servants of God by obeying his High and Holy wishes. Here we begin to be *bhaktas* and we are susceptible to further improvement in our spiritual nature, as we have described above. All this is covered by the term *abhidheya,* the second cardinal point in the supreme religious work, the *Bhāgavata.* We have now before us, the first two cardinal points in our religion, explained somehow or other in the terms and thoughts expressed by our savior who lived only four and a half centuries ago in the beautiful town of Nadia, situated on the banks of the Bhagirathi. We must now proceed to the last cardinal point termed by the great Re-establisher, *prayojana* or prospects.

What is the object of our spiritual development, our prayer, our devotion and our union with God? The *Bhāgavata* tells that the object is not enjoyment or sorrow, but continual progress in spiritual holiness and harmony.

In the common-place books of the Hindu religion in which the *rajo* and *tamo-guṇa* have been described as the ways of religion, we have descriptions of a local heaven and a local hell; the Heaven as beautiful as anything on earth and the Hell as ghastly as any picture of evil. Besides this Heaven we have many more places, where good souls are sent up in the way of promotion! There are 84 divisions of the hell itself, some more dreadful than the one which Milton has described in his "Paradise Lost." These are certainly poetical and were originally created by the rulers of the country in order to check evil deeds of the ignorant people, who are not able to understand the conclusions of philosophy. The religion of the *Bhāgavata* is free from such a poetry. Indeed, in some of the chapters we meet with descriptions of these hells and heavens, and accounts of curious tales, but we have been warned somewhere in the book, not to accept them as real facts, but as inventions to overawe the wicked and to improve the simple and the ignorant. The *Bhāgavata*, certainly tells us a state of reward and punishment in the future according to the deeds in our present situation. All poetic inventions, besides this spiritual fact, have been described as statements borrowed from other works in the way of preservation of old traditions in the book which superseded them and put an end to the necessity of their storage. If the whole stock of Hindu theological works which preceded the *Bhāgavata* were burnt like the Alexandrian library and the sacred *Bhāgavata* preserved as it is, not a part of the philosophy of the Hindus except that of the atheistic sects, would be lost. The *Bhāgavata* therefore, may be styled both as a religious work and a compendium of all Hindu history and philosophy.

The *Bhāgavata* does not allow its followers to ask anything from God except eternal love towards Him. The kingdom of the world, the beauties of the local heavens and the sovereignty over the material world are never the subjects of Vaiṣṇava prayer. The Vaiṣṇava meekly and humbly says, "Father, Master, God, Friend and Husband of my soul! Hallowed be Thy name! I do not approach You for anything which You have already given me. I have sinned against You and I now repent and solicit Your pardon. Let Thy holiness touch my soul and make me free from grossness. Let my spirit be devoted meekly to Your Holy service in absolute love towards Thee. I have called You my God, and let my soul be wrapped up in admiration at Your greatness! I have addressed You as my Master and let my soul be strongly devoted to your service. I have called You my friend, and let my soul be in reverential love towards You and not in dread or fear! I have called you my husband and let my spiritual nature be in eternal union with You, forever loving and never dreading, or feeling disgust. Father! let me have strength enough to go up to You as the consort of my soul, so that we may be one in eternal love! Peace to the world!"

Of such a nature is the prayer of the *Bhāgavata.* One who can read the book will find the highest form of prayer in the expressions of Prahlāda towards the universal and omnipresent Soul with powers to convert all unholy strength into meek submission or entire annihilation. This prayer will show what is the end and object of Vaiṣṇavas life. He does not expect to be the king of a certain part of the universe after his death, nor does he dread a local fiery and turbulent hell, the idea of which would make the hairs of young Hamlet stand erect like the forks of a *porcupine*! His idea of salvation is not total annihilation of personal existence as the Buddhists and the twenty-four gods of the Jains procured for themselves! The Vaiṣṇava the meekest of all creatures is devoid of all ambition. He wants to serve God spiritually after death as he has served Him both in spirit and matter while here. His constitution is a spirit and his highest object of life is divine and holy love.

There may be a philosophical doubt. How the human soul could have a distinct existence from the universal Soul when the gross part of the human constitution will be, no more? The Vaiṣṇava can't answer it, nor can any man on earth explain it. The Vaiṣṇava meekly answers, he feels the truth but he cannot understand it. The *Bhāgavata* merely affirms that the Vaiṣṇava soul when freed from the gross matter will distinctly exist not in time and space but spiritually in the eternal spiritual kingdom of God where love is life, and hope and charity and continual ecstasy without change are its various manifestations.

In considering about the essence of the Deity, two great errors stare before us and frighten us back to ignorance and its satisfaction. One of them is the idea that God is above all attributes both material and spiritual and is consequently above all conception. This is a noble idea but useless. If God is above conception and without any sympathy with the world, how is then this creation, this Universe composed of properties, the distinctions and phases of existence, the differences of value, man, woman, beast, trees, magnetism, animal magnetism, electricity, landscape, water and fire? In that case Śaṅkarācārya's *māyāvāda* theory would be absolute philosophy.

The other error is that God is all attribute, *i.e.* intelligence, truth, goodness and power. This is also a ludicrous idea. Scattered properties can never constitute a Being. It is more impossible in the case of belligerent principles, such as justice and mercy and fullness and creative power. Both ideas are imperfect. The truth, as stated in the *Bhāgavata* is that properties, though many of them belligerent, are united in a spiritual Being where they have full sympathy and harmony. Certainly this is beyond our comprehension. It is so owing to our nature being finite and God being infinite. Our ideas are constrained by the idea of space and time, but God is above that constraint. This is a glimpse of Truth and we must regard it as Truth itself: often, says Emerson, a glimpse of truth is better than an arranged system and he is *right.*

The *Bhāgavata* has, therefore, a personal, all-intelligent, active, absolutely free, holy, good, all-powerful, omnipresent, just and merciful and supremely spiritual deity without a second, creating, preserving all that is in the universe. The highest object of the Vaiṣṇava is to serve that Infinite Being *forever spiritually* in the activity of *Absolute Love.*

These are the main principles of the religion inculcated by the work, called the *Bhāgavata,* and Vyāsa, in his great wisdom, tried his best to explain all these principles with the aid of pictures in the material world. The shallow critic summarily rejects this great philosopher as a man-worshipper. He would go so far as to scandalize him as a teacher of material love and lust and the injurious principles of exclusive asceticism. The critic should first read deeply the pages of the *Bhāgavata* and train his mind up to the best eclectic philosophy which the world has ever obtained, and then we are sure he will pour panegyrics upon the principal of the College of Theology at Badrikashram which existed about 4,000 years ago. The shallow critic's mind will undoubtedly be changed, if he but reflects upon one great point, i.e., how is it possible that a spiritualist of the school of Vyāsa teaching the best principles of theism in the whole of the *Bhāgavata* and making the four texts quoted in the beginning as the foundation of his mighty work, could have forced upon the belief of men that the sensual connection between men with certain females is the highest object of worship! This is impossible, dear critic! Vyāsa could *not* have taught the common *vairāgī* to set up an *ākhaḍā* (a place worship) with a number of females! Vyāsa, who could teach us repeatedly in the whole of *Bhāgavata* that sensual pleasures are momentary like the pleasures of rubbing the itching hand and that man's highest duty is to have spiritual love with God, could never have prescribed the worship of sensual pleasures. His descriptions are spiritual and you must not connect matter with it. With this advice, dear critic, go through the *Bhāgavata* and I doubt not you will, in three months, weep and repent to God for despising this revelation through the heart and brain of the great Badarayan.

Yes, you nobly tell us that such philosophical comparisons produced injury in the ignorant and the thoughtless. You nobly point to the immoral deeds of the common *vairāgīs*, who call themselves "The followers of the *Bhāgavata* and the great Caitanya." You nobly tell us that Vyāsa, unless purely explained, may lead thousands of men into great trouble in time to come. But dear critic! Study the history of ages and countries! Where have you found the philosopher and the reformer fully understood by the people? The popular religion is fear of God and not the pure spiritual love which Plato, Vyāsa, Jesus, and Caitanya taught to their respective peoples! Whether you give the absolute religion in figures or simple expressions, or teach them by means of books or oral speeches, the ignorant and the thoughtless must degrade it. It is indeed very easy to tell and swift to hear that absolute truth has such an affinity with the human soul that it comes through as if intuitively. No exertion is necessary to teach the precepts of true religion. This is a deceptive idea. It may be true of ethics and of the alphabet of religion, but not of the highest form of faith which requires an exalted soul to understand. It certainly requires previous training of the soul in the elements of religion just as the student of fractions must have a previous attainment in elemental numbers and figures in arithmetic and geometry. Truth is good, is an elemental truth, which is easily grasped by the common people. But if you tell a common patient, that God is infinitely intelligent and powerful in His spiritual nature, He will conceive a different idea from what you entertain of the expression. All higher truths, though intuitive, require previous education in the simpler ones. That religion is the purest, which gives you the purest idea of God, and the absolute religion requires an absolute conception by man of his own spiritual nature. How then is it possible that the ignorant will ever obtain the absolute religion as long as they are ignorant? When thought awakens, the thinker is no more ignorant and is capable of obtaining an absolute idea of religion. This is a truth and God has made it such in His infinite goodness, impartiality and mercy. Labor has its wages and the idle must never be rewarded. Higher is the work, greater is the reward is an useful truth. The thoughtless must be satisfied with superstition till he wakes and opens his eyes to the God of love. The reformers, out of their universal love and anxiety for good endeavor by some means or other to make the thoughtless drink the cup of salvation, but the latter drink it with wine and fall into the ground under the influence of intoxication for the imagination has also the power of making a thing what it never was. Thus it is that the evils of nunneries and the corruptions of the *ākhaḍā* proceeded. No, we are not to scandalize the Savior of Jerusalem or the Savior of Nadia for these subsequent evils. Luthers, instead of critics, are what we want for the correction of those evils by the true interpretation of the original precepts.

Two more principles characterize the *Bhāgavata, viz.*, liberty and progress of the soul throughout eternity. The *Bhāgavata* teaches us that God gives us truth and He gave it to Vyāsa, when we earnestly seek for it. Truth is eternal and unexhausted. The soul receives a revelation when it is anxious for it. The souls of the great thinkers of the by-gone ages, who now live spiritually, often approach our inquiring spirit and assist it in its development. Thus Vyāsa was assisted by Nārada and Brahmā. Our *śastras,* or in other words, books of thought do not contain all that we could get from the infinite Father. No book is without its errors. God's revelation is absolute truth, but it is scarcely received and preserved in its natural purity. We have been advised in the 14th Chapter of 11th *skandha* of the *Bhāgavata* to believe that truth when revealed is absolute, but it gets the tincture of the nature of the receiver in course of time and is converted into error by continual exchange of hands from age to age. New revelations, therefore, are continually necessary in order to keep truth in its original purity. We are thus warned to be careful in our studies of old authors, however wise they are reputed to be. Here we have full liberty to reject the wrong idea, which is not sanctioned by the peace of conscience. Vyāsa was not satisfied with what he collected in the *Vedas,* arranged in the *Purāṇas* and composed in the *Mahābhārata.* The peace of his conscience did not sanction his labors. It told him from inside "No, Vyāsa! you can't rest contented with the erroneous picture of truth which was necessarily presented to you by the sages of by-gone days! You must yourself knock at the door of the inexhaustible store of truth from which the former ages drew their wealth. Go, go up to the Fountain-head of truth where no pilgrim meets with disappointment of any kind." Vyāsa did it and obtained what he wanted. We have been all advised to do so. Liberty then is the principle, which we must consider as the most valuable gift of God. We must not allow ourselves to be led by those who lived and thought before us. We must think for ourselves and try to get further truths which are still undiscovered. In the 23rd text 21st Chapter 11th *skandha* of the *Bhāgavata* we have been advised to take the spirit of the *śāstras* and not the words. The *Bhāgavata* is therefore a religion of liberty, unmixed truth and absolute love.

The other characteristic is progress. Liberty certainly is the father of all progress. Holy liberty is the cause of progress upwards and upwards in eternity and endless activity of love. Liberty abused causes degradation and the Vaiṣṇava must always carefully use this high and beautiful gift of God. The progress of the *Bhāgavata* described as the rise of the soul from Nature up to Nature's God, from *māyā,* the absolute and the infinite. Hence the *Bhāgavata* says of itself:

nigama-kalpa-taror galitaṁ phalaṁ
śuka-mukhād amṛta-drava-saṁyutam/
pibata-bhāgavataṁ rasam ālayaṁ
muhur aho rasikā bhuvi bhāvukāḥ//
(Bhāg. 1/1/3)

> "It is the fruit of the tree of thought, mixed with the nectar of the speech of Śukadeva. It is the temple of spiritual love! O! Men of piety! Drink deep this nectar of *Bhāgavata* repeatedly till you are taken from this mortal frame!"

Then the *sāragrāhī* or the progressive Vaiṣṇava adds:

surasa-sāra-yutaṁ phalam matra yat
virasāt ādi-viruddha-guṇaṁ ca tat/
tyāga-viragamito madhu-pāyinaḥ
rasika-sāra-rasaṁ piba bhāvukāḥ//

> "That fruit of the tree of thought is a composition, as a matter of course of the sweet and the opposite principles. O! Men of piety, like the bee taking honey from the flower, drink the sweet principle and reject that which is not so."

The *Bhāgavata* is undoubtedly a difficult work and where it does not relate to a picturesque description of traditional and poetical life, its literature is stiff and its branches are covered in the garb of an unusual form of Sanskrit poetry. Works on philosophy must necessarily be of this character. Commentaries and notes are therefore required to assist us in our study of the book. The best commentator is Śrīdhara Svāmī and the truest interpreter is our great and noble Caitanyadeva. God bless the spirit of our noble guides.

These great souls were not like comets appearing in the firmament for a while and disappearing as soon as their mission is over. They are like so many suns shining all along to give light and heat to the succeeding generations. Long time yet they will be succeeded by others of their mind, beauty and caliber. The texts of Vyāsa are still ringing in the ears of all theists as if some great spirit is singing them from a distance! Badrikashram! The seat of Vyāsa and the selected religion of thought! What a powerful name! The pilgrim tells us that the land is cold! How mightily did the genius of Vyāsa generate the heat of philosophy in such cold region! Not only did he heat the locality but sent its ray far to the shores of the sea! Like the great Napoleon in the political world, he knocked down empires and kingdoms of old and bygone philosophy by the mighty stroke of his transcendental thoughts! This is real power! Atheists, philosophy of Sāṅkhya, Cārvāka, the Jains and the Buddhists shuddered with fear at the approach of the spiritual sentiments and creations of the *Bhāgavata* philosopher! The army of atheists was composed of gross and impotent creatures like the legions that stood under the banner of the fallen Lucifer; but the pure, holy and spiritual soldiers of Vyāsa, sent by his Almighty Father were invincibly fierce to the enemy and destructive of the unholy and the unfounded. He that works in the light of God, sees the minutest things in creation, he that works the power of God is invincible and great, and he that works with God's Holiness in his heart, finds no difficulty against unholy things and thoughts. God works through His agents and these agents are styled by Vyāsa himself as the Incarnation of the power of God. All great souls were incarnations of this class and we have the authority of this fact in the *Bhāgavata* itself:

avatārā hy asaṅkhyeyā hareḥ sattva-nidher dvijāḥ/
yathāvidāsinaḥ kulyāḥ sarasaḥ syuḥ sahasraśaḥ//
(Bhāg. 1/3/26)

> "O *Brāhmaṇas*! God is the soul of the principle of goodness! The incarnations of that principle are innumerable! As thousands of watercourses come out of one inexhaustible fountain of water, so these incarnations are but emanations of that infinitely good energy of God which is full at all times."

The *Bhāgavata*, therefore, allows us to call Vyāsa and Nārada, as *śaktyāveśāvatāras* of the infinite energy of God, and the spirit of this text goes far to honor all great reformers and teachers who lived and will live in other countries. The Vaiṣṇava is ready to honor all great men without distinction of caste, because they are filled with the energy of God. See how universal is the religion of *Bhāgavata*. It is not intended for a certain class of the Hindus alone but it is a gift to man at large in whatever country he is born and whatever society is bred. In short Vaiṣṇavism is the Absolute Love binding all men together into the infinite unconditioned and absolute God. May it, peace reign for ever in the whole universe in the continual development of its purity by the exertion of the future heroes, who will be blessed according to the promise of the *Bhāgavata* with powers from the Almighty Father, the Creator, Preserver, and the Annihilator of all things in Heaven and Earth.

Appendix I

The Works of Kedarnath Datta Bhaktivinoda

(Arranged by Year)

n.d. *Baladeva Vidyābhūṣaṇa-carita* — A biography of Baladeva Vidyābhūṣaṇa by Bhaktivinoda in prose.

n.d. *Daśa-mūla-niryāsa* — A Bengali prose essay summarizing Caitanya's teachings in ten points of theology.

n.d. *Navadvīpa-śatakam* — A work attributed to Prabodhānanda Sarasvatī. The work describes the land of Navadwip. Bhaktivinoda translated this book into Bengali verse.

n.d. *Vedānta-sūtra* — A classic theological treatise published by Bhaktivinoda's friend, Shri Syamalal Goswami, along with the *Govinda-bhāṣya* of Baladeva Vidyābhūṣaṇa and the explanatory notes of Bhaktivinoda.

1849 *Ulā-caṇḍī-māhātmya* — Bengali verses in praise of the village deity Ulā Caṇḍī. In his autobiography Bhaktivinoda informs us that the work is lost.

1850 *Hari-kathā* — A poem in Bengali.

1850 *Līlā-kīrtana* — A poem in Bengali.

1851 *Śumbha-niśumbha-yuddha* — Bengali verses about the battle between Durgā and two demons named Śumbha and Niśumbha.

1855 Contributions to various periodicals — Bhaktivinoda wrote numerous short articles (non-Vaiṣṇava in content) from about this time. He wrote for the *Hindu Intelligencer*, *Literary Gazette* and others journals. One article is recorded by Benoy Ghosh listed as: "Speech of Kedar Nath: What should be the aim of Education," *Selections from English Periodicals of Nineteenth Century Bengal,* vols. i-v. Calcutta: Papyrus, 1978.

1856 *Poriade Part 1* — A poem in English about the activities of Porus in the days of Alexander the Great. This work is mentioned in Bhaktivinoda's autobiography and was supposed to be in twelve volumes.

1857 *Poriade Part 2* — The second part of a proposed twelve volumes. According to the *Jīvanī* only two volumes were published.

1860 *Maṭhs of Orissa* — English prose account of the various temples, monasteries and shrines in Orissa that Bhaktivinoda visited. Bhaktivinoda lived in Orissa with his paternal grandfather during this period. The work has been quoted by William Hunter in his *History of Orissa.*

1862 *Our Wants* — A work in English prose. It is mentioned in the *Jīvanī.*

1862 *Sannyāsī* — A poem in Bengali blank verse revised and republished in 1902.

1862 *Vijana-grāma* — A poem in Bengali blank verse about the destruction of Ula due to cholera during 1857. It was revised and republished in 1902.

1866 *Balide Registry* — A manual of the Government Registration Department that Bhaktivinoda translated into Urdu. It is mentioned in the autobiography.

1866 *Speech on Gautama* — A lecture in English about Gautama Muni and the philosophy of *nyāya* given at Chapra in Bihar during 1866.

1868 *Sac-cid-ānanda-premālaṅkāra* — A poem in Bengali describing the attributes of Caitanya.

1869 *The Bhagavat: Its Philosophy, Ethics and Theology* — A lecture in English on the *Bhāgavata* delivered at Dinajpur in West Bengal. Some topics covered are: the importance of the *Bhāgavata* in synthesizing many forms of theistic worship and the three truths of religion (*sambandha, abhidheya* and *prayojana*).

1870 *Garbha-stotra-vyākhyā* or *Sambandha-tattva-candrikā* — A commentary in Bengali prose on the *Garbha-stotra* from the second chapter of the tenth *skandha* of *Bhāgavata* (Prayers by the Devas for Śri Kṛṣṇa in the Womb).

1871 *A Beacon Light* — English prose. This work is only mentioned in ISKCON publications.

1871 *Ṭhākura Haridāsa* — Ten English verses about the disappearance of Haridāsa Ṭhākura, which are engraved on the *samādhi* tomb of Haridāsa by the seashore at Jagannath Puri.

1871 *Reflections* — A poem in English.

1871 *Sāragrāhī Vaiṣṇava* — A poem of twenty verses in English describing the mood of the *sāragrāhī* Vaiṣṇava. This work is only mentioned in ISKCON publications.

1871 *The Ākhaḍās in Purī* — English prose account of the various Vaiṣṇava monastaries at Puri.

1871 *The Atibaḍīs of Orissa* — A letter to the editors of the *Progress*, exposing a controversial sect of Vaiṣṇavas popular in Orissa.

1871 *The Marriage System of Bengal* — An article in English detailing Hindu marriage customs in Bengal. Bhaktivinoda gives an historical outline of the various types of traditional marriages and expresses sympathy for the women subjected to the marital practices of the *kulīna brāhmaṇas.*

1871 *The Personality of Godhead* — English prose work mentioned only in ISKCON publications.

1871 *The Temple of Jagannath at Puri* — An English prose essay describing the history of the establishment of the great temple in Puri, Orissa. This work also addresses the hypocrisy of many temple priests.

1871 *To Love God* — A short English article describing bhakti as the religion of the soul. The article is based on Christ's teaching, "Love God with all thy heart, with all thy mind, and with all thy strength, and love man as thy brother."

1872 *Vedāntādhikaraṇa-mālā* — Sanskrit verses on Vedānta philosophy with Bhaktivinoda's Bengali translation and commentary.

1873 *Datta-kaustubha* — 104 Sanskrit verses on Vaiṣṇava philosophy with Bhaktivinoda's Bengali translation and commentary.

1876 *Datta-vaṁśa-mālā* — Sanskrit verses giving a geneological description of the Datta family of Bali Samaj.

1878 *Bauddha-vijaya-kāvyam* — Sanskrit verses challenging Buddhist philosophy. The work is said by Sudarananda Vidyavinode to be in incomplete manuscript form.

1880 *Kṛṣṇa-saṁhitā* — A Sanskrit and Bengali work divided into three parts.[1]

1881 *Kalyāṇa-kalpataru* — A book of sixty-three Bengali songs describing devotion. This songbook became popular immediately upon its publication, and its songs have been popular in Bengal ever since. The work is mentioned in the *Jīvanī.*

1881 *Sajjana-toṣaṇī* — A monthly Vaiṣṇava periodical in Bengali that was first published in 1881. There are seventeen volumes extant. The last extant publication date by Bhaktivinoda is 1904.

---

1. Bhaktivinoda begins with an *Upakramaṇikā,* or introduction, in Bengali. The introduction is an 80 page study showing the development of Indian religion from an historical and geographical perspective. The *Upakramaṇikā* is specifically written according to what Bhaktivinoda calls the *ādhunika-vāda* or the "modern approach." The *Upakramaṇikā* first establishes the date of many important events of Indian history. For example, the coming of the Aryans into Brahmavarta (India), their progressive migration from north to south, and the date of the *Mahābhārata* war were all presented according to the methodology of what was then modern scholarship.

The *Saṁhitā,* middle portion, is a collection of 281 Sanskrit verses with Bengali commentary. It is divided into ten chapters discussing various aspects of Vaiṣṇava theology. Chapter one describes the ultimate relationship between the soul and God and includes a brief description of heaven (*Vaikuṇṭha).* Chapter two describes the energies of God (Nārāyaṇa) in terms of the ontological construction of *Vaikuṇṭha* and its relationship to this physical world. Chapter three describes the incarnations *(avatāras)* of Śri Hari in relation to the evolutionary development of the living entity (*jīva)* in the material world. Chapters four, five and six summarize the main pastimes of Śri Kṛṣṇa. Chapter seven explains the relationship between human language and man's ability to comprehend and communicate Kṛṣṇa *līlā.*

1883 Review in English of Pundit Upendra Mohan Goswami's Sanskrit thesis, *Nitya-rūpa-saṁsthāpanam* — This was included in the only English edition of *Sajjana-toṣaṇī.*

1886 *Bhajana-darpana-bhāṣya* — A Sanskrit commentary on Raghunātha Dāsa Gosvāmī's *Manaḥ-śikṣā.*

1886 *Bhāvāvalī* — Sanskrit verses on the subject of *rasa* written by various Caitanya Vaiṣṇava teachers, compiled and edited by Bhaktivinoda with his own Bengali translations of the verses.

1886 *Caitanya-śikṣāmṛta* — A philosophical work in Bengali prose based on Caitanya's teachings to Rūpa and Sanātana as found in *Caitanya-caritāmṛta.*

1886 *Daśopaniṣad-cūrṇikā* — A book of Bengali prose containing essential information gleaned from ten principal *Upaniṣads.*

1886 *Manaḥ-śikṣā* — Bengali verse translation of Raghunātha Dāsa's Sanskrit work *Manaḥ-śikṣā.*

1886 *Prema-pradīpa* — A philosophical Vaiṣṇava novel in Bengali prose.

Chapter eight discusses the metaphoric dimension of Kṛṣṇa *līlā* by interpreting the various *asuras* in Kṛṣṇa's life at Vraja as obstacles on the spiritual path. Chapter nine outlines the meditative process of *sahaja-samādhi* or mystic intuition, and shows how it can be employed to perceive higher spiritual reality. Finally, chapter ten depicts the character and activities of an *uttamādhikārī,* or one who has obtained spiritual maturity.

Finally, the *Upasaṁhāra,* or the summary portion of the *Kṛṣṇa-saṁhitā,* written in Bengali prose, provides a systematic explanation of Caitanya's philosophy arranged according to three topics: *sambandha, prayojana* and *abhidheya.* The *sambandha* section discusses the relationship between God, the soul and matter. *Prayojana* describes the goal of life, Kṛṣṇa *prema* (love), and *abhidheya* outlines the means by which that goal may be attained.

I have been able to determine five publications of the *Kṛṣṇa-saṁhitā.* The first was Bhaktivinoda's original 1880 edition that he refers to in his autobiography, the second was in two installments in the January/February and March 1903 editions of *Sajjana-toṣaṇī,* and in the April, May and June editions of that same year. Three printings seem to have been made by the Gaudiya Math, as evidenced by a third reprinting by the Śri Caitanya Math in 1960. I have not been able to determine when the previous two Gaudiya Math editions were made, but it is likely that at least one printing was made during the lifetime of Bhaktisiddhanta Sarasvati Maharaja.

1886 *Bhagavad-gītā* — The text of the *Gītā* with the Sanskrit commentary of Viśvanātha Cakravartī entitled, *Sārārthavarṣaṇī.* The work includes an elaborate introduction in Bengali, a Bengali translation, and a commentary for each verse, entitled *Rasika-rañjana.*

1886 *Sammodana-bhāṣyam* — A lengthy Sanskrit commentary on Caitanya's eight verses of instruction called *Śikṣāṣṭakam.*

1886 *Viṣṇu-sahasra-nāma* of the *Mahābhārata* — Published and edited by Bhaktivinoda with the Sanskrit commentary of Baladeva Vidyābhuṣaṇa called *Nāmārtha-sudhā.*

1887 *Caitanyopaniṣad* (of the Atharva Veda) — An Upanishadic treatise of nineteen Sanskrit verses dealing with Kṛṣṇa's appearance as Caitanya Mahāprabhu. Published and edited by Bhaktivinoda with his own Sanskrit commentary called *Caitanya-caraṇāmṛta* and Madhusūdana Dāsa's *Amṛta-bindu* translation of the original Sanskrit verses.

1887 *Kṛṣṇa-vijaya* — A famous Bengali epic on the *līlā* of Kṛṣṇa written in the fifteenth century by Māladhara Vasu (Gunaraj Khan). Published and edited by Bhaktivinoda with his own introduction in Bengali.

1888 *Vaiṣṇava-siddhānta-mālā* — A Bengali prose work that summarizes all the basic tenets of Caitanya Vaiṣṇava theology.

1890 *Āmnāya-sūtram* — A Sanskrit composition based largely on the Upaniṣads, presented as 130 aphorisms, with a short commentary on each aphorism in Sanskrit comprising quotes from various scriptures. Included is a Bengali translation called the *Laghu-bhāṣya.*

1890 *Navadvīpa Dhāma Māhātmyam (Parikramā Khaṇḍa)* — Eighteen chapters of Bengali verse in which Bhaktivinoda describes the complete tour of the land of Navadwip as traversed by Nityānanda and Jīva Gosvāmī.

1890 *Navadvīpa Dhāma-māhātmyam (Pramāṇa Khaṇḍa)* — Five chapters collected from various *śāstras* in Sanskrit glorifing the land of Navadwip.[2]

2. I have been unable to find a copy of the *Navadvīpa-dhāma-māhātmyam* which includes the engineer's map. Recent Gaudiya Math editions do not include the

1890 *Viṣṇu Priyā o Ānanda Bājār Patrikā* — A montly journal in Bengali published by Sisir Kumar Ghosh and edited by Bhaktivinoda for a short time.

1890 *Siddhānta-darpaṇam* — A philosophical Sanskrit work by Baladeva Vidyābhūṣaṇa. Published and edited by Bhaktivinoda with his own Bengali prose translations.

1891 *Godruma Kalpataru* — Collected Bengali essays describing Bhaktivinoda's program of *Nāma-haṭṭa.* He describes the personnel of the marketplace, how the holy name is purchased, various officers of the market, qualifications of the participants, and descriptions of his actual preaching activities.

1891 *Śrīmad Bhagavad-gītā* — Edited and published by Bhaktivinoda with Baladeva Vidyābhūṣaṇa's Sanskrit commentary, *Gītā-bhūṣaṇa,* and his own Bengali translation-commentary called *Vidvad-rañjana.*

1892 *Nāma* — The third chapter of the *Vaiṣṇava-siddhānta-mālā,* excerpted and published in pamphlet form. Used for distribution during the *Nāma-haṭṭa.*

1892 *Nāma-mahimā* — The fifth chapter of the *Vaiṣṇava-siddhān-*

---

map and Bhaktivinoda unfortunately did not serialize the *Navadvīpa-dhāma-māhātmyam* in his *Sajjana-toṣaṇī* as he did with most of his writings. There seems to be no way to determine the original contents of the work. Neither have we seen any published documentation where Bhaktivinoda specifically outlines his case for Mayapur as the site of Caitanya's birth. What little information we have can be found in the *Jīvanī* and one or two articles in the *Toṣaṇī* where the above mentioned verse and some other verses from the *Bhakti-ratnākara* are found. From what is said in the *Jīvanī* I expected that the *Navadvīpa-dhāma-māhātmyam* was the place where Bhaktivinoda presented his arguments for Mayapur as the birth site of Caitanyadeva, but the work as it exists today is a mystical work that has little to do with the textual and geographic research that the *Jīvanī* says Bhaktivinoda undertook. The *Māhātmyam* is divided into two parts, the *Parikramā* and the *Pramāṇa.* The *Parikramā* is a mystical tour of Navadvip involving a dialogue between Nityānanda Prabhu and Jīva Gosvāmī in which the geography and personalities of *Caitanya-līlā* are spiritually linked to the geography and personalities of Kṛṣṇa *līlā.* The *Pramāṇa* is a theological justification for the *Parikramā* wherein numerous verses from *śāstra* are quoted.

ta-mālā, printed in pamphlet form.

1892 *Nāma-pracāra* — The sixth chapter of *Vaiṣṇava-siddhānta-mālā*, printed as above in pamphlet form.

1892 *Nāma-tattva-śikṣāṣṭaka* — The fourth chapter of *Vaiṣṇava-siddhānta-mālā*, similarly printed as a pamphlet.

1892 *Hari-nāma* — The second chapter of the *Vaiṣṇava-siddhānta-mālā*, printed and published in pamphlet form.

1892 *Mahāprabhura Śikṣā* — A work of eleven chapters. The first chapter summaries Caitanya's philosophy in ten points. The following ten chapters explain each point in detail with Sanskrit quotations from numerous *śāstras*. The work includes Bengali prose translations and explanations.

1893 *Śaraṇāgati* — A Bengali songbook of fifty songs about the process of surrender to Śri Kṛṣṇa.

1893 *Bāul-saṅgīta* — A collection of twelve Vaiṣṇava songs in Bengali verse.

1893 *Dālāler Gītā* — A song in Bengali verse describing Nityānanda as the proprietor of the Marketplace of the Holy Name at Surabhikunj, which was Bhaktivinoda's home on the island of Godruma in Navadwip.

1893 *Gītāvalī* — A Bengali songbook of seventy-three songs.

1893 *Gītā-mālā* — A Bengali songbook of eighty songs arranged in five chapters.

1893 *Jaiva-dharma* — A philosophical Vaiṣṇava novel in Bengali prose. Most of the work is presented as a dialogue of questions and answers between various characters.

1893 *Nāma-bhajana* — A small booklet in English prose describing the divine name of Kṛṣṇa.

1893 *Śoka-śātana* — A small booklet of thirteen Bengali songs that Bhaktivinoda composed between 1888 and 1890.

1893 *Tattva-sūtra* — Fifty Sanskrit aphorisms divided into five chapters. Bhaktivinoda gives a Sanskrit commentary on each verse, plus an elaborate Bengali commentary. All the conclusions presented in this book are backed up with quotations from the *Upaniṣads*, the *Purāṇas*, *Bhagavad-gītā*, *Nārada-pañcarātra*, and other sources.

1893 *Tattva-viveka* subtitled *Sac-cid-ānandānubhūtiḥ* — This work discusses the different precepts of the Vaiṣṇavas in relation to the ideas of prominent Oriental and Western philosophers such as Plato, Aristotle, Comte, Schopenhauer, Berkeley, and so on. The work is composed in 48 Sanskrit verses with detailed Bengali commentary on each verse.

1894 *Amṛta-pravāha-bhāṣya* — A Bengali commentary on Kṛṣṇa Dāsa Kavirāja's *Caitanya-caritāmṛta.*

1894 *Tattva-muktāvalī* subtitled *Māyāvāda Śata-dūṣaṇī* — 119 Sanskrit verses by Madhvācārya refuting *advaita-vedānta* of Śaṅkarācārya. Bhaktivinoda includes a Bengali prose translation for each verse.

1894 *Vedārka-dīdhiti* — A Sanskrit commentary on the *Iśopaṇiṣad.* This commentary by Bhaktivinoda was published along with the Sanskrit explanation of Baladeva Vidyābhūṣaṇa's work entitled *Iśopaṇiṣad-bhāṣya.*

1895 *Bāla-kṛṣṇa-sahasra-nāma-stotra, Gopāla-sahasra-nāma-stotra, Kṛṣṇāṣṭottara-śata-nāma-stotra, Rādhikā-sahasra-nāma-stotra* — Four *nāma-stotras* from *Nārada-pañcarātra* published and edited by Bhaktivinoda with the Sanskrit only.

1895 *Hari-bhakti-kalpa-latikā* — A Sanskrit work on bhakti by an unknown author. Edited and published by Bhaktivinoda with the Sanskrit text only. This manuscript was found while Bhaktivinoda was living in Jagannath Puri.

1895 *Lakṣmī-carita* — A short work in Bengali verse by Mālādhara Vasu (Guṇarāja Khān), the author of *Kṛṣṇa-vijaya.* Published and edited by Bhaktivinoda with original text only.

1895 *Manaḥ-santoṣaṇī* — A Bengali translation by Jagajjivan Mishra of a Sanskrit work entitled *Kṛṣṇa-caitanyodayāvalī* by Pradyumna Miśra. This work was published and edited by Bhaktivinoda with the original text only.

1895 *Mukunda-mālā-stotram* — A devotional work in Sanskrit from South India by one of the twelve Ālvārs. Published and editied by Bhaktivinoda with Sanskrit text only.

Composed in sixty-two verses.

1895 *Ṣoḍaśa Grantha* — Sixteen small Sanskrit works on Vaiṣṇava philosophy by Vallabhācārya. Published and edited by Bhaktivinoda with the Sanskrit text only.

1895 *Gaurāṅga-stava-kalpataru* — Twelve verses in Sanskrit from Raghunātha Dāsa's *Stavāvalī*. Published and edited by Bhaktivinoda with Sanskrit text only.

1895 *Mahāprabhor Aṣṭa-kālīya-līlā-smaraṇa-maṅgala-stotram* — an eleven verse Sanskrit poem on the pastimes of Caitanya by an unknown Vaiṣṇava author. Published and edited by Bhaktivinoda with the Sanskrit only.

1896 *Artha-pañcaka* — Bhaktivinoda's explanatory notes in Bengali on Pillai Lokācārya's work of the same name in which five principles of Rāmānuja's philosophy are explained.

1896 *Gaurāṅga-līlā-smaraṇa-maṅgala-stotram* — 104 Sanskrit verses giving a condensed description of the *līlās* and teachings of Caitanya that are found in *Caitanya-bhāgavata* and *Caitanya-caritāmṛta*. Bhaktivinoda included a forty-seven page introduction in English entitled, "Śrī Caitanya Mahāprabhu: His Life and Precepts." Accompanying the Sanskrit verses is a Sanskrit commentary entitled *Vikāśinī Ṭīkā* by Śitikaṇṭha Vācaspati of Navadwip.

1896 *Rāmānuja-upadeśa* — Sanskrit verses outlining the philosophy of Rāmānuja with Bhaktivinoda's own Bengali translations.

1896 *Svalikhita-jīvanī* — This book is a 200 page Bengali prose letter which Bhaktivinoda wrote to his son, Lalita Prasad Datta, in response to a request for details of his father's personal life.

1897 *Brahma-saṁhitā* (chapter 5) — Published and edited by Bhaktivinoda with the original Sanskrit verses, Jīva Gosvāmī's commentary and Bhaktivinoda's own Bengali introduction, prose translation and commentary called *Prakāśinī*.

1898 *Pīyūṣa-varṣiṇī-vṛtti* — A Bengali commentary of Rūpa

Gosvāmī's *Upadeśāmṛta*. Bhaktivinoda published this book with Rūpa Gosvāmī's original eleven Sanskrit verses accompanied by his own Bengali prose explanations.

1898 *Goloka-māhātmyam* — The second *khaṇḍa* of Sanātana Gosvāmī's *Bṛhad-bhāgavatāmṛtam* published and edited by Bhaktivinoda with the original Sanskrit text and his own Bengali translation.

1898 *Kṛṣṇa-karṇāmṛtam* — A famous Sanskrit book of prayers describing the *mādhurya-rasa* of Kṛṣṇa *līlā* by Bilvamaṅgala Ṭhākura with the original Sanskrit verses.

1898 *Bhagavad-gītā* — Published and edited by Bhaktivinoda with the Sanskrit commentary *Dvaita-bhāṣyam* of Madhvācārya.

1899 *Bhajanāmṛta* — a treatise on devotion in Sanskrit prose by Narahari Sarakāra, a contemporary of Caitanya. Published and edited by Bhaktivinoda with his own Bengali translation.

1899 *Navadvīpa-bhāva-taraṅga* — 168 Bengali verses describing the different places in the 32 sq. mile area of Navadwip as seen through devotional eyes.

1899 *The Hindu Idols* — A thirty-two page English letter written to the Tract Society of Calcutta in response to an article entitled "Professor Max Muller on Durgā," in which Kālī, Durgā, and Śiva were the objects of criticism.

1900 *Hari-nāma-cintāmaṇi* — Haridāsa Ṭhākura's teachings on the Holy Name as collected from various Caitanya Vaiṣṇava sources. Included is a discussion of the ten offenses in chanting. The work is divided into fifteen chapters and is composed in Bengali verse.

1901 *Padma-purāṇa* — Edited and published by Bhaktivinoda with the complete Sanskrit text only.

1901 *Bhāgavatārka-marīci-mālā* — The principle verses of the *Bhāgavata* arranged into twenty chapters. Each chapter explains a particular aspect of *Bhāgavata* philosophy. The work is further divided into the three divisions: *sambandha, abhidheya* and *prayojana.* Each Sanskrit verse is accompanied by a Bengali prose translation and explanation by Bhaktivinoda.

1901 *Saṅkalpa-kalpadruma* — 104 Sanskrit verses on the pastimes of Rādhā and Kṛṣṇa by Viśvanātha Cakravartī. Edited and published by Bhaktivinoda with his own Bengali prose translation.

1902 *Bhajana-rahasya* — Compiled by Bhaktivinoda as a supplement to his *Harināma-cintāmaṇi*. The work is arranged in eight chapters that correspond to the eight divisions of the day.

1904 *Sat-kriyā-sāra-dīpikā* — A Sanskrit work attributed to Gopāla Bhaṭṭa outlining the ritual practises of the Caitanya Vaiṣṇavas. Edited and published by Bhaktivinoda with his own Bengali prose translations.

1906 *Prema-vivarta* — A work by Jagadānanda Paṇḍita in Bengali verse on divine love and holy name. Edited and published by Bhaktivinoda.

1907 *Svaniyama-dvādaśakam* — A poem of twelve Sanskrit verses with Bengali translation and explanation. This was Bhaktivinoda's final work. The Bengali explanations are not complete.

In London I came across five other works by someone named Kedarnath Datta. Four of these works may be found at the India Office Library and one at the School of Oriental and African Studies Library. None of these new works are listed in any of the Gaudiya Math lists of works by Bhaktivinoda. These works are semi-secular. Two of them are novels, which shows their author experimenting with the novel as a literary form. The names and description of these works are as follows: *Deva-dāsa* (1909, pp. 152) is described as the story of a religious life; *British Māhātmya Kāvya* (1903, pp. 66) is described as the glorification of British rule in India; *Priyamvadā* (1857, pp. 211) is described as a love story; and *Bañcaka-carita* (1863, pp. 52) is the story of a swindler.

In the School of Oriental and African Studies Library I found a work entitled *Bhārata-varṣera Itihāsa,* described as a history of India in Bengali. It was published in 1859 by one Kedarnath Datta. This work includes an introduction by the Reverend J. Long. My impression of this work is that it is not a work of Bhaktivinoda's because it is too early and appears to have a different style than the other works. In preparing this book I have not utilized any of these texts because none relate directly to Vaiṣṇavism, nor have any of them yet been authenticated as an actual work of Bhaktivinoda.

Appendix II

Extract of the Work Record of Kedarnath Datta Corrected to July 1, 1888[1]

The following extract is a record of Bhaktivinoda's work history taken from *The History of Services of Gazetted Officers Employed under the The Government of Bengal (corrected up to July 1, 1888.)*

Beginning chapter 105 entitled *History of Services of Officers in the first three grades of the Subordinate Executive Services from first appointment to July 1, 1888.*

Page 114 Kedar Nath Dutt

• Special Deputy Registrar of Assurances, with powers of a Deputy Magistrate and Deputy Collector, and in the 6th grade of the Subordinate Executive Service, Sarun, fifth February 1866.
• Assessor under Act xxi of 1867 Sarun, 8th June 1867.
• Sub-registrar of Assurances of the subdistricts of Purneah and Kissengunge, 16th October 1867.
• Deputy Magistrate and Deputy Collector, Dinagepore, 17th March 1868, Ex-officio Assessor under Act ix, 1868.
• Dinagepore, with powers of Collector 29th June 1868, 3 months' privilege leave, 29th May 1869.
• Deputy Magistrate and Deputy Collector Chumparum, 25th Oct. 1869.
• Deputy Magistrate and Deputy Collector, Pooree, 14th April 1870. Sub-Registrar of Pooree, 10th September 1870
• Promoted to the 5th grade, Subordinate Executive Service, 1870 - 3 months privilege leave, 9th November 1874.
• Vested with the powers of a Magistrate of the first class, 4th May

1. The unusual place name spellings found in both this report and the following report are the actual spellings as they are found in the government records.

Extract of Work Record (con't)

1874.
• Deputy Magistrate and Deputy Collector, Arrareah, in Purneah, 12th April 1875.
• two months privilege leave, 16th July 1877.
• Deputy Magistrate and Deputy Collector, Mohesrakha in Howrah, 27th November 1877.
• Deputy Magistrate and Deputy Collector, Bhuddruck in Balasore, 12th February 1878.
• Vested with summary powers, 11th July 1878.
• Deputy Magistrate and Deputy Collector, Narail in Jessore, 14th August 1878.
• Three months privilege leave, July 1881.
• Deputy Magistrate and Deputy Collector, Jessore, 30th September, 1881. • 3 months medical leave, 10th Jan. 1882.
• 3 months medical leave in extension, 9th April 1882, the most part of which was cancelled on joining as Deputy Magistrate and Deputy Collector, Baraset.
• Deputy Magistrate and Deputy Collector, Baraset, 24 Pergunnahs, 12th May 1882.
• Promoted to the 4th grade Deputy Magistrates and Deputy Collectors, 20th March 1883.
• Deputy Magistrate and Deputy Collector, Serampore, Hooghly 1st April 1884.
• 1 month and 15 days privilege leave, 8th May 1885.
• 1 month and 24 days privilege leave, May 1886.
• Deputy Magistrate and Deputy Collector, Nuddea, 15th November 1887.
• Promoted temporarily to 3rd grade, 31st January 1888.

Extract of the Work Record of Kedarnath Datta Corrected to November 27, 1893

Kedar Nath Datta
Born, 24th September 1838
Joined the service, 16th February 1866

(Taken from *History of Services of Officers Holding Gazetted Appointments under the Government of Bengal (corrected to 1st July 1894)* Chapter 9 Sub-executive officers pages 603-4.)

Station	Substantive Appointment	Date	Officiating Appointment	Date
Saran	Dy. Magte, and Dy. Collr, 7th grade	Feb. 16, 1866	...	...
Kishanganj in Purneah	Dy. Magte, and Dy. Collr, 7th grade	Nov. 2, 1867	...	...
Dinajpur	ditto	May 7, 1868	...	...
Champarar	ditto	Nov 15, 1869	...	...
Leave without pay for 4 days from April 10, 1870				
Puri	ditto	Apr. 14, 1870	...	...
ditto	ditto, 6th grade	Nov 25, 1870	...	...
Araria in Purnea	ditto	Apr 12, 1875	...	...
ditto	ditto, 5th grade	Dec. 9, 1876	...	...
Mohesrekhar in Howrah	ditto	Dec. 11, 1877	...	...
Bhadruck in Balasore	ditto	Feb. 26, 1878	...	...
Narail in Jessore	ditto	Oct. 14, 1878	...	...
		Oct. 17, 1881	...	...
Leave of medical certificate for 4 months and 7 days from Jan. 10, 1882				

Extract of Work Record (con't)

Barasat in 24 Panganas	ditto	May 17, 1882	...	...
ditto	ditto, 4th grade	May 20, 1883	...	...
Serampore in Hooghly	ditto	Apr. 17, 1884	...	...
Privilege leave for 1 month from Oct. 7, 1884; for 1 month and 7 days from May 8, 1885, and for 1 month and 24 days from May 20, 1886.				
Nadia	ditto	Dec. 6, 1887	...	...
ditto	ditto, 3rd grade	Jan. 29, 1889	...	...
Nitrokona in Mymensiing	ditto	Feb. 20, 1889	...	...
Tangail	ditto	May 27, 1889 Sept 5, 1889	...	...
Kalra	ditto	June 17, 1890	...	...
Burdwan	ditto	Oct. 29, 1890	...	...
Dinajpur	ditto	Nov. 26, 1890	...	...
Furlough for 1 year, 7 months and 13 days from August 20, 1891				
On furlough	ditto	Sub. pro. tem Dy. Magt. and Sept 15 1891 Dy. Collr. 2nd grade.		
ditto	ditto, 2nd grade	Jan. 1, 1892		
Sasaram in Bhahabad	ditto	April 2, 1893		
Nadia	ditto	Nov 27, 1893		

Appendix III

Children born to Kedarnath Datta Bhaktivinoda

1. Annada Prasad	son	1860
2. Saudamani	daughter	1864
3. Kadambani	daughter	1867
4. child born (dies)	son	1868
5. Radhika Prasad	son	1870
6. Kamala Prasad	son	1872
7. Bimala Prasad	son	1874
8. Barada Prasad	son	1877
9. Biraja	daughter	1878
10. Lalita Prasad	son	1880
11. Krishna Vinodani	daughter	1884
12. Shyam Sarojini	daughter	1886
13. Hari Pramodini	daughter	1888
14. Shailaja Prasad	son	1891

Summary: 8 boys, 6 girls.

Appendix IV

Sanskrit Transliteration Guide

Vowels

अ a आ ā इ i ई ī उ u ऊ ū ऋ ṛ

ॠ ṝ ऌ ḷ ए e ऐ ai ओ o औ au

Consonants

Gutturals:	क ka	ख kha	ग ga	घ gha	ङ ṅa
Palatals:	च ca	छ cha	ज ja	झ jha	ञ ña
Cerebrals:	ट ṭa	ठ ṭha	ड ḍa	ढ ḍha	ण ṇa
Dentals:	त ta	थ tha	द da	ध dha	न na
Labials:	प pa	फ pha	ब ba	भ bha	म ma
Semivowels:	य ya	र ra	ल la	व va	
Sibilants:		श śa	ष ṣa	स sa	
Aspirate:	ह ha	Anusvāra: ं ṁ		Visarga: ः ḥ	

Bengali Transliteration Guide

Vowels

অ a আ ā ই i ঈ ī উ u ঊ ū ঋ ṛ

ৠ ṝ এ e ঐ ai ও o ঔ au

ং ṁ *(anusvāra)* ঁ ṅ *(candra-bindu)* ঃ ḥ *(visarga)*

Consonants

Gutterals:	ক ka	খ kha	গ ga	ঘ gha	ঙ ṅa
Palatals:	চ ca	ছ cha	জ ja	ঝ jha	ঞ ña
Cerebrals:	ট ṭa	ঠ ṭha	ড ḍa	ঢ ḍha	ণ ṇa
Dentals:	ত ta	থ tha	দ da	ধ dha	ন na
Labials:	প pa	ফ pha	ব ba	ভ bha	ম ma
Semivowels:	য ya	র ra	ল la	ব va	
Sibilants:	শ śa	ষ ṣa	স sa	হ ha	

Vowel Symbols

The vowels are written as follows after a consonant:

া ā ি i ী ī ু u ূ ū ৃ ṛ ৄ ṝ ে e ৈ ai ো o ৌ au

For example: কা kā কি ki কী kī কু ku কূ kū কৃ kṛ

কৄ kṝ কে ke কৈ kai কো ko কৌ kau

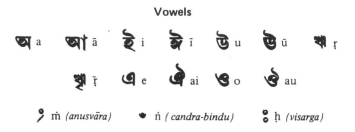

Appendix V

Sanskrit and Bengali Passages

1. ST, 1885, Vol. 2, p. 78: *iṅrāja bāṅgālira paraspara sauhārdaī svābhāvika/ iṅrāja mahāśayagaṇa ārya santāna evaṁ bhārata-vāsīgaṇao ārya santāna ataeva iṅrāja mahāśayerā evaṁ bhārata-vāsī gaṇa samparke bhrātā/svābhāvika bhrātri sneha kothāya gela? iṅrājerā āmādera śāsana kartā haiyāchena baliyā svābhāvika vṛtti kijanya lupta haibe? bhārata-vāsīgaṇa samparke jyeṣṭha, iṅrājerā kaniṣṭha/ kaniṣṭa bhrātā yakhana karmakṣetra haiyā saṁsārera bhāra grahaṇa karena, takhana jyeṣṭha bhrātā vayase vṛddha sutarāṁ bala-hīna haiyā viśeṣa prīti sahakāre kaniṣṭhera adhīnatā svīkāra karena/ ihāte doṣa ki? āmarāo yakhana yauvanāvasthāya chilāma takhana āmarā anyānya jāti sakalera upara prabhutā kariyāchi/... kaniṣṭha bhrātāke āśīrvāda kariyā sarvakṣaṇa sei paramānandamaya hari caraṇa sudhā sevana kariba, apekṣā āra saubhāgya ki āche? sarva prakāra utpāta haite kaniṣṭha bhrātā āmādigake rakṣā karivena/āmādera āra yuddha kṣetrera nirarthake kleśa svīikāra karite haibe nā/ āmārā gṛhe basiyā harināma kariba/...*

2. ST vol. 5 no. 11, 221 (1894): *śrī bhakti ratnākare pāoyā yāya ye antar-dvīpe gaṅgara pūrva-bhāge evaṁ sei antar-dvīpera madhyei śrī-māyāpura/ antardvīpa haite śrī-suvarṇa vihāra driṣṭa haya/*

3. *Bhakti-ratnākara* in *Sajjana-toṣaṇī* vol. 5 no. 11, 221 (1894) in an article entitled *Śrī-dhāma-māyāpura*. The rest of the quote is as follows: *yaiche vrindāvane yoga-pīṭha sumadhura/taiche navadvīpe yoga-pīṭha māyāpura//gaṅgā pūrva paścima tīrete-dvīpa naya/pūrve antar-dvīpa śrīsīmanta dvīpa haya//godruma dvīpa o śrīmadhya-dvīpa catuṣṭaya/kola-dvīpa jhatu jahnu modadruma āra/ rudra-dvīpa ei pañca paścime pracāra//*

4.This letter is from a Bengali publication called *Ṭhākura Bhaktivinoda* by Sundarananda Vidyavinoda, 1937, 56-57. Edited by Bhakti Pradipa Tirtha.

pranāmā nivedanam idam,

āpanāra nūtana grantha pāilāma/ bhakta-gaṇa kleśa karen, āra āmarā dīna-hīna tāhāra dvārā jīvana rakṣā kari/ āpanāke aneke "Bhaktivinoda" ākhyā diyāachena; kintu āmi āpanāke "saptama gosvāmī" bhāvi/ prakaṭa samaye chaya gosvāmī chilena, aprakaṭa samaye āpani gosvāmī/āpani dhanya o āpanāra kṛpā pāile āmi dhanya haiba/ āpani prabhu-prerita, ei śuṣkakāle āpani sanātana-dharma sajīva karitechena/ āpanāra grantha (śrī-dhāma-parikramā) ekhano pāṭha kari nāi, sparśa kariyāchi, tāhātei aṅga śītala haiyāche/ apara, navadvīpa sthāpana karilena, kintu navadvīpeśvarī kothāya? īśvarī-vyatīta navadvīpa śūnyamaya/tāṅhāke ānayana karuna, kariyā āmāra nyāya koṭī koṭī jīvake cira ṛne ābaddha karuna/

sakale dalabaddha haiyā navadvīpeśvarī viṣṇupriyādevike ṭākiyā rākhiyāchilena, ihāte śrīnavadvīpa-candra vyathita haiyā tāṅhāra priyadāsa śrī narottama ṭhākura mahāśayake darśana diyā gaurāṅga-viṣṇupriyā yugala-vigraha arpana karena/ ihāra vṛttānta "narottama vilāsa" granthe o "bhaktiratnākara" granthe dekhiyāchena/ sei vigraha adyāpi śrīkheturīte virāja karitechena/ ṭhākura, bhagavān gaurāṅgera sākṣāt ādeśa pālana karāra adhikārī kevala āpanāke nayana-gocara haya/ ei nimitta kātara haiyā āpanāra śrīcaraṇe āśraya lailāma/ devī sambanddhe aneka kathā caitanya-maṅgale āche/ bhakti-ratnākare kintu pāoyā yāya, āra viśvanātha cakravartī gaurāṅga-viṣṇupriyā-yugala-vyānera viṣaya likhiyāchena/etad-bhinna kiṁvadantī dvārā bahutara saṁvāda pāibena/ kim adhika, āmi āpanāra nitānta āśrita baliyā jānibena/
praṇāma
śrī śiśira kumāra ghoṣa dāsa

5. KS, *Upakramaṇikā,* 5*: ihāte śocanīya (viṣaya) ei ye, pūrva mahājana-kṛta aneka pariśrama-jāta adhikāra haite adhikārāntara gamanopayogī samyak sopāna parityāga-pūrvaka nirarthaka kāla-kṣepa-janaka sopānāntara gaṭhane pravṛtta hana/ madhyamādhikārīdigera śāstra-vicāra janya yadi kona grantha thākita tāhā haile āra upadharma, chala-dharma, vaidharma o dharmāntarera kalpanā-rūpa bṛhad-anartha bhārata-varṣe praveśa karita nā/uparokta abhāva paripūraṇa karāi ei śāstrera pradhāna uddeśya/*

6. KS, *Vijñāpana,* ii: *itihāsa o kāla-jñāna–ihārā artha-śāstra-viśeṣa/ yukti-dvārā itihāsa o kālera vicāra karile bhāratera aneka upakāra haibe/ tad-dvārā kramaśaḥ paramārtha-sambandheo aneka unnatira āśā karā yāya/ prācīna viśvāsa-nadīte yukti-srota saṁyoga karile bhrama-rūpa baddha śaivāla-sakala dūrībhūta haiyā paḍibe o kāla-krame aṣaśo-rūpa pūtigandha niḥśeṣita haile bhārata-vāsīdigera vijñānaṭī svāsthya lābha karibe/*

7. KS, *Upakramaṇikā,* 3: *viśvasta viṣaye yukti-yoga karite samartha haiyāo yāṅhārā pāraṁgata nā haiyāchena tāṅhārā yukty-adhikārī vā madhyamādhikārī baliyā pariganita hana/pāraṁ-gata puruṣerā sarvārtha-siddha/ tāṅhārā artha-sakala-dvārā svādhīnaceṣṭākrame paramārtha-sādhane sakṣama/ ihādera nāma uttamādhikārī/*

8. JD, 197-8: *mānava-sakala jñāna o saṁskārera tāratamya-krame adhikāra-bheda lābha kariyā thāke/ yini śuddha-cinmaya-bhāva bujhiyāchena, tinii kevala cinmaya-vigraha-upāsanāya samartha/se-viṣaye yāṅhārā yatadūra nimne āchena, tāṅhārā tatadūra mātrai bujhite pārena/ atyanta nimnādhikārīra cinmaya bhāvera upalabdhi haya nā/*

9. KS, *Upakramaṇikā,* 4: *ṭīkā ṭippanī-kārera anekei sāragrāhī chilena, kintu tāṅhārā yatadūra komala-śraddhadigera prati dayā prakāśa kariyāchena tatadūra madhyamādhikārīdigera prati karena nāi*

10. ST, Vol. 8 (1896), 150: *Tattva-sūtra: kintu svabhāva vaśata yāhāte pravṛtti haya tāhāi kare/ tāṅhādera svabhāva prāyai indriya-poṣaka, ejanya śāstra nānāvidha chala, bala o kauśalera dvārā tāhādera maṅgala vidhāna karite yatna pāna/ kakhanao narakera bhaya pradarśana karena, kakhanao vā svargera sukha-bhogera pralobhana dekhāna/ kakhanao vā pravṛtti anusāre kāryera dvārā saṁskāra karena/*

11 KS, *Upakramaṇikā,* 11: *ei śuddha vaiṣṇava-dharma asmaddeśe kon samaye udita haya o kon kon samaye unnata haiyā prakāśita haiyāche tāhā vicāra karā kartavya/ ei viṣaya*

vicāra karibāra pūrve anyānya aneka viṣaya sthira karā āvaśyaka/ ataeva āmarā prathame bhārata-bhūmira pradhāna pradhāna pūrva ghaṭanāra kāla ādhunika vicāra-mate nirūpaṇa kariyā pare sammānita grantha-sakalera ai prakāra kāla sthira kariba/ grantha-sakalera kāla nirūpita hailei tanmadhye vaiṣṇava-dharmera itihāsa, yāhā ādhunika-mate spaṣṭa haibe, tāhā prakāśa kariba/ āmarā prācīna paddhati-krame kālera vicāra kariyā thāki, kintu ekhanakāra lokadera upakārārthe ādhunika paddhati avalambana kariba/

12. KS, *Upakramaṇikā*, 79-80: *ye sakala lokera divya-cakṣu āche tāṅhārā tāṅhādigake samanvaya-yogī baliyā jānena/ yāṅhārā anabhijña vā komala-śraddha, tāṅhārā tāṅhādigake saṁsārāsakta baliyā bodha karena/ kakhana kakhana bhagavad-vimukha baliyāo sthira karite pārena/ sāragrāhī janagaṇa svadeśīya videśīya sarva-lakṣaṇa-sampanna sāragrāhī bhrātāke anāyāse jānite pārena/ tāṅhādera paricchada, bhāṣā, upāsanā, liṅga o vyavahāra-sakala bhinna bhinna haileo tāṅhārā paraspara bhrātā baliyā anāyāse sambodhana karite pārena/*

13. Ibid., 1:.*śāstra dui-prakāra, arthāt artha-prada o paramārtha-prada/ bhūgola, itihāsa, jyotiṣa, padārtha-vidyā, mānasa-vijñāna, āyur-veda, kṣudra-jīva-vivaraṇa, gaṇita, bhāṣā-vidyā, chanda-vidyā, saṁgīta, tarka-śāstra, yoga-vidyā, dharma-śāstra, danta-vidhi, śilpa, astra-vidyā, prabhṛti samasta vidyāi artha-prada śāstrera antargata/...ye śāstre ai parama phala prāptira ālocanā āche, tāhāra nāma pāramārthika śāstra/*

14. KS, *Vijñāpana*, i-ii: *prācīna-kalpa pāṭhaka mahāśayadigera nikaṭe āmāra kṛtāñjali nivedana ei ye, sthāne sthāne tāṅhādera cira-viśvāsa-virodhī kona siddhānta dekhile, tāṅhārā tad-viṣaya āpātaka ei sthira karibena ye, ai sakala siddhānta tat-tad-adhikārī jana-sambandhe kṛta haiyache/ dharma-viṣaye yāhā yāhā ukta haiyāche, tāhā sarva-lokera grāhya/ ānuṣaṅgika vṛttānta-viṣaye siddhānta-sakala kevala adhikārī janera jñāna-mārjana-rūpa phalotpatti kare/ yukti-dvārā śāstra-mīmāṁsā-pūrvaka upakramaṇikāya aitihāsika ghaṭanā o kāla-sambandhe ye sakala viṣaya kathita haiyāche, tāhā viśvāsa vā aviśvāsa karile paramārthera lābha vā hāni nāi/ itihāsa o kāla-jñāna–ihārā artha-śāstra-viśeṣa/ yukti-dvārā itihāsa o kālera vicāra bhāratera aneka upakāra haibe*|

15. KS, *Upakramaṇikā*, 61: *yata-dūra pārā gela, ghaṭanā-sakalera o grantha-sakalera ādhunika-mate kāla nirupita haila/ sāragrāhī janagaṇa vāda-niṣṭha nahena, ataeva sad-yukti dvārā ihāra viparīta kona viṣaya sthira haileo tāhā āmādera ādaraṇīya/ ataeva etat-siddhānta-sambandhe bhaviṣyat paramārthavādī vā buddhimāna artha-vādīdigera nikaṭa haite aneka āśā karā yāya/*

16. KS, *Upakramaṇikā*, 56: *vāstavika śrīmad-bhāgavata-grantha ādhunika naya, vedera nyāya nitya o prācīna.* ... p. 57: *kintu ādhunika paṇḍitadigera mate kona samaye kona deśe o kona mahātmāra caitanye ai grantharājera prathama udaya haya, tāhā nirūpaṇa karā atīva vāñjanīya/*

17. DK, vs. 12, commentary: *parera anumāna o pratyakṣa-janita baliyā śāstrera pramānatva (prāmāṇikatā) siddha haya/ "para"-śabdera dvārā brahmā haite ārambha kariyā vyāsa-prabhṛti paryanta śāstra-kāra-gaṇake bujhite haibe/ tāṅhādera anumāna o pratyakṣera dvāra śāstrake pramāṇa-rūpe gaṇya karā haiyāche/*

18. KS, *Upasaṁhāra*, 179: *cidābhāsa haite cintāra utpatti haiyāche baliyā cintā bhūtāśraya tyāga karite pāre nā, ataeva manovṛttike sthagita kariyā ātma-samādhi arthāt svadarśana*

vṛttira dvārā ātmā yakhana ālocanā karena, takhana niḥsandeha ātmopalabdhi ghaṭiyā thāke...

19. KS, *Saṁhitā*, 9/2e: *samādhi dui prakāra–savikalpa o nirvikalpa/ ... sātvata-gaṇa atyanta sahaja samādhike nirvikalpa o kūṭa-samādhike savikalpa samādhi baliyā thākena/ ātmā cid-vastu ataeva svaprakāśatā paraprakāśatā ubhaya dharmai tāhāte sahaja/ svaprakāśa-svabhāva-dvārā ātmā āpanāke āpani dekhite pāya/ para-prakāśa-dharma dvārā ātmetara sakala vastuke jñāta haite pāre/ yakhana ei dharma ātmāra svadharma haila, takhana nitānta sahaja samādhi ye nirvikalpa, tāhāte āra sandeha ki/ ātmāra viṣaya-bodhakārye yantrāntarera āśraya laite haya nā, ejanya ihāte vikalpa nāi/ kintu atan-nirasanakrame yakhana sāṅkhya-samādhi avalambana karā yāya, takhana samādhi-kārye vikalpa arthāt viparīta dharmāśraya thākāya ai samādhi savikalpa nāma prāpta haya/*

20. DK, vs. 10 commentary: *pramāṇa dui prakāra – pratyakṣa o anumāna/ ātmā o indriya-bhede pratyakṣa o dvi-vidha/ āvāra, ātmā o indriyera pratyakṣa nija o para-bhede dui prakāra/ anumāna o nija-para-bhede dvi-vidha*

21. KS, *Saṁhitā* 4/2e: *madhyamādhikārigaṇa etat-tattve saṁśaya-vaśataḥ avasthita haite pārena nā/... māyāgata samvit-karttṛka utpanna yukti-yantrera prati adhikatara viśvāsa karata mānavagaṇa prāyai sahaja samādhike kusaṁskāra baliyā tācchilya karena/*

22. Ibid., 1/33e: *yadio vākya-dvārā spaṣṭa varṇana karite aśakta haiyāchi, tathāpi sārajuṭ vṛtti-dvārā samādhi avalambana-pūrvaka bhagavad-vārtā yathā-sādhya varṇana karilāma/ vākya-sakale sāmānya artha karite gele varṇita viṣaya uttama-rūpe upalabdha haibe nā; etat-hetuka prārthanā kari ye, pāṭhaka-vṛnda samādhi avalambana-pūrvaka etat-tattvera upalabdhi karibena/... kintu ātmāra sākṣād darśana-rūpa āra ekaṭī sūkṣma-vṛtti sahaja-samādhi-nāme lakṣita haya, sei vṛtti avalambana-pūrvaka yemata āmi varṇana karilāma, pāṭhaka-vṛndao tāhā avalambana-pūrvaka sei-rūpa tattvopalabdhi karibena/*

23. ST, Vol. 8 (1896), TS 143: *jñāna sūrya svarūpa evaṁ akhila śāstra tāhāra kiraṇa mātra ei vākyera dvārā pratīta haya ye kona śāstrei samasta jñāna thākite pāre nā/ jīvera svataḥsiddha jñānai sarva śāstrera mūla evaṁ ai jñānai īśvara datta baliyā jānite haibe/sahṛdaya ṛṣigaṇa parabrahmera nikaṭa haite ai svataḥsiddha jñāna lābha kariyā anyānya jīvera upakārārtha tāhā lipibaddha karile ai mūla jñāna kiyad-aṁśe veda rūpe prakāśita haiyāche//*

24. DK, vs. 4: *Ṭīkā: sārao dui-prakāra–sāmbandhika o svarūpa/ ye sāra sakala deśa o kāla atikrama kariyā viśuddha jīva-gata, tāhāi svarūpa-sāra, tāhā avaśyai virala/ atyanta nikṛṣṭa avasthā haite ananta unnatira vidhāna avalambane jīva-gaṇera vibhinna adhikāra-gata ye sāra, tāhāi sāmbandhika/ adhikāra-vicārei tāhā pariṣkṛta haibe/*

25. KS, *Saṁhitā* 7/2e: *sei līlā goloka-dhāme svarūpa-bhāva-sampannā āche, kintu baddha-jīva-sambandhe tāhā sāmbandhikī/ baddha-jīva-sakala deśa, kāla o pātra-bhede bhinna bhinna svabhāva prāpta haoyāya ai līlā deśa-gata, kāla-gata o pātra-gata-bheda avalambana-pūrvaka bhinna-bhinnākāra-rūpe driṣṭa haya/ līlā kathanai samala haya nāi, kintu ālocakadigera mala-yukta vicāre uhāra bhinnatā paridṛśya haya/*

26. ST, Vol 8 (1896), TS, 144: *veda vākya sakalera yathārtha artha nirṇaya karaṇārthe manu, yājñavalkya, śātātapa, vaśiṣṭha, vāmadeva prabhṛti ṛṣigaṇa aneka dharma-śāstra nāmadheya granthera racanā kariyāchena/ vedavyāsa prabhṛti ṛṣigaṇao aneka purāṇa*

śāstra pracāra kariyāchena/ śrī-mahādeva anekaguli tantra vyākhyā kariyāchena/ e samudāya vyākhyāra sahita vedera vicāra karāi saṁsārī lokera karttavya/kintu e samudāya sampanna haileo nijera svataḥsiddha jñānera ālocanāo āvaśyaka yehetu vyākhyā-kartā o tāhādera ṭīkā-kartārā sarvatra svaccha nahena/kona kona sthale ṭīkā-kartādigerao sandeha dekhā yāya .... ataeva svataḥsiddha svādhīna jñānera ālocanā sarvatra prayojana ihāi śāstra vicāra sambandhe siddhānta/

27. KS, *Upakramaṇikā* p. 55-56: *viṣṇu-purāṇa-grantha kona dakṣiṇa-deśīya paṇḍita kartṛka racita haya, ihāte sandeha nahe; yehetu tad-granthe likhita āche ye, mānaverā susvādu dravya-sakala āhārānte tikta dravya avaśeṣe bhojana karibena/ei prakāra vyavahāra dakṣiṇa pradeśe pracalita āche/ grantha-kārtā svadeśa-niṣṭha āsvādaṭī grantha-madhye sanniveśita kariyāchena, sandeha nāi/...* p. 58*: svadeśa-niṣṭhatā mānava-jīvanera sambandhe svataḥ-siddha, ataeva mahāpuruṣa-gaṇao ai pravṛttira kiyat parimāṇe vaśavartī haiyā thākena/*

28. JD, 51: *nitya-tattva varṇanāra atīta/ śuddha-jīva āpana cid-vibhāge kṛṣṇa-mūrti o kṛṣṇa-līlā paridarśana karena/ vākyera dvārā varṇana karite gele, jaḍīya itihāsera nyāya kāyekāyei varṇita haiyā thāke/*

29. KS, *Saṁhitā* vs. 1/33e: *yadio vākya-dvārā spaṣṭa varṇana karite aśakta haiyāchi, tathāpi sāra-juṭ vṛtti-dvārā samādhi avalambana-pūrvaka bhagavad-vārtā yathā-sādhya varṇana karilāma/vākya-sakale sāmānya artha karite gele varṇita viṣaya uttamarūpe upalabdha haibe nā/*

30. JD, 264: *eijanya jīva viṣaye, cid-viṣaye samasta varṇanei māyika-kālera adhikāra chāḍāna yāya nā–bhūta, bhaviṣyat bhāva sutarāṁ āsiyā paḍe/.*

31. ST, Vol. 8 (1896), TS p 149: *śāstrera lāghavatā dekhā yāya kintu śāstra-kartārā ai viṣayaṭi pariṣkāra-rūpe vyakta karena nā/ tāhāra hetu ei ye, ye sakala samartha puruṣa śāstrera adhīnatā parityāga karite pāribena tāṅhārā svīya jñāna-yoge śāstra-kartādera īṅgita anuyāyī śāstra haite svabhāva vaśatai svādhīna haiyā śāstrake kevala mantrī-svarūpa varaṇa karata nija buddhi-bale evaṁ śāstrera parāmarśa-mata nirdoṣa karmācaraṇa karibena/ pakṣāntare yāṅhārā svataḥ-siddha jñāna-bale vidhi-racanā karaṇe asamartha evaṁ ajñāna vaśata kāryākāryera nirṇaya karite nā pāriyā kāmacārī haiyā kleśa pāite pārena tāṅhādera pakṣe śāstrera adhīnatā viṣayaka vidhii prayojanīya arthāt śāstra haite svādhīna haoyāra ye kona patha thāke tāhā tāṅhādera jñānā ucita nahe, yehetu tāṅhārā tadviṣayera adhikārī hailei īṅgita-krame tāhā bujhite pāribena/*

32. KS, *Saṁhitā* 7/2e: *pūrvei kathita haiyāche ye, cij-jagatera kriyā-sakala baddha-jīve svarūpa-bhāve spaṣṭa paridṛśya haya nā, kevala samādhi-dvārā kiyat parimāṇe anubhūta haya. tāhāo ai svarūpa bhāvera māyika praticchāyāke lakṣya kariyā siddha haya/ etat-hetuka braja-līlādite ye sakala deśa (vṛndāvana-mathūrādi sthāyīya bhūmi) nidarśana, kāla (dvāparādi kāla) nidarśana o vyakti (yadu-vaṁśa o gopa-vaṁśa-jāta puruṣa-gaṇa) nidarśana lakṣita haya, ai sakala nidarśana/*

33. JD, 318: *ābāra balena ye, bhagavānke māyāśrita baliyā tāṅhāke jaḍa-jagate āsite haile māyāra āśraya grahaṇa karite haya–tini ekaṭi māyika-svarūpa grahaṇa nā karile prapañce udita haite pārena nā; kenanā, brahmāvasthāya tāṅhāra vigraha nāi, īśvarāvasthāya tāṅhāra māyika-vigraha haya; avatāra-sakala māyika śarīrake grahaṇa kariyā jagate*

avatīrṇa haiyā bṛhat bṛhat kārya karena, ābāra māyika-śarīrake ei jagate rākhiyā svadhāme gamana karena/... ei samasta māyāvādīra asat siddhānta/.

34. Ibid., 268: *āmi pūrvei baliyāchi "cit" ivastu evaṁ "jaḍa" tāhāra vikāra/ vikṛta-vastute o śuddha vastute aneka viṣayera sausādṛśya thāke; śuddha-vastu haite vikṛta-vastu bhinna haiyā paḍe, kintu aneka viṣaye sausādṛśya yāya nā–karakā jalera vikāra haoyāya jala haite karakā pṛthak vastu haiyā paḍe, kintu śaityādi-guṇera sādṛśya thāke; śītala-jala o uṣṇa-jale śaityādi-guṇa-sādṛśya thāke, ... jaḍa-jagat cij-jagatera vikṛti haileo jaḍe cid-guṇera sādṛśya pāoyā yāya...*

35. Ibid., 244: *ādarśa nara-śarīrera ākṛti samatala kāca-darpaṇe yemana moṭera upara samāna dṛśya pratibhāta haya, aṅga-sakala viparyayakrame lakṣita haya, arthāt dakṣiṇa-hastake vāma-hasta o vāma-hastake dakṣiṇa-hasta ityādi dekhā yāya, tad-rūpa cij-jagatera vaicitrya o māyika-jagatera vaicitrya sthūla-darśane samabodha haileo sūkṣma-darśane viparyasta/*

36. CS, 15 and 17: *śrī-kṛṣṇa-caritāmṛta pāṭha vā śravaṇa karile adhikāra-bhede jīvera dui-prakāra pratīti haya/ ai dui-prakāra pratītira nāma vidvat-pratīti o avidvat-pratīti/ prakaṭa samaye ye śrī-kṛṣṇa-caritra prāpañcika cakṣu-dvārā paridṛśya haya, tāhāo vidvaj-janera pakṣe vidvat-pratīti o jaḍa-buddhidigera pakṣe avidvat-pratīti vistāra kariyā thāke/ ... prakaṭa-samaye ye samasta bhagaval-līlādi prāpañcika indriyera gocara haya, tāhāo vid-vat-pratīti vyatīta vastu-sākṣātkāra-rūpa phala-pradāna karite pāre nā/*

37. JD, 497-8: *vraje yāhā dekhite pāo, samastai goloke āche/ darśaka-gaṇera niṣṭhā-bhede sei sei viṣaye kichu kichu bhinna darśana haya/vastutaḥ goloke o vṛndāvane bheda nāi/darśakera cakṣu-bhede dṛśya-bheda mātra/atyanta tamo-guṇī vyakti vraje samastai jaḍamaya baliyā dekhena/ rajoguṇī vyakti-gaṇa tad-apekṣā kichu śubha darśana karena/ sattvānugāmī vyakti-gaṇa, yatadūra darśana-śakti haiyāche tatadūra śuddha-sattvera darśana karena/ sakala mānuṣerai adhikāra pṛthak, sutarāṁ darśana pṛthak/*

38. Ibid., 497: *keha alpa dekhitechena, keha kichu adhika, keha keha vā adhika parimāṇe dekhite pāna/ yāṅhāra prati kṛṣṇa-kṛpā ye parimāṇe haiteche, tini sei parimāṇe goloka darśana karitechena/*

39. JD, 498-499: *dekha, vraje sei sei abhimāna māyā-pratyayita sthūla haiyā lakṣita haiteche/ yaśodāra prasava, kṛṣṇera sūtikā-gṛha, abhimanyu-govardhanādira sahita nitya-siddhādigera udvāha-mūlaka parakīya abhimāna atyanta sthūlarūpe lakṣita haya/ esamas-tai yogamāyā-kartṛka sampādita evaṁ ati sūkṣma mūla-tattve saṁyojita, kichumātra mithyā naya evaṁ golokera sampūrṇa anurūpa/ kevala draṣṭhā-gaṇera prapañca-bādhā-anusāre darśana-bheda mātra/* 495: *kṛṣṇera cinmaya līlā nitya/ yāṅhāra śuddha-cinmaya-vastu darśane adhikāra haiyāche, tini goloka darśana karena, emata ki, ei gokulei goloka darśana karena/ yāṅhāra buddhi prapañca-pīḍāya pīḍita tini goloka darśana pāna nā/ gokula golo-ka haileo gokule prāpañcika viśva darśana karena/*

40. Ibid., 268: *śrīmad-bhāgavata-varṇita vraja-līlā sampūrṇa aprākṛta evaṁ varṇita viṣaya-sakala mānava-maṇḍale yakhana paṭhita haya, takhana śrotṛ-vargera adhikāra-bhede phalodaya haya– nitānta jaḍāsakta śrotṛ-varga jaḍa-viṣayālaṅkāra avalambana-pūr-vaka sāmānya nāyaka-nāyikāra kathā śravaṇa karena, madhyamādhikāri-gaṇa "arund-hatī-darśana"- nyāya avalambana-pūrvaka jaḍa-varṇanera sannikaṭa-sthita cid-vilāsa*

dekhite thākena, uttamādhikāri-gaṇa jaḍātīta śuddha-cid-vilāsa-rase magna ha'na/

41. KS, *Saṁhitā* 7/2e: *komala-śraddha puruṣadigera pakṣe tāhārā sampūrṇa viśvāsera sthala/serūpa sthūla nirdeśa vyatīta tāṅhādera kramonnatira panthāntara nāi/*

42. Ibid., 5/7e: *bhāravāhī brāhmaṇagaṇera strīgaṇa arthāt komalaśraddha anugata lokerā vane śrī-kṛṣṇa-nikaṭe gamana karata paramātmā kṛṣṇera mādhuryavaśa haiyā tāṅhāke ātmadāna karila/ ai komalaśraddha puruṣerāi saṁsārī vaiṣṇava*

43. ST, Vol. 8 (1896), TV, 28-29: *śrī-mūrti darśanera śāstra pramāṇa prasiddha, ataeva yukti pramāṇai deoyā yāibe/ īśvarera prakṛta mūrti nāi satya, kintu sac-cid-ānanda svarūpa avaśyai svīkṛta/ ai sac-cid-ānandera pūrṇāvibhāva baddha jīve sambhava nāi ataeva manuṣya parameśvarera ye kona bhāva dhyāna kare, tāhāi asampūrṇa pauttalika bhāva haibe/ vākyera dvārā pauttalikatā sahajei parityāga haya kintu upāsanā kāṇḍe tāhā sambhava haya nā/ ātmāte prema dvārā paramākarṣaka śrī-kṛṣṇa kiyad-aṁśe pratīta han kintu mane dhyāna-yoge kiñcit prākṛta bhāvāpanna śrī-mūrtira bhāva prakāśa haya evaṁ dehendriyādi dvārā ai śrī-mūrti adhikatara gāḍha prākṛtatva grahaṇa karena/ vastuta sādhakagaṇa ei trividhi śrī-mūrtitei sampūrṇa aprākṛta bhāvake arjjana karibena ihāi vidhi/ deha mana o ātmā ai trividha adhikareṇa bhagavānera āvirbhāvake śrī-mūrti kahā yāya....*

44. JD, 197-8: *tini yakhana mānaseo īśvarake dhyāna karena, takhana jaḍa-samaṣṭira ekaṭī mūrti kāye kāyei kalpanā kariyā thākena/ mṛnmayī mūrtike īśvara-mūrti mane karā yerūpa mānase jaḍamayī mūrtira dhyāna karāo seirūpa/ ataeva sei adhikārīra pakṣe pratimā-pūjā śubhakara/ vastutaḥ pratimā-pūjā nā thākileo sādhāraṇa jīvera viśeṣa amaṅgala haya/ sādhāraṇa jīva yakhana īśvarera prati unmukha haya, takhana sammukhe īśvarera pratimā nā dekhile hatāśa haiyā paḍe/ ... ataeva pratimā-pūjā mānava-dharmera bhitti-mūla/*

45. Ibid., 196: *ye vyakti pūjā kare, tāhāra hṛdaya-niṣṭhāra upara sakalai nirbhara/ tāhāra hṛdaya yata-dūra vyut vā bhūtera saṁsargera atīta haite pāre, tata-dūrai se śuddha-vigraha pūjā karite sakṣama haya/*

46. Ibid., 198: *sei pratimāi uccādhikārīra pakṣe sarvadāi cinmaya-vigraha, madhyamādhikārīra pakṣe manomaya vigraha evaṁ nimnādhikārīra pakṣe prathamataḥ jaḍamaya-vigraha haileo, kramaśaḥ bhāva-śodhita-buddhite cinmaya-vigrahera udaya haya/ ataeva sakala adhikārīra pakṣe śrīvigrahera pratimā bhajanīya/*

47. Ibid., 408: *nāma o nāmī paraspara abheda-tattva, etan nibandhana nāmirūpa kṛṣṇera samasta cinmaya guṇa tāṅhāra nāme āche, nāma sarvadā paripūrṇa-tattva; harināme jaḍa-saṁsparśa nāi, tāhā nitya-mukta, yehetu kakhanai māyā-guṇe ābaddha haya nāi; nāma svayaṁ kṛṣṇa, ataeva caitanya-rasera vigraha-svarūpa; nāma cintāmaṇi-svarūpe yini yāhā cāna, tāṅhāke tāhā dite samartha/*

48. Ibid.: *jaḍa-jagate hari-nāmera janma haya nāi/ cit-kaṇa-svarūpa jīva śuddha-svarūpe avasthita haiyā tāhāra cinmaya-śarīre harināma-uccāraṇera adhikārī, jagate māyā-baddha haiyā jaḍendriyera dvārā śuddha-nāmera uccāraṇa karite pāre nā, kintu hlādinī-kṛpāya sva-svarūpera ye samaye kriyā haya, takhanai tāṅhāra nāmodaya haya/ sei nāmodaya manovṛttite śuddha-nāma kṛpā-pūrvaka avatīrṇa haiyā bhaktera bhakti-pūta-jihvāya nṛtya karena/ nāma akṣarākṛti na'na, kevala jaḍa-jihvāya nṛtya karibāra samaya varṇākāre prakāśita han–ihāi nāmera rahasya/*

49. CS, pt. 2, 6: *rasa jñāta haibāra viṣaya naya, kevala āsvādanera viṣaya/ jijñāsā o saṁgraha ye duiṭī jñānera–prāthamika vyāpāra, tāhā samāpta nā haile jñānera carama vyāpāra ye āsvādana, tāhā haya nā ... āsvādana vyatīta rasera sphūrti haya nā/*

50. CS, pt. 1, 8: *deśa-videśa o dvīpa-dvīpāntara nivāsī mānava-vṛndera itihāsa o vṛttānta ālocanā kariyā dekhile spaṣṭai pratīta haibe ye, īśvara-viśvāsa mānava-jātira ekaṭī sādhāraṇa dharma/ asabhya vanya-jātigaṇa paśudigera nyāya paśumāṁsa sevana dvārā kālātipāta kare, tathāpi sūrya o candra, bṛhat bṛhat parvata sakala, baḍa baḍa nada-nadī evaṁ prakāṇḍa taru-sakalake daṇḍavat-praṇāma-pūrvaka tāhādigake dātā o niyantā baliyā pūjā kare/ ihāra kāraṇa ki? jīva nitānta baddha haileo ye paryanta tāhāra cetana ācchādita haya nāi, se paryanta tāhāte cetana- dharmera paricaya-svarūpa kiyat parimāṇa īśvara-viśvāsa avaśyai prakāśita haibe/*

51. ST, vol. 8 (1896), TS p. 176-177: *para-brahmera bhajane sarva-jīverai adhikāra āche kevala sādhakera cittera malinatā prayukta bhagavānera āvirbhāva pañca-prakāra prasiddha/ śākta, saura, gāṇapatya, śaiva o vaiṣṇava ei pañca-prakāra bhagavad-upāsanā sādhakera saṁskāra-krame haiyā thāke/... sandihān haite para-tattva-jña paryanta sakalei para-brahma bhajane adhikārī/ rāgera nirmalatā o unnatii upāsanāra lakṣaṇa/ ataeva sarva jīvera svatantra sac-cid-ānanda parameśvarera upāsanā karā ucita/*

52. 1. KS, *Upakramaṇikā*, 10: *ataeva sarva-deśei ei sakala dharma kāle kāle bhinna nāme pracalita haiyā āsiyāche/ svadeśa-videśe ye sakala dharma pracalita āche, ei dharmagulike vicāra kariyā dekhile ei pañca prakārera kona nā kona prakāra rākhā yāya/*

53. CS, pt. 1, 8-9: *sabhya avasthā prāpta haiyā tini yakhana nānā-vidha vidyāra ālocanā karena, takhanai kutarka-dvārā ai viśvāsake kiyat parimāṇe ācchādana pūrvaka haya nāstikatā, naya abheda-vādera antargata nirvāṇa-vādake mane sthāna pradāna karena/ ai sakala kadarya-viśvāsa kevala aprāpta-bala cetanera asvāsthya-lakṣaṇa, –ihāi bujhite haibe/ nitānta asabhya avasthā o sundara iśvara-viśvāsopayogī avasthāra madhye mānava-jīvanera tinaṭī avāntara avasthā lakṣita haya/ sei tina avasthātei nāstikya-vāda, jaḍa-vāda, sandeha-vāda o nirvāṇa-vāda-rūpa pīḍā-sakala jīvera unnatira pratibandhaka-rūpe kona kona vyaktike kadaryāvasthāya nīta kare/*

54. ST, vol. 4 (1892), TV., 69: *brahma-deśīya bauddha-mahāśaya yāhā balilena tāhāte bodha haya ye tini bauddhamatera ālocanā karena nāi/ kevala tāṅhāra nara-svabhāva yāhā cāya tāhāi tini bauddhamata baliyā vyākhā karena/*

55. Ibid., TV, 70: *kamṭī pracārita viśva-prīti, jaimini prakāśita nirīśvara karmāntargata apūrva-rūpī īśvara o śākya-siṁha pracārita jaḍa-nirvāṇa mataṭī tattat-matopāsakagaṇa karttṛka svābhāvika dharmera ākāre avaśyai pariṇata haibe/*

56. CS, pt. 1, 140: *varṇāśrama-rūpa dharme sthita haiyā jīvana-yātrā nirvāha karite karite cittake kṛṣṇa-pāda-padme nīta karibāra janya vaidha-bhakta nirantara yatna karibena, ihākei bhakti-yoga bale/*

57. Ibid., 83: *yathārtha balite gele, ṛṣidigera haste samāja-niṣṭha-vidhira carama unnati haiyāchela, ihā samasta sahṛdaya o vaijñānika vyakti-gaṇai svīkāra karibena/ tāṅhārā vaijñānika vicāra-krame samāja-niṣṭha-vidhike dui bhāge vibhakta kariyāchilena: yathā varṇa-vidhi o āśrama-vidhi/*

58. Ibid.: *samāj-niṣṭha mānavera dui-prakāra avasthā arthāt: svabhāva o avasthāna/*

jana-niṣṭha dharma haite svabhāva o samāja-niṣṭha dharma haite avasthāna

59. Ibid., 131: *ye paryanta dharma arthake mātra uddeśa kare, se paryanta ai dharma ārthika baliyā abhihita haya/... ārthika dharmera anyatara nāma naitika vā smārta-dharma/*

60. Ibid., 109-110: *kāle manvādi śāstre ai asvābhāvika vidhi gupta-bhāve praviṣṭha haile ucca-varṇa-prāptira āśārahita haiyā ... brahma-svabhāva-vihīna nāmamātra brāhmaṇerā svārthapare dharma-śāstra racanā kariyā anyānya varṇake bañcanā karite lāgilena/*

61. Ibid., 107: *iuropīya jātidigera vartmāna samāja ālocanā karile dekhā yāibe ye, ai samāje yataṭuku saundarya āche, tāhāo svabhāvajanita varṇa-dharmake āśraya kariyā āche/ iurope ye vyakti vaṇik-svabhāva, se vāṇijyai bhālavāse o vāṇijya-dvārā unnati-sādhana kariteche/ ye vyakti kṣatra-svabhāva se "miliṭārī lāina" vā sainika-kriyā avalambana kare/ yāhārā śūdra-svabhāva, tāhārā sāmānya sevākārya bhālavāse/*

62. Ibid., 107: *vastutaḥ varṇa-dharma kiyat-parimāṇe avalambita nā haile kona samājai cale nā/*

63. Ibid., 107: *varṇa-dharma kiyat-parimāṇe avalambita haiyā iuropīya jāti-nicayera samāja saṁsthāpita haileo ai dharma tāhādera madhye vaijñānika-rūpe sampūrṇa ākāra prāpta haya nāi/*

64. Ibid., 131: *yakhana ai dharma paramārtha paryanta uddeśa kare, takhana ai dharmera nāma pāramārthika dharma/... pāramārthika vaidha-dharmera nāma–sādhana-bhakti/*

65. Ibid., 174: *pūrei kathita haiyāche ye, śuddha-bhakti-sādhana uddeśe uttama-rūpe śarīra pālana, mānasavṛttir sundara anuśīlana o unnati-sādhana, sāmājika maṅgalacarcā o ādhyātmika śikṣāi varṇāśrama-dharmera mukhya tātparya/*

66. CS, pt. 1, 174-175: *ekhana vivecya ei ye, varṇāśrama-dharme yerūpa dīrgha-sūtrī kārya, tāhā karite gele bhaktyanuśīlanera avakāśa pāoyā yāya ki nā?*

67. Ibid.: *ati śīghra mṛtyu haile, vā citta vibhramādi vyādhi upasthita haile, aprākṛta tattva śikṣā nā pāile bhaktira aṅkura ye śraddhā, tāhā kirūpe hṛdaye jāgarita haite avakāśa lābha karibe?*

68. Ibid.: *ataeva varṇāśrama kiyat-parimāṇe dīrgha-sūtrī haileo bhakti-sādhanera anukūla-rūpe svīkāra karā kartavya/*

69. Ibid.: *vaidhī-bhaktira anuśīlana-krame tāhāra dīrgha-sūtritā kramaśaḥ kharva haiyā paḍibe/ tāhāra aṅga-sakala kramaśaḥ bhaktyaṅge pariṇati lābha karibe/*

70. Ibid.: *ukta dharmera ye aṅga bhaktira pratikūla haya, se aṅgake kramaśaḥ parityāga karite thākibe/*

71. Ibid.: *avaśeṣe vaiṣṇava-jīvane varṇāśrama-dharmaṭī bhakti-pūta haiyā parama sāttvika-bhāve sādhana-bhaktira dāsa-svarūpe karma o bhaktira paraspara avirodhe vartamāna thākibe//*

72. Ibid., 20: *īśvarera tuṣṭi-sādhanai yakhana jīvanera ekamātra tātparya, takhana ye vidhi ukta tātparyake avyavahita-rūpe lakṣya kare, se vidhir nāma mukhya-viddhi/ ye vidhi kichu vyavadhānera sahita sei tātparyake lakṣya kare, se vidhi–gauṇa/*

73. Ibid., 20: *ekaṭī udāharaṇa dilei e viṣaya spaṣṭa haibe/ prātaḥ-snāna ekaṭī vidhi/ prātaḥ-snāna kariyā śarīra snigdha o roga-śūnya haile mana sthira haya/ mana sthira haile*

īśvaropāsanā karā yāya/ esthale jīvanera tātparya ye īśvaropāsanā/

74. Ibid., 63: *kṛṣṇetara viṣaye baddha-jīvera yakhana baḍa anurāga, takhana tāhāra kṛṣṇera prati rāga nā thākā-prāya baliyā bodha haya/ takhana maṅgala-prārthī jīva kevala śāstrera ājñāya kṛṣṇa-bhajana karena/ei bhajanai vaidha bhajana/*

75. Ibid., 19: *ye paryanta viśuddha rāgera udaya nā haya, se paryanta sādhaka avaśyai kartavya-buddhi-sahakāre gauṇa o mukhya-rūpa vidhi avalambana-pūrvaka kṛṣṇānuśīlana karite thākibena/*

76. Ibid.: *rāga virala/ rāgera udaya haile vidhira āra bala thāke nā/ yekāla paryanta rāgera udaya nā haya, se paryanta vidhike āśraya karāi mānava-gaṇera pradhāna kartavya/... yāṅhārā atyanta bhāgyavān o uccādhikārī, tāṅhārāi kevala ai mārge calite samartha/*

77. Ibid., 7: *bhaya o āśā nitānta heya/ sādhakera yakhana buddhi bhāla haya, takhana tini bhaya o āśā parityāga karena evaṁ kartavya-buddhii takhana tāṅhāra ekamātra āśraya haya/ parameśvarera prati rāgera ye paryanta udaya nā haya, se paryanta kartavya-buddhike sādhaka parityāga kare nā/*

78. JD, 369: *vijaya kumāra o vrajanāthera citte eka-prakāra āścarya bhāva udaya haila—ubhayai eka mane sthira karilena ye, siddha-bābājī mahāśayera nikaṭa dīkṣā grahaṇa karā āvaśyaka/... paradina prāte gaṅgā-snāna samāpti karataḥ pūrvopadiṣṭa dvādaśa tilaka dhāraṇa-pūrvaka śrīla raghunāthadāsa bābājī mahāśayera caraṇe giyā sāṣṭāṅga-daṇḍavat praṇāma karilena/*

79. Ibid.: *bābā, nijera svabhāva vicāra kariyā dekha/ ye svabhāva haite ye rucira udaya haya, tadanusāre rasake svīkāra kara, sei rasāvalambana-pūrvaka tāhāra nitya-siddhādhikārīra anugamana kara/ ihāte kevala nijera rucira parīkṣā karā āvaśyaka/ yadi rāga-mārge ruci haiyā thāke, tabe sei ruci anusāre kārya kara; ye paryanta rāga-mārge ruci haya nāi, kevala vidhi-mārge niṣṭhā kara/*

80. ibid., *āmāra mane haya ye, śrī-lalitā devī āmāke puṣpa-mālā gumphana karite ājñā dena—āmi sundara puṣpa cayana kariyā mālā gumphana kariyā tāṅhāra śrīhaste diba; tini āmāra prati kṛpā-hāsya kariyā rādhā-kṛṣṇera galadeśe arpaṇa karibena/*

81. Ibid.: *tomāra sei sevā-sādhana siddha hauka–āmi āśīrvāda kari... bābā, tumi nirantara ei bhāve rāgānugā-bhaktira sādhana kara, bāhye nirantara vaidhī-bhaktira sādhana-aṅga-sakala śobhā pāite thākuka/*

82. Ibid.: *āmi tomāke āśīrvāda kari, tumi subalera anugata haiyā kṛṣṇa-sevā karite thāka; tumi sakhya-rasera adhikārī/*

83. JD, 383: *vāki āra kichui nāi, kevala tomāra siddha-śarīrera nāma, rūpa, paricchada, ityādi tomāra jānā āvaśyaka/*

84. Ibid.: *vrajanātha o vijaya seidina āpana āpanāke kṛta-kṛtārtha jāniyā paramānande rāgānuga-mārgera sevāya niyukta hailena; bāhye pūrvavat samastai rahila–puruṣera nyāya samasta vyavahārai rahila, kintu vijaya-kumāra antare strī-svabhāva haiyā paḍilena; vrajanātha gopa-bālakera svabhāva lābha karilena/*

85. Ibid., 484: *śrī-dhyānacandra gosvāmī sarva-śāstre paṇḍita chilena/ viśeṣataḥ hari-bhajana-tantre tāṅhāra tulya pāradarśī āra keha chila nā/ śrī-gopāla guru-gosvāmīra śiṣya-gaṇera madhye tini agra-gaṇya/ vijaya o vrajanāthake bhajana-viṣaye parama yogya jñāna*

kariyā bhajana-paddhatira samasta tattva śikṣā diyāchilena/
86. KS, *Saṁhitā* 10/12: *sāragrāhī bhajana kṛṣṇaṁ yoṣit-bhāvāśrite 'tmani/ vīravat kurute bāhye śarīraṁ karma nityaśaḥ//*
87. *Jīvanī*., 155-156: *naḍāle thākāra samaye āmi saparibāre dīkṣita hai/ bahu-dina upayukta guru anveṣaṇa kariyā pāilāma nā/ baḍai duḥkhita thāki/ yāṅhāke ekaṭu śraddhā haya, tāṅhāra mata o caritra dekhiyā se śraddhā-ṭuku dūra haya/aneka cintā karitechi, prabhu svapne se duḥkha dūra karilena/ svapne ekaṭu ābhāsa pāilāma/ sei divasei mana ānandita haila/dui ekadina pare gurudeva āmake patra likhilena/ ye āmi śīghra giyā dīkṣādāna kariba/ gurudeva āsilena/ dīkṣā kārya haiyā gela/ citta baḍai praphulla haila/ sei divasa haitei māṁsa bhakṣaṇa rūpa doṣa hṛdaya haite dūra haila/ jīvera prati kichu dayā udaya haila/*
88. HC, 15/27, p. 153: *sādhite ujjvala rasa, āche bhāva ekādaśa, sambandha, vayasa, nāma, rūpa/ yūtha, veśa, ājñā, vāsa, sevā, parākāṣṭhāśvāsa, pālya-dāsī ei aparūpa//*
89. Ibid., 15/28, p. 154: *ei ekādaśa bhāva sampūrṇa sādhane/ pañca-daśā lakṣya haya sādhaka-jīvane// śravaṇa, varaṇa, āra smaraṇa, āpana/ sampatti e-pañca-vidha daśāya gaṇana//*
90. Ibid., 15/ 29, p. 155: *nijāpekṣā śreṣṭha-śuddha-bhāvuka ye jana/ bhāva-mārge gurudeva sei mahājana// tāṅhāra śrīmukhe bhāva-tattvera śravaṇa/ haile śravaṇa daśā haya prakaṭana// bhāva-tattva dvi-prakāra karaha vicāra/ nija ekādaśa bhāva, kṛṣṇa-līlā āra/*
91. Ibid., *rādhā-kṛṣṇa aṣṭakāla sei līlā kare/ tāhāra śravaṇe lobha haya ataḥpare// lobha haile gurupade jijñāsā udaya/ kemane pāiba līlā kaha mahāśaya// gurudeva kṛpā kari' karibe varṇana/ līlā-tattve ekādaśa bhāva-saṅghaṭana// prasanna haiyā prabhu karibe ādeśa/ ei bhāve līlā madhye karaha praveśa// śuddha-rupe siddha-bhāva kariyā śravaṇa/ sei bhāva svīya citte karibe varaṇa//*
92. JD, 616: *tumi yakhana rūpa-yauvana-sampannā kiśorī, takhana tomāra siddha-rūpa ruci anusārei śrī-gurudeva nirṇaya kariyāchena/ acintya-cinmaya-rūpa-viśiṣṭha nā haile śrīrādhikāra paricārikā ke haite pāre?*
93. JD, 616: *śrīmatī rādhikāi yūtheśvarī; rādhikāra aṣṭa-sakhīra madhye kāhāra o gaṇe thākite haibe/ tomāra ruci-krame śrī-gurudeva tomāke śrī-lalitāra gaṇe rākhiyāchena/*
94. JD, 617: *ye sevā karibe sei sevāra upayogī nānā-vidha śilpa-kalāya tumi abhijña tad anurūpa-guṇa o veśa tomāra gurudeva nidiṣṭha kariyāchena/*
95. Ibid.: *ājñā dui prakāra arthāt nitya o naimittika/ karuṇāmayī sakhī ye nitya-sevā tomāke ājñā kariyāchena, tāhā tumi nirapekṣa haiyā aṣṭakālera madhye yakhana yāhā kartavya tāhā karibe/ ābāra upasthita anya kona sevā prayojana-mata ājñā karena, tāhā naimittika ājñā; tāhāo viśeṣa yatnera sahita pālana karibe/*
96. JD, 617-618: *vraje nitya-vāsai vāsa/ vrajera madhye kona grāme tomāra gopī haiyā janma haya, ābāra grāmāntarera kona gopera sahita tomāra vivāha haya; kintu kṛṣṇera muralīrabe ākriṣṭa haiyā, tumi sakhīra anugata haiyā tāṅhāra rādhā-kuṇḍastha kuñje ekaṭī kuṭīre vāsa karitecha–ei abhimāna-siddha vāsai tomāra vāsa/ tomāra parakīya bhāvai nitya-siddha-bhāva/*
97. Ibid., 618: *tumi rādhikāra anucarī–tāṅhāra sevāi tomāra sevā/ tāṅhāra dvārā prerita haiyā nirjane kṛṣṇa-sannidhāne gele, kṛṣṇa yadi tomāra prati rati pradāna karena, tumi*

tāhā svīkāra karibe nā/ tumi rādhikāra dāsī, rādhikāra anumati vyatīta kṛṣṇa-sevā svatantra haiyā karibe nā/ rādhā-kṛṣṇe samāna sneha rākhiyāo, rādhikāra dāsya-preme kṛṣṇera dāsya-prema apekṣā adhikatara āgraha karibe ihārai nāma 'sevā'/ śrī-rādhāra aṣṭakālīna sevāi tomāra sevā/

98. HC, 15/30, p. 156: *varaṇa-kālete nija ruci vicāriyā/ gurupade jānāibe sarala haiyā, prabhu, tumi kṛpā kari' yei paricaya dile more tāhe mora pūrṇa prīti haya// svabhāvata mora ei bhāve āche ruci/ ataeva ājñā śire dhari haye śuci//*

99. Ibid., 15/30, p. 157: *ruci yadi nahe tabe akapaṭa mane/ nivedibe nija ruci śrīguru-caraṇe// vicāriyā gurudeva dibe anyabhāva/ tāhe ruci haile prakāśibe nija-bhāva//*

100. Ibid., 15/31, p. 158: *śrī-guru-caraṇe paḍi balibe takhana/ tavādiṣṭa bhāva āmi karinu varaṇa// e-bhāva kakhana āmi nā chāḍiba āra/ jīvane maraṇe ei saṅgī ye āmāra//*

101. Ibid., 15/32, p. 158: *nija siddha ekādaśabhāve vratī haye/smaribe sudṛḍha-citte nija-bhāvacaye// smaraṇe vicāra eka āche ta' sundara/ āpanera yogya-smṛti kara nirantara// āpanera ayogya smaraṇa yadi haya/ bahu yuga sādhileo siddhi kabhu naya//*

102. Ibid., 15/33, p. 158: *āpana-sādhane smṛti yabe ha'ye vratī/ acire āpana-daśā haya śuddha ati// nija śuddha-bhāvera ye nirantara smṛti/ tāhe dūra haya śīghra jaḍa-baddha-mati//*

103. Ibid., 15/36. p. 162: *samādhi-svarūpa smṛti ye samaye haya/ bhāvāpana daśā āsi' haibe udaya// sei kāle nija siddha-deha abhimāna/ parājiyā jaḍa-deha ha'be adhiṣṭhāna// takhana svarūpe vraja-vāsa kṣaṇe kṣaṇa/*

104. Kedarnath Datta Bhaktivinoda, *Gītā-mālā*, ed. Śrila Bhaktikusuma Sramana (Sridham Mayapur, Nadiya: Shri Caitanya Math), 498 Śri-gaurābda: *Siddhi-lālasā* VIII/1-4; IX/1–3. (Translations by Haridhāma Dāsa.)

varaṇe taḍit, bāsa tārābalī,
kamalā mañjarī nāma
sāḍe vāra varṣa vayasa satata,
svānanda-sukhada-dhāma (1)

karpūra sevā, lalitāra gaṇa
rādhā yūtheśvarī hana
mameśvarī-nātha, śrī nandanandana
āmāra parāṇa dhana (2)

śrī rūpa mañjarī, prabhṛtira sama,
yugala sevāya āśa
avaśya se rūpa, sevā pābo āmi
parākāṣṭhā suviśvāsa (3)

kabe bā e dāsī, saṁsiddhi lābhibe,
rādhā-kuṇḍe bāsa kari'
rādhā-krishna-sevā satata karibe,

purva smṛti parihari' (4)

vṛṣabhānu-sutā, caraṇa sevane,
haibo je pālyadāsī
śrī rādhāra sukha, satata sādhane,
rahibo āmi prayāsī (1)

śrī rādhāra sukhe, kṛṣṇera je sukha,
jānibo manete āmi
rādhā-pada chāḍi', śrī kṛṣṇa-saṅgame,
kabhu nā haibo kāmī (2)

sakhī-gaṇa mama, parama suhṛt,
yugala-premera guru
tad anuga ha'ye, sevibo rādhāra,
caraṇa kalpa-taru (IX/ 3)

105. Kedarnath Datta Bhaktivinoda, *Gītā-mālā,* ed. Srila Bhaktikusuma Sramana (Shridham Mayapur, Nadiya: Sree Caitanya Math), 498 Śri-gaurābda: (The *Siddhi-lālasā* is one part of the *Gītā-mālā.*) Translations by Haridhāma Dāsa

hena kāle kabe, vilāsa mañjarī,
anaṅga mañjarī āra
āmāre heriyā, ati kṛpā kari',
balibe vacana sāra (3.1)

106. Ibid.,

vilāsa mañjarī, anaṅga mañjarī,
śrī rūpa mañjarī āra
āmāke tuliyā, laha nija pade,
deha' more siddhi sāra (10.4)

107. Kedarnath Datta Bhaktivinoda, *Bhāgavatārka-marīci-māla,* ed. Bhaktivilāsa Tīrtha (Śrīdhāma Māyāpura: Śrī Caitanya Maṭha, 470 Gaurābdīya (Bengali)), 436:

vipina-vihārī prabhu mama prabhu-vara/
śrī-vaṁśī-vadanānanda-vaṁśa-śaśadhara//
sei prabhupādera anujñā śire dhari/

108. *Jīvanī,* 176-177*: śrī-patu-bāghanāpāḍā-nivāsibhir gosvāmibhiḥ śrī-kedāranātha-dattāya bhaktāya siṣyāya kṛpayā bhaktivinodopādhiḥ pradattaḥ/... śrī-śrī-caitanyābda 400 māgha-māsa/* ***śrī-vipina-vihārī-gosvāminā****/ śrī-tinakaḍi-gosvāminā, śrī-gopāla-candra-gosvāminā, śrī-gorāṅcandra gosvāminā śrī-rāmacandra-gosvāminā/ śrī-yajñeśvara-gosvāminā/ śrī-vinoda-vihāri-gosvāminā śrī-yadunātha-gosvāminā, śrī-vinoda-vihāri-gosvāminā śrī-yogendra-candra-gosvāminā, śrī-gopāla-candra-gosvāminā, śrī-hemacandra-gosvāminā/ śrī-candrabhūṣana-gosvāminā/ śrī-kānāilāla-gosvāminā/ śrī-hārādhana-gosvāminā/*

109. JD, 397-8: *tomarā kṛṣṇa-kṛpā-pātra, tomādera saṁsārake kṛṣṇa-saṁsāra kariyā kṛṣṇa-sevā kara/ āmāra mahāprabhu jagatke yāhā śikṣā diyāchena, jagat sei ājñānusāre caluka/... erūpa mane kario nā ye, gṛhasthāśrama-avasthāya kṛṣṇa-premera parākāṣṭhā lābha haite pāre nā/ mahāprabhu adhikāṁśa kṛpā-pātrai gṛhastha*

110. CS, pt. 1, 67: *bāhya abhyantara ihāra dui ta' sādhana/ bāhye sādhaka-dehe kare śravaṇa-kīrtana/ mane nija siddha-deha kariyā bhāvana/ rātri-dina kare vraje kṛṣṇera sevana/ nijābhīṣṭa kṛṣṇapreṣṭha pācheta lāgiyā/ nirantara sevā kare antarmanā hañā/* These verses are also found in CC *Madhya-līlā* 22/156-159.

111. JD, 374: *vaidhī-niṣṭhāra sahita bahu-kāla sevā karile ye phala nā haya, rāgānugā-bhaktite svalpa-kālei sei phalera udaya haya/ vaidha-mārgera bhakti vidhi-sāpekṣa haoyāya durbalā, rāgānugā-bhakti svatantra prakṛti thākāra svabhāvataḥ prabalā ...*

112. CS, pt. 1, 70*: vaidhī o rāgānugā sādhanera dharma-bheda ei ye, vaidhī kichu vilambe bhāvāvasthā prāpta haya/ rāgānugā bhakti ati alpei bhāvāvāsthā pāiyā thākena/ śraddhā rāgānugā bhaktadigera hṛdaye niṣṭhāke kroḍībhūta kariyā ruci-rūpe udaya haya/ sutarāṁ bhāva haite tāhāte vilamba haya nā//* A similar passage also exists in JD, 374.

113. CS, pt. 1, p. 127- 128: *bhakta sannyāsīdigera varṇāśrama lopa-rūpa dharma-pravartana evaṁ neḍā bāula, kartābhajā, daraveśa, kumbhapaṭiyā, atibāḍī, svecchācārī, bhākta, brahma-vādīdigera varṇāśrama-viruddha ceṣṭāsakala atyanta ahitakara/ ai samasta kārya dvārā tāhārā ye pāpa pracalita kare, tāhā jagannāśa-kārya-viśeṣa/ sahajiyā, neḍā, bāula, kartābhajā prabhṛtira ye avaidha strī-saṁsarga sarvadā lakṣita haya, tāhā nitānta dharma-viruddha/*

114. ST, vol. 4 (1892), 64: *bāulerā kona prakāra vaidhī bhakti ācaraṇa kare nā/ rāgānugā bhaktira chale nānāvidha asadācaraṇa kariyā thāke/ vastutaḥ rāgānugā bhakti atiśaya pavitra tāhāte leśamātra jaḍīya vyāpāra nāi/*

115. Ibid., 192-3: *saṁkṣepataḥ ei saṁbandhe vaktavya ye ukta mahātmādera lokātīta sādhana ati sūkṣma o pavitratama/ tāhāte prākṛta deha vā indriyādera kona sambandha nāi/*

116. Ibid., 115: s*amprati ye dharmake sahajiyā dharma bale tāhā sarva śāstra viruddha/ vrajendra nandana prāptira janya prakṛti saṅga karā kona śāstrera vā sādhura upadeśa naya/*

117. KS *Saṁhitā* 5/19e: *jaḍa-dehagata strī-puruṣatva — cit-gata bhoktā-bhoktṛtvera asat pratiphalana/ samasta abhidhāna anveśaṇa kariyā emata ekaṭī vākya pāoyā yāibe nā, yad-dvārā cit-svarūpadigera parama caitanyera sahita aprākṛta saṁyoga-līlā samyak varṇita haite pāre/ etan nibandhana māyika strī-puruṣera saṁyoga-sambandhīya vākya-sakala tad-viṣaye sarva-prakāre samyak vyañjaka baliyā vyavahṛta haila/ ihāte aślīla cintāra kona prayojana vā āśaṅka nāi/ yadi aślīla baliyā āmarā parityāga kari, tāhā haile āra ai parama-tattvera ālocanā sambhava haya nā/ vāstavika vaikuṇṭha-gata bhāva-nicayera pratiphalana-rūpa māyika bhāva-sakala varṇana-dvārā vaikuṇṭha-tattvera varṇane āmarā samartha hai/ tad-viṣaye anya upāya nāi/*

118. ST, vol. 4 (1892), 115 & 116: *gṛhasthera pakṣe vivāhita strī-saṅga kona bhajanera saṅga naya/ ataeva kevale saṁsāra-yātrā nirvāhera janya tāhā niṣpāpa baliyā svīkṛta haya/ samprati ye dharmake sahajiyā dharma bale tāhā sarva śāstra viruddha/ se dharme vaiṣṇavadigera praveśa karā ucita naya/*

119. ST, vol. 4 (1892), 3: *āja kāla gauḍīya saṁpradāyastha vaiṣṇavagaṇa cāri bhāge vibhakta haite pārena/ yathā*
1. *pūjyapāda mantrācāryagaṇa*
2. *bhikṣāśrama abhyāgata vaiṣṇavagaṇa*
3. *varṇāśrama vyavasthāsthita prāpta-bhagavad-dīkṣā puruṣagaṇa*
4. *vaiṣṇava jāti baliyā paricita vyaktigaṇa*

120. ST, vol. 4 (1892), 3: *etat sambandhe paraspara parīkṣā vidhi śrī-haribhakti-vilāse ullikhita haiteo kārye pracalita haya nā/*

121. ST, vol. 4 (1892), 3-4: *bikṣāśramī vaiṣṇavadigera madhyeo adhikāra vicāra-bhraṣṭha haoyāya aneka pravāra anartha upasthita haiyāche/ bhikṣāśrama gamanera pūrvei sei āśramera adhikāra lābha karā ucita/ ājakāle tāhā uṭhiyā giyāche/* Melville Kennedy is similarly critical of Vaiṣṇava practices during the nineteenth century. See Melville T Kennedy, *The Chaitanya Movement; A Study of the Vaishnavism of Bengal* (Calcutta: Association Press (Y.M.C.A.) 1925). For Ramakanta Chakrabarty's views on this matter see: Chakrabarty, *Vaiṣṇavism in Bengal*, 332-335.

122. Ibid., 4: *varṇāśramasthita vaiṣṇavadigera bhakti-tattva carcāra nitānta abhāva haoyāya sadasat vivecanāśūnya haiyā tāṅhārā yāra tāra saṅga o ayathā sanmāna kariyā nijera citta kaluṣita karitechena/*

123. Ibid., 4: *ājakāla mantrācāryadigera amanoyoge vaiṣṇavadigera śuddha bhaktir vicāra prāya rahita haitechi/ jāti vaiṣṇavagaṇa viśuddha bhakti rahita haileo vaiṣṇava baliyā sammāna pāivāra dāvī kariyā thākena evaṁ sei dāvī avivecaka varṇāśramī vaiṣṇavera dvāra sammanita haiteche/*

124. ST, vol. 4 (1892), 4: *ei sakala anartha vidurita karivāra janya uparokta cāri prakāra vaiṣṇavera sammalana-pūrvaka ekaṭī sampradāya doṣaśe dhanī sabhā haoyāra āvaśyaka/*

125. ST, vol. 2 (1885), 142: *viśeṣa satarka thākā ucita ye kona prakāre samāja yena janma dvāra nirṇīta ayathā varṇa vidhi o anadhikāra dūṣita āśrama vidhi grahaṇa nā kare/*

Kedarnath Datta Bhaktivinoda's Astrological Chart

Birth time: Sunday, September 2, 1838 7:05 a.m. (estimated time of day)
Birnagar, West Bengal, India. 88E 33 23 N 14

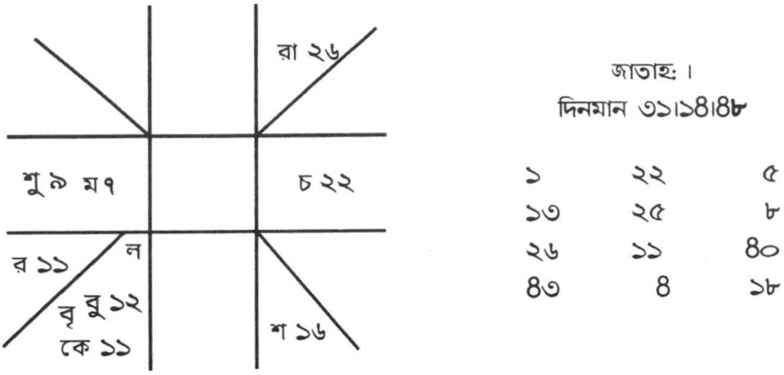

Kedarnath Datta Bhaktivinoda's astrological chart and birth time as shown in his autobiography, *Svalikhita-jīvanī.*

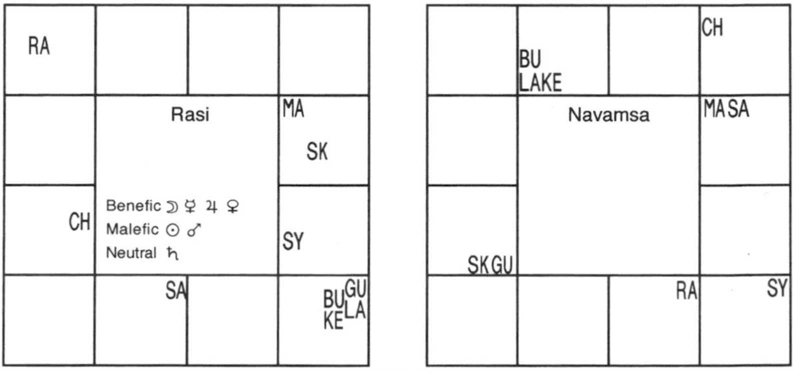

Name	Ret	Sign	Degrees	Star	Qtr.	Lord	Sub	Bindus	Shasti	B/M
Ascendant		Virgo	10° 39'	Hasta	1	Moon	Moon		Brahma	B
☉ Sun		Leo	17° 29'	Purvaphalguni	2	Ven	Mars	5	Yama	M
☽ Moon		Capricorn	16° 45'	Shravan	3	Moon	Sat	5	Ghora	M
♂ Mars		Cancer	0° 51'	Punarvasu	4	Jup	Mars	5	Rakshas	M
☿ Mercury		Virgo	12° 13'	Hasta	1	Moon	Rahu	4	Deva	B
♃ Jupiter		Virgo	3° 9'	Uttaraphalgun	2	Sun	Sat	5	Bhrasht	M
♀ Venus		Cancer	20° 39'	Ashlesha	2	Merc	Ven	6	Vamsaks	M
♄ Saturn		Scorpio	1° 39'	Visakha	4	Jup	Rahu	4	Kuvera	B
☊ Rahu		Pisces	12° 38'	Uttarabhadrap	3	Sat	Mars		Ardra	B
☋ Ketu		Virgo	12° 38'	Hasta	1	Moon	Rahu		Ardra	B
										M
										M
										M

Kedarnath Datta Bhaktivinoda's astrological chart in modern format.

Bibliography

Works in Sanskrit, Bengali and Hindi
(including translations)

Datta, Kedarnath. (Ṭhākura Bhaktivinoda). *Sajjana-toṣaṇī.* A monthly periodical that was published from 1881 to 1904. There are seventeen volumes extant published by Bhaktivinoda Ṭhākura. Edited by Radhika Prasad Datta. Calcutta: Vaishnav Depository, from 1881. (Bengali).

———. *Svalikhhita-jīvanī.* Edited by Lalita Prasad Datta. Calcutta: Lalita Prasad Datta, 1916. (Bengali).

———. *Datta-kaustubha,* edited by Bhaktipradīpa Tīrthagosvāmī. Māyāpura: The Gaudiya Mission, 1942. (Sanskrit and Bengali).

———. *The Bhagavat, Its Philosophy, Ethics and Theology,* edited by Bhaktivilas Tirtha, 2d ed. Madras: Madras Gaudiya Math, 1959. (English).

______. *Kṛṣṇa-saṁhitā.* Third edition edited by Bhaktivilāsa Tīrtha. Māyāpura: Shree Chaitanya Math, 474 Gaurābda (1960). (Sanskrit and Bengali).

______. *Jaiva-dharma.* Māyāpura: Caitanya Math, 1378 Baṅgābda (1972). (Bengali)

______. *Caitanya-śikṣāmṛta.* Māyāpura: Caityana Maṭh, 488 Gaurābda. (1974).

______. *Jaiva Dharma.* Madras: Sree Gaudiya Math. 1975. (English Translation of Bengali original.)

———. *Bhāgavata-ārka Marichimāla.* Madras: Sree Gaudiya Math, 1978. (English Translation of Sanskrit and Bengali original).

______. *Tattva-viveka, Tattva-sutra, Amnaya-sutra.* Madras: Sree Gaudiya Math 1979. (English Translation of Sanskrit and Bengali original.)

______. *Shri Chaitanya Shikshāmritam.* Madras: Sree Gaudiya Math, 1983. (English Translation of Bengali original.)

Bhaktisagar, Vasu A. *Śrīla Bhaktitīrtha Ṭhākurera: Saṁkṣipta Jīvanī.* Saurī Prapannāśrama: Prasadagopāl Dāsa, 1366 Baṅgābda (1960). (Bengali)

Bharadwaj, Banarasinath. *Kedāranātha Datta.* Calcutta: Caitanya Research Institute, 1989. (Bengali)

Chatterjee, Bankim Chandra. *Baṅkima Racanāvalī.* 2 vols. Edited by Yogesh Chandra Bagal. Calcutta: Sahitya Samsad, 1st edition 1360 Baṅgābda (1966). (Bengali)

Dāsa, Haridāsa. *Gauḍīya-vaiṣṇava-sāhitya.* Navadwip: Haridas Das, 483 Gaurābda (1969). (Bengali)

______. *Gauḍīya-vaiṣṇava-jīvana.* 2 Vols. Navadwip: Haribol Kutir, 465 Gaurābda (1951). (Bengali)

Dasa, Krishna. *Bhaktivinoda-carita.* Svananda Sukhada Kunja, Nadiya: Rajendranath Rāy Sharma, 1321 Baṅgābda (1915).

Dasa, Kunja Bihari. *Mañjarī-svarūpa-nirūpaṇa.* Sanskrit translation and edited by Jan K. Brzezinski. *Journal of Vaiṣṇava Studies,* Vol. 1, No. 3 (Spring 1993.): 59-71.

Dhyānacandra Gosvāmī. *Gaura-govindārcana-smaraṇa-paddhati.* Translated and edited by Haridhāma Dāsa. Fullerton: Sanskrit Religions Institute, 1993. (Translation from Sanskrit and Bengali.)

Ghosh, Benoy. *Sāmayikpatre Bāṅglār Samāj Chitra.* Calcutta: Bengal Publishers, 1962. (Bengali)

Gopālaguru Gosvāmī. *Gaura-govindārcana-smaraṇa-paddhati.* In *Paddhati-trayam,* pp. 1- 69. Edited by Haridāsa Dāsa. Navadwip: Haribol Kuṭīr, 1948. (Bengali)

Gopālaguru Gosvāmī. *Śrī-rādhā-kṛṣṇayor Aṣṭa-kālīya-līlā-smaraṇa-krama-paddhati.* In *Paddhati-trayam,* pp. 70 –88. Edited by Haridāsa Dāsa. Navadwip: Haribol Kuṭīr, 1948. (Bengali and Sanskrit)

Haridāsa Dāsa. *Gauḍīya-vaiṣṇava-abhidhāna.* 2 vols. Navadwip: Haribol Kutir, 1956-57. (Bengali)

Kṛṣṇa Dāsa Kavirāja. *Caitanya-caritāmṛta.* Translated from Bengali (with Sanskrit portions) by A.C. Bhaktivedanta Swami. Los

Angeles: Bhaktivedanta Book Trust, 1975.

______. *Caitanya-caritāmṛta.* Edited by Śaśībhūṣaṇa Bandyopādhyāya. Ambikā Kālnā: Gopendubhuṣaṇa Bandyopādhyāya, 1330 Baṅgābda (1923). (Bengali)

______. *Caitanya-caritāmṛta.* With the commentaries of Saccidānanda Bhaktivinoda Ṭhākura and Vārṣobhānavīdayita Dāsa. Calcutta: Gaudīya Maṭh, 1958. (Bengali)

Kapoor, O. B. L. *Vrajake Bhakta.* Mathura: Śrī Kṛṣṇa Janmasthāna Sevā Saṁsthāna, 1983. (Hindi)

Majumdar, Biman Bihari. *Śrī-caitanya-caritera Upādāna.* Calcutta: Calcutta University. 2nd ed. 1959. (Bengali)

Narahari Cakravartī. *Bhaktiratnākara.* Edited by Navīnakṛṣṇa Paravidyālaṅkāra. Calcutta: Gauḍīya Maṭh, 1940. (Bengali)

Premadāsa. *Vaṁśī-śikṣā,* Edited by Nimāicānd Gosvāmī. Navadwip, Nimāicand Gosvāmī, n. d.

Rādhāgovinda Nāth. *Gauḍīya-vaiṣṇava-darśana.* (5 vols.) Calcutta: Prācyabāṇī Mandir, 1957–60. (Bengali)

Rājavallabha Gosvāmī. *Muralī-vilāsa.* Edited by Nīlakaṇṭha Gosvāmī and Binodabihārī Gosvāmī. Baghnapara: Surendranath Bandyopadhyay, 409 Gaurābda (1895). (Bengali)

Rūpa Gosvāmī. *"Aṣṭa-kālīya-līlā-smaraṇa-stotram."* (Sanskrit) In *Early History of the Vaisnava Faith and Movement in Bengal,* Edited by S. K. De. Calcutta: Firma K. L. Mukhopadyay, 1961, 673–75.

______. *Bhaktirasāmṛta-sindhu.* (Sanskrit) With the commentaries of Jīva Gosvāmī, Mukundadāsa Gosvāmī, and Viśvanātha Cakravartī. Edited with a Bengali translation by Haridāsa Dāsa. Navadwip: Haribol Kutir, 1961.

______. *Bhaktirasāmṛta-sindhu.* (English) Vol. 1. Edited with an English translation and notes on the commentaries of Jīva Gosvāmī, Mukundadāsa Gosvāmī, and Viśvanātha Cakravartī by Swami Bon Maharaj. Vrindavan: Institute of Oriental Philosophy, 1965.

Saccidānanda Bhaktivinoda. *Smaraṇa-maṅgala-stotram tathā Svaniyama-dvādaśakam.* Māyāpura: The Gaudiya Mission,

1942. (Sanskrit)

Sanātana Gosvāmī. *Bṛhad-bhāgavatāmṛta.* Edited with a Hindi translation by Śyāma Dāsa. Vrindavan: Harinam Press, 1975. (Sanskrit)

_____. *Hari-bhakti-vilāsaḥ* edited by Haridāsa Dāsa. Vrindavan: Haridas Shastri, n. d. (Sanskrit)

Shriman, Bhaktikusum. *Prabhupāda Śrīla Sarasvatī Ṭhākura.* Māyāpura: Sri Chaitanya Math, 1983. (Bengali)

Śrīmad Bhāgavatam, Translated from Sanskrit and edited by A. C. Bhaktivedanta Swami. Los Angeles: Bhaktivedanta Book Trust, 1987.

Vṛndāvana Dāsa. *Caitanya-bhāgavata.* Calcutta: Sucārukānti Ghosh, Amṛtabāzār Patrikā Office, 1356 Baṅgābda (1949). (Bengali)

_____. *Caitanya-bhāgavata.* Edited by Bhaktisiddhānta Sarasvatī. Māyāpura: Shree Chaitanya Math, 479 Gaurābda (1965). (Bengali)

Vidyāvinoda, Sundarānanda. *Ṭhākura Bhaktivinoda.* Calcutta: Madhva Gaudiya Math, 1937. (Bengali)

———. *Bhaktivinoda-prasaṅga.* Māyāpura: Śrī Supatirañjana Nāga, 1345 Baṅgābda (1938). (Bengali)

———. *Bhaktivinoda-vānī-vaibhava.* Māyāpura: Śrī Supatirañjana Nāga, 1345 Baṅgābda (1938). (Bengali)

———. *Chātradera Śrī-bhaktivinoda.* 2nd ed. Māyāpura: Śrī Supatirañjana Nāga, 452 Gaurābda (1938). (Bengali)

———. *Gīti-sāhitye Śrī-bhaktivinoda.* Śrī Māyāpura: Śrī Niśikānta Sānyāl, 1345 Baṅgābda (1938). (Bengali)

———. *Vaiṣṇava-siddhānte Śrī-gurusvarūpa.* Calcutta: Karuna Das, 1964.

Viśvanātha Cakravartin. "*Rāgavartmacandrikā* of Viśvanātha Cakravartin." (Sanskrit) Translated by Joseph T. O' Connell, in *A Corpus of Indian Studies,* pp. 185-209. Edited by Gopikamohan Bhattacharya and Manabendu Banerjee. Calcutta: Sanskrit Pustak Bhandar, 1980.

Works in English

Albrecht, R. C. *Theodore Parker.* New York: Twayne Publishers, 1971.
Archer, W. G. *The Loves of Krishna in Indian Painting and Poetry.* New York: Grove Press, 1957.
Baird, R. D., ed. *Religion in Modern India.* New Delhi: Manohar, 1981.
Baumer, R., ed. *Aspects of Bengali History and Society.* Honolulu: University Press of Hawaii, 1975.
Bengal District Gazetteers. *History of Services of Officers Holding Gazetted Appointments Under the Government of Bengal (Corrected to 1st July 1894).* Calcutta: Government of West Bengal, 1894.
Bhaṭṭācārya, Siddheśvara. *The Philosophy of the Śrīmad-Bhāgavata.* Two vols. Santiniketan: Visva-Bharati, 1960.
Bhakti Pradip Tirtha. *Thakura Bhaktivinoda.* Ahol, Bengal: Sri Sacinath Roy Chakravarti, 1939.
Bhattacharya, Aparna. *Religious Movements of Bengal and Their Socio-Economic Ideas, 1800-1850.* Foreword by K. K. Datta. Calcutta: Vidyasagar Pustak Mandir, 1981.
Bhattacharya, Bhabani. *Socio-Political Currents in Bengal.* Sahibabad, Dist. Ghazibad: Vikas, 1980.
Bhattacharya, Sivaprasad. "Bhoja's Rasa-Ideology and Its Influence on Bengal Rasa-Sastra." *Journal of the Oriental Institute* (University of Baroda) 13, no. 2 (December 1963): 106-19.
Borthwick, Meredith. *The Changing Role of Women in Bengal, 1849-1905.* Princeton: Princeton University Press, 1984.
Bose, B. C. *Hindu Customs in Bengal.* Calcutta: The Book Co., 1929.
Bose, M. M. *Post-Caitanya Sahajiya Cult of Bengal.* Calcutta: University of Calcutta, 1930.
Bose, N. S. *The Indian Awakening and Bengal.* Calcutta: Firma K. L. Mukhopadhyay, 1960.
Bowes, Pratima. *Between Cultures.* New Delhi: Allied Publishers, 1986.
Bradley-Birt, F. B. *Twelve Men of Bengal in the 19th Century.* Calcutta: S. K. Lahiri and Co., 1925.

Brahmachari, Mahanambrata. *Vaiṣṇava Vedānta: The Philosophy of Śrī Jīva Gosvāmī.* Calcutta: Das Gupta and Co., 1974.

Bromley, David G., and Larry D. Shinn, eds., *Krishna Consciousness in the West.* Lewisburg: Bucknell University Press, 1989.

Brooks, Charles R. *The Hare Krishnas in India.* Princeton: Princeton University Press, 1989.

Broomfield, J. H. *Elite Conflict in a Plural Society: Twentieth-Century Bengal.* Berkeley: University of California Press, 1968.

______ . *Mostly About Bengal.* New Delhi: Manohar, 1982.

Brown, Mackenzie, ed., *Ultimate Concern: Tillich in Dialogue.* New York: Harper and Row, 1965.

Bultmann, Rudolf. *Kerygma and Myth: A Theological Debate.* Edited by Hans Werner Bartsch. New York: Harper and Row, 1961.

Campbell, Joseph. *The Power of Myth with Bill Moyers.* Edited by Betty Sue Flowers. New York, Doubleday, 1988.

Carman, John Braisted. *The Theology of Rāmānuja.* New Haven: Yale University Press, 1974.

Cassels, Nancy Gardner. *Religion and Pilgrim Tax Under the Company Raj.* New Delhi: Monohar, 1988.

Chakraborty, U. *Condition of Bengali Women Around the Second Half of the Nineteenth Century.* Calcutta: University of Calcutta: 1963.

Chakravarti, Amiya, ed. *A Tagore Reader.* New York: Macmillan, 1961.

Chakravarti, Janardan. *Bengal Vaishnavism and Sri Chaitanya.* Calcutta: The Asiatic Society, 1975.

Chakrabarty, Ramakanta. *Vaiṣṇavism in Bengal 1486-1900.* Calcutta: Sanskrit Pustak Bhandar, 1985.

Chakravarti, Sudhindra C. *Philosophical Foundation of Bengal Vaishnavism.* Calcutta: Academic Publishers, 1969.

Chakravarti, Surath Chandra. *Bauls: The Spritual Vikings.* Calcutta: Firma KLM, 1980.

Chatterjee, A. N. *Śrī Kṛṣṇa Caitanya.* New Delhi: Associated Publishing Co. 1983.

Chattopadhyay, Satkari. *A Glimpse into the Life of Thakur Bhakti-vinode.* Calcutta: Bhakti Vinode Memorial Committee, 1916.

Chattopadhyaya, G. *Bengal: Early Nineteenth Century*. Calcutta: Research India Publications, 1978.

Chaudhuri, Haridas. *The Integral Philosophy of Sri Aurobindo: A Commemorative Symposium*. London: Allen and Unwin, 1960.

Chunder, Bholanauth. *The Travels of a Hindoo to Various Parts of Bengal and Upper India*. London: N. Trubner and Co., 1869.

Collet, S. D. *The Life and Letters of Raja Rammohan Roy*. Calcutta: Sadharan Brahmo Samaj, 1962.

Commager, Henry Steele. *Theodore Parker: An Anthology*. Boston: Beacon Press, 1960.

Coward, Harold. *Pluralism: Challenge to World Religions*. Maryknoll, New York: Orbis Books, 1985.

______ . *Sacred Word and Sacred Text: Scripture in World Religions*. Maryknoll N.Y.: Orbis Books, 1988.

Das Gupta, Shashibhusan. *Obscure Religious Cults*. Calcutta: Firma KLM, 1969.

Das, Matilal. *Bankim Chandra: Prophet of the Indian Renaissance*. Calcutta: G. Majumdar, 1938.

Dasa, Gadadhar Pran. "Rāgānugā Bhakti Defined." *Journal of Vaiṣṇava Studies,* Vol. 1 No. 3, (Spring 1993.): 9-17.

Dasa, Rupavilasa. *The Seventh Gosvami*. Washington MS: New Jaipur Press, 1989.

Dasgupta, Surendranath. *A History of Indian Philosophy*. (5 vols.) Delhi: Motilal Banarsidass, 1975.

Datta, Kalikinkar. *Renaissance, Nationalism and Social Changes in Modern India*. Calcutta: Bookland, 1965.

______ . *Anti-British Plots and Movements Before 1857*. Meerut: Meenakshi Prakashan, 1970.

Davies, C. Collin. *Historical Atlas of the Indian Peninsula*. Bombay: Oxford University Press, 1949.

De, S. K. *Bengal's Contribution to Sanskrit Literature and Studies in Bengal Vaiṣṇavism*. Calcutta: Firma KLM, 1960.

______ . *History of Sanskrit Poetics*. 2 vols. 2nd ed. Calcutta: Firma KLM, 1960.

______ . *The Early History of the Vaiṣṇava Faith and Movement in Bengal*. 2d ed. Calcutta: Firma KLM, 1961.

______. *Sanskrit Poetics as a Study of Aesthetics.* With notes by Edwin Gerow. Berkeley: University of California Press, 1963.

Delmonico, Neal, ed. *Gifts of Sacred Wonder.* Calcutta: Subarnarekha, 1986.

______. "Rūpa Gosvāmin: His Life, Family, and Early Vraja Commentators" *Journal of Vaiṣṇava Studies.* Vol. 1, No. 2 (Winter 1993).

______. "Time Enough for Play: Religious Use of Time in Bengal Vaishnavism." Paper presented at Bengal Studies Conference, June 1982.

Desai, A.R. *Social Background of Indian Nationalism.* Bombay: Popular Prakashan, 1966.

Desai, N. *Woman in Modern India.* Bombay: Vora, 1957.

Deutsch, Eliot. *Advaita Vedanta: A Philosophical Reconstruction.* Honolulu: University of Hawaii Press, 1973.

Devanandan, P. D. *Preparation for Dialogue: A Collection of Essays on Hinduism and Christianity in New India.* Bangalore: Christian Institute for the Study of Religion and Society, 1964.

Dimock, Edward C. Jr., and Denise Levertov, trans. *In Praise of Krishna.* New York: Doubleday & Co., 1967.

______. *The Place of the Hidden Moon: Erotic Mysticism in the Vaiṣṇava Sahajiyā Cult of Bengal.* Chicago: The University of Chicago Press, 1966.

Dirks, John Edwards. *The Critical Theology of Theodore Parker.* New York: Columbia University Press, 1948.

Dumont, Louis. *Homo Hierarchicus: The Caste System and Its Implications.* Chicago: University of Chicago Press, 1980.

Dutt, Lalita Prasad. *The Ruins of Muhammadpur.* Calcutta: the author, 1925.

Dutt, Nripendra Kumar. *Origin and Growth of Caste in Bengal.* Calcutta: Firma KLM, 1968.

Eck, Diana. *Darśan: Seeing the Divine Image in India.* Chambersburg: Anima Publications, 1981.

Edwards, Michael. *The Battle of Plassey and the Conquest of Bengal.* London: B. T. Batsford, 1963.

Eisenstadt, S. N. *Intellectuals and Tradition.* New York: Humanities

Press, 1973.
Eliade, Mircea. *The Sacred and the Profane.* New York: Harcourt, Brace and World, 1959.
______. *Myth and Reality.* New York: Harper & Row, 1963.
______. *Patterns in Comparative Religion.* Translated by Rosemary Sheed. New York: Meridian Books, 1963.
Elkman, S. M. *Jīva Gosvāmī's Tattvasandarbha: A Study on the Philosophical and Sectarian Development of the Gauḍīya Vaiṣṇava Movement.* Delhi: Motilal Banarsidass, 1986.
Evans, Robert D. "A Contribution to a Bibliography of Bengali Vaisnavism." Unpublished paper. University of Chicago, December 12, 1980.
Farquhar, J. N. *An Outline of the Religious Literature of India.* Delhi: Motilal Banarsidass, 1967. (Reprint of Oxford: Oxford University Press, 1920).
______. *Modern Religious Movements in India.* Delhi: Munshiram Manoharlal, 1967. (Reprint of Oxford: Oxford University Press, 1914).
Ferguson, Wallace. *The Renaissance in Historical Thought: Five Centuries of Interpretation.* Boston: Houghton Mifflin Co., 1948.
Forbes, G. H. *Positivism in Bengal: A Case Study in the Transmission and Assimilation of an Ideology.* Colombia: South Asian Book, 1975.
French, Harold W. *The Swan's Wide Waters.* Port Washington, New York: Kennikat Press, 1974.
French, Harold W., and Arvind Sharma. *Religious Ferment in Modern India.* New Delhi: Heritage Publishers, 1981.
Frye, Northrop. *The Anatomy of Criticism.* Princeton: Princeton University Press, 1971.
Ghose, Benoy. *Selections from English Periodicals of Nineteenth Century Bengal,* vols. i-v. Calcutta: Papyrus, 1978.
Gnoli, Raniero. *The Aesthetic Experience According to Abhinavagupta.* Rev. 2nd ed. Varanasi: Chowkhamba, 1968.
Gopal, Ram. *British Rule in India.* New York: Asia Publishing House, 1963.

Gordon, Leonard A. *Bengal: The Nationalist Movement 1876 to 1940.* New York: Columbia University Press, 1974.

Grant, Colesworthey. *Rural Life in Bengal.* London: W. Thacker and Co., 1860.

Grewal, J. S. *The Sikhs of the Punjab.* Cambridge: Cambridge University Press, 1990.

Gupta, Atulchandra Pal. *Studies in the Bengal Renaissance.* Jadavpur: The National Council of Education, 1958.

Haberman, David L. *Acting as a Way of Salvation: A Study of Rāgānugā Bhakti Sādhana.* New York: Oxford University Press, 1988.

———. *Journey Through the Twelve Forests.* New York: Oxford University Press, 1994.

______. "Shrines of the Mind: A Meditative Shrine Worshipped in *Mañjarī Sādhana*". *Journal of Vaiṣṇava Studies,* Vol. 1, No. 3 (Spring 1993): 18-35.

Halbfass, Wilhelm. *India and Europe: An Essay in Understanding.* Albany: State University of New York Press, 1988.

Hamilton, William Baskerville. *The Transfer of Institutions.* London: Duke University Press, 1964.

Hawley, John S., and Srivatsa Goswami. *At Play with Krishna: Pilgrimage Dramas from Brindavan.* Princeton: Pinceton University Press, 1981.

______, and Donna M. Wulff, eds. *The Divine Consort: Radha and the Goddesses of India.* Berkeley: Graduate Theological Union, 1982.

Hay, Stephen N., ed. and trans. *A Tract Against Idolatry: Dialogue Between a Theist and an Idolater.* Calcutta: Firma KLM, 1963. Anonymous text thought to be written by Rammohun Roy.

Heimsath, Charles H. *Indian Nationalism and Hindu Social Reform.* Princeton: Princeton University Press, 1964.

Hein, Norvin. *The Miracle Plays of Mathura.* New Haven: Yale University Press, 1972.

Hoebel, E. A. *Man in the Primitive World.* New York: McGraw-Hill Book Co., 1949.

Hokins, Thomas J. "A Vital Transition: The Molding of the Hare Krishna Movement in British India", *Back to Godhead Magazine*, Vol. 16, No. 8 (August, 1981).

India, Governor-General, *Intercepted Correspondence from India: Containing Despatches from Marquis Wellesley During his Administration in India.* London: P. Hand, 1805.

Inden, Ronald B. *Marriage and Rank in Bengali Culture: A History of Caste and Clan in Middle Period Bengal.* Berkeley: University of California Press, 1976.

Inden, Ronald B., and Ralph W. Nicholas. *Kinship in Bengali Culture.* Chicago: University of Chicago Press, 1977.

James, William. *The Varieties of Religious Experience.* New York: Longmans, Green, & Co., 1902.

Joshi, V. C., ed. *Rammohun Roy and the Process of Modernization in India.* Delhi: Vikas Publishing House, 1975.

Kapoor, O. B. L. *The Philosophy and Religion of Sri Caitanya.* New Delhi: Munshriram Manoharlal Publishers, 1977.

Kaye, John W. *Christianity in India: An Historical Narrative.* London: Smith Elder, 1859.

Kennedy, Melville T. *The Chaitanya Movement: A Study of the Vaishnavism of Bengal.* Calcutta: Association Press, 1925.

Ketkar, S. V. *An Essay on Hinduism: Its Formation and Future.* London: Luzac, 1911.

Kinsley, David R. *The Divine Player: A Study of Kṛṣṇa Līlā.* Delhi: Motilal Barnasidass, 1979.

______ . *The Sword and the Flute.* Berkeley: University of California Press, 1975.

Kopf, David, ed. *Bengal Regional Identity.* East Lansing: Asian Studies Center, Michigan State University, 1969.

______ , and S. Joarder, eds. *Reflections on the Bengal Renaissance.* Rajshahi: Bangladesh Books International, 1977.

______ . *British Orientalism and the Bengal Renaissance: The Dynamics of Indian Modernization 1773-1835.* Calcutta: Firma K. L. Mukhopadhyay, 1969.

——— . *The Brahmo Samaj and the Shaping of the Modern Indian Mind.* Princeton: Princeton University Press, 1979.

______. "The Wonder that was Orientalism: In Defense of H.H. Wilson's Defense of Hinduism". *Bengal Vaiṣṇavism, Orientalism, Society and the Arts,* ed. J. T. O 'Connell. East Lansing: Asian Studies Center, Michigan State University, 1985, 75-90.

Krishnamachariar, M. *History of Classical Sanskrit Literature.* Delhi: Motilal Banarsidass, 1974.

Lamprecht, Sterling P. *Our Religious Traditions.* Cambridge: Harvard University Press, 1950.

Lavan, Spencer. *Unitarians and India.* 3rd edition. Chicago: Exploration Press, 1991.

Law, Narendra Nath. "Sri Krisna and Sri Caitanya." *The Indian Historical Quarterly* 23, no. 4 (December 1947): 261-99; and 24, no. 1 (March 1948): 19-66.

Leach, Edmund, and S. N. Mukherjee. *Elites in South Asia.* Cambridge: Cambridge University Press, 1970.

Lele, Jayant, gen. ed. *Tradition and Modernity in Bhakti Movements.* International Studies in Sociology and Social Anthropology Vol. 31. Leiden: E. J. Brill, 1981.

Lerner, Daniel. *The Passing of Traditional Society: Modernizing the Middle East.* Glencoe: The Free Press, 1958.

Lessa, William A. and Evon Z. Vogt. *Reader in Comparative Religion: An Anthropological Approach.* 2nd edition. New York: Harper and Row, 1965.

Levy, Marion J. *Modernization and the Structure of Societies.* Princeton: Princeton University Press, 1966.

Long, James (Rev.). *Calcutta and its Neighbourhood.* Edited by Sankar Sen Gupta. Calcutta: Indian Publications, 1974.

______. *Selected Papers.* edited by Mahadevaprasad Saha. Calcutta: Indian Studies, Past and Present, 1968.

______. *Selections from Unpublished Records of Government for the years 1748 to 1767.* Edited by Mahadevaprasad Saha. Calcutta: Firma K. L. M., 1973.

Majumdar, A. K. *Caitanya: His Life and Doctrine.* Bombay: Bharatiya Vidya Bhavan, 1969.

Majumdar, Bimanbehari. *History of Indian Social and Political Ideas, From Rammohan to Dayananda.* Calcutta: Bookland, 1967.

______ . *Kṛṣṇa in History and Legend.* Calcutta: University of Calcutta, 1969.

Majumdar, R. C. *Corporate Life in Ancient India.* Calcutta: Firma K. L. Mukhopadhyay, 1969.

______ . *Glimpses of Bengal in the Nineteenth Century.* Calcutta: Firma K. L. Mukhopadhyay, 1960.

______ . *History of Mediaeval Bengal.* Calcutta: G. Bharadwaj, 1973.

______ . *History of Modern Bengal.* Calcutta: G. Bharadwaj, 1978.

______ . *An Advanced History of India.* London: Macmillan, 1967.

Malinowski, B. *The Dynamics of Culture Change.* New Haven: Yale University Press, 1945.

May, Rollo. *Symbolism in Religion and Literature.* New York: G. Braziller, 1960.

McCutchion, David. *Brick Temples of Bengal.* Edited by George Michell from the archives of David McCutchion. Princeton: Princeton University Press, 1983.

McDaniel, June. *The Madness of the Saints.* Chicago: University of Chicago Press, 1989.

Mohanty, Surendra. *Lord Jagannatha.* Bhubaneswar: Orissa Sahitya Akademi, 1982.

Mohapatra, Gopinath. *Jagannatha in History and Religious Traditions of Orissa.* Calcutta: Allied Publishers, 1982.

Mozoomdar, P. C. *The Life and Teachings of Keshub Chunder Sen.* Calcutta: Thacker, Spink, 1891.

Mukherjee, K. N. "A Historico-Geographical Study for Sri Chaitanya's Birthsite." *Indian Journal of Landscape System and Ecological Studies* Vol. 7, No. II (Calcutta, 1984): 33-56.

Mukherjee, Prabhat. *History of Jagannath Temple in the Ninteenth Century.* Columbia, MO: South Asia Books, 1977.

______ . *History of the Chaitanya Faith in Orissa.* New Delhi: Asian Educational Services, 1981.

______ . *The History of Medieval Vaishnavism in Orissa.* Calcutta: R. Chatterjee, 1940.

______. *The History of the Gajapati Kings of Orissa and Their Successors.* Cuttack: Kitab Mahal, 1981.

Muller, Friedrich Max. *Keshub Chunder Sen.* Edited by Nanda Mookerjee. Calcutta: S. Gupta, 1976.

Mullick, B. *Essays on The Hindu Family in Bengal.* Calcutta: Newman and Co., 1882.

Nandy, Ashish. *At the Edge of Psychology.* Delhi: Oxford University Press, 1980.

Newman, Francis William. *Phases of Faith.* Introduction by U. C. Knoepflmacher. Reprint of the 1860 edition. New York: Leicester University Press, 1970.

Nikhilananda Swami. *Vivekananda, A Biography.* Calcutta: Advaita Ashrama, 1975.

O' Connell, Joseph T. "Jāti-Vaiṣṇavas of Bengal: "Subcaste" (Jāti) without "Caste" (Varṇa)." *Journal of Asian and African Studies* XVII, 3–4 (1981), 13 – 28.

______. "Social Implications of the Gauḍīya Vaiṣṇava Movement." Ph.D. dissertation, Harvard University, 1970.

______. "Were Caitanya's Vaiṣṇavas Really Sahajiyās? The Case of Rāmānanda Rāya." *Journal of Vaiṣṇava Studies,* Vol. 1 No. 3 (Spring 1993.): 36-58.

Oster, Akos. *The Play of the Gods: Locality, Ideology, Structure, and Time in the Festivals of a Bengali Village.* Chicago: University of Chicago Press, 1980.

Palit, C. *New Viewpoints on 19th Century Bengal.* Calcutta: Progresive Publishers, 1980.

Parke, David B. *The Epic of Unitarianism.* Boston: Beacon Press, 1969.

Poddar, A. *Renaissance in Bengal: Quests and Confrontations.* Shimla: Indian Institute of Advanced Study, 1970.

Potter, Karl. *Indian Metaphysics and Epistemology: The Tradition of Nyāya Vaiśeṣika up to Gaṅgeśa.* Princeton: Princeton University Press, 1977.

Prabhupada, A. C. Bhaktivedanta Swami. *The Nectar of Devotion.* Los Angeles: Bhaktivedanta Book Trust, 1982.

Ray, A. K. *A Short History of Calcutta.* Calcutta: Raddhi India, 1982.
______ . *The Religious Ideas of Rammohun Roy.* New Delhi: Kanak Publications, 1976.
Ray, Benoy Gopal. *Contemporary Indian Philosophers.* Allahabad: Kitabistan, 1947.
Raychaudhuri, Tapan. *Europe Reconsidered: Perceptions of the West in Nineteenth Century Bengal.* Delhi: Oxford University Press, 1988.
Risley, H. *The Tribes and Castes of Bengal: Ethnographic Glossary.* Calcutta: Bengal Secretariat Press, 1892.
Rolland, Romain. *Prophets of the New India.* New York: A. and C. Boni, 1930.
Rudolf, Lloyd I. and Susanne Hoeber. *The Modernty of Tradition: Political Development in India,* . Chicago University Press, 1967
Sarasvati, P. R. *The High-Caste Hindu Woman.* New York: Fleming H. Revell Co., 1901.
Saha, N. K. *A History of Orissa by W. W. Hunter.* Ed N. K. Saha. Calcutta: Susil Gupta, 1956.
Sarkar, Sumit. *On the Bengal Renaissance.* Calcutta: Papyrus, 1979.
______ . *A Critique of Colonial India.* Calcutta: Papyrus, 1985.
______ . *Bibliographic Survey of Social Reform Movements in the Eighteenth and Nineteenth Centuries.* New Delhi: Indian Council of Historical Research, 1975.
Sarkar, Susobhan. *Bengal Renaissance and Other Essays.* New Delhi: People's Publishing House, 1970.
Seal, Anil. *The Emergence of Indian Nationalism.* Cambridge: Cambridge University Press, 1968.
______ . *The Emergence of Indian Nationalism.* London: Cambridge, 1968.
Sen, Asok. *Iswar Chandra Vidyasagar and His Elusive Milestones.* Calcutta: Riddhi. 1977.
Sen, Dinesh Chandra. *Glimpses of Bengal Life.* Calcutta: University of Calcutta Press, 1925.
______ . *History of Bengali Language and Literature.* Calcutta: University of Calcutta, 1911.

______ . *Chaitanya and His Age.* Calcutta: University of Calcutta, 1924.

Sen Gupta, K. P. *The Christian Missionaries in Bengal.* Calcutta: Firma KLM, 1971.

Sen Gupta, Sankar. *A Study of Women of Bengal.* Calcutta: Indian Publications, 1970.

Sen, P. *Western Influence in Bengali Literature.* Calcutta: Academic Publishers, 1966.

Sen, S. P. *Social and Religious Reform Movements in the Nineteenth and Twentieth Centuries.* Calcutta: Institute of Historical Studies, 1979.

Sen, Sukumar. *History of Bengali Literature.* New Delhi: Sahitya Akademi, 1960.

Sharpe, Eric J. *Comparative Religion: A History.* New York: Scribner, 1975.

Sheridan, Daniel P. *The Advaitic Theism of The Bhāgavata Purāṇa.* Delhi: Motilal Banarsidass, 1986.

Shils, Edward. *The Intellectual Between Tradition and Modernity: The Indian Situation.* The Hague: Mouton and Co, 1961.

______ .*Tradition.* Chicago: University of Chicago Press, 1981.

Singer, Milton. ed. *Krishna: Myths, Rites and Attitudes.* Chicago: University of Chicago Press, 1968.

______ , and Bernard S. Cohn. *Structure and Change in Indian Society.* Chicago: Aldine Publishing, 1968.

______ , *When a Great Tradition Modernizes.* New York: Praeger Publishers, 1972.

Singh, Yogendra. *Modernization of Indian Tradition.* Faridabad: Thompson Press, 1977.

Sinha, Narendra Krishna. *The History of Bengal (1757-1905).* Calcutta: University of Calcutta, 1967.

Sinha, P. *Calcutta in Urban History.* Calcutta: Firma KLM, 1978.

Smith, G. *The Life of Alexander Duff.* New York: A. C. Armstrong and Son, 1880.

Smith, Wilfred Cantwell. *The Meaning and End of Religion.* New York: Macmillan, 1963.

______. *Religious Diversity*. Edited by Willard G. Oxtoby. New York: Harper and Row, 1976.
______. *Faith and Belief*. Princeton: Princeton University Press, 1979.
______. *Towards a World Theology*. Philadelphia: Westminster Press, 1981.
______. *What is Scripture?* Minneapolis: Fortress Press, 1994.
Spratt, Philip. *Hindu Culture and Personality; a Psycho-analytic Study*. Bombay: Manaktalas, 1966.
Sri Chaitanya Math. *Shrila Thakur Bhaktivinoda*. Mayapur: Sri Chaitanya Math, 1971.
Srinivas, Mysore N. *Social Change in Modern India*. Berkeley: University of California Press, 1966.
Srivastava, S. K. *Tradition and Modernization*. Allahabad: Indian International Publications, 1976.
Stewart, Tony K. "The Biographical Images of Krisna-Caitanya: A Study in the Perception of Divinity." Ph.D. dissertation, University of Chicago, 1985.
Thomas, M. M. *The Acknowledged Christ of the Indian Renaissance*. London: S. C. M. Press, 1969.
Thompson, Edward John. *Rabindranath Tagore, His Life and Work*. Calcutta: Y. M. C. A. Publishing House, 1961.
Tillich, Paul. *The Shaking of the Foundations*. New York: Scribner's Sons, 1948.
______. *Dynamics of Faith*. New York: Harper and Row, 1956.
______. *Christianity and the Encounter of the World Religions*. New York: Columbia University Press, 1963.
______. *Systematic Theology*. Chicago: University of Chicago Press, 1967.
Tripathi, R. S. *History of Ancient India*. Delhi: Motilal Banarsidass, 1960.
Upadhyaya, G. P. *The Origin, Scope and Mission of the Arya Samaj*. Allahabad: Arya Samaj, 1954.
Vidyarthi, L. P. *The Sacred Complex in Hindu Gaya*, New Delhi: Asia Publishing House, 1961.

Wach, Joachim. *Sociology of Religion.* Chicago: University of Chicago Press, 1944.

______. *The Comparative Study of Religion.* Edited by Joseph M. Kitagawa. New York: Columbia University Press, 1958.

______. *Understanding and Believing.* New York: Harper and Row, 1968.

Weber, Max. *The Religion of India: The Sociology of Hinduism and Buddhism.* Translated and edited by Hans H. Gerth and Don Martindale. Glencoe: Free Press, 1958.

Weiner, Myron. *Modernization: the Dynamics of Growth.* New York: Basic Books, 1966.

Weiss, John. *Life and Correspondence of Theodore Parker.* New York: Arno Press, 1969.

Wilson, H. H. *Religious Sects of the Hindus.* 2d ed. Calcutta: Susil Gupta, 1958.

Wintersteen, Precott Browning. *Christology in American Unitarianism.* Boston: The Unitarian Universalist Christian Fellowship, 1977.

Wise, James. *Races, Castes and Tribes of Eastern Bengal.* Calcutta: James Wise, 1883.

Wright, Conrad. *Three Prophets of Religious Liberalism: Channing, Emerson, Parker.* 2nd ed. Boston: Unitarian Universalist Association, 1980.

Yadav, K. C. *Autobiography of Swami Dayanand Saraswati.* New Delhi: Manohar Book Service, 1976.

Zimmer, Heinrich. *Myths and Symbols in Indian Art and Civilization.* Princeton: Princeton University Press, 1972.

Index

A. C. Bhaktivedanta Swami, 7n, 83, 172
Absolute (*tattva*), 65, 154-155, 166, 176
Academic Association (1828), 20
Adhikāra (competence), **132-140**, 163-164, 167-168, 200-201, 251, 255-256
  Holy Name (*nāma*) understood according to, 195, 197-200
  līlā understood according to, 185-190
  śrī-mūrti understood according to, 190-194
Ādhunika-vāda (modern approach), *2*, **128-132**, 132-133, 136-138, 140-146, 149, 168, 252
Ādiśura, King, 34
Advaitācārya, 114
Agnosticism, 207
Ajāmila, 198-199
Alexander the Great, 54
Allegory, 172-174
Amherst, Lord, 19
Āmnāya Sūtras, 100
Amṛta Bazaar Patrikā, 6, 97, 111
Amṛta-pravāha-bhāṣya, 94
Ānanda (bliss), 181
Anurāga (spiritual yearning), 73
Arabic, 18
Arjuna, 131-132
Arrareah, 85
Arundhatī, 179, 188
Aryans, 24, 81, 128
Ascetics (*vairāgīs*), 244, 246, 258
Aṣṭa-kāliya-līlā-smaraṇa, 93, 221, 231-238
Atheism, 207, 252
Atibaḍīs, 79-80, 240-241
Ātmā-samādhi, 158
Attachment. *See rāga*
Avatāra Viṣakiṣaṇa, 80

Bāghnāpāḍā Vaiṣṇavas, ix, 93, 101
Baghnapara, 93, 102
Baladeva, 78, 234-236
Ballaldighi, 105, 108
Bandyopadhyay, Hemachandra, 66
Bannerjee, Krishna Mohan, 27, 48
Barasat, 98
Basu, Raj Narayan, 63, 68
Bathing, 215
Battle of Plassey, 16
Bāuls, 240-242, 247
Belief, 141, 148-151, 251, 256
Believers, three types of, 133
Bengal Renaissance, 4-7, **16-31**
Bengal, 7, 9, 11, 15-31, 47, 73
  Bhaktivinoda in, 3, 63, 69, 74, 83, 85, 253
Bentham, Jeremy, 27
Bentinck, Lord, 27
Beverley Sahib, 72
Bhadrak, 63
Bhadraloka, 4-7, 15-31, 47, 53, 64, 68-69, 73, 80-82, 96, 97, 206
  abandoned religious traditions, 121, 135
  alcoholism and family breakdown, 28, 71-72
  alienated from tradition, 119, 196
  appeal to tradition, 89
  Bhaktivinoda and, viii-ix, 48, 53, 65, 74, 106-107, 110, 136-137, 141, 201
  Bhaktivinoda's presentation to, 141, 254
  crisis of faith, 120-123
  definition of, **17**
  Hindu ethical basis challenged, 87-88
  interpret *līlā*, 175
  lacked access to intellectual Hindu tradition, 134
  madhyamādhikārīs, 133
  new perspective, 252
  re-interpret ancestral traditions, 122, 210
  religious and cultural identity, 121
  religious experience, ix
  religious literalism, 182
  shunned image worship, 190-192
  stripped of Indian identity, 28
  theological understanding of, 168
  Unitarian influence on, 57, 156, 165
  wives, 70, 85-86
Bhagavad-gītā, 100, 116, 124
Bhagavān, 154-155, 159, 160, 175-176, 180, 209
Bhagavat Samsad, 78
Bhagavat, The, 8-9, 15, 74, 119, 137, 138, 153, 203,